빠르게 통하는 영문법 핵심 1200제

LEVEL 3

How to Study 이 책의 구성과 특징

Step 1 문법 개념을 확인하고 대표 기출 유형으로 연습하세요.

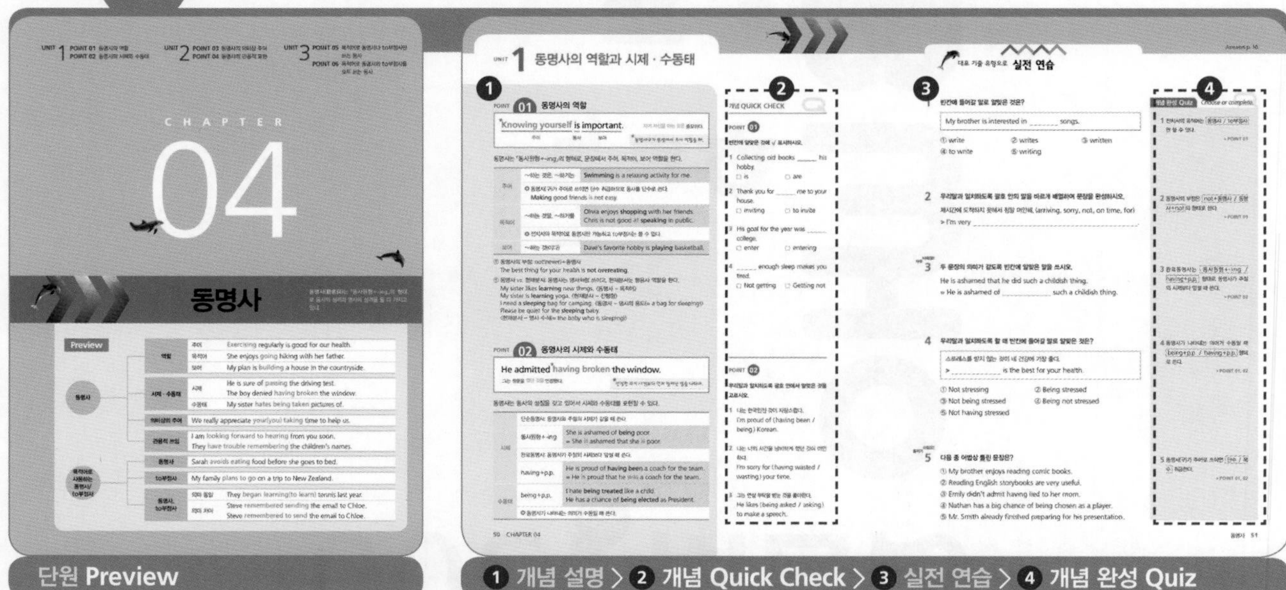

단원 Preview

① 개념 설명 > ② 개념 Quick Check > ③ 실전 연습 > ④ 개념 완성 Quiz

각 Chapter에서 배우게 될 문법 용어 설명을 쉽게 이해하고, 단원에서 배우게 될 내용과 예문을 도식화하여 한눈에 이해할 수 있습니다.

핵심 문법을 이해하기 쉽게 표로 정리했습니다. 대표 예문으로 문법 사항을 직관적으로 접한 후, 개념 설명으로 내용을 익힙니다. 배운 문법 개념을 잘 이해했는지 개념 Quick Check에서 바로 확인합니다.

학습한 내용을 대표 기출 유형의 실전 문제에 적용합니다. 자주 나오거나 틀리기 쉬운 문제를 통해 실전 감각을 효율적으로 익힙니다. 실전 연습 문제를 풀고 나면, 개념 완성 Quiz를 통해 개념을 다시 한 번 다집니다.

Step 2 다양한 유형으로 서술형 실전에 대비하세요.

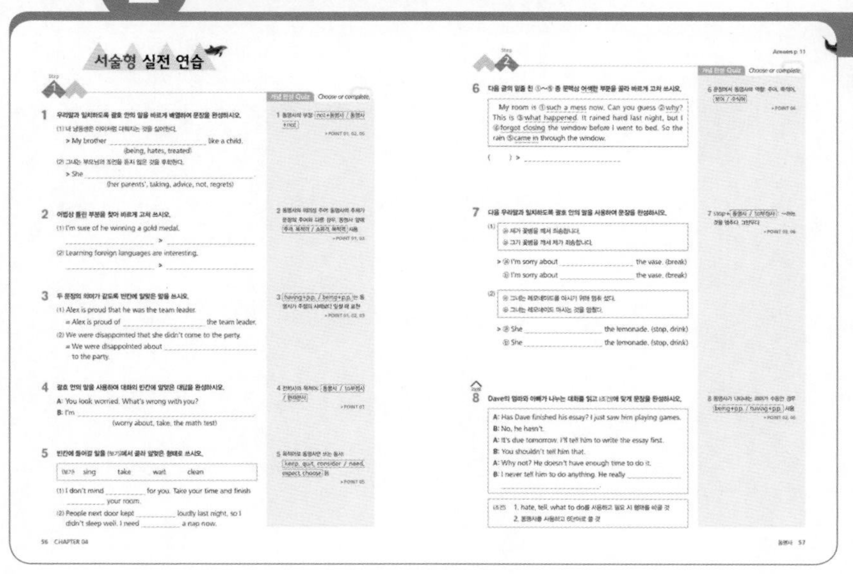

서술형 실전 연습

단계별로 다양한 유형의 서술형 문제를 풀면서 서술형 실전에 대비할 수 있습니다.

- Step 1에서 기본 서술형 문제로 준비 운동을 합니다.
- Step 2에서는 표, 도표, 그림 활용 문제, 조건형 서술형 문제와 같은 응용 문제들을 풀어 봅니다.
- 개념 완성 Quiz로 핵심 개념을 완벽히 이해합니다.

실전 문제로 중학 내신과 실력 완성에

빠르게 통하는 영문법 핵심 1200제

LEVEL 3

빠르게 통하는 영문법 핵심 1200제로 영어 자신감을 키우세요!

- 도표화된 문법 개념 정리로 문법 개념 이해 빠르게 通(통)
- 대표 기출 유형과 다양한 실전 문제로 실전 문제 풀이력 빠르게 通(통)
- 서술형, 고난도, 신유형 문항으로 내신 만점 빠르게 通(통)

학습자의 마음을 읽는 동아영어콘텐츠연구팀

동아영어콘텐츠연구팀은 동아출판의 영어 개발 연구원, 현장 선생님,
그리고 전문 원고 집필자들이 공동 연구를 통해 최적의 콘텐츠를 개발하는 연구 조직입니다.

원고 개발에 참여하신 분들

고미라 김경희 김수현 김유경 송유진 신채영 이남연 이윤희 진선호 진성인 하주영 홍미정

교재 기획·검토에 참여하신 분들

강군필 강선이 강은주 고미선 권동일 김민규 김설희 김은영 김은주 김지영 김하나 김학범
김한식 김호성 김효성 박용근 박지현 설명옥 신명균 안태정 이상훈 이성민 이지혜 정나래
조수진 김시은 최재천 최현진 하주영 한지영 한지원 한희정

Step 3 실제 학교 시험 유형으로 내신에 완벽하게 대비합니다.

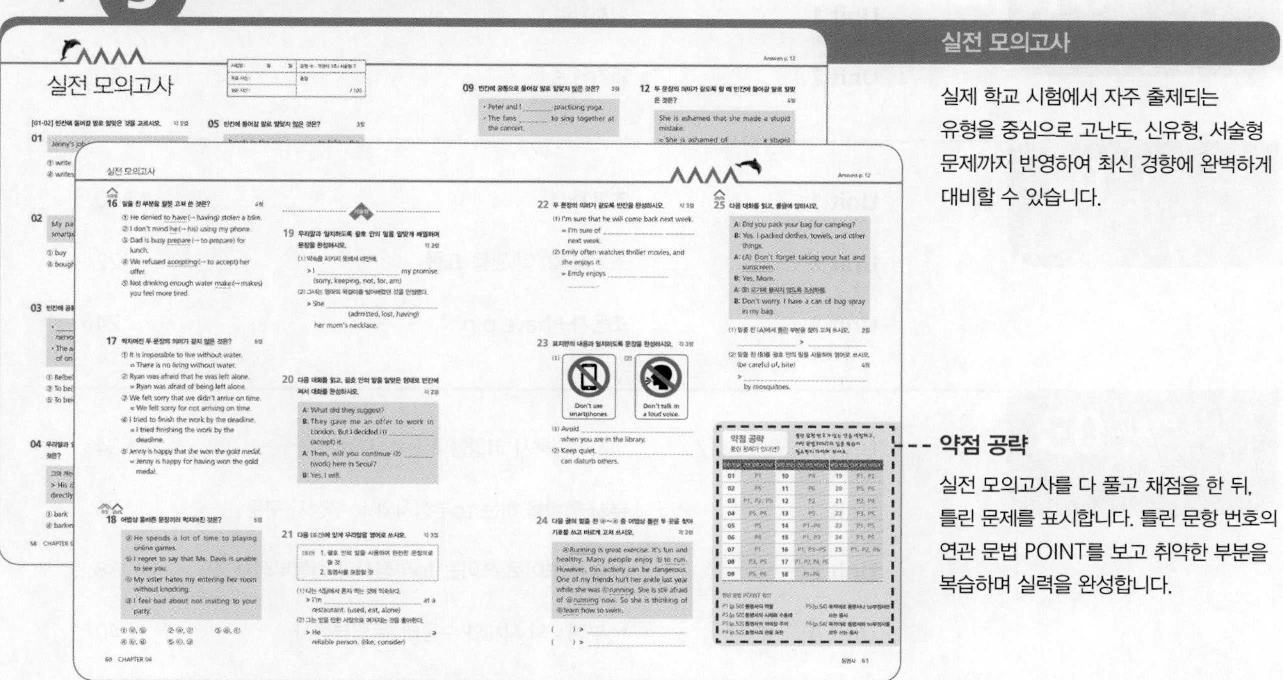

실전 모의고사

실제 학교 시험에서 자주 출제되는 유형을 중심으로 고난도, 신유형, 서술형 문제까지 반영하여 최신 경향에 완벽하게 대비할 수 있습니다.

약점 공략

실전 모의고사를 다 풀고 채점을 한 뒤, 틀린 문제를 표시합니다. 틀린 문항 번호의 연관 문법 POINT를 보고 취약한 부분을 복습하며 실력을 완성합니다.

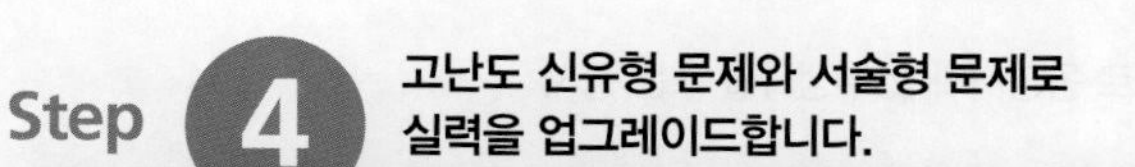

Step 4 고난도 신유형 문제와 서술형 문제로 실력을 업그레이드합니다.

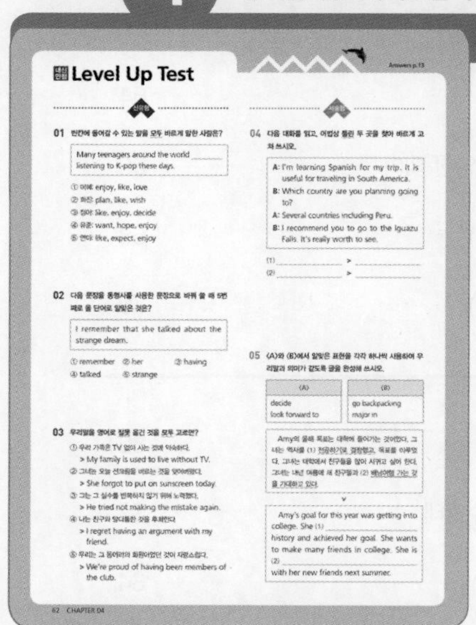

Level Up Test

고난도의 신유형 문제와 서술형 실전 문제에 도전! 최고 난이도의 내신 문제를 만나도 당황하지 않을 힘을 길러 줍니다.

Final Test

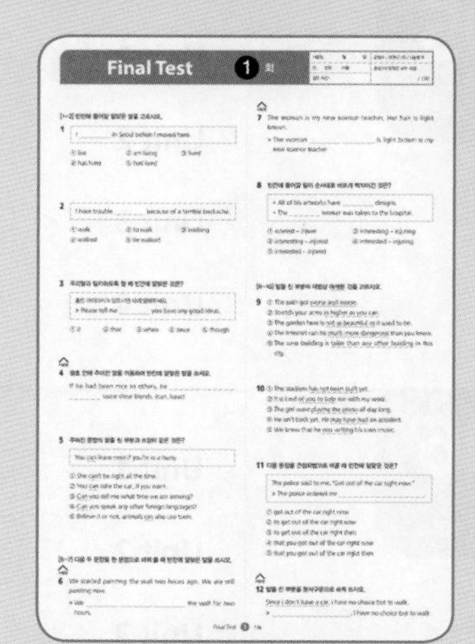

전체 문법 사항을 고르게 평가할 수 있는 3회분의 Final Test를 통해 실전 감각을 완성할 수 있습니다.

CONTENTS 차례

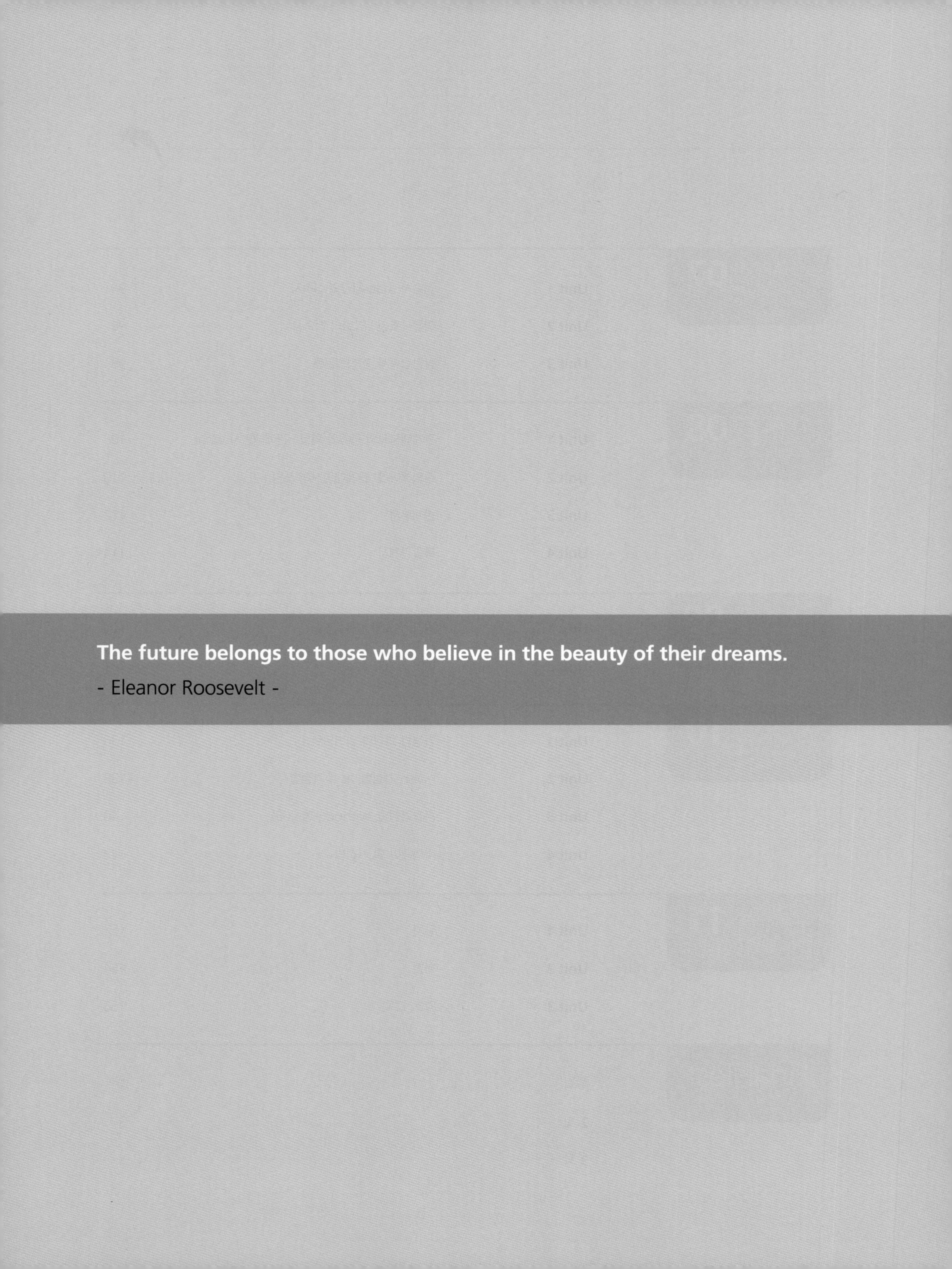
The future belongs to those who believe in the beauty of their dreams.
- Eleanor Roosevelt -

UNIT 1 POINT 01 현재완료의 쓰임
POINT 02 현재완료 진행형

UNIT 2 POINT 03 과거완료
POINT 04 과거완료의 쓰임

CHAPTER 01

시제

시제는 동사의 형태를 바꾸어 시간의 관계를 나타내는 것을 말한다.

Preview

시제

현재완료 (have+p.p.)		
	완료	I have already finished my homework.
	계속	We have known each other for ten years.
	경험	Jenny has never ridden a horse before.
	결과	Andrew has gone to New York for a trip.

현재완료 진행형 (have been+-ing)	
	Jake has been talking on the phone for two hours.

과거완료 (had+p.p.)		
	완료	The play had already begun when I got to the theater.
	계속	Tom had worked at the bank before he moved to Canada.
	경험	Mia had never learned to dance before she became a singer.
	결과	I couldn't call you because I had lost my smartphone.
	대과거	Jim lost the bike that his mom had bought him.

UNIT 1 현재완료

POINT 01 현재완료의 쓰임

We *have already finished our lunch.

우리는 이미 점심 식사를 끝마쳤다.

*과거의 일이 최근에 이미 끝났음을 나타내.

완료	(막/이미) ~했다	I **have** just **checked** the email from Sam. The train **has** not **arrived** yet.
	과거의 일이 최근에 완료됨을 표현하며, 주로 just, already, yet과 함께 쓴다. ⊕ just와 already는 주로 have(has)와 과거분사 사이에 쓰고, yet은 문장 끝에 쓴다.	
계속	~해 오고 있다	Tony **has had** a toothache since last week. My parents **have lived** in Busan for ten years.
	과거부터 현재까지 계속되는 상황을 표현하며, 주로 since, for와 함께 쓴다. ⊕ since 뒤에는 시작 시점을 나타내는 말이, for 뒤에는 구체적인 기간이 쓰인다.	
경험	~한 적이 있다	Chloe **has visited** New York before. I **have** never **sung** in front of many people.
	과거부터 현재까지의 경험을 표현하며, 주로 ever, never, before 또는 once, twice, three times 등과 같이 횟수를 나타내는 말과 함께 쓴다.	
결과	~해 버렸다 (그래서 지금 …하다)	My brother **has sold** his old computer.
	과거의 일의 결과가 현재까지 영향을 미치는 것을 표현한다.	

① 과거 시점을 나타내는 부사(구) yesterday, ~ ago 등과 when은 현재완료와 함께 쓰지 않는다.
① **have been to *vs.* have gone to** 서술형 빈출
have been to ~: '~에 가 본 적이 있다'의 의미로 경험을 나타냄
have gone to ~: '~에 가 버려서 지금 여기에 없다'의 의미로 결과를 나타냄

POINT 02 현재완료 진행형

It *has been snowing since last night.

어젯밤 이후로 계속 눈이 오고 있다.

*과거부터 지금까지 계속 진행되는 것을 나타내.

현재완료 진행형	have(has) been+-ing	I **have been watching** TV for three hours.
	'~해 오고 있는 중이다'라는 의미로, 과거에 시작된 일이 현재까지 계속 진행되고 있음을 나타낸다.	

① have(소유), know, love 등과 같이 상태를 나타내는 동사는 완료 진행형으로 쓰지 않는다.
We **have known** each other for ten years. (○)
We **have been knowing** each other for ten years. (×)

개념 QUICK CHECK

POINT 01

밑줄 친 부분의 쓰임에 해당하는 것에 √ 표시하시오.

1 Have you ever been to Spain?
□ 완료 □ 계속 □ 경험 □ 결과

2 Mia has lost her dog at the park.
□ 완료 □ 계속 □ 경험 □ 결과

3 I have just heard the bad news.
□ 완료 □ 계속 □ 경험 □ 결과

4 He has worked at the bank for 20 years.
□ 완료 □ 계속 □ 경험 □ 결과

POINT 02

다음 빈칸에 알맞은 것을 고르시오.

1 I __________ Chinese since last month.
a. have been learning
b. am learning

2 The girl __________ for an hour, so she's sweating.
a. has been run
b. has been running

대표 기출 유형으로 실전 연습

1 빈칸에 들어갈 말이 순서대로 바르게 짝지어진 것은?

> 나는 어렸을 때부터 이 집에서 살아 왔다.
> > I ________ in this house ________ I was a child.

① live – for ② lives – since ③ have lived – for
④ have lived – since ⑤ have been living – when

자주 나와요!
2 다음 중 [보기]의 밑줄 친 부분과 쓰임이 같은 것은?

> [보기] He has eaten Mexican food many times.

① The bookstore hasn't opened yet.
② How long have you kept your diary?
③ Jane has left her homework at home.
④ I have just got a text message from Mike.
⑤ My brother has never watched a horror movie.

3 다음 두 문장을 한 문장으로 바꿔 쓸 때, 빈칸에 알맞은 말을 쓰시오.

Tom began playing the game three hours ago. He is still playing it now.

> Tom ________ ________ ________ the game for three hours.

틀리기 쉬워요!
4 밑줄 친 ①~⑤ 중 어법상 틀린 부분을 골라 바르게 고쳐 쓰시오.

Mark ①has never ②gone to Vietnam, so he ③wants ④to go there ⑤someday.

( ) > ________________

5 다음 중 어법상 틀린 문장은?

① Sally has been doing yoga for two years.
② James has lived in London five years ago.
③ Have you ever seen a shooting star before?
④ I have forgotten the password for my smartphone.
⑤ My brother has gone out, so you can't meet him now.

개념 완성 Quiz *Choose or complete.*

1 과거의 일이 현재에 영향을 미칠 때에는 [have+p.p. / be동사+p.p.] 형태를 쓴다.
> POINT 01

2 [완료 / 계속 / 경험 / 결과]을(를) 나타내는 현재완료는 주로 횟수를 나타내는 표현과 함께 쓴다.
> POINT 01

3 과거의 일이 현재까지 계속되고 있음을 나타낼 때는 [have been+-ing / had been+-ing] 형태를 쓴다.
> POINT 02

4 have [gone / been] to는 '~에 가 버려서 지금 여기 없다'는 의미로 결과를 나타낸다.
> POINT 01

5 특정한 과거 시점을 나타내는 표현이 쓰이면 [현재완료 / 과거시제]를 써야 한다.
> POINT 01, 02

UNIT 2 과거완료

POINT 03 과거완료

She *had worked as a teacher until she retired.

그녀는 은퇴할 때까지 선생님으로 일했었다.

*과거에 은퇴한 시점까지 계속 했던 일을 나타내.

과거시제	과거에 일어난 상황만을 나타냄	I **lived** in Busan five years ago. (5년 전에 부산에 살았고, 지금 어디 사는지 알 수 없음)
현재완료	과거의 일과 현재의 일의 연관성을 나타냄	I **have lived** in Seoul for five years. (5년 전부터 지금까지 서울에 살고 있음)
과거완료	과거의 특정 시점을 기준으로 그 시점 이전에 완료되었거나, 그 시점까지 계속된 동작이나 상태를 나타냄	I **had lived** in Busan before we moved to Seoul. (이사하기 전부터 이사한 과거 시점까지 부산에 살았음)

ⓘ 과거완료 부정문: had not(never)+p.p.
I **had not played** tennis before then.

ⓘ 과거완료 의문문: Had+주어+p.p. ~?
Had the train **left** when you arrived?

ⓘ 과거완료 진행형: 「had been+-ing」의 형태로 과거의 특정 시점까지 계속됨을 강조한다.
The fans **had been waiting** for hours when the singer got there.

ⓘ after, before, until 등의 접속사가 있으면 과거완료 대신 과거시제를 쓸 수 있다.
My brother did the dishes after he **ate(had eaten)** dinner.

POINT 04 과거완료의 쓰임

The bank *had already closed when I got there.

내가 도착했을 때 은행은 이미 문을 닫았다.

*과거에 도착한 시점 전에 이미 완료된 일을 나타내.

완료	(막/이미) ~했었다	The bus **had** already **left** when I got to the bus stop.
	과거 이전에 시작된 일이 과거의 한 시점에 완료된 것을 표현한다.	
계속	~해 오고 있었다	She **had been** ill for a week, so she couldn't go camping.
	과거 이전부터 시작해서 과거의 한 시점까지 계속된 상황을 표현한다.	
경험	~한 적이 있었다	I **had** never **traveled** abroad until last year.
	과거 이전부터 과거의 한 시점까지의 경험을 표현한다.	
결과	~해 버렸었다	Ted found that he **had left** his smartphone at home.

ⓘ 대과거: 과거의 여러 일 중 먼저 일어난 일을 대과거라고 하며 「had+p.p.」의 형태로 쓴다.
Lucy told me that she **had** already **seen** the new movie.

개념 QUICK CHECK

POINT 03

괄호 안에서 알맞은 것을 고르시오.

1 They (finished / had finished) dinner when I came home.

2 Amy knew his name because she (has met / had met) him before.

3 The kid (had been crying / has been crying) when his mom came home.

POINT 04

밑줄 친 부분의 쓰임을 아래에서 골라 기호를 쓰시오.

a. 완료	b. 계속
c. 경험	d. 결과

1 I was tired because I hadn't slept well for several days. _____

2 He had lost his wallet, so he had no money. _____

3 The show had already finished when I turned on TV. _____

4 She had never eaten raw fish before she visited Japan. _____

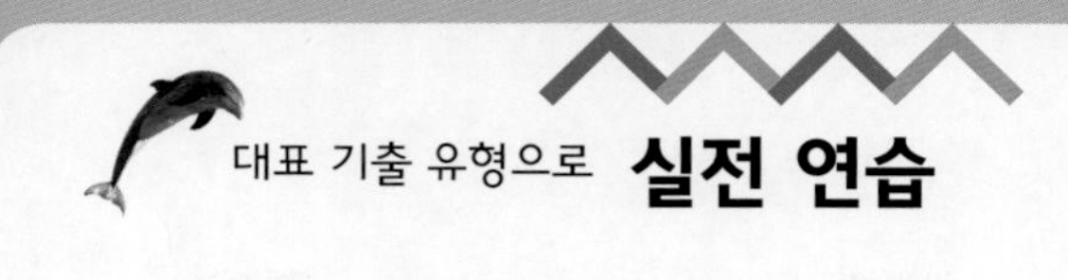

1 괄호 안의 단어를 알맞은 형태로 빈칸에 쓰시오.

Dave ________ (go) back to Canada last week. He ________ ________ (travel) to Korea before then.

2 빈칸에 들어갈 말로 알맞은 것을 모두 고르면?

She felt better after she ________ some medicine.

① takes ② took ③ will take
④ have taken ⑤ had taken

3 다음 중 밑줄 친 부분의 쓰임이 나머지와 다른 하나는?

① I had never ridden a bike until I was ten.
② My sister had been sick before she went to the doctor.
③ How long had you lived in Rome before you moved here?
④ Ryan had driven the car for ten years when it broke down.
⑤ Olivia had waited for him for two hours when Tom arrived.

틀리기 쉬워요!
4 다음 대화의 밑줄 친 부분 중 어법상 틀린 것은?

A: Why did you ① miss your flight?
B: The traffic ② was too ③ heavy. When I ④ arrived at the airport, the plane ⑤ has already taken off.

자주 나와요!
5 빈칸에 들어갈 말이 순서대로 바르게 짝지어진 것은?

• Sue found the phone that someone ________ on the bus. • Mom ________ TV for hours when I came back home.

① left – has watched
② has left – had watched
③ had left – had been watching
④ has left – has been watching
⑤ had left – has been watching

개념 완성 Quiz *Choose or complete.*

1 과거의 어느 시점보다 먼저 일어난 일이 그 시점까지 영향을 줄 때에는 [have+p.p. / had+p.p.] 형태를 쓴다.
> POINT 03

2 접속사로 시간의 전후 관계를 분명히 알 수 있을 때는 과거완료 대신 ________를 쓸 수 있다.
> POINT 03

3 [완료 / 계속 / 경험 / 결과]을(를) 나타내는 과거완료는 주로 기간을 나타내는 for나 how long과 함께 쓴다.
> POINT 04

4 과거에 시작된 일이 과거의 어느 시점에서 이미 완료되었을 때에는 ________를 쓴다.
> POINT 03, 04

5 과거의 여러 일 중 더 먼저 일어난 일을 ________라고 하며, ________의 형태로 쓴다.
> POINT 03, 04

서술형 실전 연습

개념 완성 Quiz *Choose or complete.*

1 괄호 안의 말을 사용하여 우리말을 영어로 쓰시오.

(1) Ms. Davis는 2015년부터 영어를 가르쳐 왔다. (teach English)

> Ms. Davis _______ _______ _______ _______ 2015.

(2) 나는 전에 한 번도 해돋이를 본 적이 없다. (see a sunrise)

> I _______ _______ _______ _______ _______ before.

2 괄호 안의 말을 바르게 배열하여 대화를 완성하시오.

A: Jason looked upset. What's wrong with him?

B: He ______________________________ for his birthday.

(the watch, had, lost, him, his dad, given, that)

3 다음 두 문장을 완료시제를 사용하여 한 문장으로 바꿔 쓰시오.

(1) Mike went to New York for business. He is not here now.

> Mike ______________________________ for business.

(2) I ate a hot dog on the way home. So I wasn't hungry then.

> I wasn't hungry because I ______________________________ on the way home.

4 밑줄 친 부분에서 어법상 틀린 부분을 찾아 바르게 고쳐 쓰시오.

(1) Have you gone camping with your family last weekend?

______________________ > ______________________

(2) Tom has used the bag for years when he bought a new bag.

______________________ > ______________________

5 그림을 보고, 괄호 안의 말과 완료 진행형을 사용하여 문장을 완성하시오.

two hours ago

now

(1) Jane ______________________________ for two hours. (read a book)

(2) Mina and Tom ______________________________ for two hours. (play badminton)

개념 완성 Quiz

1 과거의 일이 현재에 영향을 미치는 경우: have+p.p. / be동사+p.p. 의 형태 사용

> POINT 01

2 _______ : 과거의 여러 일 중 더 먼저 일어난 일

> POINT 04

3 have _______ to: ~에 가버려서 지금 여기 없다

> POINT 01, 04

4 완료형과 함께 쓰이지 않는 표현: ago, when, last / since, for, until

> POINT 01, 04

5 현재완료 진행형의 형태: have been+-ing / have been +p.p.

> POINT 02

Answers p. 1

개념 완성 Quiz *Choose or complete.*

6 현재완료의 경험 / 결과의 의미:
'(과거에) ~해서 (지금은) …하다'
> POINT 01

7 계속적 쓰임의 완료시제와 함께 주로 쓰이는 표현:
_____+시작 시점: ~ 이래로
_____+구체적 기간: ~ 동안
> POINT 01, 03

8 과거 특정 시점에 일어난 상황을 나타내는 경우: 과거시제 / 과거완료 사용
> POINT 01, 04

6 다음 대화를 읽고, Kate의 상황을 [조건]에 맞게 한 문장으로 쓰시오.

A: Kate, is anything wrong?
B: I can't find my umbrella. I think I lost it.
A: Do you remember when you used it last?
B: I remember taking it out of my bag on the bus. Oh, then it must be there.

[조건] 1. Kate를 주어로 하고 완료시제를 사용할 것
2. leave, umbrella, bus를 사용하고 필요 시 형태를 바꿀 것

> ______________________________

7 Tom이 수강한 강좌 목록을 보고, 동사 learn과 [보기]의 단어를 사용해 문장을 완성하시오. (단, 완료시제로 쓸 것)

Today: May 31

Class Name	Duration
Dance Class	February 1 ~ March 31
Guitar Class	April 1 ~ May 31
Baking Class	March 1 ~ May 31

[보기] for until since

(1) Tom ______________ dancing ________ March 31.
(2) Tom ______________ the guitar ________ April 1.
(3) Tom ______________ baking ________ three months.

고난도
8 밑줄 친 ⓐ~ⓔ 중 어법상 틀린 부분 두 곳을 찾아 바르게 고쳐 쓰시오.

Angela ⓐ has participated in a singing contest yesterday. She ⓑ had never sung in front of anyone before then. However, she ⓒ was not nervous because she ⓓ has practiced very hard. Also, her friends ⓔ came to cheer for her. She finally got on the stage and sang beautifully. Angela won first prize!

(1) (　　) > ______________
(2) (　　) > ______________

실전 모의고사

시험일 : 월 일	문항 수 : 객관식 18 / 서술형 7
목표 시간 :	총점
걸린 시간 :	/ 100

[01-02] 빈칸에 들어갈 말로 알맞은 것을 고르시오. 각 2점

01

Liam ________ in L.A. since his childhood.

① will live ② live ③ has lived
④ have lived ⑤ have been living

02

We ________ for hours on the sofa when the doorbell rang.

① sleep ② have slept
③ are sleeping ④ had been sleeping
⑤ have been sleeping

03 빈칸에 들어갈 말로 알맞지 않은 것은? 3점

I have visited Jeju-do with my family ________.

① once ② twice ③ before
④ many times ⑤ last summer

04 빈칸에 들어갈 말이 순서대로 바르게 짝지어진 것은? 3점

- He hasn't met his dad ________ over a year.
- Amy and I have been friends ________ we were five.

① in – for ② since – in ③ since – until
④ for – since ⑤ for – until

05 다음 대화의 밑줄 친 부분을 바르게 고친 것은? 3점

A: Did you talk to Chris last night?
B: No, I didn't. When I got home late, he goes to bed already.

① is going ② had gone ③ has gone
④ was going ⑤ has been going

06 [보기]의 밑줄 친 부분과 쓰임이 같은 것은? 3점

[보기] Jim hasn't arrived at the airport yet.

① The train has just left the station.
② Dave has been ill since last weekend.
③ Have you ever eaten Indian food before?
④ I have never seen such a beautiful painting.
⑤ How long have you taken swimming lessons?

07 우리말과 일치하도록 할 때 빈칸에 들어갈 말로 알맞은 것은? 3점

내 남동생은 세 시간째 방 청소를 하고 있는 중이다.
> My brother ________ his room for three hours.

① cleaned ② had cleaned
③ was cleaning ④ had been cleaning
⑤ has been cleaning

08 두 문장을 한 문장으로 바꿔 쓸 때 빈칸에 들어갈 말로 알맞은 것은? 3점

I forgot the man's name. I still don't remember it.
> I ________ the man's name.

① forget ② forgot
③ had forgotten ④ have forgotten
⑤ have been forgetting

[09-10] 어법상 틀린 문장을 고르시오. 각 4점

09 ① Have you eaten anything yet?
② Lisa has bought the shoes last week.
③ Andy has been talking on the phone for an hour.
④ I had lived in Seoul for five years when I graduated.
⑤ They had already left the island when the storm came.

통합

10 ① The Korean War ended in 1953.
② Sue has just got a call from her mom.
③ The movie has been showing for two months.
④ Brian had never been abroad until he turned 20.
⑤ After I finished my homework, I had gone to bed.

11 대화의 빈칸에 들어갈 말이 순서대로 짝지어진 것은? 4점

> **A:** Why were you late for school today?
> **B:** I ________ the bus this morning. The bus ________ when I got to the bus stop.

① miss – had left ② missed – left
③ has missed – left ④ missed – had left
⑤ had missed – has left

12 다음 중 빈칸에 들어갈 말이 나머지와 다른 것은? 4점

① I found that someone ________ stolen my bike.
② It ________ been raining for a week until now.
③ The package ________ arrived when we got home.
④ The party ________ been boring before Judy came.
⑤ He ________ used the computer for six years when it broke down.

[13-14] 우리말을 영어로 바르게 옮긴 것을 고르시오. 각 4점

13

> 그가 집에 도착했을 때 저녁 식사가 준비되어 있었다.

① When he arrives home, dinner is prepared.
② When he arrives home, dinner was prepared.
③ When he arrives home, dinner has been prepared.
④ When he arrived home, dinner had been prepared.
⑤ When he arrived home, dinner has been preparing.

14

> 너는 미국에 가 본 적이 있니?

① Did you go to America?
② Have you go to America?
③ Have you gone to America?
④ Have you been to America?
⑤ Have you been going to America?

고난도

15 어법상 올바른 문장끼리 짝지어진 것은? 5점

> ⓐ Have you met Michael before?
> ⓑ Jack was very tired because he has stayed up late.
> ⓒ Mia had studied a lot before she took the exam.
> ⓓ He had working in the garden before it began to rain.

① ⓐ, ⓑ ② ⓐ, ⓒ ③ ⓐ, ⓓ
④ ⓑ, ⓒ ⑤ ⓒ, ⓓ

통합 신유형

16 **빈칸 ①~⑤에 들어갈 말로 알맞지 않은 것은?** 4점

- I'm sure we ___①___ before.
- I ___②___ French for six years.
- Amy ___③___ before I arrived home.
- Jake and Kate ___④___ each other since 2016.
- J. K. Rowling ___⑤___ writing the Harry Potter series in 1990.

① have met　　② have been learning
③ had left　　④ have been knowing
⑤ started

17 **두 문장을 한 문장으로 바르게 바꿔 쓴 것은?** 4점

I lost my dog in the park three days ago.
I found the dog yesterday.

① I had found my dog that I lost in the park.
② I found my dog that I had lost in the park.
③ I found my dog that I have lost in the park.
④ I have found my dog that I lost in the park.
⑤ I had found my dog that I have lost in the park.

고난도

18 **다음 글의 밑줄 친 부분 중 어법상 틀린 것은?** 5점

Richard is a ①45-year-old man ②who lives ③with his wife and two ④boys in Texas. He ⑤works at a local radio station for twenty years.

19 **우리말과 일치하도록 괄호 안의 말을 바르게 배열하시오.** 각 2점

(1) 너는 전에 영화배우를 만나 본 적이 있니?
> ______________________
(before, met, have, ever, you, a movie star)

(2) Jane은 그 문제를 이미 해결했다고 내게 말했다.
> Jane told me ______________________ the matter. (already, solved, she, had)

20 **두 문장의 의미가 같도록 완료 진행형을 써서 문장을 완성하시오.** 각 2점

(1) The author started writing the novel two years ago, and she is still writing it.
> The author ______________________ for two years.

(2) Alex moved to Madrid six months after he began learning Spanish.
> Alex ______________________ for six months when he moved to Madrid.

21 **그림을 보고, 괄호 안의 말을 사용하여 문장을 완성하시오.** 각 3점

(1) Jisu ______________________ on the phone for two hours. (talk)

(2) Mr. Jones ______________________ the computer. (fix)

Answers p. 2

22 두 문장을 [조건]에 맞게 한 문장으로 바꿔 쓰시오. 4점

Ann went to Paris to study art last month.
She is not here now.

[조건] 1. Ann을 주어로 하고 완료시제를 사용할 것
2. 총 8단어의 완전한 문장으로 쓸 것

> ________________________________

23 우리말과 일치하도록 [조건]에 맞게 문장을 완성해 쓰시오. 4점

어제 남동생이 내게 가르쳐 주기 전까지 나는 스케이트보드를 타 본 적이 없었다.

[조건] 1. ride a skateboard를 사용할 것
2. 필요 시 단어의 형태를 바꿀 것
3. 5단어를 추가하여 문장을 완성할 것

> I ________________________ until my brother taught me yesterday.

24 그림을 보고, 괄호 안의 말을 사용하여 다음 글을 완성하시오. 각 2점

<Last Saturday> <Last Saturday> <Today>

When Minho (1) ____________ (get home), he found the window (2) ____________ (be broken). He was so scared and (3) ____________ (call) the police. However, the police officers (4) ____________ (not, find) the criminals yet.

고난도
25 Tim의 오후 일과표를 보고, 문장을 완성하시오. 각 3점

2:00 p.m.	The soccer game started.
2:20 p.m.	Tim arrived at the soccer stadium.
2:30 p.m.	Tim remembered leaving his ticket at home.
2:40 p.m.	Tim didn't have a ticket, so he had to go back home.

(1) When Tim ________ at the soccer stadium, the game ________ ________ ________.

(2) Tim had to go back home because he ________ ________ ________ ________ there.

약점 공략
틀린 문제가 있다면?

틀린 문항 번호가 있는 칸을 색칠하고, 어떤 문법 POINT의 집중 복습이 필요한지 파악해 보세요.

문항 번호	연관 문법 POINT	문항 번호	연관 문법 POINT	문항 번호	연관 문법 POINT
01	P1	10	P1~P4	19	P1, P4
02	P3	11	P3, P4	20	P2, P3
03	P1	12	P2~P4	21	P1, P2
04	P1	13	P4	22	P1
05	P4	14	P1	23	P3, P4
06	P1	15	P1, P3, P4	24	P1, P3, P4
07	P2	16	P1~P4	25	P3, P4
08	P1	17	P4		
09	P1~P4	18	P1		

연관 문법 POINT 참고

P1 (p.8) 현재완료의 쓰임
P2 (p.8) 현재완료 진행형
P3 (p.10) 과거완료
P4 (p.10) 과거완료의 쓰임

내신만점 Level Up Test

신유형

01 우리말과 뜻이 같도록 다음 단어들을 배열하여 문장을 완성할 때, 6번째로 오는 단어는?

> Sally가 이탈리아로 이사를 간 이후로 나는 그녀에게서 아무 소식을 듣지 못했다.
> (moved, haven't, since, Italy, heard, I, from, she, to, Sally)

① heard ② from ③ since ④ haven't ⑤ moved

02 다음 중 밑줄 친 부분의 쓰임이 같은 것끼리 짝지어진 것은?

> ⓐ She found that she had lost her ring.
> ⓑ I recognized him because I had seen him before.
> ⓒ He had been ill for a week when he went to the doctor.
> ⓓ The movie had already begun when I arrived at the theater.
> ⓔ My brother has used this computer for 3 years.

① ⓐ, ⓒ ② ⓑ, ⓓ ③ ⓑ, ⓔ ④ ⓒ, ⓓ ⑤ ⓒ, ⓔ

03 다음 중 어법상 올바른 문장의 개수는?

> ⓐ Andrew has never had a job until he was fifty.
> ⓑ They have been running this restaurant for two years.
> ⓒ My mom had given a ride to me before she went to work.
> ⓓ When I entered the room, Laura had been looking for her ring.

① 없음 ② 1개 ③ 2개 ④ 3개 ⑤ 4개

서술형

04 대화를 읽고, [조건]에 맞게 우리말을 영어로 쓰시오.

> A: Fiona looks upset. Do you know why?
> B: (1) 그녀는 Henry를 두 시간째 기다리고 있어.
> A: What happened to him?
> B: I don't know. (2) Henry가 아직 전화를 받지 않아.
> A: I understand her. I've also had a similar experience.

> [조건] 1. 괄호 안의 말을 사용할 것
> 2. 완료/완료진행 시제를 사용하여 문장을 완성할 것

(1) She ________ ________ ________ ________ ________ for two hours. (wait for)

(2) Henry ________ ________ ________ ________ ________ yet. (answer the phone)

05 다음 대화의 밑줄 친 ⓐ~ⓔ 중 어법상 틀린 두 곳을 골라 바르게 고쳐 쓰고, 틀린 이유를 우리말로 쓰시오.

> A: Stephanie, ⓐ did you pass the math test?
> B: No, I ⓑ haven't.
> A: What happened? You ⓒ studied very hard.
> B: I ⓓ was late for the test because I ⓔ have overslept on that day.

(1) 틀린 부분: (   ) > ________
틀린 이유: ________

(2) 틀린 부분: (   ) > ________
틀린 이유: ________

UNIT 1 POINT 01 can, could
POINT 02 may, might

UNIT 2 POINT 03 must, should, ought to
POINT 04 used to, would rather, had better

UNIT 3 POINT 05 조동사+have p.p.

CHAPTER 02

조동사

조동사는 동사 앞에 쓰여서 의미를 더해 주는 말로 능력, 허락, 요청, 추측, 의무 등 다양한 의미를 나타낸다.

Preview

조동사	can, could	능력	Lisa can play the violin well.
		허락	You can go if you finish your work.
		요청·부탁	Can(Could) you carry the boxes for me?
		가능성·추측	Eric cannot have stolen my wallet.
	may, might	허락	You may leave when you finish cleaning here.
		추측	He may(might) have left his bag on the bus.
	must (= have to)	의무	Drivers must follow traffic rules. (= Drivers have to follow traffic rules.)
		확신	They must have known the truth at that time.
	should / ought to	의무·충고	You should(ought to) go to bed early.
		후회	They should have listened to my advice.
	used to	과거의 습관	She used to play soccer with her friends.
		과거의 상태	I used to be very shy when I was a child.
관용 표현	would rather	선택	I would rather fail the exam than cheat.
	had better	의무	You had better see a doctor at once.

UNIT 1 조동사 (1)

POINT 01 can, could

Henry *can speak four languages. Henry는 4개 국어를 말할 수 있다.

*능력을 나타내는 말이야.

능력	~할 수 있다	Blue whales **can** dive for up to an hour.
	⊕ be able to로 바꿔 쓸 수 있고, 이때 be동사는 주어의 수와 문장의 시제에 맞춘다. I **was able to** finish the work thanks to you. 서술형 빈출 ⊕ 조동사는 두 개 이상 이어서 쓸 수 없으므로 can이 다른 조동사와 함께 올 경우에는 be able to를 사용한다. We **will be able to** go to Canada next year.	
허락	~해도 좋다	You **can** bring your dog inside the store.
	⊕ 허락의 의미를 나타내는 can은 may로 바꿔 쓸 수 있다.	
요청·부탁	~해 주겠니?	**Can** you help me with my science homework?
	⊕ can 대신 could를 쓰면 더 공손한 요청의 의미를 나타낸다. **Could** you tell me how to get to the library?	
가능성·추측	~일 수도 있다	An accident **can** happen anywhere, at any time.
	⊕ can't는 '~일 리가 없다'는 강한 부정적 추측의 의미로 쓰일 수 있다. The rumor **can't** be true.	

개념 QUICK CHECK

POINT 01

밑줄 친 부분의 쓰임을 아래에서 골라 기호를 쓰시오.

a. 능력	b. 허락
c. 요청	d. 추측

1 Can I sit on the grass? ______

2 He can't be Mark. He is in L.A. ______

3 My brother can drive a car. ______

4 Could you open the window? ______

POINT 02 may, might

*May I use your smartphone? 당신의 스마트폰을 써도 될까요?

*허락을 구하는 표현이야.

허락	~해도 좋다	You **may** take a rest any time.
	⊕ 허락을 나타내는 may는 can보다 더 정중한 표현으로, 일상생활에서는 may보다 can을 더 많이 쓴다.	
추측	~일지도 모른다	Emma **may** become a famous actress.
	⊕ might는 may보다 실현 가능성이 낮은 불확실한 추측을 나타낸다. Kevin **might** win a prize but I doubt it.	

① 허락을 나타내는 may와 can의 부정은 '~해서는 안 된다'의 의미를 나타낸다.
You **may not(cannot)** go out alone late at night.

POINT 02

밑줄 친 부분의 쓰임에 해당하는 것에 ✓ 표시하시오.

1 Emily may be in her room.
☐ 허락 ☐ 추측

2 May I enter the house now?
☐ 허락 ☐ 추측

3 We might move to Jeju-do next year.
☐ 허락 ☐ 추측

대표 기출 유형으로 실전 연습

1 우리말과 일치하도록 괄호 안의 말을 사용하여 문장을 완성하시오.

나는 열심히 공부해서 좋은 성적을 받을 수 있었다. (able, get)

> I studied hard and ______________________________ good grades.

2 두 문장의 의미가 같도록 조동사를 사용하여 빈칸에 알맞은 말을 쓰시오.

It is not possible that the boy is a middle school student.

= The boy __________ __________ a middle school student.

3 다음 중 밑줄 친 may의 쓰임이 나머지와 다른 것은?

① Your phone is ringing. It may be Alex.
② You may wear my new jacket if you want to.
③ Jessica walked a lot. Her legs may hurt later.
④ It may rain this afternoon. It's very cloudy now.
⑤ The traffic is very bad, so he may be a little late.

자주 나와요!

4 빈칸에 들어갈 말이 순서대로 바르게 짝지어진 것은?

- __________ you carry the bag for the old lady?
- You __________ watch TV after you have dinner.
- Will you __________ finish the report by next Monday?

① May – can – could ② Might – may – can
③ Might – can – be able to ④ Could – may – be able to
⑤ Could – are able to – can

틀리기 쉬워요!

5 다음 중 밑줄 친 부분의 쓰임이 어법상 틀린 것은?

① You may not bring your pet here.
② Don't worry. Anyone can make a mistake.
③ Andrew will can't pick you up this evening.
④ I might go to the concert tomorrow, but I'm not sure.
⑤ I have something to tell you. Can I talk to you for a minute?

개념 완성 Quiz *Choose or complete.*

1 능력을 나타내는 can은 __________로 바꿔 쓸 수 있고, 이때 be동사는 주어의 수와 문장의 시제에 맞춘다.
> POINT 01

2 [can't / may not]은(는) 강한 부정적 추측의 의미로 사용된다.
> POINT 01

3 may는 '~해도 좋다'는 ________의 의미와 '~일지도 모른다'는 ________의 의미를 나타낸다.
> POINT 02

4 can 대신 [might / could]를 쓰면 좀 더 공손한 요청의 의미를 나타낸다.
> POINT 01, 02

5 [might / can]은(는) may보다 실현 가능성이 낮은 불확실한 추측을 나타낸다.
> POINT 01, 02

UNIT 2 조동사 (2) 및 관용 표현

POINT 03 must, should, ought to

You *must follow the school rules. 너희들은 교칙을 지켜야 한다.

*해야 할 의무를 나타내.

must	~해야 한다(의무) (= have to)	You **must** wear a life vest on the boat. = You **have to** wear a life vest on the boat.
	~임에 틀림없다 (강한 추측)	Susan stayed up all night. She **must** be tired.
	⊕ must가 의무(~해야 한다)를 나타낼 때 have to로 바꿔 쓸 수 있다. You **have to** fasten your seat belt. ⊕ 부정형 must not은 금지(~하면 안 된다)를 나타낸다. You **must not** take pictures in the museum. ⊕ 부정형 don't have to는 불필요(~할 필요가 없다)를 나타낸다. You **don't have to(don't need to / need not)** bring your lunch. ⊕ 의무를 나타낼 때 과거형은 had to, 미래형은 will have to로 쓴다. She **had to** get up early this morning. You **will have to** go to bed early tonight.	
should, ought to	~해야 한다 (당연한 의무, 충고)	You **should(ought to)** exercise regularly. You **shouldn't(ought not to)** go to bed late.

POINT 04 used to, would rather, had better

You *had better bring your umbrella.
너는 우산을 가져가는 게 좋겠다.

*강한 충고의 의미를 나타내.

used to	~하곤 했다(습관) ~이었다(상태)	I **used to** go fishing with Dad every weekend. He **used to** be a troublemaker in our school.
	⊕ would는 과거의 불규칙한 습관을 나타낼 때 쓰이고, 동작만을 나타낸다. He **would** go for a walk after dinner. (○)	
would rather	~하는 편이 낫다, 차라리 ~하겠다	I **would rather** buy this blue shirt. We **would rather not** go out today.
	⊕ would rather *A* than *B*: *B* 하느니 차라리 *A* 하겠다 (*A*와 *B*는 같은 형태) I **would rather** walk **than** take a bus.	
had better	~하는 게 좋겠다	You **had better** tell the truth. You'**d better not** eat too much fast food.
	should보다 강한 충고나 명령의 의미를 나타낸다.	

ⓘ be used to+동사원형: ~하기 위해 사용되다 It **is used to cut** wood.
be used to+-ing: ~하는 데 익숙하다 She **is used to living** alone.

개념 QUICK CHECK

POINT 03

밑줄 친 부분의 쓰임을 아래에서 골라 기호를 쓰시오.

a. 의무 b. 강한 추측
c. 불필요

1 You ought to be quiet in the library. ______

2 We don't have to go to school today. ______

3 The visitor must be Dennis. I've seen his bike outside. ______

POINT 04

밑줄 친 부분이 어법상 올바르면 O, 틀리면 X를 쓰시오.

1 I would rather sleep than have breakfast. ( )

2 My parents are used to getting up early. ( )

3 Jake used to collecting toy cars when he was a little boy. ( )

4 You had not better drive today because of the snow. ( )

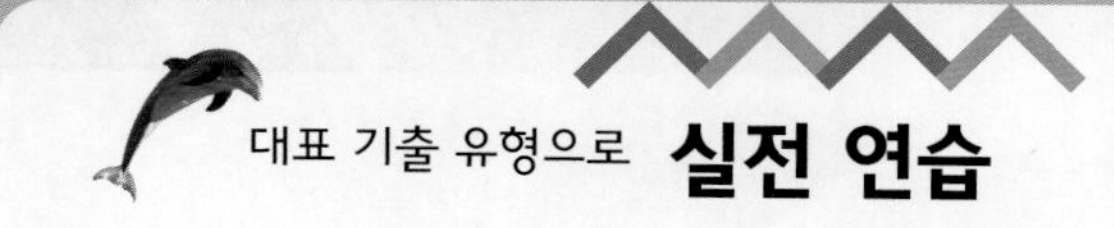

1 **빈칸에 들어갈 말로 알맞지 않은 것은?**

> This is an English speaking club, so you ________ speak English only.

① must ② have to ③ used to
④ should ⑤ ought to

자주 나와요!
2 **빈칸에 공통으로 들어갈 조동사를 쓰시오.**

• You ________ wear a helmet when you ride a bike.
• The boy ________ be Tom's brother. He looks very similar to Tom.

틀리기 쉬워요!
3 **두 문장의 뜻이 같도록 할 때 빈칸에 들어갈 말로 알맞은 것은?**

> Mary was a model when she was young, but she isn't anymore.
> = Mary ________ a model when she was young.

① would be ② ought to be ③ had better be
④ used to be ⑤ used to being

4 **우리말과 일치하도록 괄호 안의 말을 바르게 배열하여 문장을 완성하시오.**

나는 버스를 기다리느니 차라리 택시를 타겠어.

> ____

(than, rather, wait for, a taxi, would, I, take, a bus)

5 **빈칸에 들어갈 말이 순서대로 바르게 짝지어진 것은?**

> • You ________ go to the party if you don't want to.
> • I think you ________ leave your bag on the floor. It'll get dirty.

① must – would not
② must not – would not rather
③ must not – would rather not
④ don't have to – had better not
⑤ don't have to – had not better

개념 완성 Quiz *Choose or complete.*

1 should, ought to / used to, have to는 모두 의무를 나타낸다.
> POINT 03

2 의무와 강한 추측의 의미로 모두 사용되는 조동사는 ________이다.
> POINT 03

3 과거의 습관이나 상태를 나타낼 때에는 ________을(를) 사용한다.
> POINT 04

4 '*B* 하느니 차라리 *A* 하겠다'는 뜻을 나타낼 때에는 ________ ________ *A* than *B*를 사용한다.
> POINT 04

5 '~할 필요가 없다'라는 의미로 불필요를 나타낼 때에는 must not / don't have to을(를) 쓴다.
> POINT 03, 04

UNIT 3 조동사+have p.p.

POINT 05 조동사+have p.p.

(1) must have p.p.

I *must have left my smartphone on the bus.
버스에 스마트폰을 두고 내렸음에 틀림없다.
*강한 추측을 나타내.

과거의 일에 대한 강한 추측	~했음에 틀림없다	You look happy. You **must have heard** the good news.
	⊕ must have p.p.의 부정은 cannot have p.p.이다.	

(2) should have p.p.

It's raining. I *should have brought my umbrella.
비가 와. 나는 우산을 가져왔어야 했어.
*후회나 유감을 나타내.

과거의 일에 대한 후회나 유감	~했어야 했다 (그런데 하지 못했다)	The flowers died. I **should have watered** them more often.
	⊕ should have p.p.의 부정은 shouldn't(should not) have p.p.이며 '~하지 말았어야 했다 (그런데 했다)'는 의미이다. 서술형 빈출 I'm so tired. I **should not have watched** TV so late last night.	

(3) may(might) have p.p.

She *may have forgotten my birthday.
그녀는 내 생일을 잊었을지도 모른다.
*불확실한 추측을 나타내.

과거의 일에 대한 불확실한 추측	~했을지도 모른다	Mike hasn't arrived yet. He **might have taken** the wrong bus.
	⊕ might have p.p.는 may have p.p.보다 더 불확실한 추측을 나타낸다.	

(4) cannot have p.p.

Liam *cannot have done such a thing.
Liam이 그런 짓을 했을 리가 없다.
*강한 부정적 추측을 나타내.

과거의 일에 대한 강한 부정적 추측	~했을 리가 없다	Mason **cannot have passed** the exam. He didn't study at all.

개념 QUICK CHECK

POINT  05 – (1), (2)

밑줄 친 부분의 의미로 알맞은 것에 √ 표시하시오.

1 You must have taken the wrong train.
□ 탔을지도 모른다
□ 탔음에 틀림없다

2 I should have gone to bed earlier.
□ 일찍 잤다
□ 일찍 자지 않았다

3 Jack must have stopped at the red light.
□ 멈췄음에 틀림없다
□ 멈췄어야 했다

POINT  05 – (3), (4)

우리말과 일치하도록 빈칸에 알맞은 조동사를 아래에서 골라 문장을 완성하시오.

can	might
cannot	may not

1 Jack은 어젯밤에 그곳에 도착했을지도 모른다.
Jack ___________ have arrived there last night.

2 그들이 하루 만에 이탈리아에서 프랑스를 여행했을 리가 없다.
They ___________ have traveled from Italy to France in one day.

3 내 학생들은 내 말을 이해하지 못했을지도 모른다.
My students ___________ have understood my words.

대표 기출 유형으로 실전 연습

1 빈칸에 들어갈 말로 알맞은 것은?

Kate is an honest girl. She ________ to her teacher.

① might lie ② would rather lie ③ must have lied
④ cannot have lied ⑤ should have lied

자주 나와요!
2 주어진 문장과 뜻이 같은 것은?

It is possible that my sister wore my new jacket.

① My sister may have worn my new jacket.
② My sister mustn't have worn my new jacket.
③ My sister cannot have worn my new jacket.
④ My sister should have worn my new jacket.
⑤ My sister shouldn't have worn my new jacket.

3 다음 우리말을 영어로 옮긴 문장에서 틀린 부분을 찾아 바르게 고쳐 쓰시오.

Dave의 눈이 붉고 촉촉하다. 그는 많이 울었음에 틀림없다.
Dave's eyes are red and watery. He should have cried a lot.

________________ > ________________

4 빈칸에 들어갈 말이 순서대로 바르게 짝지어진 것은?

• Ann won the contest. She ________ have practiced hard. • I have a sore foot. I ________ have walked so long.

① must – cannot ② must – shouldn't ③ cannot – should
④ might – cannot ⑤ cannot – shouldn't

틀리기 쉬워요!
5 빈칸에 들어갈 말이 나머지와 다른 하나는?

① We ________ have listened to Steve. He was right.
② Karen is still angry. I ________ have apologized to her.
③ He ________ have driven a car. He doesn't have a license.
④ I'm so tired. I ________ have gone to bed early last night.
⑤ I have a toothache. I ________ have eaten chocolate less.

개념 완성 Quiz *Choose or complete.*

1 과거의 일에 대한 강한 부정적 추측을 나타낼 때에는 ________________를 사용한다.
> POINT 05

2 과거의 일에 대한 불확실한 추측을 나타낼 때에는 ________________를 사용한다.
> POINT 05

3 과거의 일에 대한 강한 추측을 나타낼 때에는 ________________를 사용한다.
> POINT 05

4 '~하지 말았어야 했다'는 의미로 과거의 일에 대한 후회나 유감을 나타낼 때에는 [shouldn't have p.p. / cannot have p.p.]를 사용한다.
> POINT 05

5 '~했어야 했다'는 의미로 과거의 일에 대한 후회나 유감을 나타낼 때에는 ________________를 사용한다.
> POINT 05

서술형 실전 연습

Step 1

개념 완성 Quiz *Choose or complete.*

1 **괄호 안의 말과 can을 사용하여 우리말을 영어로 쓰시오.**

Mike가 여기에 올 리가 없다. 그는 캠핑 갔다. (come here)

> Mike ______________________. He has gone camping.

2 **빈칸에 들어갈 말을 〈A〉와 〈B〉에서 각각 하나씩 골라 알맞은 형태로 쓰시오.**

〈A〉 must have to	〈B〉 get up be

(1) There __________ someone in the house. The lights are on.

(2) I had a meeting this morning, so I ______________ early.

3 **두 문장의 의미가 같도록 조동사를 사용하여 문장을 완성하시오.**

(1) It is not necessary that you bring your lunch.

= You ________ ________ ________ ________ your lunch.

(2) I don't believe that Alex cleaned his messy room.

= Alex ________ ________ ________ his messy room.

4 **그림을 보고, 괄호 안의 말을 사용하여 문장을 완성하시오.**

(1) <before> <now>

Sue ______________________ when she was in middle school. (used, wear glasses)

(2) I ______________________ with my friends ______________________ at home. (rather, watch TV, play soccer)

5 **우리말과 일치하도록 괄호 안의 단어를 사용하여 문장을 완성하시오.**

(1) 그것은 네 잘못이야. 너는 Kate에게 사과해야 해. (apologize)

> It's your fault. You ________ ________ ________ to Kate.

(2) 내 스마트폰을 못 찾겠어. 나는 그것을 집에 두고 왔을지도 몰라. (leave)

> I can't find my smartphone. I ________ ________ ________ it at home.

개념 완성 Quiz

1 [can't / shouldn't]: 강한 부정적 추측의 의미
> POINT 01

2 [had to / used to]: 의무를 나타내는 조동사의 과거형
> POINT 03

3 ____________: '~할 필요가 없다'는 의미로 불필요를 나타냄
> POINT 03, 05

4 ________ to: 과거의 습관이나 상태를 나타냄
> POINT 04

5 [should / might] have p.p.: 과거의 일에 대한 불확실한 추측의 의미
> POINT 03, 05

통합

6 **밑줄 친 부분의 쓰임이 틀린 것을 2개 골라 기호를 쓰고 바르게 고쳐 문장을 다시 쓰시오.**

ⓐ You may leave the table after you finish your meal.
ⓑ You will can speak English well someday.
ⓒ Lula had not better make the same mistake again.
ⓓ Chris ought to leave early if he wants to catch the train.

(   ) > ______________________

(   ) > ______________________

7 **다음 대화를 읽고, (조건)에 맞게 빈칸에 알맞은 말을 쓰시오.**

A: Mom, I saw a dragon in the garden.
B: It couldn't be a dragon. There aren't any dragons in the real world. They only exist in story books.
A: What did I see, then?
B: You ______ ______ ______ ______ ______.
There are some lizards in our garden.

(조건) 1. 과거의 일에 대한 강한 추측을 나타낼 것
2. see, a lizard를 사용하고 필요 시 형태를 바꿀 것

고난도

8 **다음 글을 읽고, Ron에게 해 줄 말을 (조건)에 맞게 쓰시오.**

Ron left the door open, and his dog got out. As soon as he knew she was gone, he went out to find her. Luckily, he found her at the park hours later, but he had a terrible time looking for the dog.

(조건) 1. 과거의 일에 대한 후회나 유감을 나타낼 것
2. You를 주어로 하고 총 7단어의 완전한 문장으로 쓸 것
3. leave the door open을 사용하고 필요 시 형태를 바꿀 것

____

개념 완성 Quiz *Choose or complete.*

6 had ____________: '~하지 않는 게 좋다'는 의미의 강한 충고
> POINT 01, 02, 03, 04

7 [may / must] have p.p.: 과거의 일에 대한 강한 추측의 의미
> POINT 05

8 [should / might] have p.p.: 과거의 일에 대한 후회나 유감의 의미
> POINT 05

실전 모의고사

시험일 : 월 일	문항 수 : 객관식 18 / 서술형 7
목표 시간 :	총점
걸린 시간 :	/ 100

[01-02] 빈칸에 들어갈 말로 알맞은 것을 고르시오. 각 2점

01

Tom hasn't eaten anything all day. He ________ be hungry.

① must ② cannot ③ should
④ had better ⑤ ought to

02

I ________ save money than buy this dress. It's too expensive.

① might ② used to
③ should not ④ would rather
⑤ didn't have to

03 다음 밑줄 친 부분과 바꿔 쓸 수 있는 것은? 2점

Children under school age <u>don't have to</u> pay the entrance fee.

① must not ② cannot ③ would not
④ might not ⑤ need not

04 빈칸에 공통으로 들어갈 말로 알맞은 것은? 3점

- You ________ wear my jacket if you are cold.
- Emily ________ solve the problem on her own.
- Excuse me, ________ you tell me where the hospital is?

① may ② can ③ must
④ ought to ⑤ have to

05 빈칸에 들어갈 말로 알맞지 <u>않은</u> 것은? 3점

You ________ go out alone at night in this city. It's dangerous.

① must not ② should not ③ ought not to
④ have to ⑤ had better not

06 두 문장의 의미가 같도록 할 때 빈칸에 들어갈 말로 알맞은 것은? 3점

Tracy didn't take her teacher's advice, but she should have.
> Tracy ________ her teacher's advice.

① must take ② might take
③ would take ④ cannot have taken
⑤ should have taken

[07-08] 대화의 빈칸에 들어갈 말이 순서대로 바르게 짝지어진 것을 고르시오. 각 3점

07

A: Ms. Evans, ________ I finish the assignment by tomorrow?
B: No, you ________. You can hand it in next week.

① may – can't ② have to – may not
③ should – must not ④ could – shouldn't
⑤ should – don't have to

08

A: ________ I speak to Racheal?
B: Sorry, there's nobody here by that name. You ________ have dialed the wrong number.

① Can – must ② Can – should
③ May – cannot ④ May – used to
⑤ Should – might

09 〈보기〉의 밑줄 친 부분과 의미가 같은 것은? 3점

〈보기〉 May I use your laptop for a while?

① Lisa may not want to see me.
② Take an umbrella. It may rain this afternoon.
③ If you have any questions, you may call me anytime.
④ The kid may be Ryan's son. He looks like Ryan a lot.
⑤ Jamie didn't answer my phone call. He may be sleeping.

10 밑줄 친 부분의 의미가 나머지와 다른 하나는? 3점

① Students must keep quiet in the library.
② James must be very sad to lose his dog.
③ Sophia must do her homework by herself.
④ You must take this medicine twice a day.
⑤ We must wear sunglasses to protect our eyes.

[11-12] 밑줄 친 부분 중 어법상 틀린 것을 고르시오. 각 4점

11 ① We had better listen to what Ms. Jones said.
② I broke Amy's bike. She must be angry at me.
③ I don't like singing. I would rather dance at the festival.
④ You ought to not play mobile games too much.
⑤ This elevator is out of order. You have to take the stairs.

통합
12 ① You shouldn't throw waste on the street.
② There would be a library next to the bank.
③ We were able to get there on time thanks to Eric.
④ You may not park here. Please move your car.
⑤ This food tastes terrible. The chef cannot have cooked it.

13 우리말을 영어로 바르게 옮긴 것은? 3점

지금 밖에 나가지 않는 것이 좋겠어.

① You can go out now.
② You might go out now.
③ You would rather go out now.
④ You had better not go out now.
⑤ You shouldn't have gone out now.

고난도
14 짝지어진 두 문장의 의미가 다른 것은? 5점

① My answers must be right.
= My answers can't be wrong.
② Chickens are birds, but they can't fly.
= Chickens are birds, but they aren't able to fly.
③ I'm sure that she passed the math exam.
= She must have passed the math exam.
④ We don't have much time, so we should hurry.
= We don't have much time, so we ought to hurry.
⑤ I went camping with my dad when young, but I don't go now.
= I'm used to going camping with my dad.

고난도 신유형
15 밑줄 친 ①~⑤ 중 어법상 틀린 것을 바르게 고친 것은? 5점

A: Ted ① hasn't arrived at the party yet. What if he doesn't come?
B: I'm sure he ② will come soon.
A: He ③ might have forgotten my birthday.
B: I don't think so. He ④ must have forgotten that. He ⑤ talked about your party this morning.

① haven't ② can't ③ should
④ cannot ⑤ has talked

16 괄호 안에서 알맞은 말을 골라 순서대로 짝지은 것은? 4점

- You should (go / went / have gone) to the concert. It was amazing.
- The actor (used to / had better) be my role model when I was young.

① go – used to
② went – used to
③ went – had better
④ have gone – had better
⑤ have gone – used to

17 우리말을 영어로 옮긴 것 중 틀린 것은? 5점

① 너는 나쁜 습관을 고쳐야 해.
> You ought to fix your bad habit.
② 그녀의 결정이 옳았음에 틀림없다.
> Her decision might have been right.
③ 내 남동생이 그런 말을 했을 리가 없어.
> My brother cannot have said such a thing.
④ 길이 막혀. 나는 차라리 택시를 타지 않겠어.
> Traffic is heavy. I would rather not take a taxi.
⑤ 그는 어렸을 때 오이 먹는 것을 싫어했다.
> He used to hate eating cucumbers when he was a child.

통합 고난도

18 어법상 올바른 문장끼리 짝지어진 것은? 5점

ⓐ What Jim said might be true, but I doubt it.
ⓑ You will must go to the dentist tomorrow.
ⓒ I would rather read a book than to watch the TV show.
ⓓ Emily checked the list many times. She cannot have made a mistake.

① ⓐ, ⓑ ② ⓐ, ⓓ ③ ⓑ, ⓒ
④ ⓑ, ⓓ ⑤ ⓒ, ⓓ

서술형

19 우리말과 일치하도록 괄호 안의 말을 바르게 배열하시오. 각 2점

(1) 너는 부모님께 아무것도 숨기지 않는 게 좋겠다.
> You ______________________ anything from your parents.
(hide, better, had, not)

(2) Jane은 똑똑해서 이 문제를 풀 수 있을지도 모른다.
> Jane is smart, so she ______________ ______________ this problem.
(able, solve, may, to, be)

20 다음 문장의 밑줄 친 부분을 문맥상 바르게 고쳐 쓰시오. 각 3점

(1) The waves are high. You <u>don't have to</u> swim in the sea.
> ______________________

(2) Mark <u>might</u> have gone hiking. He was sick in bed all day then.
> ______________________

21 다음 대화를 읽고, 괄호 안의 말과 조동사를 사용하여 우리말을 영어로 쓰시오. 4점

A: Do you want to go see this movie with me?
B: Sorry. I don't like horror movies.
A: Hmm.... If you don't go, <u>난 그 영화를 혼자 보느니 차라리 집에 있을래.</u>
B: Then, let's play computer games together.

> ______________________
(stay at home, see the movie alone)

Answers p. 5

22 그림을 보고, [조건]에 맞게 빈칸에 알맞은 말을 쓰시오. 각 4점

[조건] 1. 조동사를 이용하여 과거의 일에 대한 강한 추측을 나타낼 것 2. 괄호 안의 표현을 활용할 것

>

(1) Somi's hair is damaged and dry. She ________________ too often. (dye one's hair)

(2) Somi ________________ with her hair. (be upset)

23 다음 [조건]에 맞게 우리말을 영어로 쓰시오. 각 3점

[조건] 1. 과거의 일에 대한 후회나 유감을 나타낼 것 2. 괄호 안의 단어와 조동사를 사용할 것

(1) 그는 자신의 약속을 지켰어야 했지만, 그것을 어겼어.

> He ____________ his promise, but he broke it. (keep)

(2) 그녀는 마음이 상했어. 난 그녀의 마음에 상처를 주지 말았어야 했는데.

> She got upset. I ____________ her feelings. (hurt)

24 밑줄 친 부분 중 어법상 틀린 것을 골라 기호를 쓰고 바르게 고쳐 쓰시오. 4점

We ⓐ will go on a field trip to the National Museum of Korea tomorrow. The museum is free of charge. So we ⓑ don't have to pay for admission to enter the museum. We ⓒ will can experience traditional Korean culture there.

(　　) > ________________

25 다음 대화를 읽고, 물음에 답하시오. 각 3점

A: Your friend called while you were out. I think it's Jenny.
B: (A) 그건 Jenny일 리가 없어요. She just saw a movie with me.
A: She told me that she called you about her project.
B: (B) Amy may call me. She hasn't done it yet.

(1) 조동사를 사용하여 밑줄 친 우리말 (A)를 영어로 완성하시오.

> It ________________ Jenny.

(2) 밑줄 친 문장 (B)에서 문맥상 어색한 부분을 찾아 바르게 고쳐 쓰시오.

__________ > __________

약점 공략 틀린 문제가 있다면?

틀린 문항 번호가 있는 칸을 색칠하고, 어떤 문법 POINT의 집중 복습이 필요한지 파악해 보세요.

문항 번호	연관 문법 POINT	문항 번호	연관 문법 POINT	문항 번호	연관 문법 POINT
01	P3	10	P3	19	P1, P2, P4
02	P4	11	P3, P4	20	P3, P5
03	P3	12	P1~P5	21	P4
04	P1	13	P4	22	P5
05	P2~P4	14	P1, P3~P5	23	P5
06	P5	15	P5	24	P1, P3
07	P3	16	P4, P5	25	P1, P5
08	P1, P5	17	P3~P5		
09	P2	18	P1~P5		

연관 문법 POINT 참고

P1 (p.20) can, could
P2 (p.20) may, might
P3 (p.22) must, should, ought to
P4 (p.22) used to, would rather, had better
P5 (p.24) 조동사+have p.p.

Answers p. 6

내신만점 Level Up Test

01 문맥상 밑줄 친 부분의 쓰임이 어색한 것은?

① It's cloudy now. It may rain tonight.
② He's a thief! Someone can't call the police.
③ She hasn't eaten anything since last night. She must be hungry.
④ My old dog would take a walk every day when it was young.
⑤ You had better visit Jane today. She may leave tomorrow.

02 다음 중 어법상 틀린 문장의 개수는?

ⓐ Tourists will can see koalas in the zoo.
ⓑ You should not bring food here.
ⓒ Jessy can't be here. She has gone to Chicago.
ⓓ I had not better go out tonight because of the snow.
ⓔ I was used to visit museums every week when I was a student.

① 1개 ② 2개 ③ 3개 ④ 4개 ⑤ 없음

03 다음 중 의미가 같은 것끼리 바르게 짝지어진 것은?

(1) Amy might have told lies to me.
(2) Amy cannot have told lies to me.
(3) Amy must have told lies to me.

ⓐ It is certain that Amy told lies to me.
ⓑ It is possible that Amy told lies to me.
ⓒ I don't believe that Amy told lies to me.

① (1) – ⓐ ② (1) – ⓒ ③ (2) – ⓑ
④ (3) – ⓐ ⑤ (3) – ⓑ

04 우리말과 일치하도록 빈칸에 알맞은 말을 〈A〉와 〈B〉에서 각각 하나씩 골라 쓰시오. (한 번씩만 사용할 것)

〈A〉 might would used to

〈B〉 be hide have

유리는 나의 하나뿐인 조카이다. 나는 유리가 어린아이였을 때를 기억한다. 그녀는 수줍음이 매우 많았었다. 집에 낯선 사람이 오면, 그녀는 방에 숨곤 했었다.

v

Yuri is my only niece. I remember Yuri when she was a little child. She ________________ very shy. When a stranger came to her house, she ________________ in her room.

05 빈칸에 알맞은 조동사를 [보기]에서 골라 한 번씩만 쓰고 괄호 안의 말을 사용하여 대화를 완성하시오. (필요 시 형태를 바꿀 것)

[보기] have to should had better

A: The musical will start soon, but Ryan is not here yet.
B: Really? I (1) ________________ (remind) him of it yesterday, but I forgot. I'll call him now.
A: You (2) ________________ (call) him. I already called, but he didn't answer.
B: He (3) ________________ (come) right away, or he'll miss the musical.

UNIT 1 POINT 01 명사 역할을 하는 to부정사
POINT 02 형용사 역할을 하는 to부정사

UNIT 2 POINT 03 부사 역할을 하는 to부정사
POINT 04 to부정사 구문

UNIT 3 POINT 05 목적격 보어로 쓰이는 to부정사
POINT 06 목적격 보어로 쓰이는 원형부정사

UNIT 4 POINT 07 to부정사의 시제와 수동태
POINT 08 독립부정사

CHAPTER 03

to부정사

부정사(不定詞)는 '품사가 정해지지 않은 말'이라는 뜻이며, 인칭의 제한을 받지 않아 형태가 변하지 않고, **to부정사**는 「to+동사원형」의 형태로 쓴다.

Preview

to부정사 (to+동사원형)

역할	명사	My sister decided to study abroad.
	형용사	I have enough time to finish my project. James and I are to go hiking tomorrow.
	부사	He went to the grocery store to buy some fruit.
구문	too ~ to ...	The boy is too short to ride a roller coaster.
	enough to ...	She is smart enough to solve the problem.
목적격 보어 역할	to부정사	My teacher expected me to read many books.
	cf. 원형부정사	My parents made me clean my room.
수동태 · 시제	수동태	The computer needs to be repaired.
	시제	Jane seems to be an actress. Jane seems to have played the main role.
독립부정사		To be honest, I couldn't understand the film at all.
		To make matters worse, I don't have any money with me.

UNIT 1 명사·형용사 역할을 하는 to부정사

POINT 01 명사 역할을 하는 to부정사

*To exercise regularly isn't easy. 규칙적으로 운동하는 것은 쉽지 않다.
주어 / 동사 / 보어
*문장의 주어 역할을 해.

주어	~하는 것은, ~하기는	To ride a roller coaster is thrilling. = It is thrilling to ride a roller coaster.
	⊕ 주어나 목적어로 쓰인 to부정사(구)가 길면 가주어 또는 가목적어 it을 쓰고 to부정사(구)는 문장 뒤로 보낸다. 서술형 빈출 I found it hard to break bad habits. 〈가목적어〉 ⊕ to부정사(구)가 주어로 쓰이면 단수 취급하므로 단수 동사를 쓴다. To read books is my favorite thing.	
목적어	~하는 것을, ~하기를	He wants to be a pilot when he grows up.
보어	~하는 것(이다)	My duty in my class is to water the plants.

① to부정사의 부정형은 「not+to부정사」로 나타낸다.
I promise not to be late again.

POINT 02 형용사 역할을 하는 to부정사

He needs a friend *to talk to. 그는 이야기를 나눌 친구가 필요하다.
명사 수식
*명사 뒤에서 명사를 꾸며 줘.

명사 수식	~하는, ~할		Do you have time to help us?
	⊕ -thing, -body, -one으로 끝나는 대명사를 형용사와 to부정사가 동시에 꾸밀 때 「대명사+형용사+to부정사」 순서로 쓴다. I'm looking for something interesting to watch. ⊕ to부정사의 수식을 받는 명사가 전치사의 목적어일 때, to부정사 뒤에 전치사를 반드시 써야 한다. 서술형 빈출 Please lend me a pen to write with.		
be동사 + to부정사	예정	~할 예정이다	The plane is to take off within 10 minutes.
	의무	~해야 한다	You are to knock before you enter my room.
	의도	~하려면	If you are to get good grades, study harder.
	가능	~할 수 있다	My wallet was not to be found.
	운명	~할 운명이다	Romeo and Juliet were to fall in love with each other.

개념 QUICK CHECK

POINT 01

밑줄 친 부분의 역할에 해당하는 것에 √ 표시하시오.

1 My dream is to travel around the world.
□ 주어 □ 목적어 □ 보어

2 To walk fast burns a lot of calories.
□ 주어 □ 목적어 □ 보어

3 She hopes to visit the museum in Paris.
□ 주어 □ 목적어 □ 보어

4 A traffic jam makes it hard to arrive on time.
□ 주어 □ 목적어 □ 보어

POINT 02

밑줄 친 부분이 어법상 올바르면 ○, 틀리면 × 를 쓰시오.

1 나는 차가운 마실 것이 필요해.
I need cold something to drink. ( )

2 Amy는 영화를 볼 예정이다.
Amy is to watch a movie. ( )

3 Mike는 함께 놀 애완동물이 없다.
Mike doesn't have any pets to play. ( )

대표 기출 유형으로 실전 연습

1 우리말과 일치하도록 빈칸에 알맞은 말을 쓰시오.

건강에 좋은 식습관을 갖는 것은 중요하다.

> ________ is important ________ ________ healthy eating habits.

2 우리말과 일치하도록 괄호 안의 말을 사용하여 문장을 완성하시오.

(1) 나는 몇 시간째 서 있었어. 내게 앉을 의자를 줘. (sit on, a chair)

> I have been standing for hours. Give me ________________.

(2) Mike는 너무 추워서 따뜻한 마실 것이 필요했다. (drink, warm, something)

> Mike was very cold, so he needed ________________.

자주 나와요!

3 밑줄 친 부분의 쓰임이 나머지와 다른 하나는?

① To visit Singapore is our plan for this summer.
② The app makes it easier to find a destination.
③ Judy didn't have a chance to watch the movie.
④ My daily routine is to walk my dog in the park.
⑤ Chris wants to send these postcards to his friends.

4 두 문장의 의미가 같도록 할 때 빈칸에 들어갈 말로 알맞은 것은?

All the students are to follow the school rules.
= All the students ________________ the school rules.

① will not follow ② must follow ③ have followed
④ were following ⑤ don't have to follow

틀리기 쉬워요!

5 빈칸에 들어갈 말이 순서대로 바르게 짝지어진 것은?

• Is there a bench ________ in the park?
• I promise ________ late for the club meeting.

① sit – to be
② to sit – to be
③ to sit on – to not be
④ to sit with – not to be
⑤ to sit on – not to be

개념 완성 Quiz *Choose or complete.*

1 주어로 쓰인 to부정사가 긴 경우 주로 가주어 ________을(를) 쓰고 to부정사는 뒤로 보낸다.
> POINT 01

2 -thing으로 끝나는 대명사가 형용사와 to부정사의 꾸밈을 동시에 받을 때는 「대명사+________+________」 순서로 쓴다.
> POINT 02

3 to부정사가 명사처럼 쓰이면 문장에서 ______, ______, ______ 역할을 한다.
> POINT 01, 02

4 형용사 역할을 하는 「__________+to부정사」는 예정, 의무, 의도, 가능, 운명 등을 나타낸다.
> POINT 02

5 to부정사의 부정형은 not+to부정사 / to부정사+not 의 형태로 쓴다.
> POINT 01, 02

UNIT **2**

부사 역할을 하는 to부정사와 to부정사 구문

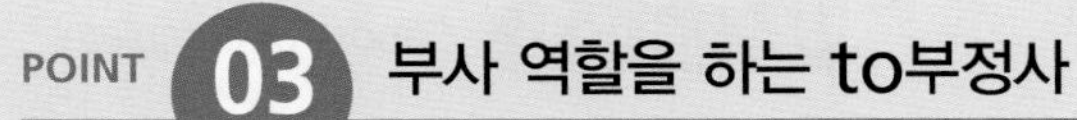

POINT 03 부사 역할을 하는 to부정사

> We went to the bakery* **to buy** a cake.
> 우리는 케이크를 사러 빵집에 갔다.
> *동사 went를 꾸며 빵집에 간 목적을 나타내.

to부정사가 부사처럼 쓰여 동사, 형용사, 부사를 수식한다.

구분	의미	예문
목적	~하기 위해	He has practiced hard **to win** the game.
	⊕ 목적을 나타낼 때 to부정사는 in order to 또는 so as to로 바꿔 쓸 수 있다. He has practiced hard **in order(so as) to win** the game.	
결과	~해서 (결국) …하다	She grew up **to be** a fashion model.
	⊕ 「only+to부정사」는 '(…했지만 결국) ~했다'의 의미로 결과를 나타낸다. Jason did his best **only to fail**.	
감정의 원인	~해서, ~하게 되어	I am happy **to win** first prize at the contest.
	⊕ 감정을 나타내는 형용사(happy, sad, glad, excited, pleased, afraid 등) 뒤에서 감정의 원인을 나타낸다.	
판단의 근거	~하다니, ~하는 것을 보니	Mia must be very angry **not to say** a word.
형용사 수식	~하기에	His theory is difficult **to understand**.

POINT 04 to부정사 구문

> This soup is* **too** hot **to** eat. 이 수프는 너무 뜨거워서 먹을 수 없다.
> *'너무 ~해서 …할 수 없다'는 의미를 나타내.

구문	의미	예문
too+형용사/부사+to부정사	너무 ~해서 …할 수 없다	I'm **too tired to do** any work today. = I'm **so tired that I can't do** any work today.
	⊕ 「so+형용사/부사+that+주어+can't+동사원형」으로 바꿔 쓸 수 있다.	
형용사/부사+enough+to부정사	~할 만큼(하기에) 충분히 …하다	He is **strong enough to climb** the wall. = He is **so strong that he can climb** the wall.
	⊕ 「so+형용사/부사+that+주어+can+동사원형」으로 바꿔 쓸 수 있다.	

① to부정사 구문 전환 시 유의점: so ~ that … 구문으로 바꿀 때, to부정사의 의미상 주어를 that절의 주어로 쓴다. 또한, that절에 타동사가 있으면 목적어를 반드시 써야 한다.
The project was **too complicated** for us **to finish** on time.
→ The project was **so complicated that** we **couldn't finish** it on time.

개념 QUICK CHECK

POINT 03

밑줄 친 부분이 나타내는 의미나 역할을 아래에서 골라 기호를 쓰시오.

a. 목적	b. 감정의 원인
c. 결과	d. 판단의 근거

1 I was surprised to hear the news. ______

2 She bought some vegetables to make a salad. ______

3 Grandma lived to be 95 years old. ______

4 He must be a genius to solve the math problem. ______

POINT 04

빈칸에 알맞은 것을 골라 기호를 쓰시오.

a. too heavy	b. too young
c. tall enough	

1 The kids are five years old. They are __________ to go to school.

2 He is __________ to reach the book on the shelf.

3 The box is __________ for me to lift.

대표 기출 유형으로 **실전 연습**

1 우리말과 일치하도록 괄호 안의 말을 바르게 배열하여 문장을 완성하시오.

(1) 그들은 딸을 보기 위해 뉴욕을 방문했다. (see, New York, to, visited)

> They ________________ their daughter.

(2) 그 남자아이는 자라서 유명한 댄서가 되었다. (be, grew up, to)

> The boy ________________ a famous dancer.

틀리기 쉬워요!

2 밑줄 친 to부정사의 쓰임이 [보기]와 같은 것은?

[보기] We were so excited to win the soccer game.

① The theory is not easy to explain.
② He will go to the shop to fix his bike.
③ Sharon must be happy to keep smiling.
④ They played computer games to stay up all night.
⑤ John was sad to hear that his friend was moving to Canada.

자주 나와요!

3 두 문장의 의미가 같도록 so ~ that ... 구문을 사용하여 문장을 완성하시오.

My brother was too sleepy to read the novel.
= My brother ________________ the novel.

4 다음 중 주어진 문장과 의미가 같은 것은?

Emily is so fit that she can finish a marathon.

① Emily is so fit to finish a marathon.
② Emily is enough fit to finish a marathon.
③ Emily is fit enough to finish a marathon.
④ Emily is too fit enough to finish a marathon.
⑤ Emily is fit that she cannot finish a marathon.

5 빈칸에 들어갈 말이 순서대로 바르게 짝지어진 것은?

• I was embarrassed ________ that I made a mistake. • The math problem was ________ for me to solve by myself.

① finding – that hard ② to find – that hard
③ finding – too hard ④ to find – too hard
⑤ to find – enough hard

개념 완성 Quiz *Choose or complete.*

1 to부정사는 문장에서 [부사 / 형용사]처럼 쓰여 목적이나 결과 등을 나타낸다.
> POINT 03

2 부사 역할을 하는 to부정사는 감정을 나타내는 형용사 뒤에서 감정의 [원인 / 결과]을(를) 나타낸다.
> POINT 03

3 '너무 ~해서 …할 수 없다'는 의미는 [enough to ~ / too ~ to …]로 나타낸다.
> POINT 04

4 '~할 만큼 충분히 …하다'는 의미는 「형용사/부사+________+to부정사」로 나타낸다.
> POINT 04

5 to부정사 구문에서 동작의 주체가 주어와 다를 때 의미상의 주어는 대부분의 경우 [from+목적격 / for+목적격]으로 쓴다.
> POINT 03, 04

UNIT **3** 목적격 보어로 쓰이는 to부정사와 원형부정사

UNIT 3 목적격 보어로 쓰이는 to부정사와 원형부정사

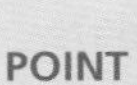

POINT 05 목적격 보어로 쓰이는 to부정사

Mom wants me* to become a lawyer.
엄마는 내가 변호사가 되기를 바라신다.
*want는 목적격 보어로 to부정사를 써.

5형식 문장에서 to부정사는 목적어를 보충 설명해주는 목적격 보어로 쓰일 수 있다.

주어+동사+목적어+to부정사	(목적어)가 …하는 것을(하도록) ~하다	The doctor advised him **to stop** smoking. Dad won't allow me **to become** a singer.
	⊕ 목적격 보어로 to부정사를 쓰는 동사 want(원하다), tell(말하다), ask(요청하다), advise(충고하다), allow(허락하다), expect(기대하다), encourage(장려하다), persuade(설득하다) 등 I will ask him **to come** with me. The doctor advised me **not to eat** fast food too much.	

POINT 06 목적격 보어로 쓰이는 원형부정사

Let me* know your email address. 네 이메일 주소를 알려 줘.
*사역동사 let은 목적격 보어로 원형부정사를 써.

to 없이 동사원형의 형태로 부정사의 역할을 하는 것을 원형부정사라고 하며, 주로 사역동사와 지각동사의 목적격 보어로 원형부정사가 쓰인다.

사역동사+목적어+원형부정사	(목적어)가 ~하게 시키다	Let me **introduce** my sister to you. The English teacher had us **write** an essay.
	⊕ get: '~가 …하게 하다'는 사역의 의미일 때, 목적격 보어로 to부정사를 쓴다. She finally got her kids **to go** to bed early. ⊕ help: '~하는 것을 돕다'는 의미일 때, 목적격 보어로 원형부정사와 to부정사를 모두 쓸 수 있다. This material helps students **(to) understand** the lesson.	
지각동사+목적어+원형부정사	(목적어)가 ~하는 것을 보다/듣다/느끼다	We saw the sun **rise** over the mountains. Did you hear somebody **shout** for help?
	⊕ 동작이 진행 중임을 강조할 때는 지각동사의 목적격 보어로 현재분사를 쓴다. Can you feel the ground **shaking**?	

① 사역동사와 지각동사의 목적어와 목적격 보어의 관계가 수동인 경우 목적격 보어로 과거분사를 쓴다.
My dad had the TV set **repaired**.
Jack heard his name **called**.

개념 QUICK CHECK

POINT 05

우리말과 뜻이 같도록 괄호 안의 말을 사용하여 빈칸에 쓰시오.

1 엄마는 내가 캠핑을 가도록 허락하셨다.
Mom allowed me ________ camping. (go)

2 나는 그녀에게 서두르라고 말했다.
I told her ________. (hurry)

3 그는 내가 동아리에 가입하도록 설득했다.
He persuaded me ________ his club. (join)

POINT 06

빈칸에 알맞은 말에 ✓ 표시하시오.

1 Don't make her ______.
□ cry □ to cry

2 Can you get your brothers ______ fighting?
□ stop □ to stop

3 I saw a man ______ a stone into the river.
□ throw □ to throw

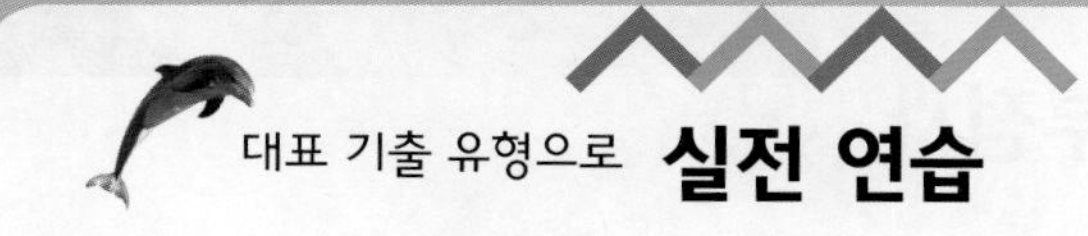

자주 나와요!

1 빈칸에 들어갈 말로 알맞지 않은 것은?

Ms. Davis ________ me to enter the violin contest.

① let ② wanted ③ advised
④ expected ⑤ encouraged

2 빈칸에 들어갈 말로 알맞은 것을 모두 고르면?

Writing a diary in English helps you ________ English.

① practice ② practices ③ to practice
④ practicing ⑤ have practiced

3 빈칸에 들어갈 말을 [보기]에서 골라 알맞은 형태로 쓰시오.

[보기] think ride buy

(1) My parents allowed me __________ a new smartphone.
(2) Jessica saw some children __________ bikes at the park.
(3) The teacher had us __________ about the message of the book.

4 밑줄 친 ①~⑤ 중 어법상 틀린 부분을 골라 바르게 고쳐 쓰시오.

Dad ①made my sister ②apologize ③to me, and ④told us ⑤not fight again.

(   ) > ____________________

틀리기 쉬워요!

5 다음 중 밑줄 친 부분의 쓰임이 어법상 틀린 것은?

① Jason had his car washed at the shop.
② Mom got me clean my room after dinner.
③ The man felt someone touch his shoulder.
④ Let me explain what happened to us yesterday.
⑤ Laura persuaded me to think again before I decided.

개념 완성 Quiz *Choose or complete.*

1 ask, tell, advise 등의 동사는 목적격 보어로 [to부정사 / 원형부정사]를 쓴다.
> POINT 05

2 help는 목적격 보어로 ________와 ________를 모두 쓸 수 있다.
> POINT 06

3 [지각동사 / 사역동사]는 목적격 보어로 원형부정사 또는 현재분사를 쓸 수 있다.
> POINT 05, 06

4 사역동사는 목적격 보어로 [현재분사 / 원형부정사]를 쓴다.
> POINT 05, 06

5 [let / get / have]은(는) '~가 …하게 하다'라는 의미일 때, 목적격 보어로 to부정사를 쓴다.
> POINT 05, 06

POINT 07 to부정사의 시제와 수동태

Noel seems to be very shy. Noel은 무척 수줍어하는 것 같다.

(1) 시제 표현

단순부정사(to+동사원형)는 to부정사의 시제와 주절의 시제가 같을 때 쓰고, 완료부정사(to+have p.p.)는 to부정사의 시제가 주절의 시제보다 앞설 때 쓴다.

seem+to +동사원형	Romeo **seems to love** Juliet. = It **seems** that Romeo loves Juliet.
seem+to+ have p.p.	Romeo **seems to have loved** Juliet. = It **seems** that Romeo loved Juliet.

⊕ 「It seems(seemed) that ~.」 구문을 「seem+to부정사」로 전환 시 seem과 that절의 동사가 같은 시제이면 단순부정사를, seem보다 한 시제 앞서면 완료부정사를 쓴다.

(2) 수동태 표현

to be+p.p.	I don't want you **to be stressed out**. His new album is going **to be released** soon.

⊕ to부정사와 의미상 주어의 관계가 수동일 때 「to be+p.p.」 형태로 쓴다.

POINT  독립부정사

***To be honest**, I don't like your gift.*

솔직히, 나는 네 선물이 마음에 안 든다. *독립적으로 쓰여 문장 전체를 수식해.

to부정사구가 관용적으로 쓰여 부사구처럼 문장 전체를 수식하는 것을 독립부정사라고 한다.

to be sure	확실히	**To be sure**, she is the best dancer.
to begin with	우선, 무엇보다도	**To begin with**, he changed his habit.
to be honest	솔직히 말하면	I don't like Scott, **to be honest**.
strange to say	이상한 말이지만	**Strange to say**, I dreamed the same dream twice.
needless to say	말할 필요도 없이	**Needless to say**, I'm going to miss you.
so to speak	말하자면	He is, **so to speak**, a walking dictionary.
to make matters worse	설상가상으로	**To make matters worse**, it started to rain.
to tell the truth	사실을 말하자면	**To tell the truth**, the movie was boring.

개념 QUICK CHECK

POINT 07

우리말과 일치하도록 괄호 안에서 알맞은 것을 고르시오.

1 그녀는 울었던 것 같다.
She seems (to have cried / to cry).

2 모두가 파티를 즐기는 것 같았다.
Everyone seemed (to enjoy / to have enjoyed) the party.

3 옷장을 정리할 필요가 있다.
The closet needs (to organize / to be organized).

4 나는 그가 잊혀지길 원하지 않는다.
I don't want him (to forget / to be forgotten).

POINT 

밑줄 친 부분의 의미로 알맞은 것을 아래에서 골라 기호를 쓰시오.

a. 우선	b. 솔직히 말하면
c. 설상가상으로	d. 말하자면

1 He is, so to speak, a genius scientist. ______

2 I don't like the color, to begin with. ______

3 To be honest, I don't remember his name. ______

4 To make matters worse, I lost my bag. ______

대표 기출 유형으로 실전 연습

1 빈칸에 들어갈 말이 순서대로 바르게 짝지어진 것은?

> Samantha seems to be happy to hear the news.
> = It _______ that Samantha _______ happy to hear the news.

① seemed – is ② seems – is
③ seemed – to be ④ seems – has been
⑤ has seemed – had been

2 문맥상 빈칸에 들어갈 말로 가장 알맞은 것은?

> I got lost in the city. ________, I had my wallet stolen on the street.

① So to speak ② To be sure
③ Needless to say ④ Strange to say
⑤ To make matters worse

자주 나와요!
3 우리말과 일치하도록 괄호 안의 말을 바르게 배열하여 문장을 완성하시오.

나는 내 친구들이 비난받는 것을 원하지 않는다.

> I don't want ______________________.
(blamed, to, my friends, be)

4 두 문장의 의미가 같도록 to부정사를 사용하여 문장을 완성하시오.

It seemed that Chelsey had lost a lot of weight.
= Chelsey seemed ______________________ a lot of weight.

틀리기 쉬워요!
5 문맥상 빈칸에 들어갈 말이 순서대로 바르게 짝지어진 것은?

> Cathy gave me a dress for my birthday. ______________, I didn't like the color. But I didn't say so because I didn't want her ______________.

① To be sure – to hurt ② So to speak – to hurt
③ To be honest – to be hurt ④ Needless to say – to be hurt
⑤ To tell the truth – to hurt

개념 완성 Quiz *Choose or complete.*

1 to부정사의 시제와 주절의 시제가 같을 때 쓰는 단순부정사는 [to+동사원형 / to+have p.p.]의 형태이다.
> POINT 07

2 설상가상으로: [so to speak / to make matters worse / strange to say]
> POINT 08

3 to부정사와 의미상 주어의 관계가 수동일 때 [be to+p.p. / to be+p.p.] 형태로 쓴다.
> POINT 07

4 주절의 시제보다 to부정사의 시제가 앞설 때 쓰는 완료부정사는 [have been to+동사원형 / to have+p.p.]의 형태이다.
> POINT 07

5 솔직히 말하면: [to be honest / to be sure / so to speak]
> POINT 07, 08

서술형 실전 연습

개념 완성 Quiz *Choose or complete.*

1 **우리말과 일치하도록 괄호 안의 말을 바르게 배열하여 문장을 완성하시오.**

(1) 강에서 수영하는 것은 위험하다.

> ______________________________ in the river.

(is, to, dangerous, swim, it)

(2) 우리는 꽃을 사기 위해 시장에 갔다.

> We went ______________________________.

(to, buy, to, the market, flowers)

1 가주어·진주어 구문: It / That + be동사 ~+ to부정사 / 동사원형

> POINT 01, 03

2 **두 문장의 의미가 같도록 괄호 안의 말과 to부정사를 사용하여 문장을 완성하시오.**

(1) I went to bed early to get enough sleep.

> I went to bed early ________ ________ ________ ________ enough sleep. (order)

(2) This train is going to leave in ten minutes.

> This train ________ ________ ________ in ten minutes. (be)

2 목적을 나타내는 to부정사는 「________ ________ ________ +동사원형」으로 바꿔 쓸 수 있다.

> POINT 02, 03

3 **괄호 안의 말을 바르게 배열하여 문맥상 알맞은 문장을 완성하시오.**

(1) The flood had destroyed their house. They ______________ ______________________. (to, needed, in, a house, live)

(2) Sadly, the owner of the dog passed away. We are looking for ____________________. (the dog, someone, take care of, to)

3 형용사 역할을 하는 to부정사: 뒤에서 명사 / 부사를 수식함

> POINT 02

4 **밑줄 친 ⓐ~ⓒ 중 어법상 틀린 부분을 골라 바르게 고쳐 쓰시오.**

(1) My dad had me ⓐ to go ⓑ to the gym ⓒ for an hour every day.

(   ) > ______________________

(2) Naomi asked ⓐ her older brother ⓑ lend ⓒ her the laptop.

(   ) > ______________________

4 사역동사의 목적격 보어의 형태: to부정사 / 동사원형

> POINT 05, 06

5 **그림을 보고, 괄호 안의 표현을 사용하여 내가 본 것이나 들은 것을 쓰시오.**

(1) I saw a girl ______________ ________. (eat an ice cream cone)

(2) I heard a man ______________ ________. (play my favorite song)

5 지각동사의 목적격 보어의 형태: to부정사, 과거분사 / 동사원형, 현재분사

> POINT 06

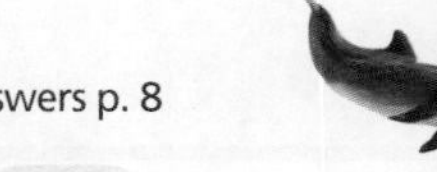

Step 2

Answers p. 8

6 다음 글의 밑줄 친 문장과 뜻이 같도록 to부정사를 사용해서 문장을 완성하시오.

> I saw Ms. Smith in front of my house. She was looking for something in a hurry. It seemed that she had lost her belongings. I asked her "What's wrong?" but she only said "Nothing," and suddenly went away.

> She seemed ________________________________.

7 그림을 보고, (조건)에 맞게 대화를 완성하시오.

(1)  (2) 

(조건) 1. 괄호 안의 말을 사용하여 완전한 문장으로 쓸 것
2. too ~ to ... 구문이나 enough to ... 구문을 사용할 것

(1) **A:** I'm sweating now. The weather ____________________
____________________. (hot, wear, this coat)
B: Then, why don't you take it off?

(2) **A:** Excuse me. Can I ride this roller coaster?
B: Sorry, you can't. You're not ____________________
____________________. (tall, get on the ride)

고난도

8 다음 대화의 내용을 요약한 문장을 (조건)에 맞게 완성하시오.

A: James must be a genius.
B: James? What makes you think so?
A: I was solving some puzzles. They were so difficult that I couldn't solve them for a long time. Then, James came and solved all the puzzles in five minutes.
B: Oh, he is, so to speak, very smart.

(조건) 1. 본문에 나온 표현과 to부정사를 사용할 것
2. 8단어를 추가하여 문장을 완성할 것

> James must be a genius ____________________________.

개념 완성 Quiz *Choose or complete.*

6 완료부정사 [to+have p.p. / to be+p.p.]: 주절인 seem의 시제보다 that절의 시제가 한 시제 앞설 때 사용
> POINT 07

7 ________: 너무 ~해서 …할 수 없다
> POINT 04

8 [부사 / 형용사] 역할을 하는 to부정사: 목적, 판단의 근거, 감정의 원인, 결과 등의 의미로 사용
> POINT 03

실전 모의고사

시험일 : 월 일	문항 수 : 객관식 18 / 서술형 7
목표 시간 :	총점
걸린 시간 :	/ 100

[01-02] 빈칸에 들어갈 말로 알맞은 것을 고르시오. 각 2점

01

Maria made her son ______________ his homework after school.

① do ② did ③ does
④ doing ⑤ to do

02

Mr. Lee always encourages his students ________ a dream.

① have ② had ③ having
④ to have ⑤ have had

03 빈칸에 공통으로 들어갈 말로 알맞은 것은? 3점

- She needs a friend to talk ________.
- I don't have any toys to play ________.

① on ② to ③ for
④ with ⑤ about

04 빈칸에 들어갈 말로 알맞지 <u>않은</u> 것은? 3점

Kate ________ me to take care of her cats while she was on vacation.

① had ② asked ③ wanted
④ allowed ⑤ expected

05 두 문장의 의미가 같도록 할 때 빈칸에 알맞은 것은? 3점

It seemed that Alex had failed the exam.
= Alex seemed to ________ the exam.

① fail ② be failed
③ had failed ④ have failed
⑤ have been failed

06 대화의 빈칸에 들어갈 말로 알맞은 것은? 3점

A: I heard the test was difficult to pass.
B: Mark passed it. He studied ________ it.
A: Oh, good for him. I'm glad to hear that.

① hard to not pass ② hard not to pass
③ too hard to pass ④ enough hard to pass
⑤ hard enough to pass

07 우리말과 일치하도록 할 때 빈칸에 알맞은 것은? 3점

우리는 모두 당신이 올해의 선수로 선정되기를 기대한다.
> We all expect you ________ as the Player of the Year.

① select ② to select
③ be selected ④ to be selected
⑤ to being selected

08 밑줄 친 부분의 쓰임이 나머지와 <u>다른</u> 것은? 3점

① The sandwich is very easy <u>to make</u>.
② We have a lot of work <u>to finish</u> today.
③ I was very disappointed <u>to fail</u> the test.
④ She grew up <u>to be</u> a famous singer.
⑤ Jenny practiced very hard <u>to win</u> the competition.

09 다음 중 나머지 문장과 의미가 <u>다른</u> 하나는? 3점

① John is too tired to study anymore.
② John isn't too tired, so he can study more.
③ John is so tired that he can't study anymore.
④ John is very tired, so he can't study anymore.
⑤ John can't study anymore because he is very tired.

10 [보기]의 밑줄 친 부분과 쓰임이 같은 것은? 4점

[보기] We need a lot of people to help us.

① It was foolish of me to believe his lie.
② Did you decide to visit Rome this year?
③ His goal is to win the school debate contest.
④ Do you have some time to talk this afternoon?
⑤ I was surprised to see the big shadow behind me.

[11-12] 빈칸에 들어갈 말이 순서대로 바르게 짝지어진 것을 고르시오. 각 3점

11

- This map will help you ________ your destination.
- Mr. Parker persuaded us ________ at a nursing home.

① find – volunteer
② to find – volunteer
③ find – to volunteer
④ finding – to volunteer
⑤ found – volunteered

12

- Linda was excited ________ for the team.
- Tim and I heard someone ________ on the door.

① to choose – knock
② to be chosen – knock
③ to choose – knocking
④ to be chosen – to knock
⑤ to choose – to knock

13 다음 중 밑줄 친 부분의 우리말 뜻이 올바른 것은? 3점

① To begin with, I'd like to thank you all. (확실히)
② The child is a genius, so to speak. (말하자면)
③ Strange to say, I'm not interested in money. (무엇보다도)
④ To tell the truth, Sally and I lied to the teacher. (말할 필요도 없이)
⑤ To make matters worse, I missed an important exam. (이상한 말이지만)

14 다음 중 빈칸에 to가 들어갈 수 없는 것은? 4점

① It's difficult ________ make new friends.
② There are many things ________ see and do in Paris.
③ Rachael didn't expect ________ be given first prize.
④ Jamie has saved money in order ________ buy new shoes.
⑤ People watched the firefighter ________ save a little girl.

[15-16] 밑줄 친 부분 중 어법상 틀린 것을 고르시오. 각 4점

15 ① The machine is very convenient to use.
② I took the express train so as arrive on time.
③ The doctor advised me not to eat junk food too much.
④ You must be brave to travel around the world by yourself.
⑤ Sarah was shocked to hear that her son got into an accident.

16 ① Can you get your dog to stop barking?
② I promised not to waste time playing games.
③ Could you recommend some music to listen?
④ She does many things to protect the environment.
⑤ We're pleased to hear that Jake was accepted to college.

17 짝지어진 두 문장의 의미가 다른 것은? 5점

① Daniel seems to be an actor.
= It seems that Daniel is an actor.

② If you are to pass the exam, study hard.
= If you want to pass the exam, study hard.

③ Angela heard someone call her nickname.
= Angela heard her nickname called.

④ Bob is strong enough to move the box.
= Bob is so strong that he can move the box.

⑤ It was so noisy outside that we couldn't fall asleep.
= It was too noisy outside for us not to fall asleep.

18 ①~⑤의 밑줄 친 부분을 바르게 고쳐 쓴 것 중 어법상 틀린 것은? 5점

> ① I don't want to see as a coward.
> ② To paint sunflowers give Cynthia comfort.
> ③ Be honest, the chef isn't good at cooking.
> ④ Megan got her son do the dishes after dinner.
> ⑤ Our soccer team did their best only lose the game.

① to see > to be seen
② give > gives
③ Be honest > To be honest
④ do > done
⑤ only lose > only to lose

서술형

19 우리말과 일치하도록 괄호 안의 말을 바르게 배열하시오. 각 2점

(1) 그 비밀번호는 기억하기에 어렵다.
> The password ____________________.
(is, difficult, remember, to)

(2) 가족과 함께 시간을 보내는 것은 중요하다.
> ________________________________ with family.
(time, is, spend, to, it, important)

20 두 문장의 의미가 같도록 to부정사를 사용하여 빈칸에 알맞은 말을 쓰시오. 각 3점

(1) You must not leave during the exam.
= You ________ ________ ________ ________ during the exam.

(2) Sophia was so brave that she could tell the truth.
= Sophia was ________ ________ ________ ________ the truth.

(3) It seemed that Jake and Tom had fought with each other.
= Jake and Tom seemed ________ ________ ________ with each other.

21 괄호 안의 말과 to부정사를 사용하여 대화를 완성하시오. 3점

> **A:** Do you want to go see a movie?
> **B:** Not really. There's ________________ ____________ (interesting, see, nothing) at the theater right now.
> **A:** Then, let's just stay at home and play games.
> **B:** That sounds good.

Answers p. 8

22 다음 [조건]에 맞게 우리말을 영어로 완성하시오. 각 3점

[조건] 1. 괄호 안의 말을 사용할 것
2. too ~ to ... 구문을 사용할 것

(1) Daisy는 너무 긴장해서 아무 말도 하지 못했다.
> Daisy was ______________________ ______________________. (nervous, say a word)

(2) 그 실험은 너무 위험해서 학생들이 할 수 없다.
> The experiment is ______________________ ______________________. (the students, dangerous, do)

23 밑줄 친 부분의 쓰임이 어법상 틀린 문장을 2개 찾아 기호를 쓰고 바르게 고쳐 문장을 다시 쓰시오. 각 3점

ⓐ My parents had the old fence paint.
ⓑ The doctor made her stay in bed all day.
ⓒ Last night, I heard the rain to fall on the roof.
ⓓ The woman helped me to find the way to the hospital.

( ) > ______________________
( ) > ______________________

24 빈칸에 알맞은 말을 [보기]에서 골라 알맞은 형태로 써넣어 글을 완성하시오. 각 2점

[보기] find live in move

Sam and Alice planned (1)__________ next spring. Their purpose was to raise their sons in a new house, so they wanted a big house (2)__________. They also wanted a big beautiful garden. It was not easy (3)__________ a house they really liked.

고난도
25 다음 대화를 읽고, 물음에 답하시오. 각 3점

A: I want to sign up for a Spanish class. What should I do?
B: Fill out this application form, please.
A: (A) 저는 쓸 펜이 없어요. Can I borrow yours?
B: Of course. Here it is.
A: Can I register for the same class for my friend, too?
B: No. (B) We don't allow anyone apply for a class for others.

(1) 밑줄 친 우리말 (A)를 괄호 안의 말을 사용하여 영어로 쓰시오. (have, a pen, write)
> ______________________

(2) 밑줄 친 (B)에서 틀린 부분을 찾아 바르게 고쳐 쓰시오.
__________ > __________

약점 공략
틀린 문제가 있다면?

틀린 문항 번호가 있는 칸을 색칠하고, 어떤 문법 POINT의 집중 복습이 필요한지 파악해 보세요.

문항 번호	연관 문법 POINT	문항 번호	연관 문법 POINT	문항 번호	연관 문법 POINT
01	P6	10	P1~P3	19	P1, P2
02	P5	11	P5, P6	20	P2, P4, P7
03	P2	12	P3, P6	21	P2
04	P5, P6	13	P8	22	P4
05	P7	14	P1~P3, P6, P7	23	P6
06	P4	15	P3, P5	24	P1, P2
07	P7	16	P1~P3, P6	25	P2, P5
08	P2, P3	17	P2, P4, P6, P7		
09	P4	18	P1, P3, P6~P8		

연관 문법 POINT 참고

P1 (p.34) 명사 역할을 하는 to부정사
P2 (p.34) 형용사 역할을 하는 to부정사
P3 (p.36) 부사 역할을 하는 to부정사
P4 (p.36) to부정사 구문
P5 (p.38) 목적격 보어로 쓰이는 to부정사
P6 (p.38) 목적격 보어로 쓰이는 원형부정사
P7 (p.40) to부정사의 시제와 수동태
P8 (p.40) 독립부정사

내신만점 Level Up Test

신유형

01 빈칸에 들어갈 수 있는 동사의 개수는?

Christina ________ me to join the magic club.

ⓐ wanted ⓑ let ⓒ had
ⓓ persuaded ⓔ allowed ⓕ helped

① 1개 ② 2개 ③ 3개 ④ 4개 ⑤ 5개

02 다음 글의 밑줄 친 부분 중 [보기]와 쓰임이 같은 것은?

[보기] I went to the library to borrow some books.

Ken wanted ① to stay healthy. He made a list of things ② to do for his health. First, he planned ③ to work out regularly. Second, he decided not to eat too much junk food ④ to avoid gaining weight. Lastly, he promised ⑤ to go to bed early.

03 밑줄 친 부분에 대한 설명으로 틀린 것은?

① I'm looking for an apartment to live in.
→ 명사를 수식하는 형용사 역할을 한다.

② The package is to be delivered this afternoon.
→ 「be동사+to부정사」의 형태로 예정을 나타낸다.

③ She found it difficult to learn a new language.
→ it은 가목적어이고 to learn ~은 진목적어이다.

④ The man got me to carry all the boxes.
→ 사역의 의미를 나타내는 got의 목적격 보어로 쓰인 to부정사이다.

⑤ I'm happy to apply for the volunteer program.
→ 판단의 근거를 나타내는 부사 역할을 한다.

서술형

04 두 문장이 같은 뜻이 되도록 [조건]에 맞게 문장을 완성하시오.

The questions of the interviewers were too difficult for me to answer.
= The questions of the interviewers were ________________________.

[조건] 1. so ~ that ... 구문을 사용할 것
2. them을 포함하고 시제에 유의할 것

05 밑줄 친 (A)와 (B)의 우리말과 뜻이 같도록 [보기]에 주어진 말을 이용하여 빈칸에 알맞은 말을 쓰시오. (필요 시 형태를 바꿀 것)

[보기] advise help write become a good writer

Jason은 작가가 되고 싶었지만 무엇을 해야 할지 몰랐다. 그는 작가에게 조언을 구했다. 그녀는 Jason에게 "다양한 책을 읽는 것이 (A) 당신이 좋은 작가가 되는 데에 도움이 된다."라고 말했다. 그녀는 또한 가능한 한 많이 (B) 쓰라고 그에게 조언했다.

∨

Jason wanted to be a writer, but he didn't know what to do. He asked a writer for advice. She said to Jason, "Reading various books (A) ________________________." She also (B) ________________ as much as possible.

UNIT 1 POINT 01 동명사의 역할
POINT 02 동명사의 시제와 수동태

UNIT 2 POINT 03 동명사의 의미상 주어
POINT 04 동명사의 관용 표현

UNIT 3 POINT 05 목적어로 동명사나 to부정사만 쓰는 동사
POINT 06 목적어로 동명사와 to부정사를 모두 쓰는 동사

CHAPTER

동명사

동명사(動名詞)는 「동사원형+-ing」의 형태로 동사의 성격과 명사의 성격을 둘 다 가지고 있다.

Preview

동명사			
역할	주어	Exercising regularly is good for our health.
	목적어	She enjoys going hiking with her father.
	보어	My plan is building a house in the countryside.
시제 · 수동태	시제	He is sure of passing the driving test. The boy denied having broken the window.
	수동태	My sister hates being taken pictures of.
의미상의 주어		We really appreciate your(you) taking time to help us.
관용 표현		I am looking forward to hearing from you soon. They have trouble remembering the children's names.

목적어로 사용하는 동명사/to부정사		
동명사		Sarah avoids eating food before she goes to bed.
to부정사		My family plans to go on a trip to New Zealand.
동명사, to부정사	의미 동일	They began learning(to learn) tennis last year.
	의미 차이	Steve remembered sending the email to Chloe. Steve remembered to send the email to Chloe.

UNIT 1 동명사의 역할과 시제 · 수동태

POINT 01 동명사의 역할

*Knowing yourself is important. 자기 자신을 아는 것은 중요하다.

주어 / 동사 / 보어

*동명사구가 문장에서 주어 역할을 해.

동명사는 「동사원형+-ing」의 형태로, 문장에서 주어, 목적어, 보어 역할을 한다.

주어	~하는 것은, ~하기는	**Swimming** is a relaxing activity for me.
	⊕ 동명사(구)가 주어로 쓰이면 단수 취급하므로 동사를 단수로 쓴다. **Making** good friends is not easy.	
목적어	~하는 것을, ~하기를	Olivia enjoys **shopping** with her friends. Chris is not good at **speaking** in public.
	⊕ 전치사의 목적어로 동명사만 가능하고 to부정사는 쓸 수 없다.	
보어	~하는 것(이다)	Dave's favorite hobby is **playing** basketball.

ⓘ 동명사의 부정: not(never)+동명사
The best thing for your health is **not overeating**.

ⓘ 동명사 *vs.* 현재분사: 동명사는 명사처럼 쓰이고, 현재분사는 형용사 역할을 한다.
My sister likes **learning** new things. 〈동명사 – 목적어〉
My sister is **learning** yoga. 〈현재분사 – 진행형〉
I need a **sleeping** bag for camping. 〈동명사 – 명사의 용도(= a bag for sleeping)〉
Please be quiet for the **sleeping** baby.
〈현재분사 – 명사 수식(= the baby who is sleeping)〉

POINT 02 동명사의 시제와 수동태

He admitted *having broken the window.
그는 창문을 깼던 것을 인정했다.

*인정한 과거 시점보다 먼저 일어난 일을 나타내.

동명사는 동사의 성질을 갖고 있어서 시제와 수동태를 표현할 수 있다.

시제	단순동명사: 동명사와 주절의 시제가 같을 때 쓴다.	
	동사원형+-ing	She is ashamed of **being** poor. = She is ashamed that she is poor.
	완료동명사: 동명사가 주절의 시제보다 앞설 때 쓴다.	
	having+p.p.	He is proud of **having been** a coach for the team. = He is proud that he was a coach for the team.
수동태	being+p.p.	I hate **being treated** like a child. He has a chance of **being elected** as President.
	⊕ 동명사가 나타내는 의미가 수동일 때 쓴다.	

개념 QUICK CHECK

POINT 01

빈칸에 알맞은 것에 √ 표시하시오.

1 Collecting old books ______ his hobby.
□ is □ are

2 Thank you for ______ me to your house.
□ inviting □ to invite

3 His goal for the year was ______ college.
□ enter □ entering

4 ______ enough sleep makes you tired.
□ Not getting □ Getting not

POINT 02

우리말과 일치하도록 괄호 안에서 알맞은 것을 고르시오.

1 나는 한국인인 것이 자랑스럽다.
I'm proud of (having been / being) Korean.

2 나는 너의 시간을 낭비하게 했던 것이 미안하다.
I'm sorry for (having wasted / wasting) your time.

3 그는 연설 부탁을 받는 것을 좋아한다.
He likes (being asked / asking) to make a speech.

1 빈칸에 들어갈 말로 알맞은 것은?

My brother is interested in ________ songs.

① write ② writes ③ written
④ to write ⑤ writing

2 우리말과 일치하도록 괄호 안의 말을 바르게 배열하여 문장을 완성하시오.

제시간에 도착하지 못해서 정말 미안해. (arriving, sorry, not, on time, for)
> I'm very ________________________________.

자주 나와요!
3 두 문장의 의미가 같도록 빈칸에 알맞은 말을 쓰시오.

He is ashamed that he did such a childish thing.
= He is ashamed of ____________ such a childish thing.

4 우리말과 일치하도록 할 때 빈칸에 들어갈 말로 알맞은 것은?

스트레스를 받지 않는 것이 네 건강에 가장 좋다.
> ____________ is the best for your health.

① Not stressing ② Being stressed
③ Not being stressed ④ Being not stressed
⑤ Not having stressed

틀리기 쉬워요!
5 다음 중 어법상 틀린 문장은?

① My brother enjoys reading comic books.
② Reading English storybooks are very useful.
③ Emily didn't admit having lied to her mom.
④ Nathan has a big chance of being chosen as a player.
⑤ Mr. Smith already finished preparing for his presentation.

개념 완성 Quiz *Choose or complete.*

1 전치사의 목적어는 동명사 / to부정사 만 쓸 수 있다.
> POINT 01

2 동명사의 부정은 not+동명사 / 동명사+not 의 형태로 쓴다.
> POINT 01

3 완료동명사는 동사원형+-ing / having+p.p. 형태로 동명사가 주절의 시제보다 앞설 때 쓴다.
> POINT 02

4 동명사가 나타내는 의미가 수동일 때 being+p.p. / having+p.p. 형태로 쓴다.
> POINT 01, 02

5 동명사(구)가 주어로 쓰이면 단수 / 복수 취급한다.
> POINT 01, 02

UNIT 2 동명사의 의미상 주어와 관용 표현

POINT 03 동명사의 의미상 주어

I don't like *her talking loudly.

나는 그녀가 크게 말하는 것을 좋아하지 않는다.

*her가 동명사 talking의 의미상 주어야.

동명사의 행위의 주체가 문장의 주어와 다를 때, 동명사 앞에 소유격이나 목적격을 써서 의미상 주어를 나타낸다.

의미상 주어	Do you mind my(me) **turning** on the radio? (라디오를 켜는 사람: 나) I'm sure of my brother('s) **winning** the game. (경기에 이기는 사람: 나의 형)

⊕ 의미상 주어가 부정대명사, 지시대명사, 무생물일 때는 목적격으로 쓴다.
I remember someone **visiting** me last night.

⊕ 동명사의 의미상 주어가 문장의 주어 또는 목적어와 같거나 일반인인 경우에는 쓰지 않는다.
I am worried about **taking** the final exams. (의미상 주어 – 문장의 주어)
Thank you for **helping** me with the work. (의미상 주어 – 문장의 목적어)
Taking pictures in this museum is not allowed. (의미상 주어 – 일반인)

POINT 04 동명사의 관용 표현

She *has trouble sleeping at night.

그녀는 밤에 자는 데 어려움을 겪는다.

*동명사가 포함된 관용적 표현이야.

look forward to -ing	~하기를 고대하다	feel like -ing	~하고 싶다
be used to -ing	~하는 데 익숙하다	It is no use -ing	~해도 소용없다
cannot help -ing	~하지 않을 수 없다	there is no -ing	~하는 것은 불가능하다
spend+시간/돈+-ing	~하는 데 시간/돈을 쓰다	on -ing	~하자마자
be busy -ing	~하느라 바쁘다	be worth -ing	~할 가치가 있다
have trouble -ing	~하는 데 어려움을 겪다	keep(prevent) *A* from -ing	*A*가 ~하지 못하게 하다

ⓘ My dad **is busy writing** his new novel.
The road was wet, so I **couldn't help falling** down.

ⓘ look forward to, be used to에 쓰인 to는 전치사이므로 뒤에 (동)명사가 온다. 서술형 빈출
We are **looking forward to** hearing from you soon.
We are **looking forward to** hear from you soon. (×)

개념 QUICK CHECK

POINT 03

우리말과 일치하도록 빈칸에 알맞은 것에 √ 표시하시오. 필요 없으면 ×표 하시오.

1 난 그가 시험에 통과할 거라고 확신한다.
I'm sure of ______ passing the exam.
□ he □ his

2 나는 그녀가 무대에서 춤을 춘 것을 기억한다.
I remember ______ dancing on the stage.
□ her □ hers

3 그는 공부하는 것을 포기했다.
He gave up ______ studying.
□ he □ his

POINT 04

밑줄 친 부분의 의미를 우리말로 쓰시오.

1 Emma <u>is used to eating</u> spicy food.
> ____________________

2 The movie <u>is worth watching twice</u>.
> ____________________

3 <u>It's no use crying</u> over spilt milk.
> ____________________

4 I <u>cannot help smiling</u> when I see you.
> ____________________

1 두 문장의 의미가 같도록 할 때 빈칸에 들어갈 말로 알맞은 것은?

Are you sure that she will come to the party tonight?
= Are you sure of ________ to the party tonight?

① she comes ② she coming ③ her come
④ her to come ⑤ her coming

2 우리말과 일치하도록 괄호 안의 말을 바르게 배열하여 문장을 완성하시오.

Smith 씨 부부는 Jake가 자신들의 차를 운전하는 것을 걱정한다.
(car, about, are, Jake, worried, their, driving)

> Mr. and Mrs. Smith ________________________________

자주 나와요!
3 빈칸에 들어갈 말로 알맞은 것은?

I'm looking forward ________ my cousin in London.

① visit ② to visit ③ to visiting
④ visited ⑤ to be visited

4 빈칸에 들어갈 말을 [보기]에서 골라 알맞은 형태로 쓰시오.

[보기] take clean make

(1) David has trouble ________ cookies at home.
(2) Maggie is busy ________ care of her new pets these days.
(3) My brother spent the whole afternoon ________ the house.

틀리기 쉬워요!
5 빈칸에 들어갈 말이 순서대로 바르게 짝지어진 것은?

• Do you mind ________ your laptop for a while?
• My brother is used ________ his bike by himself.

① I use – to fix ② I using – to fix
③ my using – fixing ④ my using – to fixing
⑤ my to use – fixing

개념 완성 Quiz *Choose or complete.*

1 동명사의 의미상 주어는 [주격, 목적격 / 목적격, 소유격]을 쓴다.
> POINT 03

2 동명사의 의미상 주어의 위치는 동명사의 [앞 / 뒤]이다.
> POINT 03

3 look forward [to+동명사 / to+동사원형]: ~하기를 고대하다
> POINT 04

4 [have trouble -ing / cannot help -ing]: ~하는 데 어려움을 겪다
> POINT 04

5 be used+[to+동명사 / to+동사원형]: ~하는 데 익숙하다
> POINT 03, 04

UNIT 3 목적어로 동명사와 to부정사를 쓰는 동사

POINT 05 목적어로 동명사나 to부정사만 쓰는 동사

He* *admitted* loving her.
그는 그녀를 사랑하는 것을 인정했다.
*admit은 목적어로 동명사만을 써.

동명사만 목적어로 쓰는 동사	enjoy, finish, stop, mind, keep, avoid, admit, consider, deny, practice, imagine, postpone(put off), give up, quit 등
	Jake enjoys **listening** to rap music. Do you mind **waiting** here for a few minutes? Avoid **talking** about people behind their backs.
to부정사만 목적어로 쓰는 동사	want, hope, plan, decide, promise, agree, choose, need, refuse, tend, wish, expect, manage 등
	I want **to watch** the movie one more time. He managed **to open** the door without the key. They decided **to build** a new school in our village.

POINT 06 목적어로 동명사와 to부정사를 모두 쓰는 동사

He* *forgot* to lock the door. 그는 문을 잠그는 것을 잊었다.
*forget은 목적어로 동명사와 to부정사를 모두 취할 수 있어.

의미 차이가 없는 동사	like, love, prefer, hate, start, begin, continue, intend 등		
	You should begin **preparing(to prepare)** for exams. Some people prefer **getting up(to get up)** early in the morning.		
의미 차이가 있는 동사	remember /forget	+동명사	(과거에) ~한 것을 기억하다/잊다
		+to부정사	(미래에) ~할 것을 기억하다/잊다
	She forgot **bringing** her textbook. (가져온 것을 잊음) She forgot **to bring** her textbook. (가져와야 하는 것을 잊음)		
	try	+동명사	(시험 삼아) ~해 보다
		+to부정사	~하려고 노력하다(애쓰다)
	He tried **making** chocolate cookies. (시험 삼아 만들어 봄) Ms. Smith tried **to find** her lost dog. (찾으려고 애씀)		
	regret	+동명사	(과거에) ~한 것을 후회하다
		+to부정사	~하게 되어 유감이다
	He regrets **lying** to his parents. I regret **to tell** you the bad news.		

① stop+동명사: ~하는 것을 멈추다/그만두다 — I stopped **playing** mobile games.
stop+to부정사: ~하기 위해 멈추다 — I stopped **to check** his text message.

개념 QUICK CHECK

POINT 05

괄호 안에서 알맞은 것을 고르시오.

1 He quit (trying / to try) to solve the problem.

2 We agreed not (saying / to say) anything.

3 I will consider (going / to go) with you.

4 I promise (bringing / to bring) you a gift.

POINT 06

우리말과 일치하도록 빈칸에 알맞은 것에 √ 표시하시오.

1 문 잠그는 것을 기억해야 해.
You should remember ______ the door.
□ locking □ to lock

2 그녀는 커피를 끊었다.
She stopped ______ coffee.
□ drinking □ to drink

3 나는 그 카메라로 사진을 한번 찍어 봤다.
I tried ______ photos with the camera.
□ taking □ to take

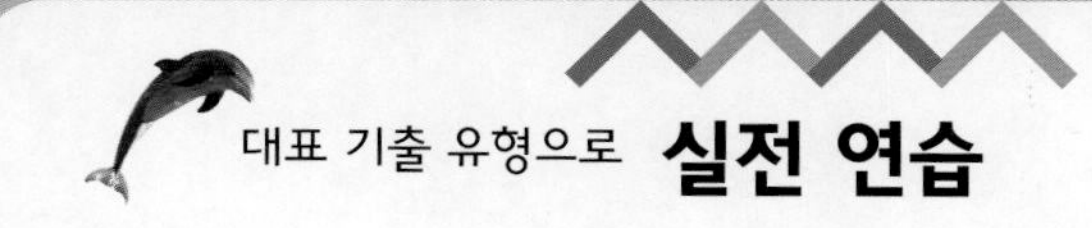

1 괄호 안의 말을 빈칸에 알맞은 형태로 쓰시오.

(1) You should avoid ______________ personal questions. (ask)

(2) We decided ______________ at the animal shelter. (volunteer)

(3) Jenny started ______________ children in kindergarten. (teach)

2 빈칸에 들어갈 말로 알맞지 않은 것은?

We ________ watching the baseball game in the stadium.

① stopped ② chose ③ enjoyed
④ put off ⑤ considered

자주 나와요!

3 우리말과 일치하도록 할 때 빈칸에 들어갈 말로 알맞은 것은?

내일 오후에 나에게 전화하는 것을 기억해. → Please ________ me tomorrow afternoon.

① forget calling ② remember calling
③ forget to call ④ remember to call
⑤ forget not to call

4 빈칸에 들어갈 말이 순서대로 바르게 짝지어진 것은?

• I have a stomachache. I regret ________ too much food. • A man was pushing his car on the road, so I stopped ________ him.

① to eat – help ② to eat – helping ③ eating – to help
④ eating – help ⑤ eating – helping

틀리기 쉬워요!

5 다음 중 어법상 틀린 문장은?

① Miranda had to give up to study abroad.
② He admitted making an important mistake.
③ The workers refused to work on the weekends.
④ Please stop complaining about your school life.
⑤ James didn't remember meeting us a few years ago.

개념 완성 Quiz *Choose or complete.*

1 [enjoy, keep, avoid / agree, promise, manage] 등의 동사는 목적어로 동명사만 쓴다.
> POINT 05, 06

2 [plan, hope, choose / consider, quit, admit] 등의 동사는 목적어로 to부정사만 쓴다.
> POINT 05

3 [remember / forget] + [동명사 / to부정사]: (미래에) ~할 것을 기억하다
> POINT 06

4 regret + [동명사 / to부정사]: ~한 것을 후회하다
> POINT 06

5 stop + [동명사 / to부정사]: ~하는 것을 멈추다
> POINT 05, 06

서술형 실전 연습

Step 1

개념 완성 Quiz *Choose or complete.*

1 **우리말과 일치하도록 괄호 안의 말을 바르게 배열하여 문장을 완성하시오.**

(1) 내 남동생은 아이처럼 다뤄지는 것을 싫어한다.

> My brother ______________________ like a child.
(being, hates, treated)

(2) 그녀는 부모님의 조언을 듣지 않은 것을 후회한다.

> She ______________________________________.
(her parents', taking, advice, not, regrets)

2 **어법상 틀린 부분을 찾아 바르게 고쳐 쓰시오.**

(1) I'm sure of he winning a gold medal.

______________ > ______________

(2) Learning foreign languages are interesting.

______________ > ______________

3 **두 문장의 의미가 같도록 빈칸에 알맞은 말을 쓰시오.**

(1) Alex is proud that he was the team leader.

= Alex is proud of ______________ the team leader.

(2) We were disappointed that she didn't come to the party.

= We were disappointed about ______________ to the party.

4 **괄호 안의 말을 사용하여 대화의 빈칸에 알맞은 대답을 완성하시오.**

A: You look worried. What's wrong with you?

B: I'm ______________________________________.

(worry about, take, the math test)

5 **빈칸에 들어갈 말을 [보기]에서 골라 알맞은 형태로 쓰시오.**

[보기] sing take wait clean

(1) I don't mind __________ for you. Take your time and finish __________ your room.

(2) People next door kept __________ loudly last night, so I didn't sleep well. I need __________ a nap now.

---

1 동명사의 부정: not+동명사 / 동명사+not
> POINT 01, 02, 06

2 동명사의 의미상 주어: 동명사의 주체가 문장의 주어와 다른 경우, 동명사 앞에 주격, 목적격 / 소유격, 목적격 사용
> POINT 01, 03

3 having+p.p. / being+p.p. 는 동명사가 주절의 시제보다 앞설 때 표현
> POINT 01, 02, 03

4 전치사의 목적어: 동명사 / to부정사 / 현재분사
> POINT 01

5 목적어로 동명사만 쓰는 동사: keep, quit, consider / need, expect, choose 등
> POINT 05

Answers p. 11

6 다음 글의 밑줄 친 ①~⑤ 중 문맥상 어색한 부분을 골라 바르게 고쳐 쓰시오.

> My room is ① such a mess now. Can you guess ② why? This is ③ what happened. It rained hard last night, but I ④ forgot closing the window before I went to bed. So the rain ⑤ came in through the window.

( ) > ____________

7 다음 우리말과 일치하도록 괄호 안의 말을 사용하여 문장을 완성하시오.

(1)
ⓐ 제가 꽃병을 깨서 죄송합니다.
ⓑ 그가 꽃병을 깨서 제가 죄송합니다.

> ⓐ I'm sorry about ____________ the vase. (break)
ⓑ I'm sorry about ____________ the vase. (break)

(2)
ⓐ 그녀는 레모네이드를 마시기 위해 멈춰 섰다.
ⓑ 그녀는 레모네이드 마시는 것을 멈췄다.

> ⓐ She ____________ the lemonade. (stop, drink)
ⓑ She ____________ the lemonade. (stop, drink)

고난도

8 Dave의 엄마와 아빠가 나누는 대화를 읽고 [조건]에 맞게 문장을 완성하시오.

A: Has Dave finished his essay? I just saw him playing games.
B: No, he hasn't.
A: It's due tomorrow. I'll tell him to write the essay first.
B: You shouldn't tell him that.
A: Why not? He doesn't have enough time to do it.
B: I never tell him to do anything. He really ____________
____________.

[조건] 1. hate, tell, what to do를 사용하고 필요 시 형태를 바꿀 것
2. 동명사를 사용하고 6단어로 쓸 것

개념 완성 Quiz *Choose or complete.*

6 문장에서 동명사의 역할: 주어, 목적어, [보어 / 수식어]
> POINT 06

7 stop+[동명사 / to부정사]: ~하는 것을 멈추다, 그만두다
> POINT 03, 06

8 동명사가 나타내는 의미가 수동인 경우 [being+p.p. / having+p.p.] 사용
> POINT 02, 06

실전 모의고사

시험일 : 월 일	문항 수 : 객관식 18 / 서술형 7
목표 시간 :	총점
걸린 시간 :	/ 100

[01-02] 빈칸에 들어갈 말로 알맞은 것을 고르시오. 각 2점

01

Jenny's job is ________ children's books.

① write ② writing ③ wrote
④ writes ⑤ to be written

02

My parents promised ________ a new smartphone for me.

① buy ② buys ③ to buy
④ bought ⑤ buying

03 빈칸에 공통으로 들어갈 말로 알맞은 것은? 3점

- ________ with strangers makes him nervous.
- The actor enjoys ________ taken pictures of on the street.

① Be(be) ② Been(been)
③ To be(to be) ④ Being(being)
⑤ To being(to being)

04 우리말과 일치하도록 할 때 빈칸에 들어갈 말로 알맞은 것은? 3점

그의 개는 짖는 것을 멈추고 나를 똑바로 쳐다보았다.
> His dog stopped ________ and looked directly at me.

① bark ② barked ③ to bark
④ barking ⑤ being barked

05 빈칸에 들어갈 말로 알맞지 않은 것은? 3점

People in the area ________ to follow the rules.

① agreed ② decided ③ considered
④ planned ⑤ refused

06 빈칸에 들어갈 말이 순서대로 짝지어진 것은? 3점

- We look forward ________ your family in Seoul.
- He couldn't help ________ since the movie was sad.

① seeing – cry ② seeing – to cry
③ to see – crying ④ to seeing – crying
⑤ to seeing – to cry

07 밑줄 친 부분의 쓰임이 나머지와 다른 하나는? 3점

① I saw a crying woman in the park.
② His new hobby is taking pictures of stars.
③ Driving too fast at night is very dangerous.
④ Jessica loves spending time with her two cats.
⑤ I'm excited about going fishing with my family.

08 밑줄 친 부분을 어법상 바르게 고친 것은? 3점

Mina studied very hard. I can't imagine she fail the exam.

① she failing ② her fails ③ hers fail
④ her to fail ⑤ her failing

09 빈칸에 공통으로 들어갈 말로 알맞지 않은 것은? 3점

• Peter and I ________ practicing yoga.
• The fans ________ to sing together at the concert.

① loved ② began ③ started
④ finished ⑤ continued

10 영어를 우리말로 잘못 옮긴 것은? 3점

① The novel is worth reading twice.
→ 그 소설은 두 번 읽을 만한 가치가 있다.
② I have trouble sleeping nowadays.
→ 나는 요즘 잠을 자는 데 어려움을 겪는다.
③ It is no use trying to persuade her.
→ 그녀를 설득하려고 해도 아무 소용없다.
④ On hearing the news, he jumped up and down.
→ 소식을 듣자마자, 그는 펄쩍펄쩍 뛰었다.
⑤ My brother is used to fixing his computer by himself.
→ 오빠는 직접 컴퓨터를 고치곤 한다.

11 대화의 빈칸에 들어갈 말이 순서대로 바르게 짝지어진 것은? 4점

A: Did you call Sam? He's still upset with you.
B: Oh, I forgot ________ him. I regret ________ such bad things to him. I'll call him right away.

① called – say ② to call – to say
③ to call – saying ④ call – saying
⑤ calling – to say

12 두 문장의 의미가 같도록 할 때 빈칸에 들어갈 말로 알맞은 것은? 4점

She is ashamed that she made a stupid mistake.
= She is ashamed of ________ a stupid mistake.

① make ② making
③ being made ④ having made
⑤ having been made

[13-14] 밑줄 친 부분이 어법상 틀린 것을 고르시오. 각 4점

13 ① We hope to graduate this summer.
② Carol postponed to visit the dentist.
③ You should quit working on weekends.
④ Jake enjoyed going hiking with his father.
⑤ He practiced speaking in front of the mirror.

통합 고난도
14 ① I don't feel like going to the magic show.
② I remember making a sandcastle with my sister last summer.
③ David is worried about getting a bad grade in science.
④ Mr. Lee considered not attending the meeting.
⑤ She has a chance of choosing as the best player.

15 주어진 우리말을 영어로 바르게 옮긴 것은? 4점

그는 진실을 말하지 않아서 나에게 화가 났다.

① He was angry at not telling the truth.
② He was angry at me telling the truth.
③ He was angry at I for not telling the truth.
④ He was angry at me for not telling the truth.
⑤ He was angry at my telling not the truth.

16 밑줄 친 부분을 잘못 고쳐 쓴 것은? 4점

① He denied to have(→ having) stolen a bike.
② I don't mind he(→ his) using my phone.
③ Dad is busy prepare(→ to prepare) for lunch.
④ We refused accepting(→ to accept) her offer.
⑤ Not drinking enough water make(→ makes) you feel more tired.

17 짝지어진 두 문장의 의미가 같지 않은 것은? 5점

① It is impossible to live without water.
= There is no living without water.
② Ryan was afraid that he was left alone.
= Ryan was afraid of being left alone.
③ We felt sorry that we didn't arrive on time.
= We felt sorry for not arriving on time.
④ I tried to finish the work by the deadline.
= I tried finishing the work by the deadline.
⑤ Jenny is happy that she won the gold medal.
= Jenny is happy for having won the gold medal.

통합 고난도
18 어법상 올바른 문장끼리 짝지어진 것은? 5점

ⓐ He spends a lot of time to playing online games.
ⓑ I regret to say that Ms. Davis is unable to see you.
ⓒ My sister hates my entering her room without knocking.
ⓓ I feel bad about not inviting to your party.

① ⓐ, ⓑ ② ⓐ, ⓒ ③ ⓑ, ⓒ
④ ⓑ, ⓓ ⑤ ⓒ, ⓓ

서술형

19 우리말과 일치하도록 괄호 안의 말을 알맞게 배열하여 문장을 완성하시오. 각 2점

(1) 약속을 지키지 못해서 미안해.
> I ____________ my promise. (sorry, keeping, not, for, am)

(2) 그녀는 엄마의 목걸이를 잃어버렸던 것을 인정했다.
> She ____________ (admitted, lost, having) her mom's necklace.

20 다음 대화를 읽고, 괄호 안의 말을 알맞은 형태로 빈칸에 써서 대화를 완성하시오. 각 2점

A: What did they suggest?
B: They gave me an offer to work in London. But I decided (1) ________ (accept) it.
A: Then, will you continue (2) ________ (work) here in Seoul?
B: Yes, I will.

21 다음 [조건]에 맞게 우리말을 영어로 쓰시오. 각 3점

[조건] 1. 괄호 안의 말을 사용하여 완전한 문장으로 쓸 것
2. 동명사를 포함할 것

(1) 나는 식당에서 혼자 먹는 것에 익숙하다.
> I'm ____________ at a restaurant. (used, eat, alone)

(2) 그는 믿을 만한 사람으로 여겨지는 것을 좋아한다.
> He ____________ a reliable person. (like, consider)

22 두 문장의 의미가 같도록 빈칸을 완성하시오. 각 3점

(1) I'm sure that he will come back next week.
= I'm sure of ________________ next week.

(2) Emily often watches thriller movies, and she enjoys it.
= Emily enjoys ________________ ________.

23 표지판의 내용과 일치하도록 문장을 완성하시오. 각 3점

(1)

(2)

(1) Avoid ________________ when you are in the library.

(2) Keep quiet. ________________ can disturb others.

24 다음 글의 밑줄 친 ⓐ~ⓔ 중 어법상 틀린 두 곳을 찾아 기호를 쓰고 바르게 고쳐 쓰시오. 각 3점

ⓐ Running is great exercise. It's fun and healthy. Many people enjoy ⓑ to run. However, this activity can be dangerous. One of my friends hurt her ankle last year while she was ⓒ running. She is still afraid of ⓓ running now. So she is thinking of ⓔ learn how to swim.

(　　) > ________________

(　　) > ________________

고난도
25 다음 대화를 읽고, 물음에 답하시오.

A: Did you pack your bag for camping?
B: Yes. I packed clothes, towels, and other things.
A: (A) Don't forget taking your hat and sunscreen.
B: Yes, Mom.
A: (B) 모기에 물리지 않도록 조심하렴.
B: Don't worry. I have a can of bug spray in my bag.

(1) 밑줄 친 (A)에서 틀린 부분을 찾아 고쳐 쓰시오. 2점

________ > ________

(2) 밑줄 친 (B)를 괄호 안의 말을 사용하여 영어로 쓰시오. (be careful of, bite) 4점

> ________________ by mosquitoes.

약점 공략
틀린 문제가 있다면?

틀린 문항 번호가 있는 칸을 색칠하고, 어떤 문법 POINT의 집중 복습이 필요한지 파악해 보세요.

문항 번호	연관 문법 POINT	문항 번호	연관 문법 POINT	문항 번호	연관 문법 POINT
01	P1	10	P4	19	P1, P2
02	P5	11	P6	20	P5, P6
03	P1, P2, P5	12	P2	21	P2, P4
04	P5, P6	13	P5	22	P3, P5
05	P5	14	P1~P6	23	P1, P5
06	P4	15	P1, P3	24	P1, P5
07	P1	16	P1, P3~P5	25	P1, P2, P6
08	P3, P5	17	P1, P2, P4, P6		
09	P5, P6	18	P1~P6		

연관 문법 POINT 참고

P1 (p.50) 동명사의 역할
P2 (p.50) 동명사의 시제와 수동태
P3 (p.52) 동명사의 의미상 주어
P4 (p.52) 동명사의 관용 표현
P5 (p.54) 목적어로 동명사나 to부정사만 쓰는 동사
P6 (p.54) 목적어로 동명사와 to부정사를 모두 쓰는 동사

Answers p.13

내신만점 Level Up Test

신유형

01 빈칸에 들어갈 수 있는 말을 모두 바르게 말한 사람은?

Many teenagers around the world ________ listening to K-pop these days.

① 미혜: enjoy, like, love
② 희진: plan, like, wish
③ 정아: like, enjoy, decide
④ 유준: want, hope, enjoy
⑤ 연아: like, expect, enjoy

02 다음 문장을 동명사를 사용한 문장으로 바꿔 쓸 때 5번째로 올 단어로 알맞은 것은?

I remember that she talked about the strange dream.

① remember ② her ③ having
④ talked ⑤ strange

03 우리말을 영어로 잘못 옮긴 것을 모두 고르면?

① 우리 가족은 TV 없이 사는 것에 익숙하다.
> My family is used to live without TV.

② 그녀는 오늘 선크림을 바르는 것을 잊어버렸다.
> She forgot to put on sunscreen today.

③ 그는 그 실수를 반복하지 않기 위해 노력했다.
> He tried not making the mistake again.

④ 나는 친구와 말다툼한 것을 후회한다.
> I regret having an argument with my friend.

⑤ 우리는 그 동아리의 회원이었던 것이 자랑스럽다.
> We're proud of having been members of the club.

서술형

04 다음 대화를 읽고, 어법상 틀린 두 곳을 찾아 바르게 고쳐 쓰시오.

A: I'm learning Spanish for my trip. It is useful for traveling in South America.
B: Which country are you planning going to?
A: Several countries including Peru.
B: I recommend you to go to the Iguazu Falls. It's really worth to see.

(1) ________________ > ________________
(2) ________________ > ________________

05 〈A〉와 〈B〉에서 알맞은 표현을 각각 하나씩 사용하여 우리말과 의미가 같도록 글을 완성해 쓰시오.

〈A〉	〈B〉
decide look forward to	go backpacking major in

Amy의 올해 목표는 대학에 들어가는 것이었다. 그녀는 역사를 (1) 전공하기로 결정했고, 목표를 이루었다. 그녀는 대학에서 친구들을 많이 사귀고 싶어 한다. 그녀는 내년 여름에 새 친구들과 (2) 배낭여행 가는 것을 기대하고 있다.

v

Amy's goal for this year was getting into college. She (1) ________________ history and achieved her goal. She wants to make many friends in college. She is (2) ________________ with her new friends next summer.

UNIT 1 POINT 01 현재분사와 과거분사
POINT 02 형용사 역할을 하는 분사

UNIT 2 POINT 03 분사구문 만들기
POINT 04 분사구문의 의미

UNIT 3 POINT 05 완료형 분사구문
POINT 06 수동형 분사구문

UNIT 4 POINT 07 주어가 있는 분사구문
POINT 08 with+(대)명사+분사

CHAPTER 05

분사

분사는 동사와 형용사의 성질을 함께 지니고 있는 것으로, 현재분사(-ing)와 과거분사(-ed) 두 가지가 있다. 형용사적 기능 외에, 동사와 접속사의 기능을 겸하는 **분사구문**이 중요하다.

Preview

분사	종류	현재분사	Don't wake up the sleeping baby.
		과거분사	She is peeling the hard boiled eggs.
	쓰임	명사 수식	The girl playing with a cat is my sister.
		보어 역할	Dad had his smartphone repaired at the shop.
분사구문	의미	시간	Leaving the house, you should turn off the lights.
		이유	Being sick in bed, I couldn't go to the party.
		조건	Taking this train, you can get to the airport.
		양보	Living close to school, he is always late for classes.
		동시동작	Singing a song, my mom watered the plants.
	완료형		Having met him before, I know what he looks like.
	수동형		Chosen to be class president, she was excited.
	주어가 있는 형태		The weather being fine, they will go on a camping trip.
	with+(대)명사+분사		The woman was sitting on the chair with her legs crossed.

UNIT 1 현재분사와 과거분사

POINT 01 현재분사와 과거분사

The *sleeping baby is my nephew. 잠자는 아기는 내 조카다.

*분사가 뒤에 있는 명사를 수식해 줘.

현재분사는 능동과 진행의 의미를 나타내고, 과거분사는 수동과 완료의 의미를 나타낸다.

현재분사	동사원형+-ing	The students are **studying** grammar. (진행: ~하고 있는) The man **making** a speech is my principal. (능동: ~하는)
	⊕ 현재분사 *vs.* 동명사: 현재분사는 형용사 역할을, 동명사는 명사 역할을 한다. He is **reading** a comic book. (현재분사: 진행시제) His hobby is **reading** comic books. (동명사: 보어)	
과거분사	동사원형+-ed	Our school was **built** in 1960. (수동: ~된) The cherry blossoms have already **gone**. (완료: ~한)

POINT 02 형용사 역할을 하는 분사

The action movie was *exciting. 그 액션 영화는 흥미진진했다.

*분사가 주어의 상태를 보충해서 설명하는 역할을 해.

분사는 명사를 앞이나 뒤에서 꾸미거나 주어나 목적어의 상태를 보충해서 설명한다.

명사 수식	분사+명사	Don't walk on that **broken** glass.
	명사+분사구	The boy **living** next door is very handsome.
	⊕ 분사가 단독으로 명사를 꾸밀 때는 명사 앞에, 분사가 구를 이루어 명사를 꾸밀 때는 명사 뒤에 온다. 서술형 빈출 Look at the bird **singing in the tree**. (○) Look at the **singing in the tree** bird. (×)	
보어 역할	주격 보어	She just stood **looking** at her children.
	목적격 보어	He had his smartwatch **repaired**.
	주어 또는 목적어와 보어와의 관계가 능동일 때는 현재분사, 수동일 때는 과거분사를 쓴다. ⊕ 목적격 보어로 분사를 쓰는 주요 동사: keep, leave, find, have, let, make, see, hear, feel 등 We heard a baby **crying**. They found the classroom door **locked**.	

① 감정을 나타내는 분사: '~한 감정을 느끼게 하는'의 의미일 때는 현재분사를, '~한 감정을 느끼는'의 의미일 때는 과거분사를 쓴다.
The new book was not **satisfying**. Oliver was **moved** by the short story.

개념 QUICK CHECK 

POINT 01

우리말에 맞는 표현에 √ 표시하시오.

1 얼린 과일
□ freezing fruit
□ frozen fruit

2 짖는 개
□ a barking dog
□ a barked dog

3 한국어로 번역된 책
□ a book translating in Korean
□ a book translated in Korean

POINT 02

괄호 안에서 알맞은 것을 고르시오.

1 He bought (a used car / a car used).

2 I want to have my hair (cutting / cut).

3 Sleeping late makes me feel (tiring / tired).

4 The rules of chess are very (confusing / confused).

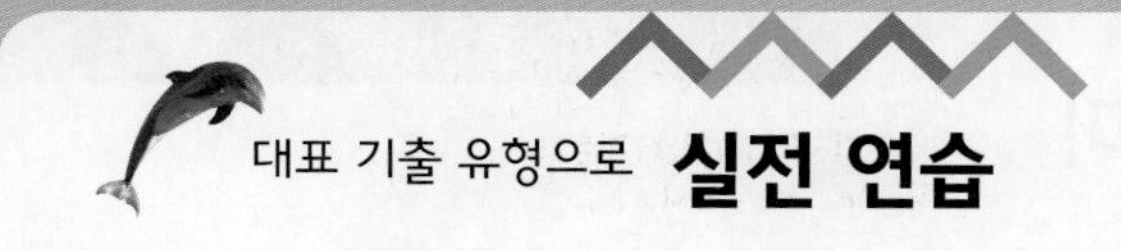

1 우리말과 일치하도록 괄호 안의 말을 알맞은 형태로 빈칸에 쓰시오.

(1) 우리는 잠긴 문을 열기 위해 사람을 불렀다.

> We called a man to open the ________ door. (lock)

(2) 나를 기다리고 계신 저 여자분은 우리 할머니시다.

> The woman ________ for me is my grandmother. (wait)

2 밑줄 친 부분의 쓰임이 나머지와 다른 하나는?

① Dad is watching a soccer game on TV.
② The girl crossing the street is my sister.
③ I was talking on the phone with my friend.
④ Her job is taking care of dogs at the animal shelter.
⑤ Some children are building sandcastles on the beach.

자주 나와요!

3 빈칸에 들어갈 말로 알맞은 것은?

The science fiction book ________ by Dr. Smith was interesting.

① writes ② wrote ③ written
④ writing ⑤ has written

4 빈칸에 들어갈 말이 순서대로 바르게 짝지어진 것은?

- My brother sat on the sofa ________ a TV show.
- Jessy and I are ________ about going on a camping trip.

① watches – excited ② watched – excited
③ watching – excited ④ watched – exciting
⑤ watching – exciting

틀리기 쉬워요!

5 밑줄 친 부분의 쓰임이 어법상 틀린 것은?

① I heard someone screaming last night.
② The songs are very confused to understand.
③ The test result made him feel discouraged.
④ Mr. Davis had his old car repaired at the shop.
⑤ He took a picture of a girl playing with her puppy.

개념 완성 Quiz *Choose or complete.*

1 「동사원형+-ing」 형태의 현재분사는 [진행, 능동 / 완료, 수동]을 나타낸다.
> POINT 01

2 동명사와 현재분사는 형태가 같지만, 현재분사는 [형용사 / 부사] 역할을, 동명사는 [동사 / 명사] 역할을 한다.
> POINT 01

3 분사구가 명사를 꾸밀 때는 명사 [앞 / 뒤]에 온다.
> POINT 01, 02

4 '~한 감정을 느끼는'이라는 의미일 때 [현재분사 / 과거분사]를 쓴다.
> POINT 02

5 주어와 주격 보어, 목적어와 목적격 보어의 관계가 수동일 때는 [현재분사 / 과거분사]를 쓴다.
> POINT 01, 02

UNIT 2 분사구문 만드는 법과 다양한 의미

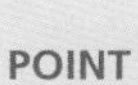

POINT 03 분사구문 만들기

***Knowing** the answer, I raised my hand.

나는 답을 알아서 손을 들었다.

*이유를 나타내는 분사구문이야.

분사구문은 분사를 이용하여 「접속사+주어+동사」의 부사절을 부사구로 대신한 구문이다.

부사절	① ~~When~~ ② ~~he~~ **left** the plane,	he switched on his smartphone.
	↓	
분사구문	③ **Leaving** the plane,	he switched on his smartphone.

⊕ 분사구문 만드는 법: ① 부사절의 접속사를 생략한다. (When 생략)
② 부사절의 주어가 주절의 주어와 같으면 생략한다. (he 생략)
③ 부사절의 동사를 현재분사 형태로 바꾼다. (left → leaving)

① 분사구문의 부정형: 분사 앞에 not이나 never를 쓴다.
Not being tall enough, she can't get on the ride.
(← As she is not tall enough, she can't get on the ride.)

POINT 04 분사구문의 의미

***Hearing** the bell, he rushed to the door.

그는 벨 소리를 들었을 때 문으로 달려갔다.

*시간을 나타내는 분사구문이야.

분사구문은 문맥에 따라서 시간, 이유, 조건, 양보, 동시동작 등 다양한 의미를 가진다.

시간	~할 때, ~하기 전/후에 등 (when, after 등)	**Walking** the dog, he watched a movie on TV. (← After he walked the dog, he watched ~.)
이유	~ 때문에 (because, since, as)	**Not liking** spinach, he ordered beans instead. (← As he didn't like spinach, he ordered ~.)
조건	만약 ~하면 (if)	**Going** straight two blocks, you will see the park. (← If you go straight two blocks, you will see ~.)
양보	비록 ~이지만 (although, (even) though)	**Taking** off so late, our plane arrived on time. (← Although our plane took off so late, it arrived ~.)
동시동작	~하면서 (while, as)	**Making** breakfast, she listened to music. (← While she was making breakfast, she listened ~.)

① 분사구문의 의미를 명확하게 하기 위해 접속사를 생략하지 않고 남겨 두기도 한다.
Though being sick, she finished her report.
(← Though she was sick, she finished her report.)

개념 QUICK CHECK

POINT 03

밑줄 친 부사절을 분사구문으로 바르게 바꾼 것에 √ 표시하시오.

1 After she turned off the lights, she left the house.
□ Turning off the lights
□ Turned off the lights

2 While I walked along the street, I saw a boy with a parrot.
□ Walk along the street
□ Walking along the street

3 Because he was not hungry, he skipped dinner.
□ Be not hungry
□ Not being hungry

POINT 04

밑줄 친 부분의 의미를 아래에서 골라 기호를 쓰시오.

a. 시간 b. 동시동작 c. 이유
d. 조건 e. 양보

1 They were watching TV, sitting on the couch. ______

2 Training every day, we'll be able to win the game. ______

3 Studying very hard, he didn't pass the exam. ______

4 Being fluent in French, he understands the book. ______

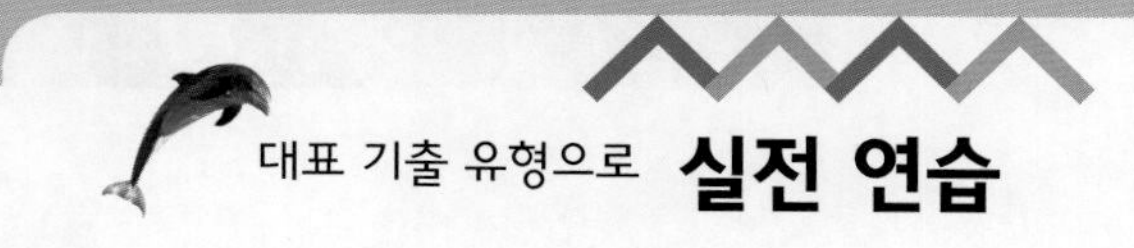

대표 기출 유형으로 실전 연습

1 밑줄 친 부분을 분사구문으로 바꿔 쓰시오.

(1) When they heard the news, they cheered loudly.
> ________________________, they cheered loudly.

(2) While I listened to the radio, I cleaned the windows.
> ________________________, I cleaned the windows.

듣기 쉬워요!
2 밑줄 친 부분과 바꿔 쓸 수 있는 것은?

Leaving right now, you won't be late for school.

① If you leave right now ② Before you leave right now
③ While you leave right now ④ Unless you leave right now
⑤ Although you leave right now

자주 나와요!
3 다음 중 밑줄 친 분사구문이 양보의 의미를 나타내는 것은?

① Playing basketball, she hurt her little finger.
② Being very rich, she is not happy with her life.
③ Eating some cookies, we watched a movie on TV.
④ Having a terrible cold, he was absent from school.
⑤ Walking along the street, I saw a man with six dogs.

4 두 문장의 의미가 같도록 빈칸에 알맞은 말을 쓰시오.

Although we attended the same school, we didn't know each other.
= Although ________ ________ ________ ________, we didn't know each other.

5 우리말과 일치하도록 할 때 빈칸에 들어갈 말로 알맞은 것은?

스페인어를 몰랐기 때문에, 그는 강의를 전혀 이해하지 못했다. > ____________, he didn't understand the lecture at all.

① Knows Spanish ② Knowing Spanish
③ Knowing not Spanish ④ Not known Spanish
⑤ Not knowing Spanish

개념 완성 Quiz *Choose or complete.*

1 분사구문을 만들 때에는 부사절의 동사를 [to부정사 / 현재분사]로 바꾼다.
> POINT 03

2 주어진 문장의 밑줄 친 부분은 [조건 / 시간 / 양보]을(를) 나타내는 분사구문이다.
> POINT 04

3 접속사 while과 as가 이끄는 부사절은 [이유 / 양보 / 동시동작]을(를) 나타내는 분사구문으로 바꿀 수 있다.
> POINT 04

4 부사절을 분사구문으로 쓸 때 주절과 같은 [주어 / 목적어 / 보어]는 생략한다.
> POINT 04

5 분사구문의 부정형은 [not+분사구문 / 분사구문+not]으로 나타낸다.
> POINT 03, 04

UNIT 3 주의해야 할 분사구문 (1)

POINT 05 완료형 분사구문

***Having lost all my money, I went home.**

나는 돈을 모두 잃어버려서 집에 갔다. *'집에 간 것'보다 '돈을 잃어버린 것'이 먼저 일어난 일임을 나타내.

부사절의 시제가 주절의 시제보다 앞선 경우 「having+p.p.」 형태로 쓴다.

부사절	After she had won the match,	she **jumped** for joy.
	↓	
분사구문	Having won the match,	she **jumped** for joy.

ⓘ As Jiho **grew up** in New York, he **speaks** English fluently. (과거 – 현재)
→ **Having grown** up in New York, Jiho **speaks** English fluently.
As we **had missed** the train, we **could not be** on time. (대과거 – 과거)
→ **Having missed** the train, we **could not be** on time.

POINT 06 수동형 분사구문

***Being invited to the party, he was happy.**

그는 파티에 초대받아서 기뻤다. *수동의 의미를 나타내는 분사구문이야.

수동적인 동작·상태를 나타내는 분사구문은 「being+p.p.」의 형태로 쓴다. 부사절의 시제가 주절의 시제보다 이전인 경우에는 「having been+p.p.」 형태로 쓴다.

부사절	When she was asked the reason for being late,	she didn't say anything.
	↓	
분사구문	(Being) Asked the reason for being late,	she didn't say anything.

부사절	As he had been injured badly,	he couldn't join the game.
	↓	
분사구문	(Having been) Injured badly,	he couldn't join the game.

ⓘ being, having been은 주로 생략되는데, 뒤에 형용사나 명사가 바로 나오면 생략하지 않는다.
Being very kind, Emily is popular with her friends.

ⓘ 주절의 주어와 분사의 관계가 능동이면 현재분사, 수동이면 과거분사로 쓴다.
Having a lot of work to do, I can't go out to play.
Located on a hill, the hotel has a fine view.

개념 QUICK CHECK

POINT 05

밑줄 친 부분을 분사구문으로 바르게 고친 것에 √ 표시하시오.

1 As I watched the movie, I want to watch a different one.
☐ Watching the movie
☐ Having watched the movie

2 When I walked down the street, I saw my English teacher.
☐ Walking down the street
☐ Having walked down the street

POINT 06

빈칸에 알맞은 것을 고르시오.

1 ________ their glasses, they wished Darren a happy birthday.
a. Raising
b. Raised

2 ________ from a distance, the rock looks like an elephant.
a. Seeing
b. Seen

3 ________ his money on his computer, he can't buy the shoes.
a. Having spent
b. Having been spent

Answers p. 14

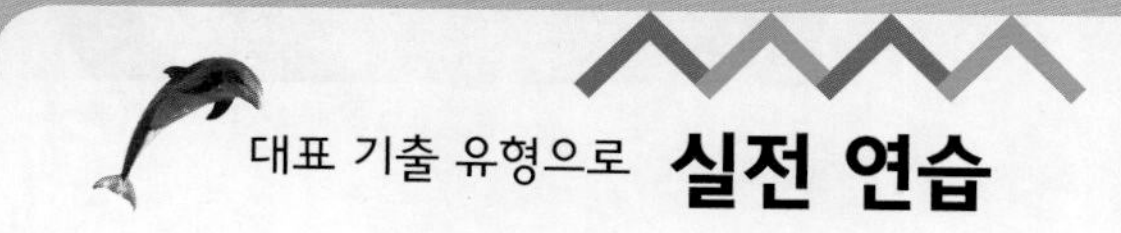

1 밑줄 친 부분을 분사구문으로 바꿔 쓰시오.

(1) As he had a car accident, he is in the hospital.

> __________________________, he is in the hospital.

(2) After she had taken the medicine for days, she felt better.

> __________________________, she felt better.

2 우리말과 일치하도록 괄호 안의 말을 사용하여 분사구문을 완성하시오.

어렸을 때 해외에서 살았기 때문에, 지수는 4개 언어를 구사한다. (live)

> ____________________ abroad as a child, Jisu speaks four languages.

자주 나와요!

3 빈칸에 들어갈 말이 순서대로 바르게 짝지어진 것은?

- ________ alone, she began to play mobile games.
- ________ a song, the man was washing the dishes.

① Left – Sing
② Be left – Singing
③ Left – Singing
④ Leaving – Sang
⑤ Leaving – Singing

4 밑줄 친 ⓐ~ⓒ 중 어법상 틀린 부분을 골라 바르게 고쳐 쓰시오.

ⓐHaving offered ⓑa teaching job last year, she ⓒwill work at the school this year.

(   ) > ____________________

틀리기 쉬워요!

5 밑줄 친 부분 중 어법상 틀린 것은?

① Waving his hand, he walked out of the house.
② Having eaten too much, I have a stomachache.
③ Seeing from the sky, all the houses look very small.
④ Being exhausted after the race, I lay down on the field.
⑤ Having arrived late, Lucas couldn't enter the concert hall.

개념 완성 Quiz *Choose or complete.*

1 부사절의 시제가 주절의 시제보다 앞서는 경우 완료형 / 수동형 분사구문으로 쓴다.

> POINT 05

2 분사구문의 시제가 주절보다 앞설 때 having+p.p. / being+p.p. 형태를 쓴다.

> POINT 05

3 분사구문에서 being, having been / been, have+-ing은(는) 주로 생략된다.

> POINT 06

4 분사구문의 시제가 주절보다 앞서고, 주어와 분사의 관계가 수동인 경우 having been+p.p. / have being+p.p.의 형태로 쓴다.

> POINT 06

5 분사구문에서 주어와 분사의 관계가 수동이고 분사구문과 주절의 시제가 같은 경우 being+p.p. / having+p.p.의 형태로 쓴다.

> POINT 05, 06

UNIT 4 주의해야 할 분사구문 (2)

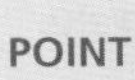

POINT 07 주어가 있는 분사구문

*Weather permitting, we'll go hiking.

날씨가 괜찮다면 우리는 하이킹하러 갈 거야.

*주절의 주어와 분사구문의 주어가 일치하지 않는 경우야.

분사구문의 주어와 주절의 주어가 같지 않을 경우에는 분사 앞에 분사구문의 주어를 쓴다.

부사절	As the elevator was out of order,	we had to use the stairs.
	↓	
분사구문	The elevator being out of order,	we had to use the stairs.

⊕ 완료형 분사구문인 경우에도 분사 having 앞에 주어를 쓴다.
As the rain had already begun, they decided to call off the game.
→ The rain having already begun, they decided to call off the game.

① 분사구문의 관용 표현: 주어가 일반인인 경우 주어를 생략하고 숙어처럼 쓴다.

- frankly speaking(솔직히 말해서)
- generally speaking(일반적으로 말해서)
- strictly speaking(엄밀히 말해서)
- judging from(~으로 판단하건대)
- speaking of(~에 관해 말하자면)
- considering(~을 고려하면)

Generally speaking, women live longer than men.

POINT 08 with+(대)명사+분사

I listened to music *with my eyes closed.

나는 눈을 감은 채로 음악을 들었다.

*'눈을 감은 채로'의 의미로 동시동작을 나타내.

with+(대)명사+현재분사	~가 …한 채로 ((대)명사와 분사가 능동 관계)	She lay on the sofa with her brother watching TV by her. (← She lay on the sofa and her brother watched TV by her.)
with+(대)명사+과거분사	~가 …된 채로 ((대)명사와 분사가 수동 관계)	He was looking at me with his arms folded. (← He was looking at me and his arms were folded.)

① 신체가 주어의 의지와 상관없이 움직일 경우에는 과거분사가 아니라 현재분사를 쓴다.
He stood by me with his legs shaking. (공포나 긴장 등으로 자동으로 떨림)

개념 QUICK CHECK

POINT 07

밑줄 친 부분을 분사구문으로 바르게 고친 것에 √ 표시하시오.

1 As Mom is sick, we will have to do the housework.
□ Being sick
□ Mom being sick

2 As school was over, they played soccer.
□ School been over
□ School being over

3 When dinner was ready, Mom called us.
□ Dinner being ready
□ Being dinner ready

POINT 08

괄호 안에서 알맞은 것을 고르시오.

1 He fell asleep with the TV (turning / turned) on.

2 With night (coming / come) on, we left for home.

3 She is staring at them with her eyebrows (raising / raised).

4 She stood on the beach with her hair (blowing / blown) in the wind.

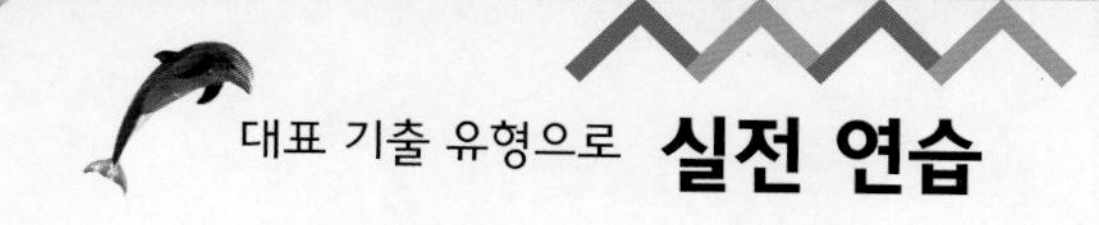

대표 기출 유형으로 실전 연습

1 밑줄 친 부분을 분사구문으로 바꿔 쓰시오.

(1) As it rained heavily, the baseball game was cancelled.

> ____________________, the baseball game was cancelled.

(2) As the room was getting dark, Jennifer looked for a candle.

> ____________________, Jennifer looked for a candle.

2 빈칸에 들어갈 말로 알맞은 것은?

The coach entered the stadium with players ________ him.

① follow ② followed ③ following
④ to follow ⑤ having followed

자주 나와요!
3 우리말과 일치하도록 괄호 안의 말을 바르게 배열하여 문장을 완성하시오.

그 남자는 팔짱을 낀 채 벽에 기대어 서 있었다. (arms, with, his, crossed)

> The man was standing ____________________ against the wall.

틀리기 쉬워요!
4 우리말을 영어로 바르게 옮긴 것은?

학교가 끝나서, 학생들은 서둘러 집으로 갔다.

① Being over, the students hurried home.
② The class was over, the students hurried home.
③ The class being over, the students hurried home.
④ The class having over, the students had hurried home.
⑤ The class having be over, the students hurried home.

5 빈칸에 들어갈 말이 순서대로 바르게 짝지어진 것은?

• ________ Monday, the art museum is closed.
• Robin went out with the computer ________ on.

① Being – turned ② Being – turning
③ It being – turned ④ It being – turning
⑤ It was – be turned

개념 완성 Quiz *Choose or complete.*

1 분사구문의 주어와 주절의 주어가 다를 경우, 분사 [앞 / 뒤]에 주어를 쓴다.
> POINT 07

2 (대)명사와 분사의 관계가 능동인 경우 [현재분사 / 과거분사]를 쓴다.
> POINT 08

3 「[with / by]+(대)명사+분사」는 '~한 채로, ~하면서'의 의미로 동시동작을 나타낸다.
> POINT 08

4 being 뒤에 형용사나 명사가 올 때는 being을 [생략한다 / 생략하지 않는다].
> POINT 07

5 (대)명사와 분사의 관계가 수동인 경우 [현재분사 / 과거분사]를 쓴다.
> POINT 07, 08

서술형 실전 연습

Step 1

개념 완성 Quiz *Choose or complete.*

1 **다음 그림을 보고, 괄호 안의 말을 알맞은 형태로 써서 문장을 완성하시오.**

(1) Watch out for the ______________________!
(fly, baseball)

(2) Did you see the ______________________?
(break, window)

2 **밑줄 친 부분을 어법상 알맞게 고쳐 쓰시오.**

(1) The ending of the novel was not satisfy to me.
> ______________________

(2) You should keep your phone turn off during the class.
> ______________________

3 **밑줄 친 부분을 분사구문으로 바꿔 쓰시오.**

As I didn't want to hurt your feelings, I couldn't tell you the truth.
> ______________________, I couldn't tell you the truth.

4 **두 문장의 의미가 같도록 [보기]에서 알맞은 접속사를 골라 문장을 완성하시오.**

[보기] since	although	if	before

(1) Turning left at the corner, you'll find the bookstore.
= ______________________, you'll find the bookstore.

(2) Having had a big lunch, I don't really feel like eating dinner.
= ______________________, I don't really feel like eating dinner.

5 **우리말과 일치하도록 괄호 안의 말을 사용하여 분사구문을 쓰시오.**

개에게 물렸던 적이 있어서, 나는 지금도 개를 무서워한다. (bite, by a dog)
> ______________________, I'm still scared of dogs.

---

1 현재분사는 [수동, 완료 / 능동, 진행]을(를), 과거분사는 [수동, 완료/ 능동, 진행]을(를) 나타낸다.
> POINT 01

2 목적어와 목적격 보어와의 관계가 수동일 때: [현재분사 / 과거분사]
> POINT 02

3 분사구문의 부정형: [not+분사 / 분사+not]
> POINT 03

4 완료형 분사구문 [having+p.p. / being+p.p.]: 주절보다 분사구문의 시제가 앞설 때 사용
> POINT 04, 05

5 수동형 분사구문 [being+p.p. / having+p.p.]: 분사와 주어의 관계가 수동일 때 사용
> POINT 06

Answers p. 15

6 다음 대화를 읽고, 괄호 안의 말을 바르게 배열하여 대화를 완성하시오.

> A: What did you do on the weekend?
> B: (1) ______________________, I went to the beach.
> (being, the weather, fine)
> A: Sounds great. Did you have fun there?
> B: Yes. (2) ______________________, I found a starfish.
> (on, the beach, while, walking)
> A: Really? If you have a picture of it, please show me!

신유형
7 〈A〉와 〈B〉에서 의미상 연결되는 문장을 골라, 분사구문을 포함한 한 문장으로 쓰시오.

〈A〉	〈B〉
• Mike grew up in Korea. • Sam is interested in animals.	• He wants to become a vet. • He speaks Korean fluently.

(1) ______________________
(2) ______________________

고난도
8 다음 글을 읽고, [조건]에 맞게 밑줄 친 우리말을 영어로 쓰시오.

> Ms. Smith went out for dinner (1) 현관문이 잠기지 않은 채로. A thief broke into her house and stole her jewelry. A police officer, Mr. Davis, saw the thief, while walking around the town. (2) 빠르게 달려서, he caught the thief.

[보기] unlock run fast the front door

[조건] 1. (1)은 with를 포함한 분사구문으로 쓸 것
2. (2)는 분사구문으로 쓸 것
3. [보기]의 주어진 표현을 사용할 것

(1) ______________________
(2) ______________________

개념 완성 Quiz *Choose or complete.*

6 주절과 분사구문의 주어가 다르면 분사구문의 주어 생략 [가능 / 불가능]
> POINT 04, 07

7 과거분사 앞의 [Been, Had been / Being, Having been] 은 생략 가능
> POINT 05, 06

8 [with / by]+(대)명사+분사: '~한 채로, ~하면서'라는 의미로 [동시동작 / 양보]을(를) 나타냄
> POINT 03, 04, 08

실전 모의고사

시험일 : 월 일	문항 수 : 객관식 18 / 서술형 7
목표 시간 :	총점
걸린 시간 :	/ 100

[01-02] 빈칸에 들어갈 말로 알맞은 것을 고르시오. 각 2점

01

He took a picture of his daughter ________ a puppy.

① holds ② held ③ holding
④ to hold ⑤ to be held

02

The visitors were ________ to see a ghostly figure.

① frighten ② to frighten ③ frightening
④ frightened ⑤ having frightened

03 **빈칸에 들어갈 말이 순서대로 짝지어진 것은?** 3점

- Amy found her cat ________ under the sofa.
- The man ________ to the hospital had an operation.

① hide – takes ② hiding – taken
③ hiding – taking ④ hidden – taking
⑤ hidden – taken

04 **밑줄 친 부분의 쓰임이 어법상 올바른 것은?** 4점

① Waited for Ted, I played mobile games.
② Left work, she turned off her computer.
③ Feeling so hungry, we ordered a large pizza.
④ You getting off at the next stop, you'll find the gallery.
⑤ Having living next door for years, we hardly know each other.

05 **우리말을 영어로 바르게 옮긴 것은?** 3점

그는 길에서 자신의 이름이 불리는 것을 들었다.

① He called his name in the street.
② He heard him calling in the street.
③ He heard his name calls in the street.
④ He heard his name called in the street.
⑤ He heard his name calling in the street.

06 **밑줄 친 부분의 쓰임이 나머지와 다른 것은?** 3점

① My hobby is collecting old records.
② Tina is posting her pictures on her blog.
③ Have you ever seen a falling star before?
④ Daniel sat listening to music on the bench.
⑤ Hearing of the accident, Jack was shocked.

[07-08] 두 문장의 의미가 같도록 할 때 빈칸에 알맞은 것을 고르시오. 각 3점

07

While I was cooking dinner, I listened to the radio.
= ________ dinner, I listened to the radio.

① Cooked ② Cooking
③ To cook ④ Being cooked
⑤ While cooked

08

Since my best friend moved to another school, I feel lonely.
= ________ to another school, I feel lonely.

① Moving
② Having moved
③ My best friend moving
④ My best friend has moved
⑤ My best friend having moved

[09-10] 밑줄 친 부분의 쓰임이 어법상 틀린 것을 고르시오.
각 3점

09 ① Frankly speaking, the food is terrible.
② Speaking of Jason, he's a good leader.
③ Ms. Davis is energetic considered her age.
④ Strictly speaking, the answer is not correct.
⑤ Judging from my experience, you'd better listen to her.

10 ① We heard dogs barking loudly outside.
② I don't want to watch a bored documentary.
③ The woman waving her hand to me is my mom.
④ You can add some dried fruits or nuts to the yogurt.
⑤ The thief caught by the police looked very young.

[11-12] 밑줄 친 부분과 바꿔 쓸 수 있는 것을 고르시오. 각 4점

11

Taken pictures of by reporters, she felt embarrassed.

① As she taken pictures of
② Before she taken pictures of
③ When she was taken pictures of
④ If she has been taken pictures of
⑤ Even if she was taken pictures of

12

Not having received an invitation, he went to the party.

① If he didn't receive
② As he didn't receive
③ When he hadn't received
④ Because he hadn't received
⑤ Although he hadn't received

13 대화의 빈칸에 들어갈 말이 순서대로 바르게 짝지어진 것은? 4점

A: Did you go to the dentist?
B: Yes. ________ a cavity, I got a terrible toothache. So, I had the tooth ________ out.

① Had – pulled ② Had – pulling
③ Having – pulls ④ Having – pulled
⑤ Being had – pulling

고난도
14 밑줄 친 부분을 잘못 바꿔 쓴 것은? 5점

① Singing a song, he washed the dishes.
(= While he was singing a song)
② The rumor being true, we didn't believe it.
(= Although the rumor was true)
③ Not having slept well last night, I felt tired.
(= As I didn't sleep well last night)
④ Taking the express train, you won't be late.
(= If you take the express train)
⑤ Raised by her grandparents, she respects elders.
(= Since she was raised by her grandparents)

15 우리말과 일치하도록 할 때 빈칸에 들어갈 말로 알맞은 것은? 4점

그녀는 개가 자신을 따라오도록 하면서 길을 걸었다.
→ She walked along the street ________.

① by her dog followed
② by her dog following
③ with her dog followed her
④ with her dog following her
⑤ with her followed by her dog

신유형

16 빈칸 ①~⑤에 들어갈 말로 알맞지 않은 것은? 5점

- They bought a ___①___ car for their son.
- The author's success story is very ___②___.
- Emily is watching a Korean film ___③___ into French.
- Nathan stood at the door with his umbrella ___④___.
- Laura ___⑤___ the room, her son was writing his diary.

① used ② moving ③ translated
④ folded ⑤ entered

통합

17 다음 중 어법상 틀린 문장은? 5점

① Eric fell asleep with the door unlocked.
② My two dogs sat calmly waiting for me.
③ Telling the exam results, she was discouraged.
④ Carl not eating meat, we thought him a vegetarian.
⑤ Having learned to play the drums for years, I'm not good at it.

통합 고난도

18 어법상 올바른 문장끼리 짝지어진 것은? 5점

ⓐ The cabin locating in the woods was cozy.
ⓑ Having been away for years, she wanted to go back home.
ⓒ He stood there with his body shaking from cold.
ⓓ I having heard the news of the storm, I cancelled my trip.

① ⓐ, ⓑ ② ⓐ, ⓒ ③ ⓑ, ⓒ
④ ⓑ, ⓓ ⑤ ⓒ, ⓓ

서술형

19 밑줄 친 부분을 분사구문으로 바꿔 쓰시오. 각 2점

(1) When she arrived at the library, she found it closed.
\> ____________________, she found it closed.

(2) As he has lost his wallet, he has no money now.
\> ____________________, he has no money now.

20 우리말과 일치하도록 괄호 안의 말을 바르게 배열하여 문장을 완성하시오. 각 2점

(1) 수영장에서 놀고 있는 아이들은 나의 사촌들이다.
\> ____________________
(playing, the pool, the children, in)
are my cousins.

(2) TV를 보지 않아서, 나는 그 프로그램에 대해 모른다.
\> ____________________
(I, TV, watching, don't, not, know)
about the show.

21 괄호 안의 말을 사용하여 대화를 완성하시오. 각 3점

A: I watched a film about Antonio Gaudi.
B: The architect? Did you like the film?
A: Yes. I (1) ____________________ (find, his buildings, interest) and I (2) ________________ (be, impress) by them.

Answers p. 15

22 다음 (조건)에 맞게 우리말을 영어로 쓰시오. 각 3점

(조건)	1. 분사구문으로 쓸 것 2. 괄호 안의 말을 사용하고, 필요 시 형태를 바꿀 것

(1) 내일 날씨가 좋으면, 우리는 소풍을 갈 것이다.

> ____________________,
(the weather, be, fine, tomorrow)
we will go on a picnic.

(2) 어둠 속에 혼자 남겨졌기 때문에 그녀는 매우 무서웠다.

> ____________________,
(leave alone, in the darkness)
she was very scared.

23 다음 대화의 밑줄 친 부분 중 어법상 틀린 것을 골라 바르게 고쳐 쓰시오. 4점

A: Do you have ① something to eat? ② Had not eaten lunch, I'm hungry.
B: Why didn't you ③ eat lunch?
A: I ④ played soccer ⑤ during lunch time.

(   ) > ____________________

24 밑줄 친 부분의 쓰임이 어법상 틀린 문장을 찾아 기호를 쓰고, 바르게 고쳐 쓰시오. 5점

ⓐ I sat on the sofa with my arms crossed.
ⓑ Injuring in the accident, he was taken to the hospital.
ⓒ The car breaking down, we waited for a tow truck.
ⓓ Having written the essay, I handed it in to the teacher.

(   ) > ____________________

25 다음 글을 읽고, 물음에 답하시오.

(A) 태어나서 in Korea, Mia moved to Canada at the age of 6. (B) Since she lived in Quebec for a long time, she speaks both French and English. She also speaks Korean well. She can speak three languages fluently.

(1) 밑줄 친 (A)와 일치하도록 bear를 알맞은 형태로 써서 분사구문을 완성하시오. 2점

> ____________________

(2) 밑줄 친 (B)를 분사구문으로 바꿔 쓰시오. 4점

> ____________________

약점 공략
틀린 문제가 있다면?

틀린 문항 번호가 있는 칸을 색칠하고, 어떤 문법 POINT의 집중 복습이 필요한지 파악해 보세요.

문항 번호	연관 문법 POINT	문항 번호	연관 문법 POINT	문항 번호	연관 문법 POINT
01	P1	10	P1, P2	19	P3, P5
02	P2	11	P6	20	P2, P3
03	P1, P2	12	P4, P5	21	P2
04	P3~P6	13	P2, P3	22	P6, P7
05	P2	14	P4~P7	23	P5
06	P1~P4	15	P8	24	P5~P8
07	P3	16	P1, P2, P8	25	P5, P6
08	P3, P5, P7	17	P1~P8		
09	P7	18	P1~P8		

연관 문법 POINT 참고

P1 (p.64) 현재분사와 과거분사
P2 (p.64) 형용사 역할을 하는 분사
P3 (p.66) 분사구문 만들기
P4 (p.66) 분사구문의 의미
P5 (p.68) 완료형 분사구문
P6 (p.68) 수동형 분사구문
P7 (p.70) 주어가 있는 분사구문
P8 (p.70) with+(대)명사+분사

Answers p. 16

내신만점 Level Up Test

신유형

01 다음 밑줄 친 부분을 분사구문으로 바꿀 때 2번째로 오는 단어로 알맞은 것은?

> Because she doesn't know Chinese, she can't understand the lecture.

① Spanish ② not ③ knowing
④ she ⑤ doesn't

02 다음 중 어법상 옳은 문장의 개수는?

> ⓐ Called a coward, the boy got angry.
> ⓑ I ate boiled eggs for breakfast.
> ⓒ They were moving by his speech.
> ⓓ Having not enough money, she couldn't buy the bag.
> ⓔ The result of the exam was disappointed.

① 1개 ② 2개 ③ 3개 ④ 4개 ⑤ 없음

03 ⓐ~ⓔ에 대해 틀리게 말한 사람을 모두 고르면?

> ⓐ Given the first prize, I jumped with joy.
> ⓑ Not having slept well last night, I am very tired.
> ⓒ Talking with me, Danny kept yawning.
> ⓓ The weather being bad, the trip will be cancelled.
> ⓔ Surrounding by fans, the singer couldn't move at all.

① 미나: ⓐ에는 분사 앞에 Being이 생략되었어.
② 성우: ⓑ는 As I don't sleep ~으로 바꿔 쓸 수 있어.
③ 지민: ⓒ의 Talking 앞에는 While을 쓸 수 있어.
④ 지수: ⓓ에서 The weather는 생략할 수 있어.
⑤ 유진: ⓔ는 Surrounded by fans, ~로 고쳐야 해.

서술형

04 다음 대화의 밑줄 친 우리말을 괄호 안의 말과 분사구문을 사용하여 영어로 쓰시오.

> A: Coming out of the bookstore, I saw my favorite author by chance.
> B: Wow! Did you get her autograph?
> A: No, I didn't.
> B: Why not?
> A: 수줍어서 나는 그녀에게 사인해 달라고 요청하지 못했어. (shy, ask for, her autograph)

> ______________________________
____

05 밑줄 친 (A)와 (B)의 우리말과 의미가 같도록 [조건]에 맞게 문장을 완성하시오.

> [조건] 1. 괄호 안의 말을 활용할 것
> 2. (B)는 분사구문으로 쓸 것

> (A) 요즘 이유 없이 우울함을 느끼나요? 만약 그렇다면, 여러분은 자신이 충분히 잠을 자고 있는지 확인해 보아야 합니다. (B) 잠을 충분히 자지 못하면, 여러분은 우울해질 수 있습니다. 신체적, 정신적 건강을 위해서 여러분은 충분한 수면을 취해야 합니다.

∨

> (A) ______________ for no reason these days? (feel, depress) If yes, you should make sure if you're sleeping enough. (B) ______________, you can become depressed. (get enough sleep) You should get enough sleep for your physical and mental health.

CHAPTER

수동태

능동태는 주어가 동작의 주체로 스스로 동작을 행하지만, **수동태**는 주어가 동작의 대상이 되어 영향을 받는 것으로 '~이 되다, 당하다'라는 의미를 나타낸다.

Preview

수동태 (be동사+p.p.)

구분	예문
조동사가 있는 수동태	The life jacket must be worn on the boat.
진행형 수동태	The computer is being repaired by Mr. Smith.
완료형 수동태	All the tickets have been sold.
4형식 문장의 수동태	Jane was sent a bunch of flowers by Mike. (= A bunch of flowers was sent to Jane by Mike.)
5형식 문장의 수동태	My sister is called a genius by everyone. He was advised to exercise regularly by the doctor. The cat was seen to climb a tree in my backyard by us.
동사구 수동태	The twins were taken care of by their grandparents.
by 이외의 전치사를 쓰는 수동태	I am worried about my presentation in English class.

UNIT 1 수동태의 의미와 형태

POINT 01 능동태와 수동태

Yesterday* was written by the Beatles.

"Yesterday"는 비틀즈에 의해 쓰였다.

*동작을 받는 대상에 초점을 둔 수동태 표현이야.

능동태는 주어가 동작의 주체인 반면, 수동태는 주어가 동작의 대상이 되는 표현으로 「be동사+p.p.(+by+행위자)」의 형태로 나타낸다.

능동태	My grandfather built this house.
↓	
수동태	This house was built by my grandfather.

① **「by+행위자」 생략:** 행위자가 일반인이거나, 불분명하거나 중요하지 않으면 생략한다.
My new bike **was stolen** yesterday. (행위자가 불분명)
A lot of wine **is produced** in France. (행위자가 중요하지 않음)

① **수동태로 쓰지 않는 동사:** 목적어가 필요 없는 자동사(appear, happen 등)이거나, 목적어를 갖는 타동사 중 소유나 상태를 나타내는 동사(have, resemble, lack, suit 등)는 수동태로 쓰지 않는다.
An electric scooter **is had** by Jake. (×)
A deer **was appeared** from behind the tree. (×)

POINT 02 수동태의 여러 가지 형태

Answers* must be written in ballpoint pen.

정답은 볼펜으로 쓰여야 한다.

*조동사 must가 포함된 수동태 표현이야.

조동사가 있는 수동태	조동사 +be+p.p.	This app **can be downloaded** for free. Liam **might be punished** by the teacher. The art project **should be finished** by next week.
	⊕ 미래형 수동태: will(be going to) be+p.p. The new movie **will(is going to) be released** next weekend.	
진행형 수동태	be동사 +being+p.p.	Our school gym **is being constructed**. The painting **is being shown** until next month. An old lady **was being helped** by the kind boy.
완료형 수동태	have/has been+p.p.	The package **has** not **been delivered** yet. All the cookies **have been eaten** by Scott. Gyeongbok Palace **has been visited** by many tourists.
	⊕ 과거완료 수동태: 「had been+p.p.」의 형태로 쓴다. I noticed that a window **had been left** open.	

개념 QUICK CHECK

POINT 01

괄호 안에서 알맞은 것을 고르시오.

1 The message (sent / was sent) by Amy.

2 Steve (invited / was invited) his friends to his house.

3 Spanish (speaks / is spoken) in many countries in Latin America.

4 Olivia (resembles / is resembled) her mother very much.

POINT 02

우리말을 영어로 바르게 표현한 것에 √ 표시하시오.

1 모든 생명은 존중받아야 한다.
□ All life should respect.
□ All life should be respected.

2 지붕이 수리되고 있다.
□ The roof is repairing.
□ The roof is being repaired.

3 그의 전화기는 도난당했다.
□ His phone has stolen.
□ His phone has been stolen.

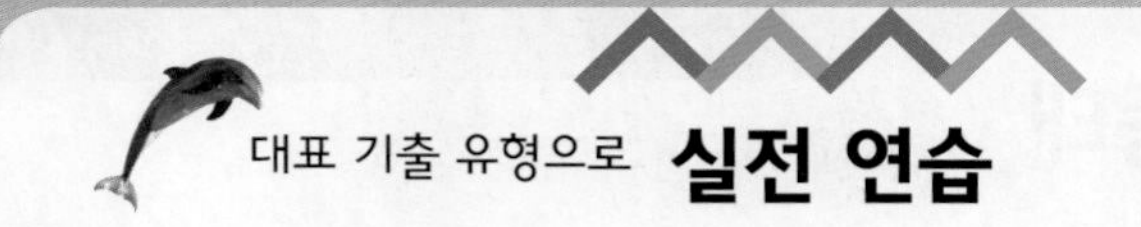

1 괄호 안의 말을 알맞은 형태로 빈칸에 쓰시오.

(1) The students ________ the wall yesterday. (paint)

(2) The museum ________ by millions of people every year. (visit)

2 우리말과 일치하도록 괄호 안의 말을 바르게 배열하여 문장을 쓰시오.

전구는 Thomas Edison에 의해 발명되었다.

(Thomas Edison, invented, the light bulb, by, was)

> ________________________________

3 다음 문장을 수동태로 바꿀 때 빈칸에 들어갈 말로 알맞은 것은?

> They are introducing the electric cars in the show.
> > The electric cars ____________ in the show.

① introduced ② will be introduced
③ are introduced ④ are being introduced
⑤ have been introduced

자주 나와요!
4 빈칸에 들어갈 말이 순서대로 바르게 짝지어진 것은?

> • The car accident ________ there last night.
> • The traffic rules must ________ by all drivers.

① happens – follow ② happened – follow
③ happened – be followed ④ was happened – follow
⑤ was happened – be followed

틀리기 쉬워요!
5 다음 중 어법상 틀린 문장은?

① This picture book was written by my aunt.
② The new library has been built since April.
③ The chocolate cake is being made by Angela.
④ The twins are resembled by their grandfather.
⑤ The book festival will be held from May 10 to 20.

개념 완성 Quiz *Choose or complete.*

1 주어가 동작을 당하는 대상이 되는 경우 [be동사+p.p. / have+p.p.]의 형태로 나타낸다.
> POINT 01

2 수동태에서 실제 동작을 행하는 주체는 문장 뒤에 「[with / by] +행위자」로 나타낸다.
> POINT 01

3 수동태의 시제가 진행형인 경우 [be동사+being+p.p. / have been+p.p.]로 나타낸다.
> POINT 02

4 조동사가 있는 수동태 문장은 [be동사+조동사+p.p. / 조동사+be+p.p.]로 나타낸다.
> POINT 01, 02

5 소유나 상태를 나타내는 타동사는 [능동태 / 수동태]로 쓰지 않는다.
> POINT 01, 02

UNIT 2 4형식과 5형식 문장의 수동태

POINT 03 4형식 문장의 수동태

A letter* **was written** to me by Mia. 편지가 Mia에 의해 내게 쓰였다.

*4형식 문장의 직접목적어를 주어로 한 수동태야.

간접목적어와 직접목적어를 각각 주어로 하는 두 가지 수동태 문장으로 바꿔 쓸 수 있다.

주어+동사+간접목적어+직접목적어	Peter **gave** her some flowers.
	↓
간접목적어를 주어로 한 수동태	주어(간접목적어)+be동사+p.p.+직접목적어+by+행위자 She **was given** some flowers by Peter.
직접목적어를 주어로 한 수동태	주어(직접목적어)+be동사+p.p.+전치사+간접목적어+by+행위자 Some flowers **were given** *to her* by Peter.

① 직접목적어가 주어일 때 간접목적어 앞에 쓰는 전치사 서술형 빈출
- to: send, give, show, lend, bring, tell, teach 등
- for: buy, make, find, cook, get 등
- of: ask, require 등

① 직접목적어만 주어로 하는 동사: buy, make, cook, write, get, choose 등

My father **made** me a sled.
→ A sled **was made** for me by my father.
→ I **was made** a sled by my father. (×)

POINT 04 5형식 문장의 수동태

Olaf* **was made** king by the people.

Olaf는 사람들에 의해 왕이 되었다.

*5형식 문장의 목적어를 주어로 한 수동태야.

5형식 문장의 목적어를 주어로 하여 수동태로 쓰고, 목적격 보어는 수동태 뒤에 남긴다.

주어+동사+목적어+목적격 보어(명사, 형용사, to부정사, 분사)	목적격 보어가 명사, 형용사, to부정사, 분사이면 그대로 쓴다. The boring movie **made** me sleepy. → I **was made** sleepy by the boring movie. He **told** us to wear a life jacket. → We **were told** to wear a life jacket by him.
주어+동사(사역동사/지각동사)+목적어+목적격 보어(동사원형)	목적격 보어로 쓰인 동사원형은 to부정사로 바꿔서 쓴다. 서술형 빈출 She **made** them wash their hands. → They **were made** to wash their hands by her. I **saw** Tom use his cell phone in class. → Tom **was seen** to use his cell phone in class by me. ⊕ 지각동사의 목적격 보어로 쓰인 현재분사는 그대로 쓴다. I **saw** Tom using his cell phone in class. → Tom **was seen** using his cell phone in class by me.

개념 QUICK CHECK

POINT 03

우리말을 영어로 바르게 표현한 것에 ✓ 표시하시오.

1 소포가 내게 보내졌다.
- □ I sent a parcel.
- □ A parcel was sent to me.

2 두 가지 수업이 우리에게 주어졌다.
- □ Two classes were given us.
- □ Two classes were given to us.

3 저녁이 우리를 위해 요리되었다.
- □ Dinner was cooked for us.
- □ Dinner was cooked to us.

POINT 

우리말과 일치하도록 괄호 안에서 알맞은 것을 고르시오.

1 Emma는 천사라고 불린다.
Emma (is called / is calling) "Angel."

2 나는 하루 종일 공부하도록 시켜졌다.
I was made (study / to study) all day long.

3 그 소년이 노래하는 소리가 들렸다.
The boy was heard (sing / singing).

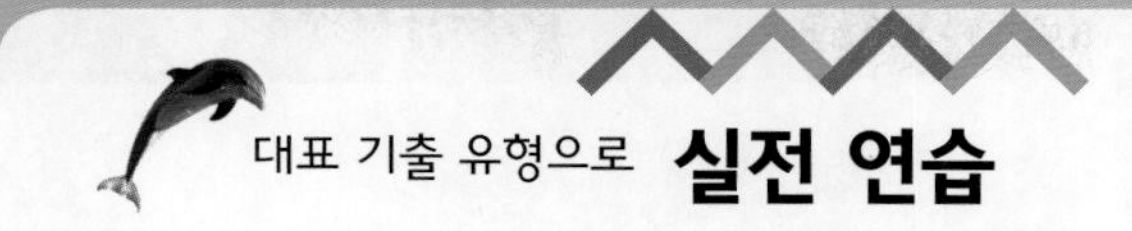

대표 기출 유형으로 **실전 연습**

1 다음 문장을 2가지의 수동태 문장으로 바꿔 쓰시오.

My mother showed me some old pictures.

> (1) I ______________________ by my mother.
> (2) Some old pictures ______________ by my mother.

2 우리말과 일치하도록 할 때 빈칸에 들어갈 말로 알맞은 것은?

John 삼촌은 내게 새 배낭을 사 주셨다. > The new backpack ______ by Uncle John.

① bought me ② bought to me ③ was bought me
④ was bought of me ⑤ was bought for me

자주 나와요!

3 다음 문장을 수동태로 바꿔 쓸 때 빈칸에 들어갈 말로 알맞은 것은?

My parents made me tell the truth. > I was made ______ the truth by my parents.

① tell ② telling ③ be told
④ to tell ⑤ to have told

4 밑줄 친 ⓐ~ⓒ 중 어법상 틀린 부분을 골라 바르게 고쳐 쓰시오.

(1) Jason ⓐwas told ⓑclean the classroom ⓒby his teacher.
( ) > ______________
(2) The concert ticket ⓐgave ⓑto Naomi ⓒby her parents.
( ) > ______________

틀리기 쉬워요!

5 다음 중 어법상 틀린 문장은?

① A letter was sent to Tom by his friend.
② The question was asked of me by Ms. Davis.
③ Sally was made a beautiful dress by her mother.
④ My dad was heard coming down the stairs by me.
⑤ I was advised to eat balanced meals by the doctor.

개념 완성 Quiz *Choose or complete.*

1 4형식 문장은 ________, ________를 각각 주어로 하는 수동태 문장으로 바꿔 쓸 수 있다.
> POINT 03

2 4형식 문장의 수동태에서 buy, make 등이 쓰인 경우 간접목적어 앞에 전치사 [of / for / to]를 쓴다.
> POINT 03

3 5형식 문장의 수동태에서 목적격 보어로 쓰인 동사원형은 [to부정사 / 현재분사]로 바꿔 쓴다.
> POINT 04

4 목적격 보어로 쓰인 [동사원형, 형용사 / to부정사, 분사]는 5형식 문장의 수동태에서 형태 변화 없이 그대로 쓴다.
> POINT 03, 04

5 [buy, make, cook / give, tell, bring] 등이 쓰인 4형식 문장에서는 직접목적어를 주어로 하는 수동태만 쓸 수 있다.
> POINT 03, 04

UNIT **3** 주의해야 할 수동태

POINT 05 동사구의 수동태

He* was made fun of by his classmates.

그는 반 친구들에게 놀림을 받았다.

*동사구 make fun of의 수동태 표현이야.

두 단어 이상으로 이루어진 동사구는 하나의 단어로 취급하여 수동태를 만든다. 이때 전치사나 부사를 생략하지 않도록 주의한다.

동사구의 능동태	A lot of students **look up to** Mr. Brady.
	↓
동사구의 수동태	Mr. Brady **is looked up to** by a lot of students.

ⓘ 주요 동사구

bring up	양육하다	turn down	~을 거절하다
take care of	~을 돌보다	put off	~을 연기하다
turn on/off	~을 켜다/끄다	laugh at	~을 비웃다
look up to	~을 존경하다	make fun of	~을 놀리다
look down on	~을 얕보다	run over	(차량이) ~을 치다

POINT  by 이외의 전치사를 쓰는 수동태

My class* is made up of 25 students.

우리 반은 25명의 학생들로 구성되어 있다.

*by 대신 of를 쓰는 수동태 표현이야.

be covered with	~로 덮여 있다	be crowded with	~로 붐비다
be filled with	~로 가득 차 있다	be pleased with	~에 기뻐하다
be satisfied with	~에 만족하다	be disappointed with(at)	~에 실망하다
be worried about	~에 대해 걱정하다	be surprised at(by)	~에 놀라다
be tired of	~에 싫증나다	be known to	~에게 알려지다
be known for	~으로 유명하다	be known as	~으로 알려져 있다
be made of(from)	~으로 만들어지다	be made up of	~로 구성되다

ⓘ He **is satisfied with** his life in middle school.
The singer **was tired of** singing the same song.

개념 QUICK CHECK 

POINT 05

우리말을 영어로 바르게 표현한 것에 √ 표시하시오.

1 경기가 연기되었다.
□ The game was put.
□ The game was put off.

2 내 제안은 거절당했다.
□ My proposal was turned down.
□ My proposal was turning down.

3 그에게 얕잡아 보이지 마라.
□ Don't be looked down by him.
□ Don't be looked down on by him.

POINT 06

우리말과 일치하도록 괄호 안에서 알맞은 것을 고르시오.

1 내 신발은 먼지로 덮여 있었다.
My shoes were covered (in / with) dust.

2 그 연극은 3막으로 구성되어 있다.
The play is composed (of / in) three acts.

3 치즈는 우유로 만들어진다.
Cheese is made (from / up) milk.

1 우리말과 일치하도록 괄호 안의 말을 사용하여 문장을 완성하시오.

(1) 그 소년은 할머니에 의해 키워졌다. (bring up)

> The boy ______________ by his grandmother.

(2) 모든 전등이 Emily에 의해 꺼졌다. (turn off)

> All the lights ______________ by Emily.

자주 나와요!
2 다음 문장을 수동태 문장으로 바꿔 쓰시오.

(1) She turned down our invitation to the party.

> Our invitation to the party ______________.

(2) The manager put the meeting off until tomorrow.

> The meeting ______________.

3 빈칸에 들어갈 말이 순서대로 바르게 짝지어진 것은?

- This restaurant is known ________ seafood.
- The dance team is composed ________ eight members.
- The National Library is filled ________ precious old books.

① as – with – of　　② as – of – with
③ for – of – in　　④ for – of – with
⑤ for – with – of

4 빈칸에 공통으로 들어갈 말로 알맞은 것은?

- Ms. Davis is tired ________ her son's excuses.
- My cats were taken care ________ by Nancy during my trip.

① in　　② at　　③ of
④ with　　⑤ about

틀리기 쉬워요!
5 빈칸에 들어갈 말이 나머지와 다른 하나는?

① We were all pleased ________ the result.
② The poor dog was run over ________ a truck.
③ The market is crowded ________ many tourists.
④ The coach was satisfied ________ the team's victory.
⑤ The hill was covered ________ various kinds of flowers.

개념 완성 Quiz *Choose or complete.*

1 동사구를 수동태로 바꿀 때에는 동사를 [be동사+p.p. / have+p.p.]로 바꾸고 나머지는 그대로 쓴다.
> POINT 05

2 행위의 대상을 강조할 때는 주로 [능동태 / 수동태] 문장을 사용한다.
> POINT 05

3 be known [as / for / to]: ~로 유명하다
> POINT 06

4 be tired [for / at / of]: ~에 싫증나다
> POINT 05, 06

5 be crowded [with / at / about]: ~로 붐비다
> POINT 05, 06

서술형 실전 연습

Step 1

개념 완성 Quiz *Choose or complete.*

1 두 문장의 의미가 같도록 빈칸에 알맞은 말을 넣어 문장을 완성하시오.

(1) The police officers were chasing the thief.
= The thief ____________ by the police officers.

(2) A famous architect will build the new stadium.
= The new stadium ____________ by a famous architect.

2 우리말과 일치하도록 괄호 안의 말을 사용하여 문장을 완성하시오.

(1) 그 문자 메시지는 누군가에 의해 내게 보내졌다. (send)
> The text message ____________ by someone.

(2) 그의 초창기 그림들은 사람들에게 비웃음을 당했다. (laugh at)
> His early paintings ____________ by people.

3 [보기]에서 알맞은 단어를 골라 문장을 완성하시오.

[보기]	of	with	at	off	to

(1) The table is covered ________ different kinds of food.
(2) The interview with the actor was put ________ until 3 p.m.
(3) Many people were surprised ________ the result of the vote.

4 밑줄 친 부분을 주어로 하는 수동태 문장으로 바꿔 쓰시오.

(1) The Italian chef cooked us a special meal.
> A special meal ____________________.

(2) We saw James and Tina go into the concert hall.
> James and Tina ____________________.

5 밑줄 친 부분을 바르게 고쳐 문장을 다시 쓰시오.

(1) The children were forced learn how to swim.
> ____________________

(2) My sister and I were brought by our grandparents up.
> ____________________

개념 완성 Quiz

1 조동사가 있는 수동태: be동사+조동사+p.p. / 조동사+be+p.p.
> POINT 02

2 간접목적어 앞에 전치사 of / to / for 를 쓰는 동사: give, send, tell, show 등
> POINT 03, 05

3 • be covered at / of / with : ~로 덮여 있다
• be surprised to / off / at : ~에 놀라다
> POINT 05, 06

4 지각동사의 목적격 보어: 능동태일 때 to부정사 / 동사원형 → 수동태일 때 to부정사 / 동사원형
> POINT 03, 04

5 동사구의 수동태 전환: 동사를 ______로 바꾸고 전치사나 부사는 그대로 연결
> POINT 04, 05

6 다음 그림을 설명하는 문장을 [조건]에 맞게 쓰시오.

(1)

(2)

(3)

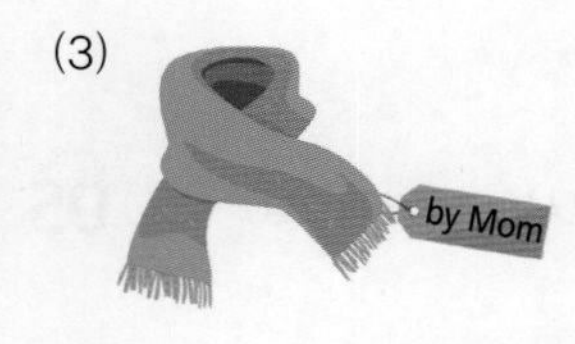

[조건] 1. 괄호 안의 말을 사용하여 수동태 문장으로 쓸 것
2. (1)은 현재시제, (2)는 현재완료, (3)은 과거시제로 쓸 것

(1) The bus ______________________. (crowd, many people)
(2) The fence ______________________. (paint, red)
(3) The scarf ______________________. (make, me)

7 다음 대화를 읽고, 밑줄 친 문장을 수동태 문장으로 바꿔 쓰시오.

A: Did you find a new owner for the dog?
B: Luckily, I did. (1) A kind lady has taken care of the dog for months.
A: How nice of her!
B: She loves the dog so much. (2) Also, our volunteers sent her dog snacks and toys.

(1) The dog ______________________ for months.
(2) Also, she ______________________.

8 다음 메모를 읽고, 괄호 안의 말을 이용하여 빈칸에 알맞게 써서 글을 완성하시오.

FACTS about NEW YORK CITY
Nickname: The Big Apple
Number of visitors: 60.5 million (2016)
62.8 million (2017)
65.2 million (2018)
Tourist attraction: Statue of Liberty (by Bartholdi)

New York City (1) ______________ (call) the Big Apple. It (2) ______________ (visit) by tens of millions of people every year recently. The Statue of Liberty is a major tourist attraction of New York City, and it (3) ______________ (design) by Bartholdi.

개념 완성 Quiz *Choose or complete.*

6 수동태의 주어로 직접목적어만 쓰는 동사: [buy, make, write / give, send, show] 등
> POINT 02, 03, 04, 06

7 간접목적어를 주어로 하는 4형식 문장의 수동태: 「주어(간접목적어)+be동사+p.p.+__________+by+행위자」
> POINT 02, 03, 05

8 완료형 수동태: [be동사+being+p.p. / have been+p.p.]
> POINT 01, 02, 04

실전 모의고사

시험일 : 월 일	문항 수 : 객관식 18 / 서술형 7
목표 시간 :	총점
걸린 시간 :	/ 100

[01-02] 빈칸에 들어갈 말로 알맞은 것을 고르시오. 각 2점

01

Maria's birthday party ________ next Saturday.

① held ② was held
③ is being held ④ will hold
⑤ will be held

02

Mr. Park was told ________ smoking by the doctor.

① stop ② to stop
③ stopping ④ to stopping
⑤ to be stopped

[03-04] 주어진 문장을 수동태 문장으로 바꿔 쓸 때 빈칸에 들어갈 말로 알맞은 것을 고르시오. 각 2점

03

The mechanic was repairing the car.
> The car ________ by the mechanic.

① had repaired ② was repaired
③ has been repaired ④ was being repaired
⑤ had been repaired

04

Ms. White teaches us English grammar.
> We ________ English grammar by Ms. White.

① taught ② have taught
③ are taught ④ are taught of
⑤ are taught to

05 밑줄 친 부분을 바르게 고쳐 쓴 것은? 3점

The art project <u>cannot complete</u> in two weeks.

① can complete ② can be not complete
③ could not complete ④ cannot be completed
⑤ can be not completed

06 우리말과 같도록 할 때 빈칸에 알맞은 것은? 3점

나는 여동생에 의해서 춤 동아리에 가입하게 되었다.
> I ________ the dance club by my sister.

① made join ② made joined
③ made to join ④ was made join
⑤ was made to join

07 다음 중 수동태 문장으로 바꿀 수 <u>없는</u> 것은? 3점

① My brother lacks a sense of humor.
② Someone broke the window in my house.
③ Laura saw her daughter sleep on the sofa.
④ They painted the school wall grey and white.
⑤ The teacher asked me an interesting question.

08 밑줄 친 부분을 <u>잘못</u> 고쳐 쓴 것은? 3점

① I was satisfied <u>from</u>(→ with) the test results.
② Our team is made up <u>for</u>(→ of) 15 members.
③ The story is known <u>for</u>(→ as) children all over the world.
④ The teacher was looked up <u>with</u>(→ to) by the students.
⑤ His proposal was turned <u>under</u>(→ down) at the meeting.

[09-10] 빈칸에 들어갈 말이 순서대로 바르게 짝지어진 것을 고르시오. 각 3점

09

- The new library ________ since last summer.
- The band's concert ________ all over the world now.

① is built – is watching
② has built – was watching
③ was built – had been watched
④ has been built – is being watched
⑤ had been built – was being watched

10

- The package was sent ________ me by my friend in the U.K.
- The cupcakes were made ________ us by my mother.
- Some questions were asked ________ the goalkeeper by the reporter.

① to – for – at
② to – of – at
③ to – for – of
④ for – to – with
⑤ for – of – with

11 **빈칸에 들어갈 말로 알맞지 않은 것은?** 4점

Peter Parker ________ by his aunt.

① was raised
② is resembled
③ was brought up
④ has been educated
⑤ will be taken care of

12 **우리말을 영어로 바르게 옮긴 것은?** 4점

미나가 교실에 들어가는 것이 목격되었다.

① Mina was seen entered the classroom.
② Mina was seen to enter the classroom.
③ Mina saw to be entered the classroom.
④ Mina saw them entering the classroom.
⑤ Mina saw someone enter the classroom.

[13-14] 주어진 문장을 수동태로 바르게 바꿔 쓴 것을 고르시오. 각 4점

13

My uncle bought me a new bike.

① A new bike was bought by my uncle.
② A new bike bought to me was my uncle.
③ A new bike is bought for me by my uncle.
④ A new bike is bought to me by my uncle.
⑤ A new bike was bought for me by my uncle.

14

People have considered 7 a lucky number.

① 7 has considered a lucky number.
② 7 has been considered a lucky number.
③ 7 has been considered to a lucky number.
④ A lucky number has been considered 7.
⑤ A lucky number has been considered as 7.

신유형
15 **빈칸 ①~⑤에 들어갈 말로 알맞지 않은 것은?** 4점

- I'm worried ___①___ the science experiment.
- The meeting may be put ___②___ by Ms. Jones.
- The cookies are made ___③___ flour, butter, and eggs.
- The historian was looked up ___④___ by all people.
- The mall will be crowded ___⑤___ a lot of people on Sunday.

① about
② off
③ at
④ to
⑤ with

16 밑줄 친 ①~⑤ 중 어법상 틀린 것은? 5점

A: Vincent van Gogh ①painted the *Mona Lisa*, didn't he?
B: No, he ②didn't. It ③was painted by Leonardo da Vinci.
A: What did van Gogh paint, then?
B: He ④is known for his sunflowers and starry night paintings. He ⑤is regarding as one of the greatest painters.

17 수동태로 바꾼 것 중 어법상 틀린 것은? 4점

① Laura looked after their dogs.
> Their dogs were looked after by Laura.
② We heard the boy playing the violin.
> The boy was heard playing the violin.
③ Dad made me an egg sandwich.
> I was made an egg sandwich by Dad.
④ The teacher persuaded me to major in math.
> I was persuaded to major in math by the teacher.
⑤ The doctors are studying the effect of the medicine.
> The effect of the medicine is being studied by the doctors.

18 다음 중 어법상 틀린 문장끼리 짝지어진 것은? 5점

ⓐ The room has been used by Liam for a year.
ⓑ My writing was laughed by my classmates.
ⓒ Tom was disappointed at the test results.
ⓓ My brother was made do the dishes by my dad.

① ⓐ, ⓒ ② ⓐ, ⓓ ③ ⓑ, ⓒ
④ ⓑ, ⓓ ⑤ ⓒ, ⓓ

19 우리말과 일치하도록 괄호 안의 말을 사용하여 문장을 완성하시오. (필요 시 형태를 바꿀 것) 각 2점

(1) 그 여자는 모두에게 천재라고 불렸다.
> The woman ____________ by everyone. (call, a genius)

(2) 나는 내 자전거가 공원에서 도둑맞았다는 것을 알았다.
> I found that my bike ____________ in the park. (steal)

20 주어진 문장을 괄호 안의 지시대로 바꿔 쓰시오. 각 3점

I gave my mom a flower basket.

(1) (my mom을 주어로)
> ____________

(2) (a flower basket을 주어로)
> ____________

21 다음 메모를 보고 괄호 안의 말을 이용하여 수진이네 가족이 오늘 해야 할 일을 완성하시오. 각 2점

오늘의 할 일
수호: 자전거 고치기
수진: 수호에게 중국어 가르쳐주기
아빠: 가족들에게 스파게티 요리해주기

(1) The bike should ____________ by Suho. (repair)
(2) Suho has to ____________ by Sujin. (teach, Chinese)
(3) Spaghetti will ____________ by Dad. (cook, the family)

22 다음 문장을 주어진 말로 시작하는 문장으로 바꿔 쓰시오. 각 3점

(1) Grandma is baking some cookies for me.
> Some cookies ____________________
____________________.

(2) Tom asked Jessica to go see a musical.
> Jessica ____________________
____________________.

23 다음 그림을 보고, [조건]에 맞게 콘서트장 이용 규칙을 완성하시오. 각 3점

(1)

(2) 

[조건]	1. 수동태 문장으로 쓸 것 2. 괄호 안의 말을 사용하고 필요 시 형태를 바꿀 것

(1) Cell phones ____________ during the concert. (must, turn off)

(2) No one ____________ food in the hall. (allow, eat)

24 다음 중 수동태로 바꿀 수 있는 문장 2개를 골라 기호를 쓰고, 수동태로 바꿔 쓰시오. 각 3점

ⓐ Andy has a fancy restaurant.
ⓑ We should recycle paper for the Earth.
ⓒ My brother bought me a nice pencil case.
ⓓ Suddenly a red car appeared in front of us.

(   ) > ____________________
(   ) > ____________________

고난도
25 다음 대화를 읽고, 물음에 답하시오.

A: Did you see Tina?
B: Yes. Are you looking for her?
A: Yes. (A) Mark sent her a box of chocolates.
B: Really? I just saw her in the club room. (B) She was heard talk on the phone.
A: OK. Thanks.

(1) (A)를 2가지의 수동태 문장으로 바꿔 쓰시오. 4점
> ____________________
> ____________________

(2) (B) 문장에서 어법상 틀린 부분을 찾아 바르게 고쳐 쓰시오. 2점
____________ > ____________

약점 공략
틀린 문제가 있다면?

틀린 문항 번호가 있는 칸을 색칠하고, 어떤 문법 POINT의 집중 복습이 필요한지 파악해 보세요.

문항 번호	연관 문법 POINT	문항 번호	연관 문법 POINT	문항 번호	연관 문법 POINT
01	P2	10	P3	19	P2, P4
02	P4	11	P1, P2, P5	20	P3
03	P2	12	P4	21	P2, P3
04	P3	13	P3	22	P2, P3, P4
05	P2	14	P2, P4	23	P2, P4, P5
06	P4	15	P5, P6	24	P1, P2, P3
07	P1, P3, P4	16	P1, P6	25	P3, P4
08	P5, P6	17	P1~P5		
09	P2	18	P1~P6		

연관 문법 POINT 참고
P1 (p.80) 능동태와 수동태
P2 (p.80) 수동태의 여러 가지 형태
P3 (p.82) 4형식 문장의 수동태
P4 (p.82) 5형식 문장의 수동태
P5 (p.84) 동사구의 수동태
P6 (p.84) by 이외의 전치사를 쓰는 수동태

Answers p. 20

내신만점 Level Up Test

신유형

01 다음 문장을 수동태로 바꿀 때 5번째로 오는 단어로 알맞은 것은?

My mother made me set the table for dinner.

① made ② set ③ table
④ dinner ⑤ mother

02 다음 백설공주 동화의 내용과 일치하는 문장을 모두 고르면?

왕비는 백설공주에게 독이 든 사과를 주었다.

① The Queen gave Snow White a poisoned apple.
② The Queen was given a poisoned apple to Snow White.
③ Snow White was given a poisoned apple by the Queen.
④ A poisoned apple was given to Snow White by the Queen.
⑤ A poisoned apple was being given for Snow White by the Queen.

03 다음 중 밑줄 친 부분을 잘못 고친 것은?

① The advice may not accept by the students. (→ may not be accepted)
② The flag of Austria is made up by two colors. (→ is made up of)
③ The direction to the hospital asked to me by him. (→ was asked for me)
④ The great scientist were looked up by all people. (→ was looked up to by)
⑤ A strange man was seeing enter the music room by us. (→ was seen to enter)

서술형

04 그림을 보고, [조건]에 맞게 문장을 완성하시오.

[조건] 1. 괄호 안의 말을 사용하여 수동태로 쓸 것
2. (1)은 현재시제, (2)는 현재진행시제를 사용할 것

(1) The restaurant ______________________.
(fill, a lot of people)
(2) The steak ______________________.
(serve, the waiter)

05 밑줄 친 (A)와 (B)의 우리말과 의미가 같도록 [조건]에 맞게 문장을 완성하시오. 각 3점

(A) 박항서 감독은 베트남 축구 팬들에게 존경을 받는다. He led the Vietnamese football team to the top of Southeast Asia in 2018, and (B) 베트남 사람들은 이것에 기뻐했다. Coach Park was even named the "Person of the Year" in Vietnam.

[조건] 1. 괄호 안의 말을 사용할 것
2. 수동태로 쓸 것

(A) Coach Park Hang-seo ______________ Vietnamese football fans. (look up to)
(B) Vietnamese people ______________. (please, this)

UNIT 1 POINT 01 접속사 that
POINT 02 시간의 접속사

UNIT 2 POINT 03 이유의 접속사
POINT 04 조건 · 양보의 접속사

UNIT 3 POINT 05 상관접속사
POINT 06 간접의문문

CHAPTER 07

접속사

접속사는 단어, 구, 절을 서로 연결해 주는 말이다.

Preview

접속사

구분	세부	예문
명사절 접속사	주어	It was a surprise that we won first prize.
	목적어	We heard that he had returned to Canada.
	보어	The problem is that she doesn't listen to me.
	동격	The idea that you will cook for your mom is wonderful.
부사절 접속사	시간	When I arrived in Norway, it was snowing.
	이유	She took some medicine because she had a fever.
	조건	If it rains tomorrow, the field trip will be postponed.
	양보	Though my grandparents live far away, I often visit them.
상관접속사		Both my sister and I are good at singing. The food is not only delicious but also healthy. Ms. Brown is going to go either London or Paris.
간접의문문	의문사가 있는 경우	Can you tell me where the post office is?
	의문사가 없는 경우	I wonder whether the rumor is true or not.

UNIT 1 접속사 that, 시간의 접속사

POINT 01 접속사 that

Remember *that honesty is the best policy.

정직이 최선의 방책이라는 것을 기억해라.

*목적어절을 이끄는 접속사야.

주어	~라는 것은	**That** my dream is to be a professional gamer is true. = It is true **that** my dream is to be a professional gamer.
	⊕ that절이 주어로 쓰이면 단수 취급하며, 주로 가주어 it을 주어 자리에 쓰고 that절은 뒤로 보낸다. 서술형 빈출	
목적어	~라는 것을	They're hoping **(that)** their missing dog will come home.
	⊕ 목적어절을 이끄는 접속사 that은 생략할 수 있다.	
보어	~라는 것(이다)	The problem is **that** we don't have enough time.
동격	~라는	I love the fact **that** you are my parents.
	⊕ 주로 fact, idea, news, truth, belief 뒤에 쓰여 내용을 구체적으로 설명한다.	

POINT 02 시간의 접속사

I like to listen to music *while I study.

나는 공부하는 동안 음악 듣는 것을 좋아한다.

*'~하는 동안'의 의미로 시간의 부사절을 이끄는 접속사야.

when	~할 때	Turn off the lights **when** you leave the house.
while	~하는 동안	He hurt his leg **while** he was playing soccer.
	⊕ while은 '~인 반면에'의 의미로 대조를 나타내는 부사절을 이끌기도 한다. Steve is very outgoing, **while** his brother is shy and quiet.	
as	~할 때, ~하면서	Ms. Parker was smiling **as** she walked into the classroom.
before	~하기 전에	Look both ways **before** you cross the street.
after	~한 후에	**After** I finish this job, I'll go out to meet my friend.
until	~할 때까지	My mom didn't go to bed **until** we got home.
since	~한 이래로	I've been swimming **since** I was five years old.
as soon as	~하자마자	I'll call you **as soon as** I hear about the results.

① 시간의 부사절에서는 현재시제로 미래를 나타낸다. 서술형 빈출

We'll wait here **until** the bus comes.

개념 QUICK CHECK

POINT 01

밑줄 친 부분의 쓰임을 아래에서 골라 기호를 쓰시오.

a. 주어	b. 목적어
c. 보어	d. 동격

1 I admit that I was wrong. ______

2 The belief is that success will come eventually. ______

3 The news that he would not recover worried them. ______

4 It's important that we look at the problem in detail. ______

POINT 02

우리말과 일치하도록 빈칸에 알맞은 말을 골라 √ 표시하시오.

1 네 일을 끝마칠 때까지 가지 마라.
Don't leave ______ you finish your work.
□ since □ until

2 그는 어렸을 때 교통사고를 당했다.
He was in a car accident ______ he was young.
□ when □ while

3 나는 해변에 도착하자마자 바다에 뛰어들 것이다.
I'll jump into the sea as soon as I ______ to the beach.
□ get □ will get

Answers p. 20

1 빈칸에 들어갈 말로 알맞은 것은?

________ was surprising that the team went to the final match.

① It ② He ③ This ④ That ⑤ What

2 (보기)의 밑줄 친 부분과 쓰임이 같은 것은?

(보기) The important thing is that we do our best.

① That she is a cheerleader is not true.
② He admitted that he had lied to his friends.
③ We don't like the idea that he will be our guide.
④ I hope that I can meet and interview my role model.
⑤ The problem was that no one could solve the problem.

3 우리말과 일치하도록 빈칸에 알맞은 말을 (보기)에서 골라 문장을 완성하시오.

(보기) until since while before

(1) 그들은 엄마가 돌아올 때까지 여기서 기다렸다.
> They waited here ________ their mother came back.

(2) 버스가 움직이는 동안에는 좌석에서 일어나지 마세요.
> Do not get up from your seat ________ the bus is moving.

자주 나와요!

4 밑줄 친 ⓐ~ⓒ에서 어법상 틀린 부분을 골라 바르게 고쳐 쓰시오.

Daniel ⓐ will call you ⓑ as soon as he ⓒ will get to the airport.

(   ) > ________________________

틀리기 쉬워요!

5 밑줄 친 부분의 쓰임이 어색한 것은?

① Carl checked his cell phone as he ate lunch.
② I have been learning English since I was 10.
③ We all think that Betty will be a great pianist.
④ Please make me dinner when you get home.
⑤ Make sure you brush your teeth after you go to bed.

개념 완성 Quiz *Choose or complete.*

1 that절이 주어인 경우, 주로 가주어 ________을 주어 자리에 쓰고 that 절은 뒤로 보낸다.
> POINT 01

2 접속사 that은 [명사절 / 부사절]을 이끈다.
> POINT 01

3 접속사 [while / until / since]: ~할 때까지
> POINT 02

4 시간의 부사절에서 미래를 나타낼 때에는 [미래시제 / 현재시제]를 쓴다.
> POINT 02

5 접속사 [as / that / after]: ~할 때, ~하면서
> POINT 01, 02

UNIT 2 이유 · 조건 · 양보의 접속사

POINT 03 이유의 접속사

We didn't go outside *because it was raining.

비가 오고 있었기 때문에 우리는 나가지 않았다.

*'~ 때문에'의 의미로 이유를 나타내.

because	~ 때문에	She decided to take a break **because** she felt tired.
as	~ 때문에	**As** the boss was ill, they postponed the meeting.
	⊕ as의 다양한 의미: '~할 때', '~ 때문에', '~인 대로', '~함에 따라' 등 They arrived **as** we were leaving. (~할 때) **As** the forecast predicted, the weather was very cold. (~인 대로) **As** you exercise more, your body produces more heat. (~함에 따라)	
since	~ 때문에	**Since** Noel was interested in acting, he joined the drama club.

① 접속사 because 뒤에는 절이, 전치사구 because of 뒤에는 명사(구)가 온다.
I missed my flight **because** there was a traffic jam. (because+주어+동사)
I missed my flight **because of** a traffic jam. (because of+명사구)

POINT 04 조건 · 양보의 접속사

***If you book now, you will get good seats.**

지금 예약하면 너는 좋은 자리를 구할 거야.

*'만약 ~하면'의 의미로 조건을 나타내.

if	만약 ~하면	**If** we miss the last bus, we will have to walk home.
unless	만약 ~하지 않으면	**Unless** you change your eating habits, you can't lose weight. = **If** you **don't** change your eating habits, ~.
	⊕ unless는 if ~ not으로 바꿔 쓸 수 있으며, 부정문과 함께 쓰지 않는다.	
as long as	~하는 한	Talking on the Internet is free **as long as** you have WiFi.
although, though	비록 ~이지만	**Although** she knew she was wrong, she refused to admit it.
even if, even though	만약 ~할지라도	**Even if** I go to bed early, it is hard to get up early in the morning.

① 조건의 부사절에서는 현재시제로 미래를 나타낸다.  서술형 빈출
I will call the teacher **if** you **don't** stop fighting.

① 양보를 나타내는 전치사(구)인 despite나 in spite of 뒤에는 명사(구)가 온다.
Despite(In spite of) being rich, Mr. Edwards leads a simple life.

개념 QUICK CHECK

POINT 03 ~ 04

A 밑줄 친 부분의 쓰임에 해당하는 것에 √ 표시하시오.

1 If she doesn't apologize, I will never speak to her again.
☐ 조건 ☐ 양보

2 I had a banana for breakfast as there was no milk for cereal.
☐ 시간 ☐ 이유

3 Even though I have the money, I won't buy the bag.
☐ 이유 ☐ 양보

B 괄호 안에서 알맞은 말을 고르시오.

1 I got wet (because / because of) I forgot to bring my umbrella.

2 If you (don't / won't) exercise, you will get fat.

3 (Although / Despite) the rain, he went to the football match.

4 (If / Unless) we have an invitation card, we can't enter inside.

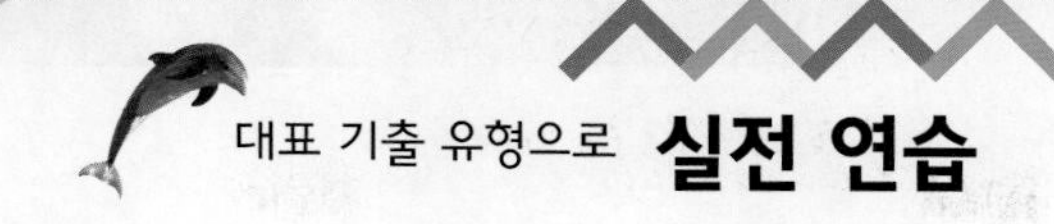

대표 기출 유형으로 실전 연습

1 빈칸에 들어갈 말로 알맞은 것은?

> We couldn't see the movie ________ the tickets were sold out.

① while ② since ③ even if
④ although ⑤ unless

2 빈칸에 공통으로 들어갈 접속사를 쓰시오.

- ________ it was noisy outside, we couldn't fall asleep.
- ________ it got darker, the weather got much colder.
- Eric came into the classroom ________ the class began.

자주 나와요!
3 두 문장의 의미가 같도록 할 때 빈칸에 들어갈 말로 알맞은 것은?

> If you haven't asked in advance, you can't take a sample.
> = ________ you have asked in advance, you can't take a sample.

① As ② Unless ③ Even if
④ Though ⑤ As long as

4 우리말과 일치하도록 할 때 빈칸에 들어갈 말로 알맞은 것은?

> Alex는 나보다 어리지만, 매우 똑똑하고 현명하다.
> \> ________ Alex is younger than me, he is very smart and wise.

① If ② Until ③ Because
④ Although ⑤ As soon as

틀리기 쉬워요!
5 밑줄 친 부분의 쓰임이 어법상 틀린 것은?

① You can stay with us as long as you want.
② The trip was canceled because it rained heavily.
③ Though the cold weather, they played outside for hours.
④ Since she was good at singing, she could join the choir.
⑤ If you make a reservation today, you can get a 20% discount.

개념 완성 Quiz *Choose or complete.*

1 접속사 [since / until / unless]은(는) 이유를 나타낸다.
> POINT 03

2 접속사 ________는 '~할 때', '~ 때문에', '~인 대로', '~함에 따라' 등 다양한 의미를 나타낸다.
> POINT 03

3 접속사 ________는 '만약 ~하지 않으면'이라는 뜻을 나타낸다.
> POINT 04

4 [although, though / if ~ not, unless]: 비록 ~이지만
> POINT 04

5 접속사 뒤에는 주어와 동사를 갖춘 절이 오고, 전치사(구) 뒤에는 [명사(구) / 부사(구)]가 온다.
> POINT 03, 04

UNIT **3** # 상관접속사, 간접의문문

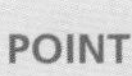

POINT 05 상관접속사

I'll eat* both pizza and spaghetti.

나는 피자와 스파게티 둘 다 먹을 거야.

* 'A와 B 둘 다'의 의미를 나타내는 상관접속사야.

두 개 이상의 단어가 짝을 이루어 접속사 역할을 하는 것을 상관접속사라고 한다.

both *A* and *B*	*A*와 *B* 둘 다	**Both** soccer **and** baseball are team sports.
either *A* or *B*	*A* 또는 *B* 둘 중 하나	Bring **either** a raincoat **or** an umbrella.
neither *A* nor *B*	*A*와 *B* 둘 다 아닌	**Neither** Norway **nor** Switzerland is in the EU.
not *A* but *B*	*A*가 아니라 *B*	**Not** Amy **but** Emily lives here with us.
not only *A* but (also) *B* = *B* as well as *A*	*A*뿐만 아니라 *B*도	**Not only** students **but also** parents can log in to the school website. = Parents **as well as** students can log in ~.

ⓘ 주어로 쓰일 때 both *A* and *B*는 복수 취급하고, 나머지는 모두 *B*에 동사의 수를 일치시킨다.

ⓘ 상관접속사의 *A*와 *B*에 들어가는 두 요소는 문법적으로 같은 형태여야 한다. 서술형 빈출

He neither **speaks** nor **understands** English.

POINT 06 간접의문문

Do you know* when the parade starts?

퍼레이드가 언제 시작하는지 아니?

* 간접의문문이 know의 목적어 역할을 해.

의문문이 다른 문장의 일부가 되어 주어, 목적어, 보어로 쓰이는 것을 간접의문문이라고 한다.

의문사 있는 간접의문문	의문사+주어+동사	Can you tell me? + Why were you absent yesterday? → Can you tell me **why you were** absent yesterday?
	⊕ 의문사가 주어인 경우: 「의문사+동사」의 순서로 쓴다. I want to know. + Who broke the vase? → I want to know **who broke** the vase. ⊕ 주절의 동사가 think, believe, guess, suppose 등인 경우 간접의문문의 의문사를 문장 맨 앞에 쓴다. 서술형 빈출 Do you think? + What should I do? → **What** do you think **I should do**?	
의문사 없는 간접의문문	if/whether +주어+동사	I wonder. + Have you finished your work? → I wonder **if(whether) you have finished** your work.
	⊕ 주어로 쓰여 문장 앞에 올 때는 whether만 쓸 수 있다. **Whether Lucy has gone to Mexico** is not certain.	

개념 QUICK CHECK

POINT 05

괄호 안에서 알맞은 것을 고르시오.

1 He is both intelligent (and / but) kind.

2 Jerry is neither good at French (or / nor) Spanish.

3 I will either go for a walk or (read / to read) a book after dinner.

4 Not your sister but you (has / have) to wash the dishes.

POINT 06

우리말을 영어로 바르게 옮긴 것에 √ 표시하시오.

1 그가 무엇을 하고 있는지 너는 아니?
- ☐ Do you know what is he doing?
- ☐ Do you know what he is doing?

2 나는 그녀가 돌아왔는지 궁금하다.
- ☐ I wonder if she came back.
- ☐ I wonder if did she come back.

3 너는 왜 외계인이 존재한다고 믿니?
- ☐ Do you believe why aliens exist?
- ☐ Why do you believe aliens exist?

Answers p. 21

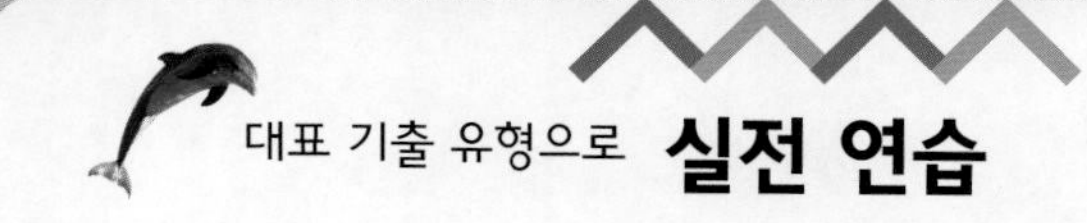

대표 기출 유형으로 실전 연습

1 우리말과 일치하도록 빈칸에 들어갈 말이 순서대로 바르게 짝지어진 것은?

> 그녀는 나를 칭찬하지도 비난하지도 않았다.
> \> She ________ praised ________ criticized me.

① both – and ② not – but ③ either – or
④ neither – nor ⑤ not only – but

자주 나와요!
2 두 문장의 의미가 같도록 빈칸에 알맞은 말을 쓰시오.

(1) Steve was absent yesterday. Eric was not absent yesterday.
\> ________ Eric ________ Steve was absent yesterday.

(2) The teacher likes the book. The students also like the book.
\> The students ________ ________ ________ the teacher like the book.

3 다음 두 문장을 한 문장으로 바꿔 쓰시오.

(1) I want to know. What does Lisa want for her birthday?
\> I want to know ________________________.

(2) I wonder. Did he go to the rock concert?
\> I wonder ________________________.

4 빈칸에 들어갈 말로 알맞지 않은 것은?

> Can you tell me ________________?

① when the bus will come ② who the contest won
③ if you are coming or not ④ why she is angry at me
⑤ what you bought at the store

틀리기 쉬워요!
5 다음 중 어법상 틀린 문장은?

① Whether she likes it or not doesn't matter.
② You should consider price as well as quality.
③ How do you think he solved the problem?
④ Can you imagine what will happen in 20 years?
⑤ I went to London not to travel but meeting my best friend.

개념 완성 Quiz *Choose or complete.*

1 either *A* or *B* / neither *A* nor *B* / not only *A* but *B* : *A*와 *B* 둘 다 아닌
> POINT 05

2 both *A* and *B* / not *A* but *B* / *B* as well as *A* : *A*가 아니라 *B*
> POINT 05

3 의문사가 없는 간접의문문은 「________+주어+동사」의 형태로 쓴다.
> POINT 06

4 의문사가 있는 간접의문문에서 의문사가 주어인 경우 의문사+동사 / 동사+의문사 의 순서로 쓴다.
> POINT 06

5 간접의문문에서 주절의 동사가 happen, matter / think, believe 등인 경우 간접의문문의 의문사를 문장 맨 앞에 쓴다.
> POINT 05, 06

Step 1

개념 완성 Quiz *Choose or complete.*

1 접속사 that을 사용하여 두 문장을 한 문장으로 바꿔 쓰시오.

(1) Andrew didn't keep his promise. It is disappointing.

> ______________________________

(2) The trouble is this. My daughter doesn't want to live here.

> ______________________________

2 우리말과 일치하도록 괄호 안의 말을 사용하여 문장을 완성하시오.

(1) 지금 집에서 출발하면, 너는 비행기를 놓치지 않을 것이다. (leave home)

> ____________________, you won't miss your flight.

(2) 초인종 소리를 듣자마자, 그녀는 문으로 뛰어갔다. (hear the doorbell)

> ____________________, she ran to the door.

3 밑줄 친 ⓐ~ⓒ 중 어법상 틀린 부분을 골라 바르게 고쳐 쓰시오.

We ⓐwill go out for dinner ⓑafter the music show ⓒwill be over.

(   ) > ____________________

4 다음 두 문장을 한 문장으로 바꿔 쓸 때 빈칸에 알맞은 말을 쓰시오.

(1) Diane doesn't have a pen. She doesn't have paper, either.

> Diane has ________ a pen ________ paper.

(2) Dr. Parker's lecture is informative. It is interesting as well.

> Dr. Parker's lecture is ________ ________ informative ________ ________ interesting.

5 [보기]에서 알맞은 말을 골라 괄호 안의 말을 사용하여 문장을 완성하시오.

[보기] because	because of	although	despite

(1) I couldn't go camping ______________________________.
(the heavy rain)

(2) ______________________________, this room is still hot.
(I turned on the air conditioner)

개념 완성 Quiz

1 that절이 주어로 쓰일 때: It / This +동사 ~+that+주어+동사 ...」
> POINT 01

2 접속사 as soon as / as long as / while : ~하자마자
> POINT 02, 04

3 시간·조건의 부사절의 시제: 현재시제 / 미래시제로 미래 표현
> POINT 02

4 not *A* but *B* / neither *A* nor *B* / either *A* or *B* : *A*도 *B*도 둘 다 아닌
> POINT 05

5 • because / because of +주어+동사 ~
• although / despite +명사(구)
> POINT 03, 04

Step 2

6 우리말과 일치하도록 (조건)에 맞게 문장을 완성하시오.

You will not go to the party.	I will clean the house.

(조건) 1. 두 개의 문장 중 알맞은 것을 골라 사용하고 필요 시 형태를 바꿀 것
2. 필요한 접속사 1개를 추가할 것

(1) 네가 파티에 가지 않으면, 나도 가지 않을 것이다.

> ________________________, I won't go there, either.

(2) 나는 집 청소를 한 후에 샤워를 할 것이다.

> I'm going to take a shower ________________________.

7 그림을 보고, 밑줄 친 부분 중 틀린 곳을 바르게 고쳐 쓰시오.

(1) SCHOOL FESTIVAL (2) SCHOOL FESTIVAL

This is the principal of Green Middle School. I'd like to tell you that our school festival will be held in any situation tomorrow. (1) If it will rain tomorrow, the school festival will be held in the gym. (2) Unless it won't rain tomorrow, the school festival will be held on the playground.

(1) ________________ > ________________

(2) ________________ > ________________

고난도

8 다음 질문을 사용하여 학교 신문 기자를 뽑는 인터뷰를 완성하시오.

- Why do you want to be a school newspaper reporter?
- Have you written any articles before?
- Are you good at talking with people?

A: Tell me (1) ________________________.

B: I want to let students know what's happening in our school.

A: OK. I'd like to know (2) ________________________.

B: Yes. My article was in the school newspaper last year.

A: I also wonder (3) ________________________.

B: Yes, I am. I like to hear about people's stories.

개념 완성 Quiz *Choose or complete.*

6 접속사 [before / after / when]: ~한 후에

> POINT 02, 04

7 접속사 [though / unless / until]: 만약 ~하지 않으면

> POINT 04

8 의문사가 없는 간접의문문의 형태: [whether, if / as, since] +주어+동사 ~

> POINT 06

실전 모의고사

시험일 : 월 일	문항 수 : 객관식 18 / 서술형 7
목표 시간 :	총점
걸린 시간 :	/ 100

[01-02] 빈칸에 들어갈 말로 알맞은 것을 고르시오. 각 2점

01

_______ you hurry up, you'll be late.

① If ② When ③ After
④ Unless ⑤ Because

02

Mina got good grades _______ she studied hard.

① before ② since ③ while
④ until ⑤ even if

03 빈칸에 공통으로 들어갈 말로 알맞은 것은? 3점

- _______ you turn left, you can see the theater on your right.
- Do you know _______ Bonnie will join the dance club?

① As(as) ② If(if)
③ When(when) ④ While(while)
⑤ Since(since)

04 주어진 문장의 밑줄 친 부분과 의미가 같은 것은? 3점

<u>As</u> he was hungry, he ate the whole pizza.

① I usually listen to music <u>as</u> I take a walk.
② <u>As</u> spring comes, it is getting warmer.
③ We will meet at the main gate at 2 <u>as</u> I told you.
④ <u>As</u> today is the school's anniversary, there is no class.
⑤ <u>As</u> he grew up, he became more interested in art.

[05-06] 빈칸에 들어갈 말이 순서대로 바르게 짝지어진 것을 고르시오. 각 3점

05

- Wash your hands _______ you come home.
- Jason didn't know his mistake _______ the teacher pointed it out.

① while – until ② while – since
③ as long as – since ④ as soon as – until
⑤ as soon as – after

06

- _______ Ben's Korean wasn't perfect, I could understand him.
- You'd better not use your smartphone _______ you're crossing the street.

① If – as ② Though – if
③ Because – while ④ When – even if
⑤ Although – while

07 밑줄 친 <u>that</u>의 쓰임이 나머지와 <u>다른</u> 것은? 3점

① The fact is <u>that</u> Pamela is not a good cook.
② I lost the ring <u>that</u> you gave me last week.
③ I don't like the idea <u>that</u> he knows my name.
④ People believe <u>that</u> dogs are loyal to their owners.
⑤ It is true <u>that</u> the couple broke up a few months ago.

08 우리말과 일치하도록 할 때 빈칸에 알맞은 것은? 3점

내 여동생뿐만 아니라 나도 요가 강좌를 듣고 있다.
> _______ my sister _______ I am taking yoga lessons.

① Not – but ② Either – or
③ Both – and ④ Neither – nor
⑤ Not only – but also

09 대화의 빈칸에 들어갈 말로 알맞은 것은? 3점

A: Where did you put your wallet?
B: I don't remember __________.

① where I put my wallet
② where you put your wallet
③ where did I put my wallet
④ did where I put your wallet
⑤ did you put where my wallet

10 대화의 빈칸에 들어갈 말이 순서대로 짝지어진 것은? 3점

A: Did you hear ________ there was an earthquake in Japan?
B: No, I didn't. When did it happen?
A: It happened ________ you left for Korea. That's a relief.

① it – after ② when – before
③ that – after ④ that – before
⑤ when – while

11 두 문장을 한 문장으로 바꿀 때 빈칸에 알맞은 것은? 4점

Someone sent me a bunch of flowers. It must be Mike or Brian.
> __________ sent me a bunch of flowers.

① Not Brian but Mike ② Either Mike or Brian
③ Both Mike and Brain ④ Brain as well as Mike
⑤ Neither Mike nor Brian

12 우리말을 영어로 바르게 옮긴 것은? 3점

그가 무엇을 닮았다고 생각하니?

① What do you think he look like?
② What do you think he looks like?
③ What do you think does he look like?
④ Do you think what he does look like?
⑤ Do you think what does he look like?

13 빈칸에 들어갈 말이 주어진 문장과 같은 것은? 3점

________ I had a terrible cold, I went to school.

① I fell asleep in class ________ I was very tired.
② ________ it began to rain, I closed the windows.
③ We got angry ________ he didn't admit he was wrong.
④ ________ the book was boring, I read it to the end.
⑤ Tell me ________ you want to change the schedule.

14 우리말을 영어로 옮긴 것 중 틀린 것은? 4점

① 아이들과 어른들 모두 이 영화를 좋아한다.
> Both children and adults like this movie.
② 나는 내 답이 맞는지 확실히 알지 못한다.
> I'm not sure what my answer is correct.
③ 네가 원하는 한 이 방을 이용할 수 있다.
> You can use this room as long as you want.
④ 우리는 5살 때부터 서로 알고 지내왔다.
> We have known each other since we were five.
⑤ 그는 프랑스가 아니라 영국으로 여행을 갈 것이다.
> He is going to travel not to France but to England.

[15-16] 어법상 틀린 문장을 고르시오. 각 4점

15 ① I can't imagine what will happen in 50 years.
② Either orange juice or soda will be provided.
③ My dad will be busy until he finishes his project.
④ As time goes by, I can understand my parents better.
⑤ Not only Kevin but also his parents enjoys watching TV.

통합

16 ① Do you know who won the final match?
② It is certain that she made the dress by herself.
③ Joan sang a song while she was taking a shower.
④ He will buy the house if its price will be reasonable.
⑤ In spite of being poor, the man never steals anything.

고난도

17 짝지어진 두 문장의 의미가 다른 것은? 5점

① Brush your teeth before you go to bed.
= Go to bed after you brush your teeth.
② I was hungry because I didn't have lunch.
= I was hungry as I didn't have lunch.
③ If you don't want it, I'll take it back.
= Unless you want it, I'll take it back.
④ Although her voice was small, I could hear her.
= Despite her small voice, I could hear her.
⑤ The movie was not interesting, and it was not touching, either.
= The movie was not interesting but touching.

고난도 신유형

18 밑줄 친 부분을 고쳐 쓴 것 중 어법상 틀린 것은? 5점

- He has a belief ⓐ though he will succeed someday.
- She will prepare dinner before her son ⓑ will arrive.
- Amy and I enjoy both skiing and ⓒ skate.
- They have no idea ⓓ if or not Tracy will join the team.
- Jason moved to London ⓔ because his father's new job.

① ⓐ → that ② ⓑ → arrives
③ ⓒ → to skate ④ ⓓ → whether or not
⑤ ⓔ → because of

19 주어진 접속사를 써서 두 문장을 한 문장으로 고쳐 쓰시오. 각 2점

(1) She stayed home all day. She didn't feel well.
> Because ______________________________.

(2) He has never been abroad. He speaks English fluently.
> Although ______________________________.

20 학생 100명에게 축구와 야구에 대한 선호도를 조사한 그래프를 보고, [보기]의 표현을 사용하여 문장을 완성하시오. 각 2점

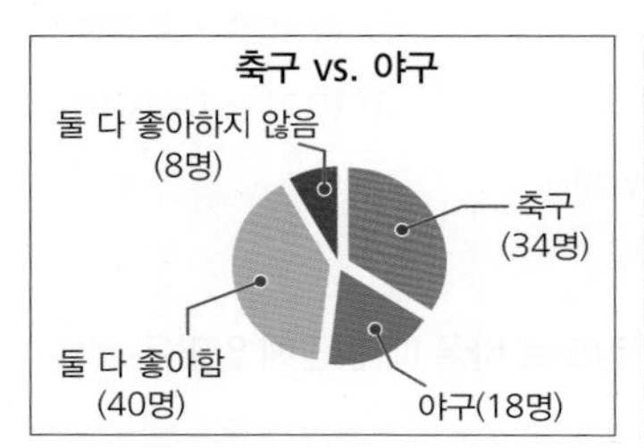

[보기]
neither ~ nor
either ~ or
both ~ and

(1) 40 students like ______________.
(2) 52 students like ______________.
(3) 8 students like ______________.

21 다음 [조건]에 맞게 우리말을 영어로 쓰시오. 각 3점

[조건] 1. 괄호 안의 말과 알맞은 접속사를 사용할 것
2. (1)은 10단어, (2)는 9단어로 쓸 것

(1) 영수증이 없다면, 너는 환불을 받을 수 없다.
> ______________________________
(the receipt, get a refund)

(2) 몇몇 동물들이 도구를 사용할 수 있다는 것은 흥미롭다.
> ______________________________
(interesting, some animals, use tools)

Answers p. 22

22 밑줄 친 부분의 쓰임이 어법상 틀린 문장 2개를 골라 기호를 쓰고 바르게 고쳐 문장을 다시 쓰시오. 각 3점

ⓐ Even if he apologizes, she won't forgive him.
ⓑ We will wait until Mr. Davis will give us a call.
ⓒ Amy neither speaks nor understanding Chinese.
ⓓ Whether or not he heard of the news is not certain.

(   ) > ____________________
(   ) > ____________________

23 다음 두 문장을 한 문장으로 바꿔 쓰시오. 각 3점

(1) Do you believe? + Who donated the valuable painting?
> ____________________

(2) I'd like to know. + Are you going to join us for dinner?
> ____________________

24 빈칸에 알맞은 접속사를 [보기]에서 골라 써넣어 글을 완성하시오. 각 2점

[보기] since though while as long as as soon as

Elsa and Anna are sisters, but they are different. (1) ________ Anna is active, Elsa is shy. (2) ________ Elsa doesn't express her feelings, it is certain that she really cares for Anna. (3) ________ they are together, they will be able to overcome any difficulties.

고난도

25 다음 대화의 밑줄 친 ①~⑤ 중 어법상 틀린 두 곳을 골라 바르게 고쳐 쓰시오. 각 3점

A: Do you know ①where is James going to travel?
B: I don't remember exactly, but he ②is traveling only one country for a month.
A: He told me that the seasons there are ③the opposite to here.
B: Then, he ④may be traveling to ⑤both Australia or New Zealand.

(1) (   ) > ____________________
(2) (   ) > ____________________

약점 공략
틀린 문제가 있다면?

틀린 문항 번호가 있는 칸을 색칠하고, 어떤 문법 POINT의 집중 복습이 필요한지 파악해 보세요.

문항 번호	연관 문법 POINT	문항 번호	연관 문법 POINT	문항 번호	연관 문법 POINT
01	P4	10	P1, P2	19	P3, P4
02	P3	11	P5	20	P5
03	P4, P6	12	P6	21	P1, P4
04	P2, P3	13	P2~P4	22	P2, P4, P5, P6
05	P2	14	P2, P4~P6	23	P6
06	P2, P4	15	P2, P3, P5, P6	24	P4
07	P1	16	P1, P2, P4, P6	25	P5, P6
08	P5	17	P2~P5		
09	P6	18	P1~P3, P5, P6		

연관 문법 POINT 참고

P1 (p.94) 접속사 that
P2 (p.94) 시간의 접속사
P3 (p.96) 이유의 접속사
P4 (p.96) 조건 · 양보의 접속사
P5 (p.98) 상관접속사
P6 (p.98) 간접의문문

내신만점 Level Up Test

01 밑줄 친 부분에 대해 잘못 설명한 사람을 모두 고르면?

① As I was sick, I went to bed early last night.
> 윤아: As는 Since로 바꿔 쓸 수 있어.

② Neither I nor Ann remembers his birthday.
> 성우: '*A*와 *B* 둘 중 하나'라는 뜻이야.

③ Unless you stop eating fast food, you will gain weight.
> 지민: Unless는 If ~ not으로 바꿔 쓸 수 있어.

④ I joined the art club, while Andy joined the magic club.
> 유정: while은 '~하는 동안에'라는 뜻으로 쓰였어.

⑤ Even though I didn't have enough time, I tried my best to finish the project.
> 다해: Even though는 '비록 ~일지라도'라는 뜻으로 쓰였어.

02 빈칸 ⓐ~ⓔ 중 어느 곳에도 들어갈 수 없는 것은?

- I wonder ___ⓐ___ he passed the exam.
- Linda won't forgive you ___ⓑ___ you apologize.
- ___ⓒ___ my grandpa is in his 70's, he is still quite active.
- The accident happened ___ⓓ___ the road was slippery.
- People are expecting ___ⓔ___ the Korean team will win the game.

① that ② after ③ unless
④ whether ⑤ although

서술형

03 다음 문장을 [조건]에 맞게 다시 쓰시오.

[조건] 1. while, though, unless, as 중 하나를 사용할 것
2. 접속사로 문장을 시작할 것

(1) The river was not safe to swim in, but he jumped in to save the girl.
> ______________________

(2) Read the instructions carefully, or you won't be able to make the model airplane.
> ______________________

04 다음 대화를 읽고, 물음에 답하시오.

A: May I take your order?
B: I'd like to know if you have a vegetarian dish.
A: Oh, are you a vegetarian? (A) 당신은 고기와 생선을 모두 드시지 않는군요.
B: No, I don't. Do you have any recommendations?
A: Then, I recommend you order Bibimbap.
B: (B) What are the ingredients?
A: Various vegetables with rice.
B: That sounds wonderful.

(1) 괄호 안의 말을 사용하여 (A)의 우리말을 6단어의 영어 문장으로 쓰시오. (eat, meat, fish, neither)
> ______________________

(2) 다음 빈칸에 (B)의 문장을 알맞게 써넣어 문장을 완성하시오.
> Can you tell me ______________?

UNIT 1
POINT 01 관계대명사의 종류와 역할
POINT 02 관계대명사 what

UNIT 2
POINT 03 전치사+관계대명사
POINT 04 관계대명사의 계속적 용법

UNIT 3
POINT 05 관계부사
POINT 06 관계대명사 *vs.* 관계부사

UNIT 4
POINT 07 복합관계대명사
POINT 08 복합관계부사

CHAPTER 08

관계사

관계사에는 접속사와 대명사의 역할을 함께 하는 관계대명사와, 접속사와 부사 역할을 함께 하는 관계부사가 있다.

Preview

관계사

구분	세부	예문
관계대명사	주격	I often visit my uncle who lives in Paris.
	목적격	The cake which he made was delicious. The man with whom I talked is my brother.
	소유격	We know a girl whose mother is a doctor.
	what	The shop didn't have what I wanted to buy.
	계속적 용법	He won the first prize in the contest, which surprised us.
관계부사	장소	This is the bookstore where I found the book.
	시간	He remembers the day when we first met at school.
	이유	Do you know the reason why they acted like that?
	방법	I wonder how my friend improved her math grade.
복합관계사	복합관계대명사	I will give the ticket to whoever wants to join us.
	복합관계부사	However tired you are, you should brush your teeth.

UNIT 1 관계대명사의 종류와 역할, 관계대명사 what

POINT 01 관계대명사의 종류와 역할

This is the boy *who helped me. 이 애가 나를 도와줬던 소년이야.

*관계대명사 who가 이끄는 절이 선행사 the boy를 수식해.

관계대명사는 「접속사+대명사」의 역할을 하며, 선행사를 꾸미는 형용사절을 이끈다. 선행사가 사람인 경우 who(m), that을, 사물이나 동물인 경우 which, that을 사용한다.

주격 관계대명사	who, which, that	Do you know the girl **who(that)** lives over there? Alice hates movies **which(that)** are scary.
목적격 관계대명사	who(m), which, that	Ms. Lee is the teacher **who(m)(that)** we all respect. I found the dog **which(that)** Jack was looking for.
소유격 관계대명사	whose	The girl **whose** skirt is blue is Ann's sister. That is the restaurant **whose** owner is my uncle.
	⊕ 선행사가 사물이나 동물일 때, whose 대신 of which를 쓸 수 있다. He stayed in a hotel **whose** name I forgot. = He stayed in a hotel the name **of which** I forgot.	

ⓘ 관계대명사 that을 주로 쓰는 경우
1. 선행사가 「사람+사물/동물」인 경우
   I know the man and his dog **that** live in the cabin.
2. 선행사가 -thing으로 끝나는 경우
   There is nothing **that** I can do about the matter.
3. 최상급, 서수, all, every, the only, the same, the very 등이 선행사에 포함된 경우
   Matilda is the best book **that** I have read.

ⓘ 목적격 관계대명사와, 뒤에 분사가 이어지는 「주격 관계대명사+be동사」는 생략할 수 있다.
The girl **(whom)** we met in France has sent us a card.
We visited the palace **(which was)** built in 1395 in Seoul.

POINT 02 관계대명사 what

***What she said made me laugh.** 그녀가 말한 것이 나를 웃게 했다.

*'~하는 것'의 의미로 선행사를 포함하는 관계대명사야.

관계대명사 what은 선행사를 포함하며, '~하는 것'의 의미로 명사절을 이끌어 문장에서 주어, 목적어, 보어 역할을 한다.

주어	~하는 것은	**What** they need most is a house to live in.
목적어	~하는 것을	She is reviewing **what** she's learned today.
보어	~하는 것(이다)	A movie director is **what** I want to be in the future.

ⓘ 관계대명사 what은 the thing that으로 바꿔 쓸 수 있다.
I will wear **what(the thing that)** I bought in Paris.

개념 QUICK CHECK

POINT 01

우리말을 영어로 바르게 옮긴 것에 √ 표시하시오.

1 내가 믿을 수 있는 친구들
- □ friends whom I can trust
- □ friends whose I can trust

2 부엌에 있는 탁자
- □ the table that stand in the kitchen
- □ the table that stands in the kitchen

3 엄마가 배우인 소년
- □ the boy who mother is an actress
- □ the boy whose mother is an actress

4 내가 본 가장 재미있는 영화
- □ the most interesting movie that I've seen
- □ the most interesting movie who I've seen

POINT 02

괄호 안에서 알맞은 것을 고르시오.

1 (That / What) I want to do is to relax at home.

2 The book (which / what) I'm reading is very interesting.

3 Did you understand (that / what) the teacher explained?

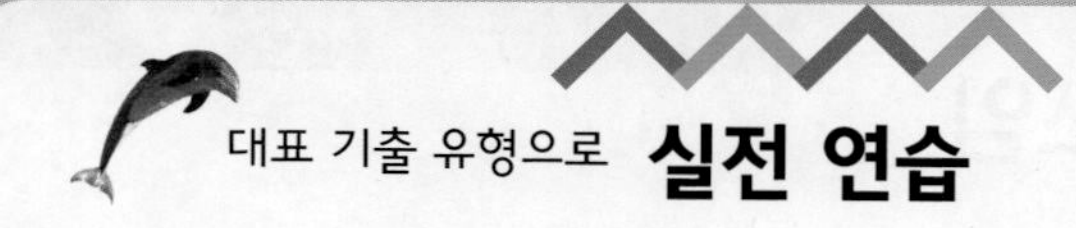

대표 기출 유형으로 실전 연습

1 빈칸에 들어갈 말을 [보기]에서 골라 문장을 완성하시오. (한 번씩 쓸 것)

[보기] which	that	whom

(1) Tina has a cat ________ is three months old.

(2) The woman ________ I met on the bus was very friendly.

(3) Volunteer work is something ________ gives me great joy.

2 다음 두 문장을 관계대명사를 사용하여 한 문장으로 바꿔 쓰시오.

(1) Look at the musician. The musician is singing on the street.

> Look at the musician ____________________.

(2) The vet takes care of animals. The animals' lives are in danger.

> The vet takes care of animals ____________________.

3 밑줄 친 부분을 생략할 수 없는 것은?

① They have a friend who grew up in France.
② The man whom I met in the shop is an animal trainer.
③ Tina has a bunch of flowers that her boyfriend bought.
④ Where did you buy the shirt which you wore yesterday?
⑤ I'm curious about the robot which was made by Dr. Wales.

자주 나와요!

4 우리말과 일치하도록 괄호 안의 말과 관계대명사를 사용하여 문장을 완성하시오. (필요 시 형태를 바꿀 것)

나는 호주 여행에서 경험한 것을 잊지 못할 것이다. (experience)

> I won't forget ________ ________ ________ during my trip to Australia.

틀리기 쉬워요!

5 빈칸에 들어갈 말이 순서대로 바르게 짝지어진 것은?

- I know a boy ________ parents are both lawyers.
- The store didn't have ________ I really needed to buy.
- Melisa wore the same dress ________ I wore at the party.

① whom – that – which
② whom – that – what
③ whose – which – that
④ whose – what – that
⑤ of which – what – which

개념 완성 Quiz *Choose or complete.*

1 선행사가 사람일 때 목적격 관계대명사로 [whom / what]을 쓸 수 있다.
> POINT 01

2 관계대명사와 뒤에 나오는 명사의 관계가 소유인 경우, 관계대명사로 [who / whose]를 쓴다.
> POINT 01

3 [주격 관계대명사 / 목적격 관계대명사]는 생략할 수 있다.
> POINT 01

4 [what / that]은 선행사를 포함하며, '~하는 것'의 의미로 명사절을 이끄는 관계대명사이다.
> POINT 02

5 최상급, 서수, the only, the same 등이 선행사에 포함된 경우 관계대명사는 주로 [that / which]을(를) 쓴다.
> POINT 01, 02

UNIT 2 주의해야 할 관계대명사의 쓰임

POINT 03 전치사+관계대명사

This is the hotel in which we are staying.
이곳이 우리가 머물고 있는 호텔이다.

*관계대명사가 전치사의 목적어 역할을 해.

관계대명사가 전치사의 목적어로 쓰일 때 전치사는 관계대명사의 앞이나 관계대명사절 끝에 올 수 있다.

전치사와 관계대명사의 위치	This is the book. + Guests can write their names in the book. → This is the book **which** guests can write their names **in**. → This is the book **in which** guests can write their names.
	⊕ who나 that은 「전치사+관계대명사」 형태로 쓸 수 없다. 서술형 빈출 The movie **that** I was talking to you **about** won an Academy Award. (○) The movie **about that** I was talking to you won an Academy Award. (×)
전치사와 관계대명사의 생략	Tony is the boy **with whom** I often play badminton. (생략 불가능)
	⊕ 목적격 관계대명사가 단독으로 쓰일 때는 생략할 수 있지만 「전치사+관계대명사」로 쓰일 때는 생략할 수 없다. Tony is the boy **(whom)** I often play badminton **with**.

POINT 04 관계대명사의 계속적 용법

My tablet PC, which is two days old, broke down.
내 태블릿 PC는 이틀 됐는데 고장이 났다.

*선행사에 대해 추가해서 설명하고 있어.

관계대명사의 계속적 용법은 「선행사+콤마(,)+관계대명사절」의 형태로, 선행사에 대한 부가적인 설명을 덧붙인다.

선행사가 단어나 어구	We met Federer, **who** is a great tennis player. ← We met Federer, **and he** is a great tennis player.
	⊕ 계속적 용법의 관계대명사는 「접속사(and, but, for)+대명사」로 바꿔 쓸 수 있다.
선행사가 앞 절 전체	He received perfect test scores, **which** surprised us a lot. ← He received perfect test scores, **and it** surprised us a lot.
	⊕ 계속적 용법의 which는 앞 문장 전체를 선행사로 취할 수 있다.

! 관계대명사 which, who만 계속적 용법으로 쓸 수 있고, that은 쓸 수 없다.
They bought a house**, which** has been empty for five years. (○)
They bought a house**, that** has been empty for five years. (×)

! 계속적 용법으로 사용될 경우, 목적격 관계대명사는 생략할 수 없다.
I met the girl, **whom** I had ever seen last year. (○)
I met the girl, I had ever seen last year. (×)

개념 QUICK CHECK

POINT 03

우리말을 영어로 바르게 옮긴 것에 √ 표시하시오.

1 내가 기다리고 있는 작가
- □ the writer for whom I'm waiting
- □ the writer whom for I'm waiting

2 그가 언급하고 있는 보고서
- □ the report to he is referring
- □ the report he is referring to

3 우리가 갔던 극장
- □ the theater to which we went
- □ the theater to that we went

POINT 04

괄호 안에서 알맞은 것을 고르시오.

1 I don't like Fred, (who / which) often lies to me.

2 Jack came home late last night, (who / which) made his mom angry.

3 Chloe is wearing a yellow dress, (which / that) is very expensive.

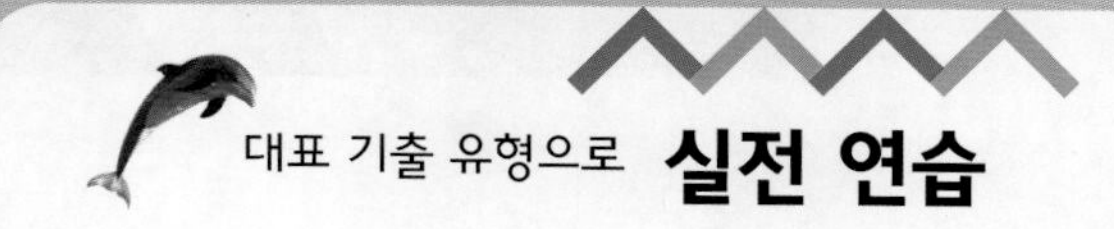

대표 기출 유형으로 **실전 연습**

1 두 문장을 한 문장으로 바꿔 쓸 때 빈칸에 들어갈 말로 알맞은 것은?

> The music was good. We listened to the music at the party.
> = The music ________ we listened at the party was good.

① which ② to that ③ to which
④ to whom ⑤ with which

2 빈칸에 들어갈 말이 순서대로 바르게 짝지어진 것은?

> • The woman is the doctor ________ I told you about.
> • We found the painting in ________ you were interested.

① that – that ② that – which ③ who – that
④ what – which ⑤ whom – that

자주 나와요!
3 빈칸에 공통으로 들어갈 말로 알맞은 것은?

> • Eric recovered from surgery, ________ pleased all of us.
> • I lent Susan *The Little Prince*, ________ is my favorite book.

① who ② that ③ whom
④ which ⑤ what

4 우리말과 일치하도록 괄호 안의 말을 바르게 배열하여 문장을 완성하시오.

(1) Evans 선생님이 말을 건네고 있는 남자아이는 Tim이다.
> ________________________ is Tim.
(to, Ms. Evans, is talking, the boy)

(2) Amy가 작가가 되었는데, 그것은 나를 놀라게 했다.
> Amy became ________________________.
(surprised, made, a writer, me, which)

틀리기 쉬워요!
5 다음 중 어법상 올바른 문장은?

① There is a waiting list on people put their names.
② Look at the big dog with that the man is running.
③ Jane purchased a used car, that is as good as new.
④ Alex is my classmate with which I learn Taekwondo.
⑤ One of my best friends is Nathan, who lives next door.

개념 완성 Quiz *Choose or complete.*

1 관계대명사가 전치사의 ________로 쓰일 때 전치사는 관계대명사의 앞이나 관계대명사절 끝에 올 수 있다.
> POINT 03

2 관계대명사 who, that / whom, which 은(는) 「전치사+관계대명사」 형태로 쓸 수 없다.
> POINT 03

3 관계대명사 which, who / whom, that 만 계속적 용법으로 쓸 수 있다.
> POINT 04

4 계속적 용법의 관계대명사는 선행사+콤마+관계대명사절 / 콤마+선행사+관계대명사절 의 형태이며 앞 문장 전체를 선행사로 취할 수 있다.
> POINT 03, 04

5 목적격 관계대명사가 「________+________」의 형태로 쓰일 때는 생략할 수 없다.
> POINT 03, 04

UNIT **3** 관계부사

POINT 05 관계부사

This is the bookstore *where I first saw her.

이곳이 내가 그녀를 처음 본 서점이다.

*장소를 나타내는 선행사를 수식하는 관계부사야.

관계부사는 「접속사+부사」의 역할을 하며 관계부사절을 이끌어 선행사를 수식한다. 선행사가 장소면 where, 시간이면 when, 이유면 why, 방법이면 how를 쓴다. 관계부사는 「전치사+관계대명사」로 바꿔 쓸 수 있다.

where = at/in/to which	I know the shop. You can buy used cameras **at** the shop. → I know the shop **where(at which)** you can buy used cameras.
when = at/in/on which	I won't forget the day. I passed the audition **on** the day. → I won't forget the day **when(on which)** I passed the audition.
why = for which	Tell me the reason. The answer is correct **for** the reason. → Tell me the reason **why(for which)** the answer is correct.
how = the way in which	I want to know the way. He could master English **in** the way. → I want to know the way **in which** he could master English. → I want to know the way(**how**) he could master English. ⊕ 관계부사 how는 선행사 the way와 함께 쓰지 않는다. 서술형 빈출

① 관계부사의 생략: 선행사가 일반적인 명사(the place, the time, the reason ...)이면 선행사나 관계부사 중 하나를 생략할 수 있다.
Do you remember the day(when) we first met?

POINT 06 관계대명사 *vs.* 관계부사

I like the new house *that we moved *into*.

난 우리가 이사한 새집이 마음에 든다.

*전치사의 목적어 역할을 하는 관계대명사가 필요해.

관계대명사 + 불완전한 문장	This is the house **which** Mozart was born in. (in의 목적어 필요) I enjoyed the time **that** we spent together. (spent의 목적어 필요) ⊕ 관계대명사는 「접속사+대명사」의 역할을 하므로 관계대명사를 제외하면 주어, 목적어, 보어 중 하나가 빠진 불완전한 문장을 이끈다.
관계부사 + 완전한 문장	This is the place **where** I saw the cat. We have not fixed the date **when** we will go on a holiday. ⊕ 관계부사는 「접속사+부사」의 역할이므로 관계부사를 제외하면 부사가 빠진 완전한 문장을 이끈다.

개념 QUICK CHECK

POINT 05

우리말을 영어로 바르게 옮긴 것에 √ 표시하시오.

1 우리가 묵을 호텔
- □ the hotel where we're going to stay
- □ the hotel when we're going to stay

2 우리가 만났던 해
- □ the year where we met
- □ the year when we met

3 내가 화가 난 이유
- □ the reason why I'm angry
- □ the reason how I'm angry

4 내가 문제를 푼 방법
- □ the way I solved the problem
- □ the way how I solved the problem

POINT 06

괄호 안에서 알맞은 것을 고르시오.

1 Do you remember the Halloween (that / when) you dressed like a fairy?

2 The house (which / where) is next to mine is very expensive.

3 We found the forest (which / where) we used to go.

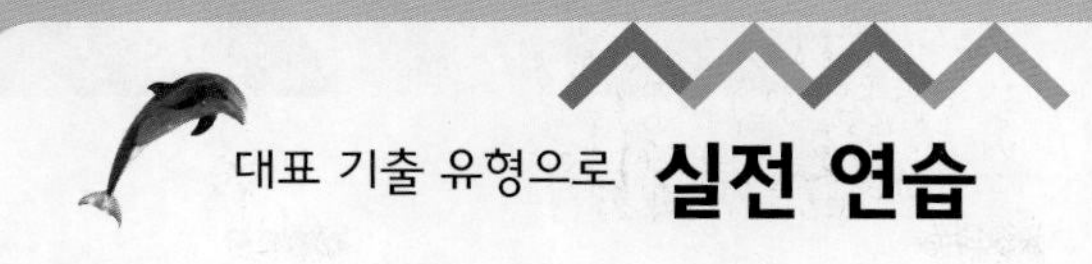

대표 기출 유형으로 **실전 연습**

1 밑줄 친 부분과 바꿔 쓸 수 있는 것은?

> Do you know the time at which the lecture will finish?

① how ② when ③ why
④ where ⑤ which

자주 나와요!
2 관계부사를 사용하여 다음 두 문장을 한 문장으로 바꿔 쓰시오.

(1) Tell me the reason. You made that decision for the reason.
> Tell me ________ ________ ________ you made that decision.

(2) March is the month. A new semester starts in that month in Korea.
> March is ________ ________ ________ a new semester starts in Korea.

3 밑줄 친 ⓐ~ⓒ 중 어법상 틀린 부분을 찾아 바르게 고쳐 쓰시오.

The woman ⓐ showed me ⓑ the way how she ⓒ trained her dogs.

(　　) > ______________________

4 빈칸에 where가 들어갈 수 없는 것은?

① This is the restaurant ________ I first met my husband.
② The company ________ my father works makes furniture.
③ She visited the palace ________ was built in 17th century.
④ I miss the cabin ________ we used to play together all day.
⑤ The hotel ________ my family stayed was very comfortable.

틀리기 쉬워요!
5 밑줄 친 부분의 쓰임이 어법상 틀린 것은?

① He hasn't decided on the place where the students will camp.
② She didn't tell us the reason she canceled the appointment.
③ I showed him the way in which I uploaded pictures online.
④ I'm looking forward to the year when I'll spend in London.
⑤ The man doesn't remember the moment when he got into an accident.

개념 완성 Quiz *Choose or complete.*

1 관계부사는 선행사의 종류에 따라 「________+관계대명사」로 바꿔 쓸 수 있다.
> POINT 05

2 관계부사 [when / how / why]의 선행사는 the reason이다.
> POINT 05

3 관계부사 [how / why]는 선행사 [the reason / the way]와(과) 함께 쓰지 않는다.
> POINT 05

4 관계부사는 「접속사+부사」의 역할을 하므로, 부사가 빠진 [완전한 / 불완전한] 문장을 이끈다.
> POINT 06

5 선행사가 일반적인 명사(the place, the time 등)이면 선행사나 관계부사 중 하나를 생략할 수 [있다 / 없다].
> POINT 05, 06

POINT 07 복합관계대명사

You can eat *whatever you like. 네가 좋아하는 것은 무엇이든 먹어도 된다.

*'~하는 것은 무엇이든'의 의미로 eat의 목적어절을 이끌어.

복합관계대명사는 「관계대명사+-ever」의 형태로 자체에 선행사를 포함하며 명사절이나 양보의 부사절을 이끈다.

whoever	~하는 누구든지 (= anyone who)	I'll play tennis with **whoever** wants to play with me.
	누가 ~할지라도 (= no matter who)	**Whoever** you are, this is off limits.
whatever	~하는 것은 무엇이든지 (= anything that)	Let's do **whatever** you want, it's your birthday!
	무엇이 ~할지라도 (= no matter what)	**Whatever** you say, I'll believe you.
whichever	~하는 것은 어느 것이든지 (= anything that)	You can have **whichever** you like.
	어느 것이 ~할지라도 (= no matter which)	**Whichever** you choose, you won't be satisfied.

POINT 08 복합관계부사

Call me *whenever you're free. 시간 날 때 언제든 내게 전화해 줘.

*'~할 때는 언제나'의 의미로 시간의 부사절을 이끌어.

복합관계부사는 「관계부사+-ever」의 형태로 자체에 선행사를 포함하며 부사절을 이끈다.

wherever	~하는 곳은 어디든지 (= at any place where)	The dog followed Mary **wherever** she went.
	어디에 ~하든지 (= no matter where)	**Wherever** you are, I hope you're happy.
whenever	~할 때는 언제나 (= at any time when)	I'm ready, so I can leave **whenever** you want to leave.
	언제 ~하든지 (= no matter when)	**Whenever** you visit him, you'll find him playing games.
however	아무리 ~할지라도 (= no matter how)	**However** much it costs, I want to buy it.
	⊕ 「however+형용사(부사)+주어+동사」의 어순에 주의한다.  서술형 빈출 **However hard I study**, my mom is never satisfied.	

개념 QUICK CHECK

POINT 07

밑줄 친 부분의 의미로 알맞은 것에  ✓ 표시하시오.

1 Whoever comes will be welcome.
☐ 오는 누구든지
☐ 누군가 올 때

2 Whatever you do, I'm with you.
☐ 네가 하는 것은
☐ 네가 무엇을 하더라도

3 You may have whichever of the desserts you like.
☐ 네가 좋아하는 디저트는 어느 것이든
☐ 네가 어느 디저트를 좋아할지라도

POINT 08

괄호 안에서 알맞은 것을 고르시오.

1 I'm busy now, but I'll do my homework (wherever / whenever) I have time.

2 He led the caravan (wherever / however) he wanted to go.

3 (However you may be hungry / However hungry you may be), you should eat slowly.

1 우리말과 일치하도록 할 때 빈칸에 들어갈 말로 알맞은 것은?

학교 교칙을 어긴 사람은 누구든지 벌을 받을 것이다.
> ________ breaks the school rules will be punished.

① However ② Whoever ③ Whenever
④ Whatever ⑤ Whichever

2 두 문장의 의미가 같도록 할 때 빈칸에 들어갈 말로 알맞은 것은?

Whatever happens, I will never give up my dream.
= ________ happens, I will never give up my dream.

① At any time ② Anyone who ③ Anything that
④ No matter how ⑤ No matter what

자주 나와요!
3 빈칸에 공통으로 들어갈 말로 알맞은 것은?

• Feel free to ask for assistance ________ you need it.
• My father watches a baseball game ________ he has time.

① whichever ② whatever ③ whenever
④ wherever ⑤ however

틀리기 쉬워요!
4 빈칸에 들어갈 말이 순서대로 바르게 짝지어진 것은?

• My family goes ________ my mom wants to travel.
• ________ you choose among them, it will suit you well.

① wherever – Whichever ② whoever – However
③ wherever – Whenever ④ whenever – However
⑤ whichever – Whatever

5 다음 중 어법상 틀린 문장은?

① You'll be able to rent a car whenever you want.
② Wherever I go, my little sister always follows me.
③ Rachel forgives her son no matter what he does wrong.
④ However the house is expensive, I'm sure they will buy it.
⑤ The patients will do anything that the doctor recommends.

개념 완성 Quiz *Choose or complete.*

1 복합관계대명사는 명사절이나 [시간의 부사절 / 양보의 부사절]을 이끈다.
> POINT 07

2 [no matter what / anything that]: 무엇이 ~할지라도
> POINT 07

3 [however / whatever / whenever]: ~할 때는 언제나, 언제 ~하든지
> POINT 08

4 [whoever / whichever / wherever]: ~하는 것은 어느 것이든지, 어느 것이 ~할지라도
> POINT 07, 08

5 however 뒤에 [주어+동사+형용사(부사) / 형용사(부사)+주어+동사]의 어순으로 쓰는 것에 주의한다.
> POINT 07, 08

서술형 실전 연습

Step 1

개념 완성 Quiz *Choose or complete.*

1 우리말과 일치하도록 괄호 안의 말을 바르게 배열하여 문장을 완성하시오.

(1) 기차에서 내 옆에 앉았던 소년은 러시아에서 왔다.

> ______________________ is from Russia.

(in the train, who, next to, sat, the boy, me)

(2) 노벨상을 탄 작가의 책은 백만 부가 팔렸다.

> ______________________ sold a million copies.

(the Nobel Prize, author, whose, won, the book)

2 다음 문장에서 어법상 틀린 부분을 찾아 바르게 고쳐 쓰시오.

(1) I couldn't understand which the teacher said.

____________ > ____________

(2) Jess loves the gallery where she often visits alone.

____________ > ____________

3 관계사를 사용하여 두 문장을 한 문장으로 바꿔 쓰시오.

(1) Do you have a friend? The friend lives in a foreign country.

> ______________________

(2) Let me know the day. The art exhibition will start on the day.

> ______________________

4 다음 문장을 괄호 안의 지시에 맞게 바꿔 쓰시오.

Julia went to the city that her parents were born in.

(1) (전치사를 관계대명사 앞에 쓸 것)

> ______________________

(2) (관계부사를 사용할 것)

> ______________________

5 [보기]에서 알맞은 관계사를 골라 넣어 문장을 바꿔 쓰시오.

[보기] that	which	however	whatever

(1) Jonny didn't clean his room, and it made his mother angry.

> Jonny didn't clean his room, ______________________.

(2) No matter how hard I try to persuade her, she won't listen to me.

> ______________________, she won't listen to me.

1 whose / which : 선행사의 종류에 관계없이 소유를 나타내는 관계대명사

> POINT 01

2 선행사+관계대명사+ 완전한 문장 / 불완전한 문장

> POINT 02, 06

3 where / when / how : the day, the time 등이 선행사인 관계부사

> POINT 01, 05

4 「전치사+관계대명사」로 쓸 수 없는 관계대명사: who, that / whom, which

> POINT 03, 05

5 계속적 용법으로 쓸 수 있는 관계대명사: who, which / whom, that

> POINT 04, 08

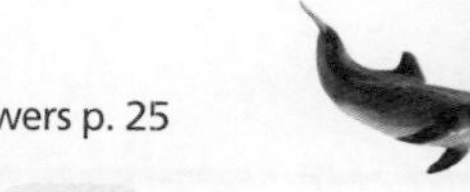

Answers p. 25

Step 2

6 그림을 보고, 괄호 안의 말과 알맞은 관계사를 사용하여 대화를 완성하시오.

(1)

(2)

(1) **A:** I'm looking for a backpack. I'd like to put my laptop in it.

B: Here is a good one ____________________. (can hold)

(2) **A:** Can you tell me the reason ________________________?

(the accident, happen)

B: It happened because it was snowy. My car suddenly slipped.

7 [보기]에서 알맞은 관계사를 골라 써넣어 다음 도서관 안내문을 완성하시오.

[보기]	whatever	whenever	wherever
	whoever	however	

Welcome to Dream Library

________ wants to read books, please visit our school library. Come ________ you want to read a book. You can sit ________ you like. We have a lot of books. You can read about ________ you want.

8 빈칸에 알맞은 관계사를 써넣어 다음 글을 완성하시오.

A long time ago, there was a girl (1) ________ became friends with a fairy. They met in a forest (2) ________ the girl liked to play. One afternoon in the winter (3) ________ it was very cold, the girl got lost. She started to cry near the lake. The fairy appeared and took her to a house (4) ________ was not very far.

개념 완성 Quiz *Choose or complete.*

6 [why / how / where]: the reason이 선행사인 관계부사

> POINT 01, 05

7 복합관계사 [however / whatever]의 의미: ~하는 것은 무엇이든지, 무엇이 ~할지라도

> POINT 07, 08

8 [who, that / what, which]: 선행사가 사람일 때 쓰는 주격 관계대명사

> POINT 01, 05

실전 모의고사

시험일 : 월 일	문항 수 : 객관식 18 / 서술형 7
목표 시간 :	총점
걸린 시간 :	/ 100

[01-03] 빈칸에 들어갈 말로 알맞은 것을 고르시오. 각 2점

01

We were moved by ________ the doctor did for children in Africa.

① who ② that ③ what
④ which ⑤ whose

02

I borrowed the book ________ cover is green from the library.

① who ② whose ③ that
④ which ⑤ where

03

The house ________ the Russian writer was born became a museum.

① that ② which ③ what
④ when ⑤ where

04 두 문장의 의미가 같도록 할 때 빈칸에 들어갈 말로 알맞은 것은? 2점

Whenever she does yoga, she feels relaxed.
= ________ she does yoga, she feels relaxed.

① At any time ② Anything that
③ Anyone who ④ No matter when
⑤ No matter which

05 빈칸에 공통으로 들어갈 말로 알맞은 것은? 2점

- We will stay at a hotel ________ is located close to the airport.
- Steve was an actor when he was a child, ________ surprised us.

① where ② that ③ what
④ which ⑤ whose

06 빈칸에 들어갈 말이 나머지와 다른 것은? 3점

① This is ________ I could do for you.
② My sister ate ________ Dad cooked for me.
③ I didn't tell him ________ I heard from Steve.
④ ________ we want to know is why he didn't come.
⑤ He packed up his things ________ he will bring to Paris.

07 우리말을 영어로 잘못 옮긴 것은? 3점

나는 우리가 처음 만났던 날을 기억한다.

① I remember when we first met.
② I remember the day we first met.
③ I remember the day when we first met.
④ I remember the day on that we first met.
⑤ I remember the day on which we first met.

08 대화의 빈칸에 들어갈 말이 순서대로 짝지어진 것은? 3점

A: Is this the smartphone ________ was released last week?
B: Yes. It's the newest phone ________ has four camera lenses.

① that – who ② that – what
③ which – who ④ what – which
⑤ which – that

[09-10] 빈칸에 들어갈 말이 순서대로 바르게 짝지어진 것을 고르시오. 각 3점

09

- She found the shoes for ________ I was looking.
- I got an email from Alex, ________ used to live next door.

① that – what ② that – whom
③ which – who ④ which – what
⑤ whose – that

10

- The store ________ I bought this shirt is closed today.
- They saw the man and his horse ________ were walking along the beach.

① that – what ② that – which
③ which – that ④ where – when
⑤ where – that

11 밑줄 친 부분을 생략할 수 있는 것은? 3점

① Amy has a cat that has big eyes.
② I forgot to bring my essay which I wrote.
③ That is the actor about whom Kelly talked.
④ There were people who were waiting for the train.
⑤ We saw a documentary film, which was about wild animals.

12 밑줄 친 부분과 바꿔 쓴 말의 의미가 다른 것은? 4점

① This is the reason why I helped him. (→ for which)
② Whatever she says will be accepted. (→ Anything that)
③ I wanted to buy the ring, but it was expensive. (→ which)
④ You can borrow my books whenever you want. (→ no matter when)
⑤ No matter who he is, he shouldn't be treated like that. (→ Whoever)

13 밑줄 친 부분의 쓰임이 어법상 틀린 것은? 4점

① I visited my cousin who lives in Busan.
② David has a big dog which kids are afraid of.
③ We don't know why he didn't tell the truth.
④ She is looking for a boy whose name is Tim Davis.
⑤ Jess likes J. K. Rowling, that is a best-selling author.

14 다음 글의 빈칸 ⓐ~ⓒ에 들어갈 말이 바르게 짝지어진 것은? 4점

> Daisy invites ___ⓐ___ wants to come to her house. Yesterday she invited me and made lunch with vegetables ___ⓑ___ she grew. I was thankful for ___ⓒ___ she did for me.

	ⓐ	ⓑ	ⓒ
①	whoever	what	that
②	whoever	which	what
③	whenever	that	what
④	whenever	what	which
⑤	wherever	which	that

[15-16] 어법상 틀린 문장을 고르시오. 각 4점

15

① Do you know the reason Jason quit his job?
② This is the city where we lived for ten years.
③ Let me know the time at which the game will start.
④ Beth waited for the weekend when she could go hiking.
⑤ Matt showed me the way how I could use this machine.

16 ① I like what I bought at the antique shop.
② This is the first story that O. Henry wrote.
③ Angela is a friend whom I can trust.
④ The man who Mia is talking to is my dad.
⑤ We went to the restaurant where Tim recommended.

고난도
17 짝지어진 문장의 의미가 다른 것은? 5점

① Look at the girl. Jim is talking to the girl.
= Look at the girl to whom Jim is talking.
② Whoever asks, I'll never tell her secret.
= No matter who asks, I'll never tell her secret.
③ He found a car. The car's windows were broken.
= He found a car whose windows were broken.
④ Whatever you say, I won't change my mind.
= Anything that you say, I won't change my mind.
⑤ We want to know the way. She stays healthy in the way.
= We want to know the way in which she stays healthy.

18 어법상 올바른 문장끼리 짝지어진 것은? 5점

ⓐ However the watch is old, I can't throw it away.
ⓑ He can travel wherever he wants for one year.
ⓒ Here are the books in what you are interested.
ⓓ Tell me whatever you know about the rumor.
ⓔ I turned down his invitation, which made him upset.

① ⓐ, ⓑ, ⓓ ② ⓐ, ⓒ, ⓔ ③ ⓑ, ⓒ, ⓓ
④ ⓑ, ⓓ, ⓔ ⑤ ⓒ, ⓓ, ⓔ

19 두 문장의 의미가 같도록 알맞은 관계사를 사용하여 문장을 바꿔 쓰시오. 각 2점

(1) The thing that happened to him made us sad.
= ________ ________ ________ ________ made us sad.

(2) My aunt will marry a man, and he is from Ireland.
= My aunt will marry a man, ________ ________ ________ ________.

20 생략된 괄호 안의 말을 알맞은 위치에 넣어 문장을 다시 쓰시오. 각 2점

(1) The girl we met in London sent us an email. (whom)
> ________________________________

(2) They visited the tower built by a famous architect. (which was)
> ________________________________

21 다음 표와 일치하도록 알맞은 관계부사를 써넣어 문장을 완성하시오. 각 2점

James Brown	was born in Michigan	1991
	learned Korean through a website	2017
	went to Korea to teach English	2018

(1) 1991 was the year ________ James Brown was born.
(2) ________ James Brown learned Korean was through a website.
(3) Korea was the country ________ James Brown went to teach English.

Answers p. 26

22 다음 [조건]에 맞게 우리말을 영어로 쓰시오. 각 4점

[조건] 1. 알맞은 관계사를 사용할 것
2. 괄호 안의 말을 사용하고 필요 시 형태를 바꿀 것
3. (1)은 10단어, (2)는 9단어로 쓸 것

(1) 내가 너에게 말했던 그 호수는 캐나다에 있다.
(the lake, tell about, in Canada)
> ______________________________

(2) 그는 어느 것을 선택하더라도 그것에 만족하지 못할 것이다. (choose, be satisfied with)
> ______________________________

23 그림을 보고, 관계사와 괄호 안의 말을 사용하여 문장을 완성하시오. 각 3점

(1) 
(2) 

(1) Jamie likes the girl ______________ ______________. (hair, long and blonde)

(2) I can't forget the day ______________ in the speech contest. (win first prize)

24 다음 대화의 밑줄 친 ①~⑤ 중 어법상 틀린 두 곳을 골라 바르게 고쳐 쓰시오. 각 3점

A: Mom, can I eat ①something now?
B: No. It's almost midnight.
A: I'm hungry. I ②want to eat the ice cream ③what Uncle John bought for us.
B: ④However you may be hungry, you shouldn't eat anything ⑤before you go to bed.

(1) (　　) > ______________________________
(2) (　　) > ______________________________

25 우리말과 일치하도록 [보기]의 말과 알맞은 관계사를 사용하여 문장을 완성하시오. 각 4점

[보기] volunteer　　is interested in
at an animal shelter
helping abandoned dogs

LovePet은 (A) 학생들이 동물 보호소에서 자원봉사를 하는 동아리입니다. 여러분이 그곳에서 무엇을 하든지, 그것은 큰 도움이 될 것입니다. (B) 유기견들을 돕는 것에 관심이 있는 사람은 누구든지 환영합니다.

⬇

LovePet is a club (A) ______________________________.
Whatever you do there, it will be a big help. (B) ______________________________ is welcome.

약점 공략
틀린 문제가 있다면?

틀린 문항 번호가 있는 칸을 색칠하고, 어떤 문법 POINT의 집중 복습이 필요한지 파악해 보세요.

문항 번호	연관 문법 POINT	문항 번호	연관 문법 POINT	문항 번호	연관 문법 POINT
01	P2	10	P1, P5, P6	19	P2, P4
02	P1	11	P1, P3, P4	20	P1
03	P5	12	P4, P5, P7, P8	21	P5
04	P8	13	P1, P3~P5	22	P3, P7
05	P1, P4	14	P1, P2, P7	23	P1, P5
06	P1, P2	15	P5	24	P1, P2, P8
07	P5	16	P1, P2, P6	25	P5, P7
08	P1	17	P1, P3, P5, P7		
09	P3, P4	18	P1~P8		

연관 문법 POINT 참고

P1 (p.108) 관계대명사의 종류와 역할
P2 (p.108) 관계대명사 what
P3 (p.110) 전치사+관계대명사
P4 (p.110) 관계대명사의 계속적 용법
P5 (p.112) 관계부사
P6 (p.112) 관계대명사 *vs.* 관계부사
P7 (p.114) 복합관계대명사
P8 (p.114) 복합관계부사

내신만점 Level Up Test

신유형

01 다음 두 문장을 관계사를 사용하여 한 문장으로 바꿀 때, 7번째로 오는 단어는?

> People want to know the way. The child could learn three languages in the way.

① know ② child ③ how ④ learn ⑤ languages

02 빈칸에 들어갈 말이 같은 것끼리 짝지어진 것은?

> ⓐ ________ you say might hurt others' feelings.
> ⓑ I know a store ________ you can buy used laptops.
> ⓒ Mary had children of ________ she had to take care.
> ⓓ Tom was elected the team leader, ________ surprised us.
> ⓔ They are interested in the dress ________ was designed by an actress.

① ⓐ, ⓑ ② ⓐ, ⓒ ③ ⓑ, ⓒ ④ ⓑ, ⓔ ⑤ ⓓ, ⓔ

03 빈칸에 들어갈 말에 대해 바르게 말한 사람은?

> This is the house ___ⓐ___ Jessy lived when she was young. She especially loved her room ___ⓑ___ she used for ten years. It was so bright and warm. She visits the house ___ⓒ___ she comes to this city.

① 성우: ⓐ에는 where가 들어갈 수 없어.
② 도현: ⓐ에는 that이 들어갈 수 있어.
③ 지민: ⓑ에는 which와 that이 모두 들어갈 수 있어.
④ 승연: ⓑ에 들어갈 관계사는 생략할 수 없어.
⑤ 예지: ⓒ에는 whatever를 쓸 수 있어.

서술형

04 다음 대화를 읽고, 물음에 답하시오.

> A: I'm going to see a new action movie. Do you want to join me?
> B: Sorry. I don't like action movies.
> A: Why not? (A) <u>난 스트레스를 받을 때마다 액션 영화를 봐.</u>
> B: (B) <u>Action movies have a lot of violent scenes, what makes me uncomfortable.</u>

(1) 복합관계부사와 괄호 안의 말을 사용하여 (A)를 영어로 바르게 옮겨 쓰시오.

> ______________________, I see action movies. (be stressed out)

(2) 밑줄 친 문장 (B)에서 어법상 <u>틀린</u> 부분을 찾아 바르게 고쳐 쓰시오.

______________ > ______________

05 다음 글의 밑줄 친 ⓐ~ⓔ 중 어법상 <u>틀린</u> 두 곳을 찾아 바르게 고치시오.

> Climbing Mt. Halla was ⓐ<u>which</u> I always wanted to do. I finally climbed Mt. Halla, ⓑ<u>which</u> is 1,950 meters high. ⓒ<u>When</u> I reached the summit, I got a certificate for climbing Mt. Halla. ⓓ<u>Whatever</u> reaches the summit can get a certificate. This is the most memorable experience ⓔ<u>that</u> I have ever had.

(1) (   ) > ______________

(2) (   ) > ______________

UNIT 1 POINT 01 원급, 비교급, 최상급
POINT 02 원급을 이용한 표현

UNIT 2 POINT 03 비교급, 최상급을 이용한 표현
POINT 04 원급과 비교급을 이용한 최상급 의미

비교

비교는 두 가지 또는 그 이상의 대상을 서로 견주어 설명하는 방법이다.

Preview

비교

구분	의미	예문
원급 비교 as ~ as	~만큼 …한(하게)	Jason can run as fast as Mike.
	~의 -배만큼 …한(하게)	Jason can run twice as fast as I can.
비교급 비교 -er than	~보다 더 …한	Jason can run faster than Mike.
	점점 더 ~한(하게)	Jason ran faster and faster.
	~할수록 더 …한(하게)	The faster Jason ran, the more famous he became.
최상급 비교 (셋 이상) the -est	~에서 가장 …한	Jason is the fastest boy in his class.
	가장 ~한 (것)들 중 하나	Jason is one of the fastest boys in his class.

UNIT 1 원급, 비교급, 최상급

POINT 01 원급, 비교급, 최상급

My sister is two years *younger than me.

내 여동생은 나보다 두 살 더 어리다.

*비교급 표현으로 '~보다 더 어린'의 의미야.

원급	as+원급+as ~만큼 …한(하게)	The race car is **as fast as** lightning.
	not as(so)+원급+as ~만큼 …하지 않은(않게)	Jake's score is **not as good as** Wendy's.
비교급	비교급+than ~보다 더 …한(하게)	The weather changes **more quickly** in winter **than** in fall.
	less+원급+than ~보다 덜 …한(하게)	I think English is **less difficult than** Chinese.
	⊕ 「not as(so)+원급+as」와 「less+원급+than」은 같은 의미를 나타낸다. Tennis is **not so popular as** baseball in Korea. = Tennis is **less popular than** baseball in Korea.	
최상급	the+최상급+in(of) ~에서 가장 …한(하게)	Last summer was **the hottest** summer **in** ten years.
	⊕ in 뒤에는 주로 '장소나 범위를 나타내는 명사'가 나오고, of 뒤에는 '비교의 대상이 되는 명사'가 나온다. He is **the best** singer **of** all the members.	

POINT 02 원급을 이용한 표현

My brother is *twice as old as I. 형은 나의 두 배만큼 나이가 많다.

*'~의 두 배만큼 …한'의 의미로 배수비교를 나타내.

배수사+as+원급+as	~의 –배만큼 …한(하게)	Your phone is **three times as expensive as** mine.
	⊕ 「배수사+비교급+than」은 '~보다 –배 더 …한(하게)'의 의미이다. Your phone is **three times more expensive than** mine.	
as+원급+as possible	가능한 한 ~한(하게)	Send me the email **as soon as possible**. = Send me the email **as soon as you can**.
	⊕ 「as+원급+as+주어+can」으로 바꿔 쓸 수 있다. 이때 주절의 동사가 과거면 can 대신 could를 쓴다. 서술형 빈출 She visited her grandma **as often as possible**. = She visited her grandma **as often as she could**.	

개념 QUICK CHECK

POINT 01

괄호 안에서 알맞은 것을 고르시오.

1 The movie was not as (good / better) as I thought.

2 English is (more important / important) than math to me.

3 This ride is less (thrilling / more thrilling) than that one.

4 Can you name the (higher / highest) building in the world?

POINT 02

우리말을 영어로 바르게 표현한 것에 √ 표시하시오.

1 네 배만큼 큰
- □ four times as big as
- □ four times as bigger as

2 이것보다 세 배 더 큰
- □ three times as bigger as this
- □ three times bigger than this

3 가능한 한 빠르게
- □ as fast as possible
- □ as possible as fast

1 괄호 안에서 알맞은 것을 고르시오.

(1) My bag is as big as (your / yours).
(2) Jane goes shopping as often (as / than) Mary.
(3) I don't like heavy things, so I will buy the (heavier / lightest) travel bag in the shop.

2 다음 대화의 빈칸에 old의 형태를 각각 알맞게 쓰시오.

A: Guess how old my brother is. My dad is 30 years ________ than my brother. My dad is three times as ________ as my brother.
B: I got it. He's 15 years old.

자주 나와요!
3 우리말과 의미가 같도록 괄호 안의 말을 이용하여 빈칸에 알맞게 쓰시오.

이 타워는 저 호텔보다 4배 더 높다. (tall)
> This tower is ______________________ as that hotel.

4 밑줄 친 부분이 어법상 틀린 것은?

① The TV show was better than I expected.
② I think Tina can jump as high as the player.
③ She tried to finish the job as soon as she could.
④ This horror movie is not more scary as I imagined.
⑤ These are the most comfortable shoes in the shop.

틀리기 쉬워요!
5 다음 표의 내용과 일치하지 않는 것은?

	cell phone	laptop	camera
price	$900	$850	$450

① The camera is the cheapest of the three.
② The camera is not as expensive as the laptop.
③ The laptop is more expensive than the camera.
④ The cell phone is not as expensive as the laptop.
⑤ The cell phone is twice more expensive than the camera.

개념 완성 Quiz *Choose or complete.*

1 '가장 ~한(하게)'의 의미를 나타낼 때는 [the+비교급 / the+최상급]으로 표현한다.
> POINT 01

2 '~만큼 …한(하게)'의 의미를 나타낼 때는 [as ... as / -er than](으)로 표현한다.
> POINT 01, 02

3 「배수사+as+[원급 / 비교급]+as」는 '~의 –배 만큼 …한(하게)'의 의미이다.
> POINT 02

4 as soon as possible은 ['~만큼 빠르게' / '가능한 한 빠르게']의 의미이다.
> POINT 01, 02

5 대부분의 3음절 이상의 형용사는 [-er 또는 -est / more 또는 most]를 사용하여 비교급과 최상급을 표현한다.
> POINT 01, 02

UNIT 2 여러 가지 비교 구문

POINT 03 비교급, 최상급을 이용한 표현

*The harder you study, the better grades you get.

너는 열심히 공부할수록 더 좋은 점수를 받는다.

*'~할수록 더 …한'의 의미를 나타내.

(1) 비교급을 이용한 표현

much(even, still, far, a lot) +비교급	훨씬 더 ~한	The test was **much more difficult** than the previous one.
	⊕ very와 so는 비교급을 수식할 수 없다. 서술형 빈출 Emily is **very prettier** than her sister. (×)	
비교급+and+비교급	점점 더 ~한(하게)	Everything will get **better and better**.
the+비교급 ~, the+비교급 …	~할수록 더 …한(하게)	**The more careful** you are, **the fewer** mistakes you make.

(2) 최상급을 이용한 표현

one of the +최상급+복수명사	가장 ~한 …(것)들 중 하나	*Cats* is **one of the most popular musicals**.
	⊕ 최상급 뒤에 복수명사가 오는 것에 주의한다. 서술형 빈출 Jack is one of the smartest **students** in our school.	
the+최상급 +명사(+that)+주어 +have(has)+p.p.	지금껏 ~한 것들 중에서 가장 …한(하게)	Hawaii is **the most beautiful island (that) I have ever visited.**

POINT 04 원급과 비교급을 이용한 최상급 의미

*No one is as kind as Kate.

누구도 Kate만큼 친절하지 않다.

*원급을 이용해서 최상급의 의미를 나타내.

비교급+than any other+단수명사	다른 어떤 ~보다 더 …한	This is **cheaper than any other smartphone** in the shop.
비교급+than all the other+복수명사	다른 모든 ~들보다 더 …한	This is **cheaper than all the other smartphones** in the shop.
부정주어 ~ as(so) +원급+as	어떤 ~도 −만큼 …하지 않은	**No** smartphone is **as(so) cheap as** this smartphone in the shop.
부정주어 ~ 비교급+than	어떤 ~도 −보다 더 …하지 않은	**No** smartphone is **cheaper than** this smartphone in the shop.

개념 QUICK CHECK

POINT 03

1 우리말을 영어로 바르게 표현한 것에 √ 표시하시오.

(1) 훨씬 더 비싼
- □ very more expensive
- □ much more expensive

(2) 점점 더 피곤한
- □ more and more tired
- □ more tired and more tired

2 괄호 안에서 알맞은 것을 고르시오.

(1) Seoul is one of the busiest (city / cities) in the world.

(2) This is the (more interesting / most interesting) book that I've ever read.

POINT 04

주어진 문장과 의미가 같은 것에 모두 √ 표시하시오.

1 Steve is the tallest boy in my class.
- □ Steve is as tall as any other boy in my class.
- □ Steve is taller than all the other boys in my class.
- □ No boy is as tall as Steve in my class.
- □ No boy is the tallest in my class.

대표 기출 유형으로 실전 연습

1 빈칸에 들어갈 말로 알맞지 않은 것은?

> This food is ________ more delicious than I expected.

① far ② even ③ very
④ much ⑤ a lot

쉬워요! 틀리기

2 우리말과 일치하도록 괄호 안의 말을 바르게 배열하여 문장을 완성하시오.

이것은 내가 본 (영화) 중에서 가장 감동적인 영화이다.

> This is ______________________________________.
(that, ever seen, film, I've, the most moving)

자주 나와요!

3 대화의 밑줄 친 ①~⑤ 중 어법상 틀린 것을 골라 바르게 고쳐 쓰시오.

A: ① How ② was your English presentation?
B: Not good. I wasn't nervous at first, but I ③ got ④ much and much ⑤ nervous before the presentation.

( ) > ______________________

4 두 문장의 의미가 같도록 할 때 빈칸에 들어갈 말로 알맞은 것은?

> No camera app in the world is as useful as this.
> = This is ____________ any other camera app in the world.

① as useful as ② not as useful as
③ not useful than ④ more useful than
⑤ the most useful

5 다음 중 어법상 올바른 문장은?

① It is getting more and more hot in May.
② The more tired I am, the more sweets I eat.
③ She is one of the most famous actress in Asia.
④ Jason is funniest than any other boy in my school.
⑤ This drama is very more popular than the previous one.

개념 완성 Quiz *Choose or complete.*

1 비교급을 수식하는 표현으로는 [much / very / so], even 등이 있으며, '훨씬'이라는 의미를 갖는다.
> POINT 03

2 '지금껏 ~한 것들 중에서 가장 …한'이라는 의미는 [one of the+최상급+복수명사 / the+최상급+명사+(that)+주어+have(has)+p.p.]로 나타낸다.
> POINT 03

3 '점점 더 ~한(하게)'라는 의미는 「________ and ________」으로 표현한다.
> POINT 03

4 「부정주어 ~ as+원급+as」는 [비교급 / 최상급]의 의미이다.
> POINT 04

5 원급과 비교급 구문을 활용하여 [원급 / 비교급 / 최상급]의 의미를 나타낼 수 있다.
> POINT 03, 04

서술형 실전 연습

Step 1

개념 완성 Quiz *Choose or complete.*

1 다음 표의 내용에 맞게 괄호 안의 말을 사용하여 문장을 완성하시오.

Name	Subin	Jina
Height	162 cm	169 cm
50m Running Speed	11 seconds	13 seconds

(1) Jina ________ ________ ________ Subin. (tall)

(2) Jina does not run ________ ________ ________ Subin. (fast, as)

2 두 문장의 의미가 같도록 빈칸에 알맞은 말을 쓰시오.

Her dog was three times as big as mine.

= Her dog was ________ ________ ________ ________ mine.

3 우리말과 일치하도록 괄호 안의 말을 이용하여 문장을 완성하시오.

"Carmen"은 세계에서 가장 유명한 오페라 중 하나이다.

> *Carmen* is ________ ________ ________ ________ ________ ________ in the world. (one, popular, opera)

4 주어진 문장과 같은 의미가 되도록 빈칸에 알맞은 말을 쓰시오.

Jupiter is the biggest planet in our solar system.

= No other planet in our solar system is ________ ________ ________ Jupiter.

= Jupiter is bigger than ________ ________ ________ in our solar system.

= No other planet in our solar system is ________ ________ Jupiter.

5 괄호 안의 말을 알맞은 위치에 넣어 문장을 다시 쓰고, 우리말로 해석하시오.

Today is colder than yesterday. (much)

> ________________________________

> 우리말 뜻: ________________________________

개념 완성 Quiz

1 • ~보다 더 …한: 비교급 / 원급 문장으로 표현
• ~만큼 …한: 비교급 / 원급 문장으로 표현

> POINT 01

2 배수사+ as+원급+as / as+비교급+as
= 배수사+ 비교급+than / 원급+than

> POINT 02

3 '가장 ~한 …(것)들 중 하나': one of the+ 비교급 / 최상급 + 단수명사/복수명사

> POINT 02

4 원급, 비교급으로 최상급 표현하기
최상급 (the -est) 문장:
= 비교급+than / as+원급+as +any other+ 단수명사 / 복수명사

> POINT 04

5 비교급을 강조하는 말: very, so / much, a lot

> POINT 03

Answers p. 28

개념 완성 Quiz *Choose or complete.*

6 빈칸에 알맞은 말을 써넣어 대화를 완성하시오.

(1) **A**: What number is 7 times more than 4?

B: It's ______________.

(2) **A**: What number is ________ ________ ________ as 2?

B: It's 4.

6 '2배'를 나타내는 말: ________ 또는 two ________

> POINT 02

고난도

7 다음 그림과 도표를 설명하는 문장을 [조건]에 맞게 완성하시오.

(1) 

(2) 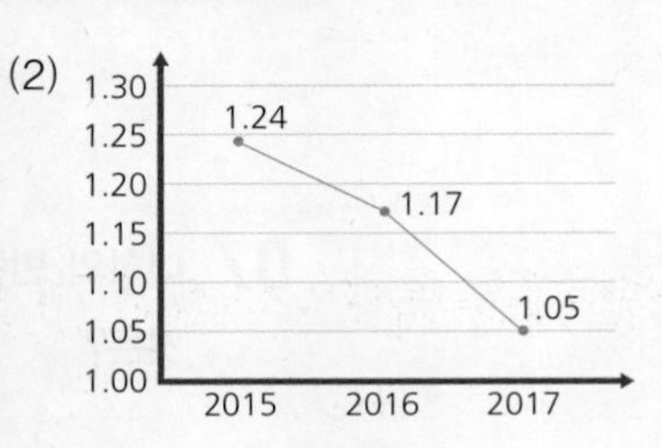

[조건]	1. 적절한 비교급 표현을 사용할 것 2. 각각 괄호 안의 말을 활용할 것

(1) ______________ we climb up the mountain, ______________ it will get. (high, cold)

(2) The birthrate is getting ____________________. (low)

7 '~할수록 더 …하다' : the+비교급, the+비교급 / 비교급+and+비교급

> POINT 03

8 자연스러운 대화가 되도록 괄호 안의 말을 바르게 배열하여 문장을 완성하시오.

A: What do you think about living in the city?

B: Well, it's (1) ______________________________.
(in the countryside, exciting, than, more, living)

A: Yes, but the city can be (2) ______________________________.
(dangerous, than, more, the countryside)

B: That's true. I think people in the city aren't (3) ______________
______________________________.
(open and friendly, those in the countryside, as, as)

A: I'm sure that the countryside is more relaxed, too.

8 '~만큼 …한': as+원급+as / 비교급+than

> POINT 01

실전 모의고사

시험일 : 월 일	문항 수 : 객관식 17 / 서술형 8
목표 시간 :	총점
걸린 시간 :	/ 100

[01-02] 빈칸에 들어갈 말로 알맞은 것을 고르시오. 각 2점

01

She looks ________ than before.

① happy ② more happy
③ happier ④ most happy
⑤ happiest

02

Computers help us to work much ________.

① efficiency ② efficient
③ more efficient ④ efficiently
⑤ more efficiently

[03-04] 빈칸에 들어갈 말로 알맞지 않은 것을 고르시오. 각 2점

03

Tiffany is more ________ than I.

① active ② careful ③ diligent
④ generous ⑤ strong

04

Bikes are ________ slower than airplanes.

① far ② still ③ much
④ a lot ⑤ very

05 빈칸에 들어갈 말이 순서대로 바르게 짝지어진 것은? 3점

- Narae works hardest ________ us all.
- Sara is the tallest ________ my class.

① of – of ② of – in
③ in – in ④ between – of
⑤ in – between

06 밑줄 친 부분을 바르게 고친 것끼리 짝지어진 것은? 3점

- E-books are cheap than laptops.
- Tom speaks quickly than Mary.

① cheap – quickly
② cheaper – quickly
③ more cheaper – quickly
④ cheaper – more quickly
⑤ more cheap – more quickly

07 대화의 빈칸에 들어갈 말이 순서대로 바르게 짝지어진 것은? 3점

A: Who do you think is the ________ soccer player in the world?
B: I think Lionel Messi is.
A: I think Cristiano Ronaldo is as ________ as Lionel Messi.

① good – better ② better – good
③ better – best ④ best – good
⑤ best – best

08 나의 가족에 대한 표의 내용과 일치하지 않는 것은? 3점

	Dad	Mom	I	Sister
age	45	40	15	12
height	178cm	165cm	170cm	155cm

① I am older than my sister.
② My mom is not as tall as my dad.
③ My dad is two times as old as me.
④ My sister is the youngest in my family.
⑤ My mom is not shorter than my sister.

09 밑줄 친 부분의 쓰임이 올바른 것은? 3점

① My brother is not as smarter as me.
② My cell phone is much expensive than yours.
③ My grandmother is the oldest in my family.
④ The more you eat, the more you gain weight.
⑤ Adell is one of the best singer in the world.

10 밑줄 친 부분의 쓰임이 틀린 것은? 4점

① This is the best movie I've ever seen.
② These days, I feel more and more tired.
③ My grade was not as good as I hoped.
④ Baseball is even more popular than soccer in America.
⑤ Mt. Everest is higher than any other mountains in the world.

11 주어진 문장과 의미가 같은 것은? 4점

The North Pole is not as cold as the South Pole.

① The North Pole is as cold as the South Pole.
② The North Pole is colder than the South Pole.
③ The North Pole is less cold than the South Pole.
④ The South Pole is not as cold as the North Pole.
⑤ The South Pole is not colder than the North Pole.

12 다음 중 의미가 나머지와 다른 하나는? 4점

① Russia is the biggest country in the world.
② Russia is as big as other countries in the world.
③ No country is as big as Russia in the world.
④ No country is bigger than Russia in the world.
⑤ Russia is bigger than all the other countries in the world.

통합
13 짝지어진 두 문장의 뜻이 같지 않은 것은? 4점

① Sean is four years younger than James.
= James is four years older than Sean.
② Twelve is three times larger than four.
= Twelve is three times as large as four.
③ I help my mom as often as possible.
= I help my mom as often as I can.
④ The higher we go up, the colder the air becomes.
= As we go up higher, the air becomes colder.
⑤ Warren Buffett is one of the richest people in the world.
= Warren Buffett is richer than all the other people in the world.

14 우리말을 영어로 옮긴 것 중 옳지 않은 것은? 4점

① 이 사과는 장미만큼 빨갛다.
> This apple is as red as a rose.
② 말은 코끼리보다 무겁지 않다.
> Horses are less heavy than elephants.
③ 코알라는 가장 게으른 동물이다.
> Koalas are the laziest animal.
④ 정직보다 중요한 것은 없다.
> There is something more important than honesty.
⑤ 너는 일찍 시작할수록 일찍 끝낼 수 있을 것이다.
> The sooner you begin, the sooner you'll finish it.

15 다음 중 어법상 올바른 문장의 개수는? 4점

ⓐ Call me back as soon as possible.
ⓑ Your dress is the prettier than mine.
ⓒ Watching movies is as exciting as going shopping.
ⓓ These days, more and more people travel abroad.

① 0개 ② 1개 ③ 2개 ④ 3개 ⑤ 4개

고난도

16 **어법상 올바른 문장끼리 짝지어진 것은?** 5점

ⓐ The older you are, the wise you become.
ⓑ You are the kindest person I've ever met.
ⓒ No river in the world is as longer as the Nile.
ⓓ Left-handed people tend to be more creative.

① ⓐ, ⓑ ② ⓐ, ⓒ ③ ⓑ, ⓒ
④ ⓑ, ⓓ ⑤ ⓒ, ⓓ

17 **그림의 내용을 잘못 말한 사람은?** 5점

① 은영: The yellow bag is cheaper than the brown bag.
② 정민: The brown bag is not bigger than the yellow bag.
③ 지윤: The pink bag is twice as expensive as the yellow bag.
④ 태현: The brown bag is less expensive than the yellow bag.
⑤ 상민: The pink bag is the smallest but the most expensive of the three.

18 **빈칸에 알맞은 말을 [보기]에서 골라 필요한 경우 올바른 형태로 바꾸어 문장을 완성하시오.** 각 2점

[보기] little quick hot handsome

(1) I earn ________ money than my sister.
(2) Greg is the ________ ________ guy I've seen in my life.
(3) I walk to school. It's just as ________ as taking the bus.

19 **주어진 문장과 의미가 같도록 빈칸을 채워 문장을 완성하시오.** 2점

Bruno visits his grandparents as often as possible.
= Bruno visits his grandparents as often as ________ ________.

20 **우리말과 일치하도록 괄호 안의 말을 사용하여 문장을 완성하시오.** 3점

나의 고향인 제주는 한국에서 가장 큰 섬이다.
> My hometown is Jeju, which ________ ________ ________ ________ in Korea. (big, island)

21 **다음 표의 내용과 일치하도록 괄호 안의 말을 이용하여 빈칸에 알맞게 쓰시오.** 각 2점

Rank	Name of Building	Height
1	Burj Khalifa	828m
2	Shanghai Tower	632m
3	Kingdom Clock Tower	601m
4	Ping An Finance Center	599m
5	Lotte World Tower	555m

(1) Burj Khalifa is ________ ________ ________ ________ building in the world. (tall)
(2) Lotte World Tower is not ________ ________ ________ Ping An Finance Center. (tall)
(3) Kingdom Clock Tower is ________ ________ Shanghai Tower. (short)

Answers p. 29

22 다음 표를 보고 빈칸에 알맞은 말을 쓰시오. 각 2점

	(dolphin)	(elephant)	(dog)
IQ	80	70	60

(1) Elephants are ________ intelligent than dolphins.

(2) Dolphins are ________ intelligent than dogs.

(3) Dogs are the ________ intelligent animal in the chart.

23 우리말과 일치하도록 괄호 안의 말을 바르게 배열하여 문장을 완성하시오. 4점

뉴욕에서 시애틀까지의 거리는 서울에서 부산까지의 거리보다 더 길다.

> The distance from New York to Seattle is ______________________________.

(is, longer, from, Busan, to, Seoul, it, than)

24 밑줄 친 부분에서 어법상 틀린 곳을 찾아 바르게 고쳐 문장을 다시 쓰시오. 각 4점

(1) The more you exercise, the more healthy you will be.

(2) It is one of the most popular TV program in Korea these days.

(1) ______________________________

____

(2) ______________________________

____

25 세 사람의 50m 달리기 속도를 나타낸 다음 표를 보고 [조건]에 맞게 영어로 쓰시오. 각 4점

[조건] 1. 일반동사의 과거시제로 쓸 것
2. 각각 괄호 안의 말을 활용할 것

Tom	David	Harry
9 sec.	7 sec.	14 sec.

(sec. = seconds)

(1) Tom ________ ________ ________ David. (slow)

(2) David ________ ________ ________ ________ ________ Harry. (fast)

약점 공략
틀린 문제가 있다면?

틀린 문항 번호가 있는 칸을 색칠하고, 어떤 문법 POINT의 집중 복습이 필요한지 파악해 보세요.

문항 번호	연관 문법 POINT	문항 번호	연관 문법 POINT	문항 번호	연관 문법 POINT
01	P1	10	P1, P3, P4	19	P2
02	P1, P3	11	P1	20	P1
03	P1	12	P1, P4	21	P1, P4
04	P3	13	P1~P4	22	P1
05	P1	14	P1, P3, P4	23	P1
06	P1	15	P1~P3	24	P3
07	P1	16	P1, P3, P4	25	P1, P2
08	P1, P2	17	P1, P2, P3		
09	P1, P3	18	P1		

연관 문법 POINT 참고

P1 (p.124) 원급, 비교급, 최상급
P2 (p.124) 원급을 이용한 표현
P3 (p.126) 비교급, 최상급을 이용한 표현
P4 (p.126) 원급과 비교급을 이용한 최상급 의미

내신 만점 Level Up Test

Answers p. 30

01 다음 중 어법상 <u>어색한</u> 문장의 개수는?

ⓐ Today is very hotter than yesterday.
ⓑ What is the biggest planet in the solar system?
ⓒ The TV show is getting more and more interesting.
ⓓ The early you start, the sooner you finish.
ⓔ Let me know the result as soon as possible.

① 1개 ② 2개 ③ 3개 ④ 4개 ⑤ 없음

02 다음 글의 내용과 일치하지 <u>않는</u> 것은?

The average *life span of human beings is 80 years. However, animals have different life spans. American Box Turtles live about 123 years, and *carp live about 100 years. Amazon Parrots live as long as human beings. Queen ants live about three years, but worker ants live only about half a year.

*life span 수명 *carp 잉어

① American Box Turtles live longer than Amazon Parrots.
② Carp don't live twice as long as human beings.
③ Amazon Parrots live about 80 years.
④ Amazon Parrots live about twenty years less than carp.
⑤ Worker ants live half as long as queen ants.

03 빈칸에 알맞은 말을 [보기]에서 <u>모두</u> 골라 기호를 빈칸에 쓰시오.

• Your soup is ________ more delicious than mine.

[보기]	a. many	b. much	c. even
	d. little	e. less	f. very

04 두 문장이 같은 뜻이 되도록 [조건]에 맞게 빈칸에 알맞은 말을 쓰시오.

[조건] 1. can을 사용할 것
2. 필요하면 형태를 바꿀 것

All the students escaped from the building as soon as possible.
= All the students ______________________
______________________________.

05 밑줄 친 ①~⑤ 중 어법상 <u>틀린</u> 것을 찾아 바르게 고치고, <u>틀린</u> 이유를 우리말로 쓰시오.

Yuna Kim is one of the ①<u>greatest</u> figure ②<u>skaters</u> in the world. To win the gold medal, she ③<u>kept practicing</u> and tried her best. Many young skaters want ④<u>to become</u> the next Yuna Kim. I hope we can see skaters as ⑤<u>better</u> as her.

틀린 부분: (   ) > ______________________

틀린 이유: ______________________
____

UNIT 1 POINT 01 가정법 과거
POINT 02 가정법 과거완료

UNIT 2 POINT 03 I wish/as if+가정법 과거
POINT 04 I wish/as if+가정법 과거완료

UNIT 3 POINT 05 혼합가정법
POINT 06 without(but for)+명사(구)

UNIT 4 POINT 07 that절 내의 가정법 현재
POINT 08 if의 생략

CHAPTER

10

가정법

가정법은 사실과 반대되거나 이룰 가능성이 없는 것을 가정하여 심정이나 희망 사항 등을 표현할 때 쓴다.

Preview

if 가정법

과거	만약 ~라면, …할 텐데	If I were you, I would study more.
과거완료	만약 ~했다면, …했을 텐데	If I had been older, I would have been wiser.
혼합가정법	만약 ~했다면, …할 텐데	If I had finished the work, I would be free today.

I wish 가정법

과거	~라면 좋을 텐데	I wish we were together.
과거완료	~였다면 좋았을 텐데	I wish we had been together.

as if 가정법

과거	마치 ~인 것처럼	He talks as if he knew about the event.
과거완료	마치 ~였던 것처럼	He talks as if he had known about the event.

UNIT 1 가정법 과거와 과거완료

POINT 01 가정법 과거

*If you were here, I would ask your opinion.

네가 여기 있다면 나는 네 의견을 물어볼 텐데.

*현재 사실과 반대되는 상황을 가정해.

가정법 과거는 현재 사실과 반대되는 상황이나 실현 가능성이 적은 일을 가정하여 말할 때 쓴다.

If+주어 +동사의 과거형, 주어+조동사의 과거형 +동사원형	만약 ~한다면/라면, …할 텐데	If I were you, I would stop playing games. If he knew her phone number, he could call her.

⊕ 가정법 과거의 조건절에서는 주어에 상관없이 be동사는 were를 쓰는 것이 원칙이지만 구어체에서는 was를 쓰기도 한다.

If it were/was not too hot, we would have lunch in the garden.

ⓘ 가정법 과거는 직설법 현재로 바꿔 쓸 수 있다. 서술형 빈출

If you didn't live far away, we could visit you often.

→ As you live far away, we can't visit you often.

POINT 02 가정법 과거완료

*If he had joined the game, we would have won the game.

그가 경기에 합류했더라면 우리가 경기를 이겼을 텐데.

*과거 사실과 반대되는 상황을 가정해.

가정법 과거완료는 과거 사실과 반대되는 상황이나 과거에 이루지 못한 소망을 가정하여 말할 때 쓴다.

If+주어+had+p.p., 주어+조동사의 과거형 +have+p.p.	만약 ~했다면/였다면, …했을 텐데	If I had brought my umbrella, I wouldn't have got all wet. If we had booked the tickets, we could have gone to the concert.

ⓘ 가정법 과거완료는 직설법 과거로 바꿔 쓸 수 있다. 서술형 빈출

If it hadn't rained heavily, they would have played soccer.

→ As it rained heavily, they didn't play soccer.

개념 QUICK CHECK

POINT 01

주어진 표현의 옳은 해석에 √ 표시하시오.

1 If I weren't sick, I could go camping.
- □ 아파서 캠핑을 갈 수 없다
- □ 아프지 않아서 캠핑을 갈 수 있다

2 If I had a car, I would give you a ride.
- □ 내가 차가 있어서 너를 데려다 주겠다
- □ 내가 차가 없어서 너를 데려다 줄 수 없다

3 If I were hungry, I would eat the pizza.
- □ 배가 고파서 피자를 먹는다
- □ 배가 고프지 않아서 피자를 안 먹는다

POINT 02

우리말과 일치하도록 괄호 안에서 알맞은 것을 고르시오.

1 내가 더 조심했더라면 실수하지 않았을 텐데.
If I (were / had been) more careful, I wouldn't (make / have made) the mistake.

2 우리가 일찍 출발하지 않았더라면 버스를 놓쳤을 텐데.
If we (didn't leave / hadn't left) early, we would (have missed / had missed) the bus.

3 내가 수영하는 법을 알았더라면 수영장에 갔을 텐데.
If I (knew / had known) how to swim, I could (go / have gone) to swimming pool.

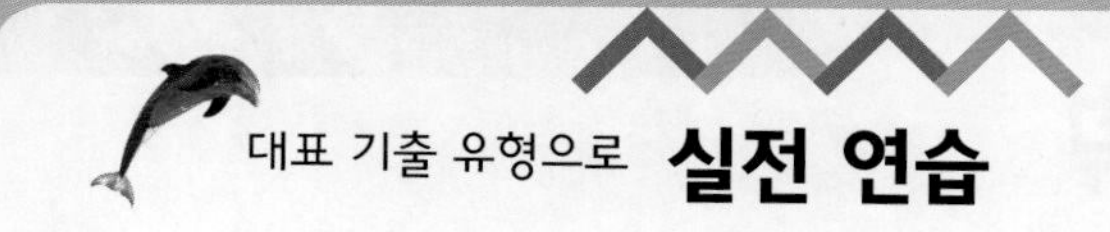

대표 기출 유형으로 **실전 연습**

1 **주어진 문장을 가정하는 문장으로 바꿔 쓸 때 빈칸에 알맞은 말을 쓰시오.**

Because we don't have enough money, we can't help them more.

> If we ________ enough money, we could help them more.

2 **대화의 빈칸에 들어갈 말이 순서대로 바르게 짝지어진 것은?**

A: I lied to my mom.
B: If I ________ you, I ________ tell her the truth and ask her for forgiveness.

① am – can ② am – will ③ am – could
④ were – would ⑤ were – would have

자주 나와요!
3 **대화의 빈칸에 들어갈 말로 알맞은 것은?**

A: Congratulations! I heard your team won the game.
B: Thank you. We couldn't have won if all the players ________ hard.

① have worked ② had worked ③ haven't worked
④ hadn't worked ⑤ will have worked

4 **우리말과 일치하도록 괄호 안의 말을 배열하여 문장을 쓸 때 앞에서 네 번째 오는 말로 알맞은 것은?**

내가 거기 있었더라면 너를 도와주었을 텐데.
(there, I, have, helped, I, if, been, would, had) you.

① would ② been ③ there
④ had ⑤ helped

틀리기 쉬워요!
5 **다음 중 어법상 틀린 문장은?**

① I would be tired if I went home late.
② If I were a college student, I would go backpacking.
③ If I had studied hard, I would have passed the exam.
④ You could have arrived on time if you had taken the subway.
⑤ If you haven't listened to his advice, you couldn't have succeeded.

개념 완성 Quiz *Choose or complete.*

1 가정법 과거는 직설법 [과거 / 현재 / 과거완료]로 바꿔 쓸 수 있다.
> POINT 01

2 가정법 과거는 「If+주어+동사의 [현재형 / 과거형 / 과거완료형], 주어+조동사의 [현재형 / 과거형]+동사원형」으로 표현한다.
> POINT 01

3 가정법 과거완료는 [과거 / 현재] 사실과 반대되는 상황을 가정하여 말할 때 쓰인다.
> POINT 02

4 가정법 과거완료는 「if+주어+had+p.p., 주어+조동사의 [과거형 / 현재형]+have+p.p.」로 표현한다.
> POINT 02

5 가정법 과거는 [과거 / 현재] 사실과 반대되는 상황을 가정하여 말할 때 쓰인다.
> POINT 01, 02

UNIT 2 I wish 가정법, as if 가정법

POINT 03 I wish/as if+가정법 과거

I wish I were a genius. 내가 천재라면 좋을 텐데.

*현재의 이루기 힘든 소망을 나타내.

I wish+가정법 과거 (주어+동사의 과거형)	~하면 좋을 텐데 (현재 사실에 대한 유감이나 이루기 힘든 현재의 소망)	**I wish** we **were** together. (→ I'm sorry we **aren't** together.) **I wish** I **could go** to the BTS concert. (→ I'm sorry I **can't go** to the BTS concert.)
	⊕ 동사의 과거형 대신 「조동사의 과거형+동사원형」으로 쓸 수 있다. ⊕ 미래에 있을 일에 대한 소망을 나타낼 때는 will 대신 would를 쓴다. **I wish** my brother **would enter** college this time.	
as if+가정법 과거 (주어+동사의 과거형)	마치 ~한 것처럼 (주절과 같은 시제의 반대를 가정)	Ann looks **as if** she **were** ill. (→ In fact, Ann **isn't** ill.) Scott behaved **as if** he **had** a good relationship with Jason. (→ In fact, Scott **didn't have** a good relationship with Jason.)

POINT 04 I wish/as if+가정법 과거완료

He speaks English as if he had lived in England.

그는 마치 영국에 살았던 것처럼 영어를 한다.

*과거 사실과 반대를 가정하는 표현이야.

I wish +가정법 과거완료 (주어+had+p.p.)	~했더라면 좋았을 텐데(과거 사실에 대한 유감이나 아쉬움)	**I wish** I **had got** good grades. (→ I'm sorry I **didn't get** good grades.) **I wish** I **hadn't lost** my student ID. (→ I'm sorry I **lost** my student ID.)
as if +가정법 과거완료 (주어+had+p.p.)	⊕ as if 가정법 과거는 주절의 동사와 같은 시제를 나타내고, as if 가정법 과거완료는 주절의 동사보다 한 시제 앞선 시제를 나타낸다.	
	마치 ~했던 것처럼(주절보다 한 시제 앞선 시점의 반대를 가정)	She looks **as if** she **had seen** a ghost. (→ In fact, she **didn't see** a ghost.) He talked **as if** he **had won** the tennis game. (→ In fact, he **hadn't won** the tennis game.)

개념 QUICK CHECK

POINT 03

주어진 표현의 옳은 해석에 √ 표시하시오.

1 I wish I watched TV in the evening.
- □ 저녁에 TV를 본다
- □ 저녁에 TV를 보지 못한다

2 She walks as if she were a model.
- □ 그녀는 모델이다
- □ 그녀는 모델이 아니다

3 I wish I were tall.
- □ 나는 키가 크다
- □ 나는 키가 크지 않다

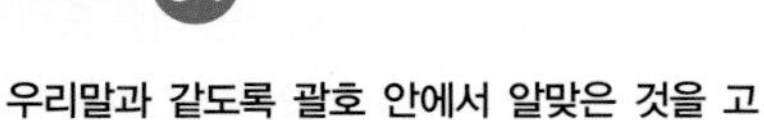

POINT 04

우리말과 같도록 괄호 안에서 알맞은 것을 고르시오.

1 그가 제시간에 도착했더라면 좋았을 텐데.
I wish he (arrived / had arrived) on time.

2 그녀는 그 책을 읽었던 것처럼 말한다.
She talks as if she (reads / had read) the book.

3 내가 그 영화를 봤더라면 좋았을 텐데.
I wish I (see / had seen) the movie.

Answers p. 31

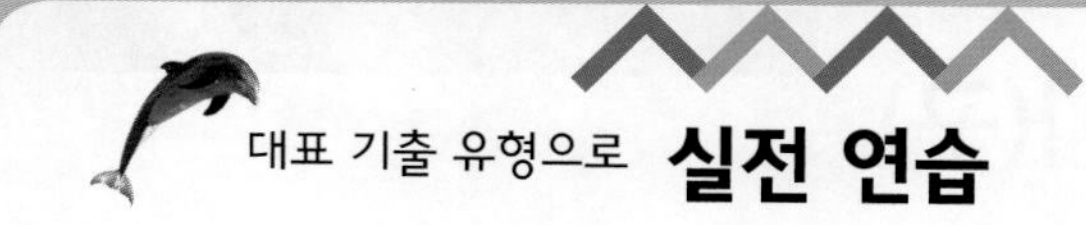

대표 기출 유형으로 실전 연습

1 우리말과 일치하도록 괄호 안의 말을 이용하여 문장을 완성하시오.

누군가 그 불쌍한 아이를 도와줬더라면 좋았을 텐데.

> I wish someone __________ the poor child. (help)

틀리기 쉬워요!

2 주어진 문장을 가정법으로 바꿔 쓸 때 빈칸에 들어갈 말로 알맞은 것은?

> I'm sorry that my grandmother is sick.
> > I wish my grandmother ________ sick.

① isn't ② was ③ were
④ weren't ⑤ won't be

자주 나와요!

3 빈칸에 들어갈 말로 알맞은 것은?

> Wayne didn't climb Mt. Halla, but he speaks as if he ________ it.

① climbs ② is climbing ③ climbed
④ has climbed ⑤ had climbed

4 우리말과 일치하도록 괄호 안의 말을 알맞은 형태로 써서 문장을 완성하시오.

나도 민영이처럼 영어를 잘 말할 수 있으면 좋을 텐데. 그녀는 외국에 살았던 것처럼 영어를 말한다.

> I wish I ⓐ __________ (speak) English well like Minyoung.
She speaks English as if she ⓑ __________ (live) abroad.

5 대화의 빈칸에 들어갈 말이 순서대로 바르게 짝지어진 것은?

> **A:** I traveled alone in Spain. I wish I ________ with Angela.
> **B:** Didn't you travel with Angela? She talks as if she ________ with you.

① traveled – has traveled ② traveled – had traveled
③ had traveled – has traveled ④ had traveled – had traveled
⑤ had traveled – would have traveled

개념 완성 Quiz *Choose or complete.*

1 과거 사실에 대한 유감이나 아쉬움은 「I wish+ 가정법 현재 / 가정법 과거 / 가정법 과거완료 」로 나타낸다.
> POINT 04

2 가정법 과거는 「주어+ 동사의 현재형 / 동사의 과거형 / 동사의 과거완료형 」으로 나타낸다.
> POINT 03

3 과거 사실의 반대를 가정할 때 「as if+ 가정법 현재 / 가정법 과거 / 가정법 과거완료 」 형태를 사용한다.
> POINT 04

4 현재 사실에 대한 유감이나 아쉬움을 나타낼 때 「I wish+ 가정법 현재 / 가정법 과거 / 가정법 과거완료 」 형태를 사용한다.
> POINT 03, 04

5 가정법 과거완료는 「주어+ have+p.p. / had+p.p. 」로 나타낸다.
> POINT 04

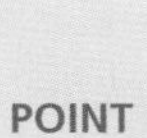

UNIT 3 혼합가정법, without+명사(구)

POINT 05 혼합가정법

If I **had finished** the work yesterday, I **would be** free now. 내가 어제 일을 끝마쳤다면 지금 한가할 텐데.

혼합가정법은 과거의 일의 결과가 현재까지 영향을 미칠 때 쓰이며, 주로 조건절에는 가정법 과거완료를, 주절에는 가정법 과거를 쓴다.

If+주어 +had+p.p., 주어+조동사의 과거형+동사원형	(과거에) ~했더라면, (현재) …할 텐데	If I **had read** the book last week, I **could lend** it to you today. (→ As I **didn't read** the book last week, I **can't lend** it to you today.)

ⓘ 과거에 일어난 일의 결과가 과거에 종료된 상황이면 가정법 과거완료를, 현재까지 영향을 미칠 때는 혼합가정법으로 쓰는 것에 주의한다. 혼합가정법의 주절에는 현재를 나타내는 부사인 now나 today 등이 자주 쓰인다. 서술형 빈출
If he **had studied** hard, he **would have passed** the exam.
If he **had studied** harder at school, he **might have** a better job now.

POINT 06 without(but for)+명사(구)

Without planes, we **would not be** able to travel far away. 비행기가 없다면 우리는 멀리 여행할 수 없을 텐데.

without (but for) +명사(구), 가정법 과거 (주어+조동사의 과거형+동사원형)	(현재) ~이 없다면	**Without(But for)** water, there **would be** no living things.
	⊕ without(but for)은 뒤에 가정법 과거가 오면 if it were not for로 바꿔 쓸 수 있다. **Without(But for)** their support, I **couldn't continue** my studies. → **If it were not for** their support, I **couldn't continue** my studies.	
without (but for) +명사(구), 가정법 과거완료 (주어+조동사의 과거형+ have+p.p.)	(과거에) ~이 없었다면	**Without(But for)** the traffic jam, we **would have arrived** long ago.
	⊕ without(but for)은 뒤에 가정법 과거완료가 오면 if it had not been for로 바꿔 쓸 수 있다. **Without(But for)** the online map, we **would have gotten** lost. → **If it had not been for** the online map, we **would have** gotten lost.	

개념 QUICK CHECK

POINT 05

우리말과 일치하도록 괄호 안에서 알맞은 것을 고르시오.

1 어젯밤에 일찍 잤더라면 지금 피곤하지 않을 텐데.
If I had gone to bed early, I (wouldn't feel / wouldn't have felt) tired now.

2 내가 시간이 있었다면 너를 도왔을 텐데.
If I had had time, I (would help / would have helped) you.

3 내가 어젯밤에 공부를 더 했더라면, 시험을 통과할 수 있을 텐데.
If I had studied more last night, I (could have passed / could pass) the exam.

POINT 06

밑줄 친 부분 대신 쓸 수 있는 것에  **표시하시오.**

1 Without your help, I couldn't finish this work.
□ If it were not for
□ If it had not been for

2 But for the comic books, I would have felt bored on the plane.
□ If it were not for
□ If it had not been for

Answers p. 31

대표 기출 유형으로 실전 연습

자주 나와요!

1 대화의 빈칸에 들어갈 말로 알맞은 것은?

> A: Why are you so tired today?
> B: I slept late yesterday. If I ________ late yesterday, I wouldn't be tired today.

① slept ② didn't sleep ③ have slept
④ hadn't slept ⑤ won't sleep

2 빈칸에 들어갈 말로 알맞은 것은?

> ________ the receipt, I couldn't exchange the clothes.

① If I had ② As it was ③ With
④ But for ⑤ If it were

3 우리말과 일치하도록 할 때 빈칸에 들어갈 말로 알맞은 것은?

> 내가 그림을 잘 그렸다면, 지금 화가가 되어 있을 텐데.
> > If I ________ good at drawing, I would be an artist now.

① am ② had been ③ have been
④ were ⑤ would have been

4 밑줄 친 부분과 바꿔 쓸 수 있는 것은?

> Without his advice, I would have done it again.

① If it is ② If it wasn't ③ If it won't be
④ If it were not for ⑤ If it had not been for

틀리기 쉬워요!

5 밑줄 친 부분의 쓰임이 어법상 틀린 것은?

① Without my sister, I would be lonely here in Texas.
② But for the compass, he would have lost his way in the desert.
③ If I have worked hard last week, I would be free this week.
④ If he had prepared enough, he wouldn't have made such a mistake.
⑤ If you hadn't transferred to another school, I could see you every day.

개념 완성 Quiz *Choose or complete.*

1 혼합가정법은 과거의 일의 결과가 [현재 / 과거 / 미래]까지 영향을 미칠 때 쓰인다.
> POINT 05

2 '(현재) ~이 없다면'의 의미의 표현은 without이나 ________가 쓰인다.
> POINT 06

3 혼합가정법의 조건절에는 [가정법 과거 / 가정법 현재 / 가정법 과거완료]를 쓰고, 주절에는 가정법 과거를 쓴다.
> POINT 05

4 without(but for) ~ 뒤에 가정법 과거완료가 오면 ['(현재) ~이 없다면, … 할 텐데' / '(과거에) ~이 없었다면, … 했을 텐데']의 의미이다.
> POINT 06

5 without(but for) ~ 뒤에 가정법 과거가 오면 ['(현재) ~이 없다면, …할 텐데' / '(과거에) ~이 없었다면, …했을 텐데']의 의미이다.
> POINT 05, 06

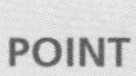 

UNIT 4 주의해야 할 가정법

POINT 07 that절 내의 가정법 현재

I* suggest that you take an umbrella with you.

나는 네가 우산을 가져가야 한다고 제안한다.

*suggest 뒤의 that 절에서 가정법 현재가 쓰이고 있어.

주어+동사+that +주어(+should) +동사원형	-가 ~해야 한다고 주장/제안/요구/명령/권고하다	My parents **require** that I **(should) be** back home early. She **recommended** that Tony **(should) keep** quiet during the lesson.
	⊕ 주장, 제안, 요구, 명령, 권고 등을 나타내는 동사(suggest, insist, demand, order, request, recommend 등) 뒤에 이어지는 that절의 동사는 (should+)동사원형으로 쓴다.	
It is+형용사+that +주어(+should) +동사원형	-가 ~해야 하는 것은 중요하다/필요하다/당연하다	It is **important** that she **(should) finish** the work by tomorrow. It is **essential** that you **(should) have** confidence when making a presentation.
	⊕ 이성적 판단, 필요, 당위 등을 나타내는 형용사(important, essential, natural, strange, necessary 등) 뒤에 이어지는 that절의 동사는 (should+)동사원형으로 쓴다.	

POINT 08 if의 생략

***Were the theme park free, we would go every day.**

놀이공원이 공짜면 우리는 매일 갈 텐데.

*if가 생략된 가정법 과거 구문이야.

가정법에서 if절의 동사가 were, had, should인 경우 if를 생략하고 주어와 동사를 도치하여 쓸 수 있다.

Were+주어 ~, 주어+조동사의 과거형 +동사원형	**Were I** you, I **would accept** the offer. (← If I were you, ~) **Were he** rich, he **could buy** the big house. (← If he were rich, ~)
Had+주어+p.p. ~, 주어+조동사의 과거형 +have+p.p.	**Had she** studied harder, she **would have gotten** better grades. (← If she had studied harder, ~) **Had he** thought carefully, he **wouldn't have made** such a decision. (← If he had thought carefully, ~)

개념 QUICK CHECK

POINT 07

괄호 안에서 알맞은 것을 고르시오.

1 The doctor suggested that he (get / got) more exercise.

2 It is important that she (sleep / slept) more.

3 I recommended that you (eat / ate) until you feel better.

4 It is necessary that we (will pack / pack / packed) enough water for hiking.

POINT 08

밑줄 친 우리말을 영어로 바르게 표현한 것을 고르시오.

1 그녀가 만약 우리 선생님이라면, we would be very happy.
- □ Was our teacher she
- □ Were she our teacher

2 내가 만약 너의 충고를 따랐더라면, I would have been happier.
- □ Had taken I your advice
- □ Had I taken your advice

3 내가 만약 키가 크다면, I would wear that dress.
- □ Were I tall
- □ Were tall I

Answers p. 32

대표 기출 유형으로 실전 연습

1 빈칸에 들어갈 말로 알맞은 것은?

> Yesterday I bought a shirt, but there was a button missing. I demanded that the clerk ________ me a refund.

① give ② gave ③ is giving
④ has given ⑤ would give

2 빈칸에 들어갈 말로 알맞지 않은 것은?

> It is ________ that the student follow the school rules.

① natural ② essential ③ important
④ necessary ⑤ possible

자주 나와요!
3 밑줄 친 부분에서 If를 생략하여 다시 쓰시오.

(1) If those jeans were cheaper, I could buy them.
> ________________________, I could buy them.

(2) If he had known the answer, he would get perfect score.
> ________________________, he would get perfect score.

4 우리말과 일치하도록 괄호 안의 말을 이용하여 문장을 완성하시오.

만약 네가 좀 더 주의했더라면, 그 사고는 일어나지 않았을 텐데.
> ________ ________ ________ ________ ________, the accident wouldn't have happened. (be, more careful)

틀리기 쉬워요!
5 빈칸에 들어갈 말이 나머지와 다른 것은?

① They requested that I ________ polite to people.
② ________ I rich, I would travel around the world.
③ Should she ________ here with me, I would be very happy.
④ It is important that every game ________ held on schedule.
⑤ It's raining. He insists that the festival ________ postponed.

개념 완성 Quiz *Choose or complete.*

1 주장, 제안, 요구, 명령, 권고 등을 나타내는 동사 뒤에 이어지는 that절의 동사는 [동사원형 / to부정사](으)로 쓴다.
> POINT 07

2 이성적 판단, 필요, 당위 등을 나타내는 형용사 뒤에 이어지는 that절의 동사는 [동사원형 / to부정사](으)로 쓴다.
> POINT 07

3 if절의 동사가 were, had, should인 경우 if를 생략하고 주어와 동사를 ________하여 쓸 수 있다.
> POINT 08

4 가정법 과거완료는 「if+주어+had+p.p., 주어+조동사의 [과거형 / 현재형]+have+p.p.」로 표현한다.
> POINT 08

5 가정법 과거의 조건절은 「주어+[동사의 현재형 / 동사의 과거형 / 동사의 과거완료형]」으로 나타낸다.
> POINT 07, 08

서술형 실전 연습

Step 1

개념 완성 Quiz *Choose or complete.*

1 **두 문장의 의미가 같도록 빈칸에 알맞은 말을 쓰시오.**

As it was rainy yesterday, the students didn't go on a picnic.

> If it ________ ________ ________ rainy yesterday, the students ________ ________ ________ on a picnic.

2 **다음 문장에서 if를 생략하여 다시 쓰시오.**

If I were an architect, I would build my own house.

> ________________________________

3 **밑줄 친 부분에 유의하여 두 문장의 뜻을 우리말로 쓰고, 의미 차이를 설명하시오.**

(1) If I <u>have</u> enough apples, I <u>will bake</u> an apple pie for you.

> ________________________________

(2) If I <u>had</u> enough apples, I <u>would bake</u> an apple pie for you.

> ________________________________

4 **우리말과 일치하도록 괄호 안의 말을 사용하여 문장을 완성하시오.**

(1) 내가 아침 식사를 했더라면, 지금 배가 고프지 않을 텐데.

> If I ________________ breakfast, I ________________ now. (eat, hungry)

(2) 그가 계단에서 미끄러지지 않았더라면, 그는 다리가 부러지지 않았을 텐데.

> If he ________________ on the stairs, he ________________ his leg. (slip, break)

5 **주어진 문장을 소망을 나타내는 문장으로 바꿔 쓸 때 빈칸에 알맞은 말을 쓰시오.**

(1) I am sorry she doesn't understand me.

> I wish she ________________________ me.

(2) I am sorry you weren't with me then.

> I wish you ________________________ then.

---

1 가정법 과거완료: 과거 / 현재 의 사실에 반대되는 내용을 가정

> POINT 02

2 가정법 문장에서 if를 생략하면 주어와 동사를 ________ 시킨다.

> POINT 08

3 조건절 / 가정법 과거 : 특정 상황에서 일어날 일을 설명한 문장으로 실제 일어날지 여부를 알 수 없음

조건절 / 가정법 과거 : 일어나지 않을 일을 가정하므로 현재 상황에 반대되는 일

> POINT 01

4 혼합가정법: If+주어+had+p.p., 주어+조동사의 현재형 / 과거형 +동사원형

> POINT 02, 05

5 과거 사실에 대한 유감이나 아쉬움을 나타내는 표현: I wish+ 가정법 현재 / 가정법 과거 / 가정법 과거완료

> POINT 03, 04

Answers p. 32

6 대화의 빈칸에 괄호 안의 말을 알맞은 형태로 써서 문장을 완성하시오.

> **A:** How come Susie didn't come to our club meeting last week?
> **B:** Because she was in the hospital then.
> **A:** I'm very sorry to hear that. If I had known that, I ________ ________ her. (visit)

7 그림을 보고, [조건]에 맞게 문장을 완성하시오.

(1) 

(2) 

> [조건] 1. as if 가정법으로 쓸 것
> 2. 괄호 안의 표현을 활용할 것

(1) My dog, Spot, is sleeping on my bed ____________________ human. (be)

(2) Bob pretended ____________________ on the wall. (scribble)

고난도

8 다음 글의 밑줄 친 부분을 주어진 말로 시작하는 문장으로 바꿔 쓰시오.

> **A Very Bad Day**
>
> It was the first day on my new job, but I overslept! (1) <u>I forgot to set my alarm clock the night before.</u> I quickly got dressed and ran out of the house, but I was never going to make it in time. I took the subway. When I got out of the subway station, it was raining heavily. (2) <u>I didn't bring my umbrella, and got all wet.</u> What a terrible day!

(1) I wish ____________________ the night before.

(2) I wish ____________________ my umbrella.

개념 완성 Quiz *Choose or complete.*

6 [가정법 과거 / 가정법 과거완료]: 과거 사실과 반대되는 상황을 가정

> POINT 02

7 과거 사실의 반대를 가정할 때: as if+[가정법 현재 / 가정법 과거 / 가정법 과거완료]

> POINT 03, 04

8 과거에 일어난 일에 대해 반대 내용을 소망하는 경우: I wish+[가정법 현재 / 가정법 과거 / 가정법 과거완료] 형태 사용

> POINT 03, 04

실전 모의고사

시험일 : 월 일	문항 수 : 객관식 18 / 서술형 7
목표 시간 :	총점
걸린 시간 :	/ 100

[01-03] 빈칸에 들어갈 말로 알맞은 것을 고르시오. 각 2점

01

If he were healthier, he ________ the army.

① will join ② joined
③ has joined ④ would join
⑤ would have joined

02

If Susan ________ her finger, she would be a world famous pianist now.

① doesn't injure ② would not injure
③ did not injure ④ has not injured
⑤ had not injured

03

It is necessary that every student ________ a school uniform.

① wear ② wears ③ wore
④ will wear ⑤ would wear

04 빈칸에 들어갈 말이 순서대로 바르게 짝지어진 것은? 3점

A: If I ________ coffee, I would be asleep now.
B: Me, too. Without coffee, I ________ be awake.

① had – could
② had had – would
③ had had – couldn't
④ hadn't had – would
⑤ hadn't had – wouldn't

05 밑줄 친 ⓐ~ⓔ 중 어법상 틀린 것은? 3점

James ⓐ speaks German as if he ⓑ were German. If you heard ⓒ him ⓓ speak German, you ⓔ take him for a German.

① ⓐ ② ⓑ ③ ⓒ ④ ⓓ ⑤ ⓔ

06 밑줄 친 were가 알맞지 않은 것은? 3점

① Tom looks as if he were sick today.
② He insisted that the issue were discussed.
③ If today were Friday, I would go to Busan to see the sea.
④ If my math teacher were here, he would help me solve this problem.
⑤ If my parents were in New York now, they could see the Statue of Liberty.

07 밑줄 친 부분의 쓰임이 어법상 올바른 것은? 4점

① I wish I have my own room.
② If I had wings, I will fly home.
③ She speaks as if she is an actress.
④ Jane would bought a more expensive bag if she had had more money.
⑤ Without his grandmother, he would not have been able to become a soccer player.

통합
08 밑줄 친 부분의 쓰임이 어법상 틀린 것은? 4점

① He acts as if he didn't know me.
② She talked as if she knew everything.
③ Were I a millionaire, I would buy a luxurious car.
④ If I took a bus, it would have been much cheaper.
⑤ If I were more talented, I would become a professional soccer player.

09 빈칸에 들어갈 말로 알맞지 않은 것은? 3점

> ________ your help, I couldn't have won the prize.

① But for ② Without
③ Because ④ Had it not been for
⑤ If it had not been for

10 밑줄 친 ①~⑤ 중 어법상 틀린 것은? 4점

> It is important that teenagers ①learn history correctly. Had I ②studied history hard, I ③could ④have explained it to my children. Instead, I recommended that they ⑤watched historical documentaries.

11 괄호 안의 단어 중 알맞은 것끼리 짝지어진 것은? 4점

> • If I (am / were) you, I wouldn't take a risk.
> • If he were here, what (will / would) he say?
> • If she (had not helped / did not help) me, I could not have finished it.

① am – will – did not help
② am – would – had not helped
③ were – will – did not help
④ were – would – did not help
⑤ were – would – had not helped

12 대화의 빈칸에 들어갈 말로 알맞은 것은? 4점

> A: Without your help, I couldn't have gotten on the bus. Thank you so much.
> B: You're welcome.
> A: If I ________ my wallet, I would buy you lunch now.
> B: That's OK.

① don't lose ② didn't lose ③ haven't lost
④ hadn't lost ⑤ won't have lost

13 다음 문장이 의미하는 바로 알맞은 것은? 3점

> If you had done it, you would regret it.

① As you do it, you regret it.
② As you did it, I don't regret it.
③ As you didn't do it, you regret it.
④ As you didn't do it, you don't regret it.
⑤ As you don't do it, you wouldn't regret it.

14 우리말을 영어로 옮긴 것 중 옳지 않은 것은? 4점

① 내가 너만큼 키가 크다면 정말 좋을 텐데.
> I really wish I were as tall as you.
② 내가 네 주소를 알았더라면, 엽서를 보냈을 텐데.
> If I had known your address, I would have sent you a postcard.
③ 그는 마치 선생님인 것처럼 나에게 영어를 가르쳐 주었다.
> He taught me English as if he were a teacher.
④ 내가 숙제를 마쳤더라면, 지금 외식하러 나갈 수 있을 텐데.
> If I had finished my homework, I could eat out now.
⑤ 알람 시계가 없다면, 아침에 일어날 수 없을 텐데.
> Without alarm clocks, we will not be able to get up in the morning.

15 우리말을 영어로 바르게 옮긴 것은? 3점

> 만약 내가 돈이 많다면, 아프리카에 있는 가난한 아이들을 도울 텐데.

① If I have lots of money, I won't help poor children in Africa.
② If I have lots of money, I would help poor children in Africa.
③ If I had lots of money, I would help poor children in Africa.
④ If I had lots of money, I will help poor children in Africa.
⑤ If I had had lots of money, I would help poor children in Africa.

16 다음 중 어법상 올바른 문장의 개수는? 5점

ⓐ I wish I were more diligent.
ⓑ If I spoke French, I could work in France.
ⓒ If I had let her practice singing, she would become a singer now.
ⓓ It were not for the rain, I would go out to exercise.

① 0개 ② 1개 ③ 2개 ④ 3개 ⑤ 4개

17 다음 문장에서 알 수 있는 것은? 4점

Without my smartphone, I wouldn't waste so much time.

① I waste so much time.
② I don't waste time at all.
③ I don't have a smartphone.
④ I want to change my smartphone.
⑤ I won't use my smartphone any more.

18 직설법으로 문장 전환이 올바르지 <u>않은</u> 것은? 5점

① If my grandma heard well, she would not need a hearing aid.
> As my grandma doesn't hear well, she needs a hearing aid.

② If I had been more careful, I wouldn't have broken the vase.
> As I wasn't more careful, I broke the vase.

③ I wish I were invited to the party.
> I'm sorry I am not invited to the party.

④ I wish I had passed the driving test.
> I'm sorry I didn't pass the driving test.

⑤ If I had known how to drive, I would have driven you home.
> As I didn't know how to drive, I don't drive you home yesterday.

19 다음 직설법 문장을 가정법으로 바꿀 때 빈칸에 알맞은 말을 쓰시오. 각 2점

(1) As I didn't take the doctor's advice, I am ill now.
> If I ________ ________ the doctor's advice, I ________ ________ ________ ________ now.

(2) As I read the book, I was disappointed in the movie version.
> If I ________ ________ the book, I ________ ________ ________ ________ in the movie version.

20 다음 문장이 가정하는 문장이 되도록 빈칸에 알맞은 말을 넣어 문장을 완성하시오. 각 3점

(1) I'm sorry I can't speak foreign languages fluently.
> I wish I ________________________________
________________________________.

(2) In fact, she didn't see the horror movie.
> She talks as if ________________________________
________________________________.

21 우리말과 일치하도록 괄호 안의 말을 이용하여 문장을 완성하시오. 각 3점

(1) Gary는 자신의 개를 마치 사람처럼 대한다. (as if)
> Gary treats his dog ________ ________ ________ ________ a human being.

(2) 공기가 없다면 모든 생물은 존재할 수 없을 텐데. (living things, exist)
> ________ ________ air, no ________ ________ ________ ________.

22 다음 문장의 밑줄 친 부분을 문맥에 맞게 고쳐 쓰시오. 각 3점

(1) If I study all three subjects at once, I would have been confused about all of the contents.

> ____________________

(2) Bryan wouldn't have been late, have he left home earlier in the morning.

> ____________________

23 우리말과 일치하도록 괄호 안의 말을 바르게 배열하여 문장을 완성하시오. 4점

만약 내가 살 수 있는 날이 오직 하루 있다면, 나는 모든 돈을 기부할 거야.
(all my money, I, would, to live, only one day, if, I, donate, had)

> ____________________

24 괄호 안의 말을 문맥에 맞게 고쳐 빈칸에 쓰시오. 각 3점

- If the company (A) ________ (advertise) well, it would sell far more products than now.
- Now I am a good musician, but I didn't know how to play any musical instruments when I was young. I wish I (B) ________ (play) the violin back then.

(A) ____________ (B) ____________

25 그림에 맞는 문장을 [보기]에서 골라 문맥에 맞게 올바른 형태로 바꿔 글을 완성하시오. 각 3점

[보기] I am alone I order beef

(1)

My home is too noisy. Everybody is enjoying the party. But I wish ____________.

(2)

I ordered chicken at the restaurant, but it didn't taste good. I wish ____________.

약점 공략
틀린 문제가 있다면?

틀린 문항 번호가 있는 칸을 색칠하고, 어떤 문법 POINT의 집중 복습이 필요한지 파악해 보세요.

문항 번호	연관 문법 POINT	문항 번호	연관 문법 POINT	문항 번호	연관 문법 POINT
01	P1	10	P2, P7, P8	19	P2, P5
02	P5	11	P1, P2	20	P3, P4
03	P7	12	P5	21	P3, P6
04	P1, P5, P6	13	P5	22	P2, P8
05	P1, P3	14	P1~P6	23	P1
06	P1, P3, P7	15	P1	24	P1, P4
07	P1~P3, P6	16	P1, P3, P5, P8	25	P3, P4
08	P1~P8	17	P6		
09	P6, P8	18	P1~P5		

연관 문법 POINT 참고

P1 (p.136) 가정법 과거
P2 (p.136) 가정법 과거완료
P3 (p.138) I wish/as if+가정법 과거
P4 (p.138) I wish/as if+가정법 과거완료
P5 (p.140) 혼합가정법
P6 (p.140) without(but for)+명사(구)
P7 (p.142) that절 내의 가정법 현재
P8 (p.142) if의 생략

내신만점 Level Up Test

Answers p. 34

01 빈칸에 들어갈 수 있는 말로 짝지어진 것은?

> ________ his father's help, he couldn't have become a champion.

> [보기] a. But for
> b. Without
> c. With
> d. If it were not for
> e. If it had not been for

① a, b, c ② a, b, e ③ b, c, d
④ b, d, e ⑤ c, d, e

02 다음 글을 읽고 Max에게 해 줄 수 있는 조언으로 가장 적절한 것은?

> Last Sunday, Max went to Gina's home. He saw an action figure on the table that he really wanted to have. He looked around quietly and hid it in his bag. Now Max regrets what he did and wants to apologize to Gina.

① If I am you, I will tell the truth and apologize to her.
② If I were you, I will tell the truth and apologize to her.
③ If I am you, I would tell the truth and apologize to her.
④ If I were you, I would tell the truth and apologize to her.
⑤ If I were you, I would have told the truth and apologized to her.

03 다음 중 어법상 틀린 문장의 개수는?

> ⓐ If I were a good guitarist, I could join the school band.
> ⓑ She requested that I locked the door.
> ⓒ He talks as if he had won the final game.
> ⓓ I wish I had finished my homework earlier.
> ⓔ If she had worked harder, she would have succeeded now.

① 1개 ② 2개 ③ 3개 ④ 4개 ⑤ 없음

04 다음 대화의 밑줄 친 ⓐ~ⓔ 중 어법상 틀린 부분을 찾아 기호를 쓰고, 바르게 고쳐 쓰시오.

> **A:** Frank, why are you still ⓐ watching TV? Your math final is tomorrow.
> **B:** It's my favorite show and ⓑ it'll end in just 20 minutes.
> **A:** ⓒ If I were you, I ⓓ won't waste a single minute watching TV.
> **B:** You're right, Mom. But I ⓔ have to see this program.

(   ) > ____________________

05 그림을 보고 [조건]에 맞게 Tony가 할 말을 완성하시오.

> [조건] 1. 가정법 과거완료로 쓸 것
> 2. more careful, break를 사용할 것

Tony: If I ____________________,
I ____________________ the vase.

UNIT 1 POINT 01 수의 일치
POINT 02 시제의 일치

UNIT 2 POINT 03 평서문의 간접화법
POINT 04 의문문과 명령문의 간접화법

UNIT 3 POINT 05 강조
POINT 06 도치

CHAPTER

11

일치, 화법, 강조, 도치

문장에서 서로 밀접한 관계에 있는 어(구)끼리 수·인칭·시제 등에 따라 어떤 일정한 형태를 취하는 것을 **일치**라고 한다. 또한, 말을 전달하는 방법을 **화법**이라고 한다. 어떤 어구를 강조하기 위해서 '주어+동사'의 어순이 '동사+주어'로 바뀌는 것을 **도치**라고 한다.

Preview

일치	수의 일치	단수	The boy **studies** English every day.
		복수	The boys **study** English every day.
	시제의 일치	주절이 현재일 때	I know that you **are** busy.
		주절이 과거일 때	I knew that you **were** busy.
화법	직접화법		He said to me, **"I am** busy."
	간접화법		He told me **(that) he was** busy.
강조	동사 강조		The boy **does** study English every day.
	명사 강조		This is **the very** book that I have been looking for.
	It ~ that ... 강조		**It was** Chris **that** sent you the gift last month.
도치	부사(구) 도치		On the top of the hill **stood an old house**.
	부정어 도치		Never **does my mom** get up late in the morning.
	so/neither+동사+주어		He is very busy, and so **am I**.

UNIT 1 일치

POINT 01 수의 일치

Every student is wearing a school uniform.*

모든 학생이 교복을 입고 있다.

*주어의 인칭과 수에 동사를 일치시키는 것을 수의 일치라고 해.

단수 취급하는 주어	every, each가 포함된 주어	**Each** of the balloons **has** a different shape.
	과목명, 국가명, 병명	**Physics is** my favorite subject.
	하나의 개념을 나타내는 「A and B」	**Trial and error is** one way of learning.
	⊕ curry and rice, time and tide, bread and butter	
	시간, 거리, 금액, 무게 단위	**Two weeks is** enough to finish the work.
복수 취급하는 주어	항상 복수로 쓰이는 명사	These **pants suit** me just fine.
	두 개의 개념을 나타내는 「(both) A and B」	**My mom and dad are** traveling together.
	the+형용사(~한 사람들)	**The rich are** not always happy.

ⓘ a number of+복수명사+복수 동사 / the number of+복수명사+단수 동사 서술형 빈출
A number of students are wearing glasses. (많은 학생들)
The number of students has been decreasing. (학생들의 수)

ⓘ 「all, some, most, half, none, the rest of+명사」는 명사의 수에 동사를 일치시킨다.
Most of the boys are interested in playing games.
None of the information was useful to me.

POINT 02 시제의 일치

I **think*** that the movie **was** not good.

나는 그 영화가 별로였다고 생각한다.

*종속절의 시제를 주절의 시제에 일치시키는 것을 시제의 일치라고 해.

주절이 현재시제인 경우	종속절은 현재, 과거, 미래 시제 가능	She **thinks** that the picture **is** beautiful. You **know** that the story **was** not true. They **are saying** that they **will win** the match.
주절이 과거시제인 경우	종속절은 과거나 과거완료 가능	He **thought** that it **would rain** the next day. She **told** me that her brother **had left** for London.

⊕ 주절이 현재시제에서 과거시제로 바뀌면 종속절은 원래 시제에서 한 단계 이전 시제로 바뀐다.
They **say** that the thief **was** caught.
→ They **said** that the thief **had been** caught.

ⓘ 시제 일치의 예외: 현재의 습관이나 사실, 진리, 격언 등은 항상 현재시제로 쓰고, 역사적 사실은 항상 과거시제로 쓴다. 서술형 빈출
We **learned** that water **freezes** at 0°C. (과학적 사실)
We **know** that World War II **broke** out in 1939. (역사적 사실)

개념 QUICK CHECK

POINT 01

괄호 안에서 알맞은 것을 고르시오.

1 The Philippines (have / has) two official languages.

2 The young (is / are) the hope of the future.

3 A number of children (is / are) playing in the playground.

4 All of the money (was / were) stolen.

POINT 02

빈칸에 알맞은 것에 모두 √ 표시하시오.

1 He thinks that he _______ hard.
☐ studies ☐ studied

2 She said that she _______ late.
☐ is ☐ was

3 The teacher said that the sun _______ in the east.
☐ rises ☐ rose

4 He told us that World War II _______ in 1945.
☐ ended ☐ had ended

Answers p. 34

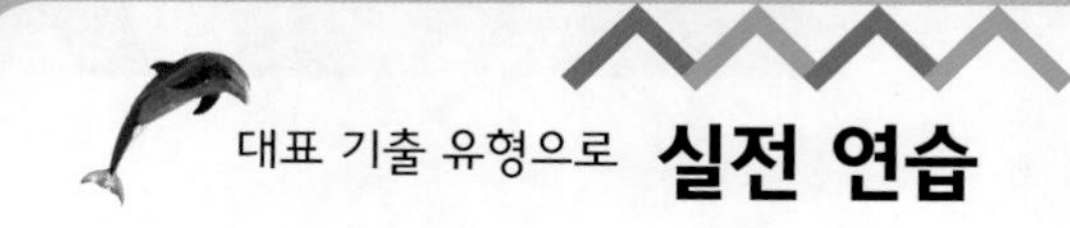

1 빈칸에 들어갈 말이 순서대로 바르게 짝지어진 것은?

> • A number of cars ________ parked in the parking lot.
> • Every student ________ his own special talent.

① is – has ② is – have ③ are – is
④ are – has ⑤ are – have

자주 나와요!
2 빈칸에 들어갈 be동사의 형태가 나머지와 다른 것은?

① I believe that each of us ________ precious.
② Fifty dollars ________ a high price for a concert ticket.
③ Those new jeans ________ too expensive for me to buy.
④ Ten kilometers ________ not a long distance for the runner.
⑤ Mathematics ________ the most interesting subject for me.

3 우리말과 일치하도록 괄호 안의 말을 알맞은 형태로 빈칸에 쓰시오.

(1) 나는 Jason이 여행에서 언제 돌아올지 알고 있다.
> I know when Jason ____________ back from the trip. (come)

(2) 그는 나에게 한 달 후에 돌아올 것이라고 말했다.
> He told me that he ______________ back in a month. (be)

4 빈칸에 들어갈 말로 알맞은 것은?

> The teacher said that water ________ at 100°C.

① boil ② is boiling ③ boils
④ boiled ⑤ has boiled

틀리기 쉬워요!
5 밑줄 친 부분의 쓰임이 어법상 틀린 것은?

① I'm expecting that he will help me.
② The unemployed want to get a job.
③ Both Alice and Ted are afraid of birds.
④ Half of the money was paid first for the trip.
⑤ The number of tourists are increasing every year.

개념 완성 Quiz *Choose or complete.*

1 「a number of+복수명사」가 주어로 쓰인 문장은 뒤에 단수 동사/ 복수 동사 가 온다.
> POINT 01

2 every, each가 포함된 주어는 단수/ 복수 취급한다.
> POINT 01

3 주절이 과거시제인 경우 종속절은 현재, 과거, 미래 / 과거, 과거완료 시제로 쓴다.
> POINT 02

4 사실, 진리, 격언 등은 항상 현재시제 / 과거시제로 쓴다.
> POINT 02

5 「the+형용사」는 '~한 사람들' / '~한 사람'이라는 의미이다.
> POINT 01, 02

UNIT **2** 화법

POINT 03 평서문의 간접화법

She *told me that she **was** happy. 그녀는 내게 행복하다고 말했다.

*그녀가 한 말을 내가 전달하는 간접화법이야.

직접화법	They said to her, "Our English teacher quizzed us yesterday."
↓	① ② ③ ④ ③ ⑤
간접화법	They told her (that) their English teacher had quizzed them the day before.

① 전달 동사를 바꾼다. (say(said) → say(said), say(said) to → tell(told))
② 콤마(,)와 인용부호(" ")를 없애고 접속사 that을 쓴다. 이때 that은 생략 가능하다.
③ 인용부호 안의 인칭대명사를 전달자 입장에 맞게 바꾼다. (1인칭 → 주절의 주어로, 2인칭 → 주절의 목적어로, 3인칭 → 그대로)
④ 동사의 시제를 알맞게 바꾼다. (전달 동사가 현재일 때는 시제 변화 없음, 전달 동사가 과거일 경우 시제 일치에 맞게 바꿈)
⑤ 지시대명사와 부사(구)를 전달자 입장에 맞게 바꾼다. (this(these) → that(those), here → there, now → then, ago → before, today → that day, yesterday → the day before (the previous day), tomorrow → the next day(the following day))

POINT 04 의문문과 명령문의 간접화법

He *asked me **how old I was**. 그는 내게 몇 살인지 물었다.

*그가 물어본 것을 내가 전달하는 간접화법이야.

(1) 의문문의 간접화법

의문사가 있는 의문문	ask(+목적어) +의문사+주어 +동사	She said to me, "What time does the shop open?" → She **asked** me **what time the shop opened**.
	⊕ 의문사가 주어인 경우에는 「의문사+동사」의 어순으로 쓴다. Please tell me **who can** solve the problem.	
의문사가 없는 의문문	ask(+목적어) +if(whether) +주어+동사	Mom said to me, "Have you finished your homework?" → Mom **asked** me **if(whether) I had finished** my homework.

(2) 명령문의 간접화법

긍정 명령문	tell/advise/order/ask/warn 등+목적어+to부정사	Mom said to me, "Clean your room." → Mom **told** me **to clean** my room.
부정 명령문	tell/advise/order/ask/warn 등+목적어+not+to부정사	He said to her, "Don't be back late." → He **ordered** her **not to be** back late.

개념 QUICK CHECK

POINT 03

다음을 간접화법으로 전환할 때 괄호 안에서 알맞은 것을 고르시오.

1 Lucy said, "The boys are here."
→ Lucy said the boys were (here / there).

2 She said to me, "I like you."
→ She told me she liked (me / you).

3 He said, "I cleaned the room."
→ He said he (cleaned / had cleaned) the room.

POINT 04

우리말을 영어로 바르게 표현한 것에 √ 표시하시오.

1 그는 내게 어디에 가고 있는지 물었다.
□ He asked me where I was going.
□ He asked me where was I going.

2 그는 내게 문을 열라고 명령했다.
□ He ordered me open the door.
□ He ordered me to open the door.

3 그녀는 내게 전화를 받지 말라고 말했다.
□ She told me not to answer the phone.
□ She told me don't answer the phone.

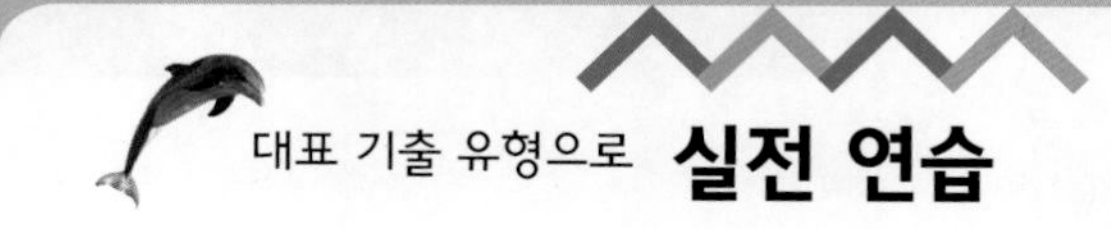

1 직접화법을 간접화법으로 바꿔 쓸 때 빈칸에 알맞은 말을 쓰시오.

(1) Sally said, "I can go shopping now."
> Sally said that ______________ shopping then.

(2) You said to me, "I bought this book yesterday."
> You told me that ______________ that book the day before.

틀리기 쉬워요!
2 직접화법을 간접화법으로 바꾼 문장에서 밑줄 친 부분 중 어법상 틀린 것은?

He said to me, "Where are you from?"
> He ① asked me ② where ③ I ④ am ⑤ from.

자주 나와요!
3 우리말과 일치하도록 할 때 빈칸에 들어갈 말로 알맞은 것은?

그들은 Nancy에게 몇 살인지 물었다. > They asked Nancy ______________.

① if how old she is
② how old are you
③ how old was she
④ how old she was
⑤ how old you were

4 다음 문장을 간접화법으로 바르게 고쳐 쓴 것은?

The officer said to his men, "Don't go out."

① The officer ordered his men not to go out.
② The officer advised his men to go out not.
③ The officer tells his men not to go out.
④ The officer orders his men to not go out.
⑤ The officer asked his men don't go out.

5 밑줄 친 부분의 쓰임이 어법상 올바른 것을 모두 고르면?

① They asked me whether my major was.
② Sarah told me that she will join my club.
③ The principal told us not to run in the hall.
④ The doctor advised me get enough sleep.
⑤ He asked me if I wanted to go see the play.

개념 완성 Quiz *Choose or complete.*

1 직접화법을 간접화법으로 전환할 때, 전달 동사인 say to는 [tell / say to]로 쓴다.
> POINT 03

2 직접화법을 간접화법으로 전환할 때 전달 동사가 [현재 / 과거]일 경우, 시제 변화가 없다.
> POINT 04

3 의문사가 있는 의문문을 간접화법으로 전환할 때 [if+주어+동사 / 의문사+동사+주어 / 의문사+주어+동사]의 어순이 된다.
> POINT 04

4 명령문을 간접화법으로 바꾸는 경우에 동사원형을 [to부정사 / 현재분사] 형태로 쓴다.
> POINT 04

5 의문사가 없는 의문문을 간접화법으로 전환할 때, 「________ +주어+동사」의 어순이 된다.
> POINT 03, 04

UNIT 3 강조, 도치

POINT 05 강조

You *do look pretty in the dress. 그 드레스를 입으니 정말 예뻐 보인다.

*do가 동사 look을 강조하는 표현이야.

동사 강조	do/does/did+동사원형 (정말 ~하다/했다)	The actress **does have** a great smile. He **did solve** the difficult math problem.
명사 강조	the very+명사 (바로 그 ~)	It's **the very watch** that I lost. This is **the very book that** I want to read.
It ~ that 강조구문	It is/was +주어/목적어/부사(구) +that ... (…인 것은 바로 ~이다/였다)	Mike hid the toy under the bed. → **It was** Mike **that(who)** hid the toy under the bed. → **It was** the toy **that(which)** Mike hid under the bed. → **It was** under the bed **that(where)** Mike hid the toy.
	⊕ 강조어구에 따라 that 대신 who(m), which, where, when을 쓸 수 있다. ⊕ It is/was ~ that 강조구문으로 동사는 강조할 수 없다. 서술형 빈출 It was **hid** that Mike the toy under the bed. (×)	

POINT 06 도치

Here *is the answer. 여기 답이 있다.

*here가 문두에 나와 주어와 동사가 도치된 구문이야.

부사(구) 도치	부사(구)+동사+주어	The dog was lying next to the bed. → **Next to the bed** was the dog lying.
	Here/There+동사+주어	**There** goes our train.
	⊕ 주어가 대명사인 경우에는 부사(구)가 문장 앞에 오더라도 주어와 동사가 도치되지 않는다. **Here** she comes back to us again.	
부정어(never, seldom, little 등) 도치	부정어+조동사/do동사+주어+동사원형	She never eats fast food. → **Never** does she eat fast food.
	부정어+be동사+주어	He was seldom as happy as that moment. → **Seldom** was he as happy as that moment.
so+동사+주어	~도 또한 그렇다	Emily likes chocolate, and **so do I**.
neither +동사+주어	~도 또한 그렇지 않다	I don't want to go, and **neither does** Tom.

개념 QUICK CHECK

POINT 05

우리말을 참고하여 빈칸에 알맞은 것을 아래에서 골라 기호를 쓰시오.

a. the very　b. that　c. did

1 나는 정말 문을 잠갔다.
I ______ lock the door.

2 그것이 내가 찾고 있는 바로 그 가방이다.
It's ______ bag I'm looking for.

3 내가 그녀를 만난 것은 바로 어제였다.
It was yesterday ______ I met her.

POINT 06

빈칸에 알맞은 것에 √ 표시하시오.

1 Behind the bushes ______.
□ the duck is
□ is the duck

2 There ______.
□ she goes
□ goes she

3 Hardly ______.
□ walks she
□ does she walk

4 My sister is outgoing, and ______.
□ so I am
□ so am I

대표 기출 유형으로 실전 연습

자주 나와요!

1 우리말과 일치하도록 할 때 빈칸에 들어갈 말로 알맞은 것은?

> Christine은 그 금빛 드레스를 입으니 정말 멋져 보였다.
> > Christine ________ look great in that golden dress.

① is ② do ③ does ④ did ⑤ the very

2 우리말을 영어로 가장 바르게 옮긴 것은?

> 어제 내가 고양이를 찾은 곳은 바로 티슈 상자 안이었다.

① It was I that found my cat in the tissue box yesterday.
② It was my cat that I found in the tissue box yesterday.
③ It was in the tissue box that I found my cat yesterday.
④ It was found that I my cat in the tissue box yesterday.
⑤ It was yesterday that I found my cat in the tissue box.

3 대화의 빈칸에 들어갈 말로 알맞은 것은?

> A: I don't like horror movies.
> B: ____________________

① So am I. ② So do I. ③ Neither am I.
④ Neither will I. ⑤ Neither do I.

4 우리말과 일치하도록 괄호 안의 말을 바르게 배열하여 문장을 완성하시오.

나는 멕시코 음식을 먹어 본 적이 전혀 없다.
> Never ____________________ Mexican food. (I, have, eaten)

틀리기 쉬워요!

5 다음 중 어법상 틀린 문장은?

① Near the lake is an old wooden house.
② It was gave that Pam me a nice wallet.
③ Hardly did he go out on the weekend.
④ It's the very movie that I wanted to see.
⑤ Be quiet! Here he comes to our classroom.

개념 완성 Quiz *Choose or complete.*

1 동사를 강조하는 경우에는 동사 앞에 [the very / do동사 / be동사]를 사용하여 표현한다.
> POINT 05

2 It is/was와 that 사이에 주어, 목적어 등이 되는 [동사 / 명사]나 부사(구) 등을 넣어 강조할 수 있다.
> POINT 05

3 '나도 그러지 않다'라는 의미는 「[So / Nor / Neither]+동사+I」를 쓴다.
> POINT 06

4 부정어를 첫머리에 두어 강조하는 경우, 뒤에 나오는 주어와 동사는 ________ 된다.
> POINT 06

5 운동의 방향이나 장소 등을 나타내는 부사(구)가 첫머리에 오면, [주어+동사 / 동사+주어]의 어순이 된다.
> POINT 05, 06

서술형 실전 연습

Step 1

개념 완성 Quiz *Choose or complete.*

1 우리말과 일치하도록 괄호 안의 말을 알맞은 형태로 빈칸에 쓰시오.

(1) 모든 학생은 한 가지 동아리에 가입해야 한다.

> Every student ______________ join a club. (have to)

(2) 정치학은 내가 전공하고 싶은 것이다.

> Politics ______________ what I want to major in. (be)

2 밑줄 친 부분을 바르게 고쳐 문장을 다시 쓰시오.

(1) Both Tom and I <u>am interested in</u> soccer.

> ______________________________

(2) The sick and poor <u>needs</u> help.

> ______________________________

3 다음 문장을 주어진 말로 시작하는 문장으로 바르게 바꿔 쓰시오.

(1) She says she will exercise regularly.

> She said ______________________________.

(2) The teacher tells us that Pluto is not a planet.

> The teacher told us that ______________________________.

4 두 문장의 의미가 같도록 빈칸에 알맞은 말을 쓰시오.

(1) He said to me, "I like your gift."

= He told me that ______________________________.

(2) The girl said to me, "I am afraid of these bees."

= The girl told me that ______________________________.

5 밑줄 친 부분을 강조하는 문장으로 바꿔 쓰시오.

(1) Chris <u>likes</u> eating chocolate ice cream.

> ______________________________

(2) He <u>seldom</u> takes part in the soccer game.

> ______________________________

개념 완성 Quiz

1 every, each+명사: 단수 / 복수 취급

> POINT 01

2 「the+형용사」가 주어로 쓰인 경우: 단수 / 복수 취급

> POINT 01

3 과학적 사실은 주절의 시제와 상관없이 항상 현재시제 / 과거시제로 쓴다.

> POINT 02

4 직접화법의 인용부호 속의 I는 주절의 주어 / 주절의 목적어 / 종속절의 주어와 일치시킨다.

> POINT 03

5 부정어를 첫머리에 두어 강조하는 경우 주어와 동사는 ________ 시킨다.

> POINT 05, 06

6 대화의 빈칸에 괄호 안의 말을 바르게 배열하여 문장을 완성하시오.

A: Did your father fix your toy?
B: No, he didn't. (1) ____________________ fixed it.
(was, my brother, it, who)
A: He must be good at fixing things.
B: Yes. Not only (2) ____________________, but he also enjoys doing it. (fix, he, things, well, does)

7 다음 [보기]와 같이 빈칸에 알맞은 말을 써서 인터뷰 질문지를 완성하시오.

[보기] The interviewer says to me, "What is your name?"
> The interviewer asks me what my name is.

(1) The interviewer says to me, "What do you enjoy doing in your free time?"
> The interviewer asks me ____________________ in my free time.

(2) The interviewer says to me, "Have you been abroad?"
> The interviewer asks me ____________________.

고난도
8 다음 글의 밑줄 친 문장을 직접화법으로 바꿔 쓰시오.

In winter, grasshopper had no food to eat. He was very hungry. (1) Grasshopper asked himself what he would do. Then, he remembered Ant had saved a lot of food during the summer. Grasshopper ran to Ant's home. He knocked on her door. (2) He told Ant to give him some food. Ant said, "I worked all summer but you only played. Now you don't have enough food to eat."

(1) > Grasshopper asked himself, "____________________"
(2) > He said to Ant, "____________________"

개념 완성 Quiz *Choose or complete.*

6 It / That is ~ that ...: …인 것은 바로 ~이다
> POINT 05, 06

7 의문문을 간접화법으로 전환할 때 의문사가 있으면 that / 의문사 / if나 whether 을(를) 인용부호 부분 앞머리에 쓴다.
> POINT 04

8 간접화법의 to부정사는 직접화법의 의문문 / 명령문 에 해당한다.
> POINT 04

실전 모의고사

시험일 : 월 일	문항 수 : 객관식 19 / 서술형 6
목표 시간 :	총점
걸린 시간 :	/ 100

01 빈칸에 공통으로 들어갈 말로 알맞은 것은? 2점

- Mason ________ like playing board games.
- Seldom ________ he hang around with his friends.

① is ② do ③ does
④ has ⑤ have

02 빈칸에 들어갈 수 있는 말을 모두 고르면? 2점

Tiffany said that she ________ hard.

① studies ② will study ③ has studied
④ studied ⑤ had studied

03 빈칸에 들어갈 말이 순서대로 바르게 짝지어진 것은? 2점

He said that there ________ a big car accident an hour ago. The injured ________ taken to a hospital.

① is – was ② is – were
③ was – was ④ was – were
⑤ has been – were

04 밑줄 친 부분의 쓰임이 나머지와 다른 것은? 4점

① Mia does hate cockroaches.
② Lily did go to school in Mexico.
③ I did my homework with my friends.
④ Jina and her sister do enjoy skiing.
⑤ Kate did do her best on the exam.

05 빈칸에 들어갈 be동사의 형태가 나머지와 다른 것은? 4점

① Bread and butter ________ my favorite breakfast.
② The number of old people ________ rapidly increasing.
③ Mathematics ________ the most difficult subject to me.
④ Measles ________ a common childhood disease.
⑤ Sunglasses ________ a necessity for children who like to play outside.

06 화법을 전환한 문장의 밑줄 친 부분 중 틀린 것은? 3점

Eric said to Kelly, "Do you live here now?"
> Eric ① asked Kelly ② whether ③ she ④ lives ⑤ there then.

[07-08] 두 문장의 의미가 같도록 할 때 빈칸에 알맞은 것을 고르시오. 각 3점

07

He told me he was tired of the rain.
> He said to me, "________ tired of the rain."

① You are ② He is ③ I am
④ He was ⑤ I was

08

Evelyn said, "I go to the bookstore every Saturday."
> Evelyn said that ________ to the bookstore every Saturday.

① I go ② I went ③ she goes
④ she'll go ⑤ she would go

09 주어진 문장을 간접화법으로 바르게 바꾼 것은? 4점

Sally said to her brother, "Don't bother me."

① Sally told her brother not to bother me.
② Sally told her brother not to bother her.
③ Sally said to her brother not to bother her.
④ Sally said to her brother to not bother me.
⑤ Sally said to her brother don't bother her.

10 주어진 문장을 직접화법으로 바르게 바꾼 것은? 4점

Isabel asked me if she might come back the following day.

① Isabel said to me, "May I come back tomorrow?"
② Isabel said to me, "Do I come back tomorrow?"
③ Isabel said to me, "If I might come back tomorrow?"
④ Isabel asked me, "If I may come back the next day?"
⑤ Isabel asked me, "May I come back the following day?"

11 빈칸에 알맞은 말이 순서대로 바르게 짝지어진 것은? 4점

The teacher informed us that Hangeul ________ in the Joseon Dynasty. Now all of the students ________ about this fact.

① creates – knows
② created – know
③ was created – know
④ was created – knows
⑤ had been created – know

12 밑줄 친 부분을 강조한 문장 중 어법상 틀린 것은? 4점

① The singer does sing very well.
② I did remember when your birthday was.
③ It is comic books that I lost yesterday.
④ He is the very man who knows the secret.
⑤ It was in 1950 when the Korean War broke out.

13 밑줄 친 부분의 쓰임이 어법상 틀린 것은? 4점

① All of the furniture were made of wood.
② Half of the cake was left over after the party.
③ Seven days have passed since the baby was born.
④ A number of boys like playing soccer in the playground.
⑤ The young in our society are the hope of our future.

14 밑줄 친 부분을 강조하는 문장으로 고쳐 쓸 때 빈칸에 알맞은 것은? 4점

I never imagined that the plant would be so big.
> Never ________ that the plant would be so big.

① I imagined ② imagined I
③ do I imagine ④ did I imagine
⑤ I did imagine

고난도
15 다음 중 어법상 올바른 문장의 개수는? 4점

ⓐ Every morning Angela gets up at six.
ⓑ Mom told me that the early bird caught the worm.
ⓒ Daniel knows that World War I had broken out in 1914.
ⓓ Yesterday, I learned that the sun rises in the east, and sets in the west.

① 1개 ② 2개 ③ 3개 ④ 4개 ⑤ 없음

신유형
16 대화의 빈칸에 들어갈 말로 가장 적절한 것은? 4점

> A: Thank you for finding my ring. By the way, where did you find it?
> B: ______________________

① I did find your ring in the drawer last night.
② It was in the drawer that I found your ring last night.
③ It was I that found your ring in the drawer last night.
④ It was last night that I found your ring in the drawer.
⑤ It was your ring that I found in the drawer last night.

17 Which of the underlined words has a different usage? 4점

① She did solve the difficult riddle.
② The shirt does look good on you.
③ He does like to read fantasy novels.
④ We do know what will happen next.
⑤ I did volunteer work at the nursing home.

18 대화의 밑줄 친 ①~⑤ 중 어법상 틀린 것은? 5점

> A: Hana asked me ①if I could lend her my notebook.
> B: Was she absent from school?
> A: Yes, ②it was yesterday that she was absent. Her sister caught a cold, and ③so she did.
> B: Oh, that's too bad. How is she now?
> A: She told me that she ④got over it.
> B: Good. We ⑤need to be careful and not get sick.

고난도
19 다음 중 간접화법으로 잘못 바꿔 쓴 것은? 5점

① Jessica said to me, "Who called me yesterday?"
> Jessica asked me who had called her the day before.

② My teacher said to us, "Be quiet in the classroom."
> My teacher told us to be quiet in the classroom.

③ Oliver said to me, "Have you been to New Zealand?"
> Oliver asked me that I had been to New Zealand.

④ Mom said to me, "Don't be late tonight."
> Mom told me not to be late that night.

⑤ Mary said, "I bought a new cell phone yesterday."
> Mary said she had bought a new cell phone the previous day.

20 각 문장을 다음과 같이 바꿔 쓸 때 빈칸에 알맞은 말을 쓰시오. 각 2점

(1) He says he will study hard to succeed.
> He said he ______________________ to succeed.

(2) They think that you broke the window.
> They thought that you ______________ ______________ the window.

(3) Do you know that Columbus discovered America in 1492?
> Did you know that Columbus __________ ______________ America in 1492?

Answers p. 36

21 다음 문장을 간접화법으로 바꿔 쓰시오. 각 2점

(1) She said to him, "Where are you from?"

> She asked him ____________________.

(2) Amy said to us, "Have you seen the movie?"

> Amy asked us ____________________.

신유형

22 다음 대화를 간접화법으로 전환한 문장으로 바르게 고쳐 쓰시오. 각 3점

Mom: When will you leave home tomorrow?

Dave: I will leave home at 8:00 in the morning.

(1) Mom asked Dave ____________________
____________________.

(2) Dave said that ____________________
____________________.

23 밑줄 친 ①~⑤ 중 어법상 틀린 부분을 골라 바르게 고쳐 쓰시오. 3점

Mom asked me ① whether I ② was hungry. I ③ said no. Then Mom ④ told me ⑤ finish my homework before dinner.

(   ) > ____________________

24 다음 문장을 괄호 안의 지시에 알맞게 고쳐 쓰시오. 각 3점

ⓐ Yuna ⓑ speaks English as well as a native speaker of English.

(1) ____________________
____
(밑줄 친 ⓐ를 강조하는 문장으로)

(2) ____________________
____
(밑줄 친 ⓑ를 강조하는 문장으로)

고난도

25 다음 글을 읽고, 물음에 답하시오. 각 3점

Today is Sports Day at Helen's school. (A) Every student who is going to participate are warming up before the event. (B) Yesterday, her teacher said to them, "Be careful not to get hurt."

(1) 윗글의 밑줄 친 (A)에서 어법상 틀린 부분을 찾아 바르게 고쳐 문장을 다시 쓰시오.

____
____

(2) 윗글의 밑줄 친 (B)를 간접화법으로 고칠 때 빈칸에 알맞은 말을 쓰시오.

> Yesterday, her teacher advised them ____________________.

약점 공략
틀린 문제가 있다면?

틀린 문항 번호가 있는 칸을 색칠하고, 어떤 문법 POINT의 집중 복습이 필요한지 파악해 보세요.

문항 번호	연관 문법 POINT	문항 번호	연관 문법 POINT	문항 번호	연관 문법 POINT
01	P5, P6	10	P4	19	P3, P4
02	P2	11	P1, P2	20	P2
03	P1, P2	12	P5	21	P4
04	P5	13	P1, P2	22	P3, P4
05	P1	14	P6	23	P4
06	P4	15	P2	24	P5
07	P3	16	P5	25	P1, P4
08	P3	17	P5		
09	P4	18	P1~P6		

연관 문법 POINT 참고

P1 (p.152) 수의 일치
P2 (p.152) 시제의 일치
P3 (p.154) 평서문의 간접화법
P4 (p.154) 의문문과 명령문의 간접화법
P5 (p.156) 강조
P6 (p.156) 도치

Answers p. 37

내신만점 Level Up Test

01 주어진 문장의 밑줄 친 부분을 강조하는 문장으로 잘못 바꾸어 쓴 것은?

> ① Daisy ② drank ③ green tea ④ at the café ⑤ last Sunday.

① It was Daisy who drank green tea at the café last Sunday.
② It was drank that Daisy green tea at the café last Sunday.
③ It was green tea that Daisy drank at the café last Sunday.
④ It was at the café where Daisy drank green tea last Sunday.
⑤ It was last Sunday when Daisy drank green tea at the café.

02 다음 중 어법상 틀린 문장끼리 짝지어진 것은?

> ⓐ Every person has his own personal opinion.
> ⓑ A number of fans are waving flags.
> ⓒ Mathematics are difficult for many students.
> ⓓ The young likes to upload pictures online.
> ⓔ None of the workers are wearing helmets.

① ⓐ, ⓑ　② ⓑ, ⓒ　③ ⓑ, ⓓ
④ ⓒ, ⓓ　⑤ ⓓ, ⓔ

03 다음 대화를 간접화법으로 옮긴 글의 밑줄 친 ①~⑤ 중 어법상 틀린 것은?

> **Mom:** Who washed the dishes?
> **Me:** Nancy washed the dishes for you.

∨

> Mom ① asked me ② who washed the dishes. I ③ told her that Nancy ④ had washed the dishes for ⑤ her.

04 우리말과 일치하도록 (조건)에 맞게 알맞은 말을 쓰시오.

> (조건) 1. so 또는 neither를 반드시 사용할 것
> 2. 각각 3단어로 쓸 것

(1) 그는 클래식 음악을 좋아하고 나도 그렇다.
> He likes classical music, and ______________________.

(2) 나는 오늘 나가고 싶지 않고 Emily도 그렇다.
> I don't want to go out today, and ______________________.

05 다음 문장에서 어법상 틀린 곳을 찾아 바르게 고쳐 쓰시오.

(1) Never I dreamed of seeing you again.
____________ > ____________

(2) I thought the Korean soccer team will beat the German team.
____________ > ____________

12 우리말과 일치하도록 할 때 빈칸에 들어갈 말이 순서대로 바르게 짝지어진 것은?

> 내가 만약 좋은 소식을 더 일찍 알았더라면 너를 위해 케이크를 만들었을 텐데.
> > If I __________ the good news earlier, I __________ a cake for you.

① knew – made
② knew – would make
③ had known – would make
④ had known – would have made
⑤ have known – would have made

13 빈칸에 들어갈 말이 나머지와 다른 것은?

① It is necessary __________ them to share ideas.
② It is easier __________ me to find out what is wrong.
③ It is rude __________ you to talk like that to your elders.
④ It was impossible __________ him to answer the question.
⑤ It is a pleasure and honor __________ me to be here today.

서술형
14 우리말과 일치하도록 괄호 안의 말을 이용하여 빈칸에 알맞은 말을 쓰시오.

내가 결과를 알게 되자마자 너에게 알려줄게. (know)
> __________ __________ __________ __________ __________ the results, I will let you know.

[15-16] 밑줄 친 부분이 어법상 틀린 것을 고르시오.

15 ① Jenny is lying in bed with her eyes closed.
② He seems to have little money to spend.
③ The dog will train for a year by professionals.
④ The children have gone to play with their friends.
⑤ There was nothing she could have done when her son broke the vase.

16 ① Nowadays, almost every family has a car.
② It was reported that acid rain hurts wild plants.
③ I thought that he would have finished his work by then.
④ Each of the girls has a different character.
⑤ We learned that the Korean War had been over in 1953.

서술형
17 두 문장의 의미가 같도록 빈칸에 알맞은 말을 쓰시오.

I'll give you whatever you want.
> I'll give you __________ __________ you want.

18 밑줄 친 부분의 쓰임이 어법상 올바른 것은?

① That store sells used books.
② The book is writing in easy English.
③ Did you see a boy danced with my daughter?
④ The girl played the guitar is one of my best friends.
⑤ That watch was giving to me years ago by my father.

19 다음 중 밑줄 친 부분을 생략할 수 있는 것을 모두 고르면?

① This is what she would like as a gift.
② He is the only trainer that can handle the dog.
③ I saw a sick kitten whose life was in danger.
④ The boy fell in love with a girl whom he saw once.
⑤ She bought a new cell phone which is made in China.

서술형
20 밑줄 친 부분에서 어법상 어색한 곳을 찾아 바르게 고쳐 쓰시오.

To lose weight, Jane stopped to eat snacks.
__________________ → __________________

21 우리말을 영어로 가장 바르게 옮겨 쓴 것은?

> 그녀가 시애틀에 도착했을 때, 일주일째 비가 내리던 중이었다.

① When she arrived in Seattle, it has been raining for a week.
② When she had arrived in Seattle, it was raining for a week.
③ When she arrived in Seattle, it had been raining for a week.
④ When she has arrived in Seattle, it has been raining for a week.
⑤ When she had arrived in Seattle, it had been raining for a week.

서술형
22 빈칸에 들어갈 말을 괄호 안에 주어진 말을 이용하여 알맞은 형태로 쓰시오.

If it were not for water, we __________________ for a single day. (live, not)

23 다음 중 빈칸에 as가 들어가기에 어색한 것은?

① Do in Rome __________ the Romans do.
② __________ you know, this needs a lot of practice.
③ He may need some help __________ he is a new member.
④ Don't come to me __________ you are ready.
⑤ __________ she grew older, she became wiser.

[24-25] 우리말과 일치하도록 괄호 안의 말을 바르게 배열하시오.

서술형
24 그녀가 산 것이 무엇일 거라고 추측하니?
(do, guess, she, you, bought, what)
> __________________________________

서술형
25 네가 더 많이 연습할수록 너는 더 잘할 것이다.
(you, will, practice, the more, do, the better, you)
> __________________________________

Final Test 3회

시험일 : 월 일	문항수 : 객관식 15 / 서술형 10
반 : 번호 : 이름 :	총점 (각 문항은 모두 4점)
걸린 시간 :	/ 100

[1–2] 빈칸에 공통으로 들어갈 알맞은 말을 고르시오.

1

- ________ you recommend a good Italian restaurant?
- If you had been there, you ________ have seen the accident.

① May[may] ② Can[can] ③ Must[must]
④ Could[could] ⑤ Should[should]

2

- We heard the news ________ she won a gold medal.
- She loves her neighbor ________ is a firefighter.

① who ② that ③ which ④ what ⑤ whom

3 주어진 문장의 밑줄 친 부분과 쓰임이 같은 것은?

It is amazing to think how the Internet has changed our lives.

① The best thing is to tell the truth.
② I advise you to take notes during class.
③ To travel around the world will be very nice.
④ I wish to talk about a book that I recently read.
⑤ I'm sorry, but I don't want to pretend to be satisfied.

4 빈칸에 들어갈 말로 알맞지 않은 것은?

The drummer ________ playing the drums.

① enjoyed ② kept ③ stopped
④ needed ⑤ practiced

서술형
5 다음 [보기]에서 알맞은 것을 골라 빈칸에 쓰시오.

[보기] have to had better be able to used to

(1) I ________ do too much exercise, so it hurt my knees.
(2) You ________ not go there. It's too dangerous.
(3) You got a speeding ticket. You will ________ pay a $50 fine.

6 두 문장을 한 문장으로 바꿔 쓸 때 빈칸에 알맞은 것은?

He was late for an appointment. But he stopped by the bakery to buy a sandwich.
> ________ he was late for an appointment, he stopped by the bakery to buy a sandwich.

① As ② Before ③ If ④ Since ⑤ Although

서술형
7 다음 문장을 분사구문으로 바꿀 때, 빈칸에 알맞은 말을 쓰시오.

As she had bought a new computer, she gave her old one to me.
> ________________, she gave her old one to me.

8 밑줄 친 부분의 쓰임이 어법상 옳은 것은?

① I have never been so happy since I left my hometown.
② No other engine is not so powerful as this.
③ She acted as if she doesn't know me at all.
④ The way how she manages her students is wonderful.
⑤ The work must completed next Monday.

9 주어진 문장을 간접화법으로 바르게 고쳐 쓴 것은?

He said to me, "You have to decide by five o'clock today."

① He told me that you have to decide by five o'clock today.
② He told me that you had to decide by five o'clock that day.
③ He told me that I have to decide by five o'clock today.
④ He told me that I had to decide by five o'clock that day.
⑤ He told me that he had to decide by five o'clock that day.

[10–11] 괄호 안의 말을 이용하여 다음 문장을 같은 뜻의 문장으로 바꿔 쓰시오.

서술형
10 Sylvia was so strong that I could not win the match.
(too ~ to)
> ________________

서술형
11 That she can speak Chinese like a native is so amazing.
(It ~ that)
> ________________

[13-14] 밑줄 친 부분의 쓰임이 주어진 문장과 같은 것을 고르시오.

13

It is nice of Bolton to talk like that.

① It is hard to say good-bye to you.
② I'm so glad to win this match.
③ Mr. Watson got a chance to see the Northern Lights.
④ They have to produce a lot of milk to win a prize.
⑤ Soyeon is smart to use that English-English dictionary.

14

Have you ever seen a ghost?

① Dave has gone to Paris.
② Susan has been sleeping for two days.
③ She has never played bowling before.
④ He has just finished her homework.
⑤ Minji has stayed in Dubai for six years.

15 다음 문장의 밑줄 친 부분을 바르게 고친 것은?

I looked for my ring but couldn't find it anywhere. I thought I lost my ring.

① lose ② have lost ③ have been lost
④ had lost ⑤ had been lost

서술형
16 밑줄 친 부분을 분사구문으로 바꿔 쓸 때 빈칸에 알맞은 말을 쓰시오.

Although you are in trouble, you have to remain cool.
> ______________, you have to remain cool.

서술형
17 밑줄 친 부분 중 어법상 틀린 부분을 찾아 바르게 고쳐 쓰고, 틀린 이유를 우리말로 쓰시오.

This unique house in that he lives is very old.
틀린 부분: ______________ > ______________
틀린 이유: ______________
____

18 밑줄 친 부분을 괄호 안의 말과 바꿔 쓸 수 없는 것은?

① You don't have to do anything this morning. (need not)
② Can you stop at the market on the way home? (Could)
③ May I have your name and phone number? (Can)
④ I cannot work with her any more. (must not)
⑤ Everyone is able to join the soccer club. (can)

서술형
19 다음 문장이 의미가 통하도록 주어진 말을 이용하여 빈칸에 알맞게 쓰시오.

Because I ________ ________ to Paris several times, I was familiar with the area. (be)

20 우리말과 일치하도록 할 때 빈칸에 들어갈 말이 바르게 짝지어진 것은?

만약 내가 충분한 돈이 있다면, 세계 일주 여행을 할 텐데. > If I ________ enough money, I ________ a trip around the world.

① have – take ② had – will take
③ had – would take ④ have had – would take
⑤ had had – would have taken

21 밑줄 친 부분의 쓰임이 어법상 틀린 것은?

① We were made to clean the floors.
② Being sunny, we went out to swim in the sea.
③ I suggest you not waste your limited time.
④ I know a French restaurant where the food is excellent.
⑤ He gave me his old camera, which is over 30 years old.

22 빈칸에 들어갈 말이 나머지와 다른 것은?

① I wonder ________ she knows the truth.
② He behaved as ________ nothing had happened.
③ Please let me know ________ she has any problems.
④ ________ you are over the age of 18, you cannot drive a car.
⑤ ________ you don't bring your membership card, you cannot get a discount.

23 빈칸에 들어갈 말이 순서대로 바르게 짝지어진 것은?

• Are you satisfied ________ your job as a teacher? • Prime Minister Margaret Thatcher was known ________ the "Iron Lady". • The South Pole is covered ________ ice and snow.

① at – to – on ② at – as – on ③ of – to – with
④ of – as – with ⑤ with – as – with

[24-25] 직접화법은 간접화법으로, 간접화법은 직접화법으로 바꿔 쓰시오.

서술형
24 My mother said to me, "I'll be home late today."
> My mother told me that ______________.

서술형
25 He asked me what I was doing then.
> He said to me, ______________

Final Test 2회

시험일 : 월 일	문항수 : 객관식 16 / 서술형 9
반 : 번호 : 이름 :	총점 (각 문항은 모두 4점)
걸린 시간 :	/ 100

[1–2] 빈칸에 들어갈 알맞은 말을 고르시오.

1

I've been a big fan of Son Heungmin ________ I was eight years old.

① if ② that ③ until ④ since ⑤ because

2

My aunt is going to get married in May, ________ the weather is beautiful.

① that ② who ③ how ④ what ⑤ when

3 두 문장이 같은 의미가 되도록 할 때 빈칸에 알맞은 것은?

He has no money to buy it. And he has no time to buy it.
= He has ________ money ________ time to buy it.

① both – and ② not – but
③ either – or ④ neither – nor
⑤ not only – but also

4 우리말을 영어로 가장 바르게 옮겨 쓴 것은?

며칠 전에 내가 그를 만난 곳은 바로 우리 집 앞이었다.

① A few days ago, I met him in front of my house.
② I did meet him a few days ago in front of my house.
③ It was him that I met a few days ago in front of my house.
④ It was in front of my house that I met him a few days ago.
⑤ It was a few days ago that I met him in front of my house.

서술형
5 다음 문장이 의미가 통하도록 빈칸에 알맞은 말을 쓰시오.

I ________ ________ stay home than go out on such a rainy day.

6 주어진 문장의 밑줄 친 부분과 바꿔 쓸 수 있는 것은?

I tried to learn ballet but it was much harder than I expected.

① so ② as ③ more ④ a lot ⑤ very

7 다음 중 밑줄 친 부분의 쓰임이 어법상 옳은 것은?

① I'm not afraid of being left alone in my house.
② Thousands of people have visited Seoul last year.
③ I saw a boy and a dog who are running in the park.
④ Not to know what to do, we were just sitting there.
⑤ This soap can be using without water.

8 주어진 문장의 밑줄 친 부분과 쓰임이 다른 것은?

The research showed that older people were seen to be more realistic.

① That he will resign as chairman is certain.
② The problem is that this car is too expensive for us.
③ The fact that I was short was a big disadvantage.
④ The girl that I met yesterday helped me with my science homework.
⑤ I heard that many people got hurt due to the strong winds.

서술형
9 괄호 안의 말을 바르게 배열하여 문장을 완성하시오.

I feel cold. Please give me ________________.
(drink, hot, to, something)

10 다음 중 의도하는 바가 나머지와 다른 것은?

① You cannot bring children under the age of 3 here.
② You must not bring children under the age of 3 here.
③ You should not bring children under the age of 3 here.
④ You ought not to bring children under the age of 3 here.
⑤ You don't have to bring children under the age of 3 here.

[11–12] 우리말과 뜻이 같도록 주어진 말을 이용하여 문장을 완성하시오.

서술형
11 나는 사람들 앞에서 노래를 할 때마다 매우 긴장이 된다.

> I am very nervous ________ ________ ________ ________ in front of people. (sing songs)

서술형
12 한국에서 가장 유명한 곳들 중의 한 곳을 소개할게.

> Let me introduce ________ ________ ________ ________ ________ ________ in Korea. (famous, place)

13 밑줄 친 부분의 쓰임이 나머지와 다른 것은?

① What have you ordered for lunch?
② Do you understand what I am saying?
③ Thank you for what you have done for me.
④ What we really need is a nice vacation.
⑤ What happened to them could happen to us.

[14-15] 빈칸에 공통으로 들어갈 알맞은 말을 고르시오.

14

- He ________ have been sad to live alone away from his family.
- Someone who has a heart disease ________ not use this medicine.

① can ② must ③ would
④ had better ⑤ used to

15

- Why don't you go to the restaurant ________ we had dinner last week?
- Could you please tell me ________ the subway station is?

① that ② which ③ what ④ when ⑤ where

16 다음 문장의 밑줄 친 부분 중 어법상 어색한 것은?

Seeing(①) the calm sea makes(②) me(③) feeling(④) peaceful(⑤).

서술형
17 밑줄 친 부분에서 어법상 틀린 곳을 바르게 고쳐 문장을 다시 쓰시오.

Not only you but also he were not at home last night.

> ________________________________

18 주어진 문장의 밑줄 친 부분과 쓰임이 같은 것은?

He has lived in this house for more than 30 years.

① The rock band has been popular since its debut.
② Angela has just solved the difficult problem.
③ He has gone to America leaving his family in Korea.
④ Jimin has ever seen shooting stars in the sky.
⑤ I have never seen this beautiful place before I visited here.

[19-20] 우리말과 일치하도록 괄호 안의 말을 이용하여 문장을 완성하시오.

서술형
19 내가 그녀의 충고를 따랐었다면 지금 편안하게 살 수 있을 텐데.

> If I had followed her advice, I ________ ________ comfortably now. (live)

서술형
20 내가 돈이 더 많이 있으면 좋을 텐데.

> I wish ________ ________ more money. (have)

21 다음 중 어법상 옳은 문장을 2개 고르면?

① Are you satisfied with your working conditions?
② Somebody asked me where was the bus stop.
③ Do you mind to excuse us for a few minutes?
④ He seemed to be surprised at the news.
⑤ My mom expected me passing the test.

22 다음 문장의 밑줄 친 부분과 바꿔 쓸 수 있는 것은?

As I didn't eat anything all day, I am hungry.

① Until ② That ③ While ④ Since ⑤ Although

서술형
23 다음을 수동태 문장으로 바꿔 쓸 때 빈칸에 알맞은 말을 쓰시오.

They will remember Korea as a beautiful country.

> Korea ________ ________ ________ as a beautiful country by them.

24 주어진 문장과 의미가 같은 것을 모두 고르면?

That is the most important point in this talk.

① No other point is as important as that in this talk.
② That is one of the most important points in this talk.
③ No other point is more important than that in this talk.
④ That is more important than any other point in this talk.
⑤ That is ten times more important than any other point in this talk.

서술형
25 다음을 두 가지 형태의 수동태 문장으로 바꿔 쓸 때 빈칸에 알맞은 말을 쓰시오.

The boss offered her a better position.

> ________________ a better position by the boss.
> A better position ________________ by the boss.

Final Test 1회

시험일 : 월 일	문항수 : 객관식 16 / 서술형 9
반 : 번호 : 이름 :	총점 (각 문항은 모두 4점)
걸린 시간 :	/ 100

[1–2] 빈칸에 들어갈 알맞은 말을 고르시오.

1

I ________ in Seoul before I moved here.

① live ② am living ③ lived
④ has lived ⑤ had lived

2

I have trouble ________ because of a terrible backache.

① walk ② to walk ③ walking
④ walked ⑤ be walked

3 우리말과 일치하도록 할 때 빈칸에 알맞은 것은?

좋은 아이디어가 있으시면 내게 말해주세요.
> Please tell me ________ you have any good ideas.

① if ② that ③ when ④ since ⑤ though

서술형
4 괄호 안에 주어진 말을 이용하여 빈칸에 알맞은 말을 쓰시오.

If he had been nice to others, he ________ ________ ________ some close friends. (can, have)

5 주어진 문장의 밑줄 친 부분과 쓰임이 같은 것은?

You can leave now if you're in a hurry.

① She can't be right all the time.
② You can take the car if you want.
③ Can you tell me what time we are arriving?
④ Can you speak any other foreign languages?
⑤ Believe it or not, animals can also use tools.

[6–7] 다음 두 문장을 한 문장으로 바꿔 쓸 때 빈칸에 알맞은 말을 쓰시오.

서술형
6 We started painting the wall two hours ago. We are still painting now.

> We ________ ________ ________ the wall for two hours.

서술형
7 The woman is my new science teacher. Her hair is light brown.

> The woman ________ ________ is light brown is my new science teacher.

8 빈칸에 들어갈 말이 순서대로 바르게 짝지어진 것은?

- All of his artworks have ________ designs.
- The ________ worker was taken to the hospital.

① interest – injure ② interesting – injuring
③ interesting – injured ④ interested – injuring
⑤ interested – injured

[9–10] 밑줄 친 부분이 어법상 어색한 것을 고르시오.

9 ① The pain got worse and worse.
② Stretch your arms as higher as you can.
③ The garden here is not as beautiful as it used to be.
④ The Internet can be much more dangerous than you know.
⑤ The new building is taller than any other building in this city.

10 ① The stadium has not been built yet.
② It is kind of you to help me with my work.
③ The girl wants playing the piano all day long.
④ He isn't back yet. He may have had an accident.
⑤ We knew that he was writing his own music.

11 다음 문장을 간접화법으로 바꿀 때 빈칸에 알맞은 것은?

The police said to me, "Get out of the car right now."
> The police ordered me ________________.

① get out of the car right now
② to get out of the car right now
③ to get out of the car right then
④ that you got out of the car right now
⑤ that you got out of the car right then

서술형
12 밑줄 친 부분을 분사구문으로 바꿔 쓰시오.

Since I don't have a car, I have no choice but to walk.
> ________________, I have no choice but to walk.

빠르게
통하는
영문법
핵심 1200제

실전 문제로 중학 내신과 실력 완성에

빠르게 통하는 영문법

핵심 1200제

Answers

LEVEL 3

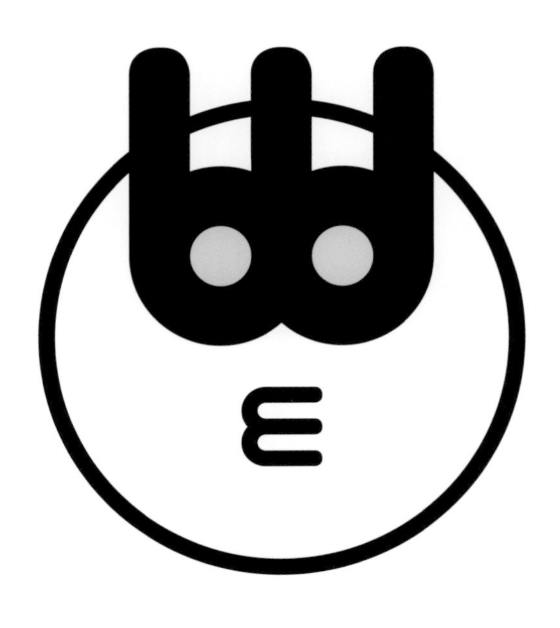

동아출판

CHAPTER 01
시제

UNIT 01 현재완료

개념 QUICK CHECK p.8

POINT 01 **1** 경험 **2** 결과 **3** 완료 **4** 계속

POINT 02 **1** a. have been learning
2 b. has been running

실전 연습 p.9

1 ④ **2** ⑤ **3** has, been, playing
4 ② → been **5** ②

1 과거부터 현재까지 계속되는 상황을 나타내야 하므로 첫 번째 빈칸에는 현재완료가 알맞고, 두 번째 빈칸에는 뒤에 시작 시점을 나타내는 표현이 나오므로 since가 알맞다.

2 [보기]와 ⑤는 '~해 본 적이 있다'는 의미로 경험을 나타낸다. ①과 ④는 완료, ②는 계속, ③은 결과를 나타낸다.

3 과거에 시작된 일이 현재까지 계속 진행되고 있음을 나타낼 때에는 현재완료 진행형(have[has] been+-ing)을 쓴다.

4 주어진 문장이 '~에 가 본 적이 없다'는 의미의 경험을 나타내므로 has never been to로 써야 한다.

5 ② 특정 과거 시점을 나타내는 부사구(five years ago)가 있으므로 현재완료와 함께 쓸 수 없다. (has lived → lived)

개념 완성 Quiz

1 have+p.p. **2** 경험 **3** have been+-ing
4 gone **5** 과거시제

UNIT 02 과거완료

개념 QUICK CHECK p.10

POINT 03 **1** had finished **2** had met
3 had been crying

POINT 04 **1** b **2** d **3** a **4** c

실전 연습 p.11

1 went, had, traveled **2** ②, ⑤
3 ① **4** ⑤ **5** ③

1 첫 번째 빈칸에는 지난주에 캐나다로 돌아간 과거 상황을 나타내므로 과거시제를 쓰고, 두 번째 빈칸에는 캐나다로 돌아간 과거 시점보다 여행을 한 것이 더 이전이므로 과거완료를 쓴다.

2 몸이 나아진 과거 시점보다 약을 먹은 시점이 더 이전이므로 과거완료를 쓴다. 시간의 전후가 나타나는 접속사 after가 쓰였으므로 과거완료 대신 과거시제를 쓸 수 있다.

3 ①은 과거완료의 경험, 나머지는 모두 계속의 의미를 나타낸다.

4 ⑤ 공항에 도착한 과거 시점 이전에 비행기가 이미 출발했으므로 완료의 의미를 나타내는 과거완료를 쓴다. (→ had already taken off)

5 첫 번째 빈칸은 휴대 전화를 발견한 시점보다 누군가가 놓고 간 것이 이전이므로 과거완료가 알맞다. 두 번째 빈칸은 집에 온 시점 이전부터 계속 TV를 보고 있었으므로 과거완료나 과거완료 진행이 알맞다.

개념 완성 Quiz

1 had+p.p. **2** 과거시제 **3** 계속
4 과거완료 **5** 대과거, had+p.p.

서술형 실전 연습 pp.12~13

1 (1) has, taught, English, since
(2) have, never, seen, a, sunrise
2 lost the watch that his dad had given him
3 (1) has gone to New York
(2) had eaten a hot dog
4 (1) Have you gone → Did you go
(2) has used → had used
5 (1) has been reading a book
(2) have been playing badminton
6 Kate has left her umbrella on the bus.
7 (1) had learned, until
(2) has learned[has been learning], since
(3) has learned[has been learning], for
8 (1) ⓐ → participated
(2) ⓓ → had practiced

1 (1) 과거부터 현재까지 계속되고 있음을 나타내므로 현재완료(have+p.p.)를 쓴다.
(2) 경험을 나타내는 현재완료의 부정이므로 「have never p.p. ~」로 쓴다.

2 시계를 잃어버린 시점 이전에 생일 선물로 받았으므로 과거완료(had+p.p.)를 쓴다.

3 (1) '뉴욕에 가서 지금 여기 없다'라는 결과를 나타내므로 have(has) gone to를 쓴다.
(2) 배가 고프지 않았다는 과거의 기준 시점보다 핫도그를 먹은 것이 더 이전이므로 과거완료(had+p.p.)로 쓴다.

4 (1) 특정한 과거 시점을 나타내는 부사구(last weekend)가 있으므로 과거시제로 써야 한다.
(2) 새 가방을 산 시점 이전에 계속 그 가방을 사용했다는 의미가 되어야 하므로 과거완료로 써야 한다.

5 과거에 시작된 일이 현재까지 계속 진행되고 있음을 나타낼 때에는 현재완료 진행형(have(has) been+-ing)을 쓴다.

6 버스에 우산을 두고 내려서 현재 우산이 없다는 결과를 나타내야 하므로 현재완료(have(has)+p.p.)로 쓴다.

7 (1) 첫 번째 빈칸에는 Dance Class가 2월 초에 시작해서 3월 말에 완료되었으므로 과거완료(had+p.p.)를 쓰고, 두 번째 빈칸은 뒤에 완료된 시점이 나오므로 '~까지'라는 의미의 until을 쓴다.
(2) (3) 첫 번째 빈칸에는 과거부터 현재까지 계속 배우고 있으므로 현재완료(have(has)+p.p.)나 현재완료 진행형(have(has) been+-ing)을 쓴다. 두 번째 빈칸은 (2)는 시작 시점이 나오므로 since가, (3)은 배운 기간이 나오므로 for가 알맞다.

8 (1) ⓐ 특정한 과거 시점을 나타내는 부사인 yesterday가 있으므로 과거시제로 써야 한다.
(2) ⓓ 과거의 기준 시점인 노래 대회 이전에 연습을 열심히 했으므로 과거완료(had+p.p.)로 쓴다.

개념 완성 Quiz

1 have+p.p. **2** 대과거 **3** gone **4** ago, when, last
5 have been+-ing **6** 결과 **7** since, for **8** 과거시제

실전 모의고사 pp. 14~17

01 ③	**02** ④	**03** ⑤	**04** ④	**05** ②	**06** ①
07 ⑤	**08** ④	**09** ②	**10** ⑤	**11** ④	**12** ②
13 ④	**14** ④	**15** ②	**16** ④	**17** ②	**18** ⑤

19 (1) Have you ever met a movie star before?
(2) she had already solved
20 (1) has been writing the novel
(2) had been learning Spanish
21 (1) has talked(has been talking)
(2) has fixed
22 Ann has gone to Paris to study art.
23 had not(never) ridden a skateboard
24 (1) got home (2) had been broken
(3) called (4) haven't found
25 (1) arrived, had, already, started
(2) had, left, his, ticket

01 어렸을 적부터 L.A.에서 계속 살았다는 의미가 되어야 하므로 현재완료인 has lived가 알맞다.

02 이전부터 초인종이 울린 과거 시점까지 몇 시간 동안 자고 있었으므로 계속을 나타내는 과거완료 진행형인 had been sleeping이 알맞다.

03 특정한 과거의 시점을 나타내는 부사구 last summer는 현재완료와 함께 쓸 수 없다.

04 for 뒤에는 구체적인 기간이, since 뒤에는 시작 시점이 쓰인다.

05 집에 온 과거 시점보다 Chris가 잠자리에 든 시점이 더 이전이므로 과거완료인 had gone으로 써야 한다.

06 [보기]와 ①은 현재완료의 완료의 의미를 나타낸다. ②와 ⑤는 계속, ③과 ④는 경험의 의미로 쓰였다.

07 3시간 전부터 지금까지 계속 청소하고 있으므로 현재완료나 현재완료 진행형을 써야 한다.

08 이름을 잊어버리고 지금도 기억하지 못하므로 결과를 나타내는 현재완료 have forgotten이 알맞다.

09 ② 특정한 과거 시점을 나타내는 부사구 last week는 현재완료와 함께 쓸 수 없다. (has bought → bought)

10 ⑤ 숙제를 끝낸 것이 잠자리에 든 것보다 이전에 일어났으므로, 주절의 동사를 과거시제로 써야 한다. (→ After I (had) finished my homework, I went to bed.)

11 첫 번째 빈칸은 과거의 상황을 나타내므로 과거시제인 missed로, 두 번째 빈칸은 정류장에 도착한 과거 시점보다 더 이전에 버스가 떠났음을 나타내는 과거완료 had left로 써야 한다.

12 ②는 지금까지 비가 계속 내리고 있음을 나타내는 현재완료 진행이 되어야 하므로 빈칸에 has가 알맞다. 나머지는 모두 과거완료나 과거완료 진행형에 쓰이는 had가 알맞다.

13 집에 도착한 과거 시점 이전에 이미 저녁 식사가 준비되어 있었으므로 과거완료를 사용한다.

14 Have you been to ~?는 '~에 가 본 적이 있니?'의 의미이다.

15 ⓑ 피곤한 과거의 시점보다 밤늦게까지 깨어 있었던 것이 더 이전이므로 과거완료로 써야 한다. (has stayed → had stayed) ⓓ 특정 과거 시점 이전부터 그 시점까지 계속됨을 나타내므로 과거완료나 과거완료 진행으로 쓴다. (had working → had worked(had been working))

16 ④ 상태를 나타내는 동사 know는 완료 진행형으로 쓰지 않는다. (have been knowing → have known)

17 ② 개를 잃어버린 것이 찾은 것보다 먼저 일어난 일이므로 대과거 (had+p.p.)를 사용한다.

18 기간을 의미하는 for twenty years로 보아 works는 현재완료인 has worked로 써야 한다.

19 (1) 현재완료의 의문문은 Have(Has)+주어+(ever)+p.p. ~?로 쓴다.
(2) 과거의 특정 시점 이전에 발생한 일은 과거완료(had+p.p.)를 쓰고, already는 주로 had와 과거분사 사이에 쓴다.

20 (1) 2년 전에 시작해서 지금도 소설을 쓰는 중이므로 현재완료 진행의 문장을 완성한다.
(2) 이사 가기 6개월 전부터 배워 왔으므로 과거완료 진행의 문장을 완성한다.

21 (1) 두 시간 전부터 지금까지 계속 전화 통화를 하고 있으므로 현재완료나 현재완료 진행형을 쓴다.
(2) 컴퓨터를 고쳤다는 결과를 나타내므로 현재완료를 쓴다.

22 '~에 가 버려서 지금 여기에 없다'의 의미를 나타낼 때는 have(has) gone to ~를 쓴다.

23 과거의 특정 시점까지 한 번도 해 보지 못한 경험을 표현할 때는 과거완료로 쓴다.

24 (1), (3) 지난 토요일에 겪은 과거 상황을 나타내므로 과거시제로 쓴다. (2) 집에 도착했을 때 이미 창문이 깨져 있었으므로 과거완료로 쓴다. (4) 범인을 아직까지 찾지 못한 상황이므로 현재완료로 쓴다.

25 과거의 특정 시점은 과거 시제로 쓰고, 과거의 특정 시점보다 먼저 일어난 일을 나타낼 때에는 과거완료로 쓴다.

내신만점 Level Up Test p.18

01 ③ 02 ⑤ 03 ④
04 (1) has been waiting for Henry
(2) has not answered the phone
05 (1) 틀린 부분: ⓑ → didn't
틀린 이유: 일반동사의 과거시제 의문문에 대한 응답이므로 didn't로 답해야 한다.
(2) 틀린 부분: ⓔ → had overslept
틀린 이유: 시험 시간에 늦은 과거의 시점보다 늦잠을 잔 것이 더 이전이므로 과거완료 시제로 써야 한다.

01 문장을 배열하면 I haven't heard from Sally since she moved to Italy.이므로 6번째로 오는 단어는 since이다.

02 ⓐ는 과거완료의 결과, ⓑ는 경험, ⓒ와 ⓔ는 계속, ⓓ는 완료의 의미를 나타낸다.

03 ⓐ 과거의 기준 시점인 50살 때까지 일을 가져 본 적이 없으므로 과거완료로 써야 한다. (has never had → had never had)

04 (1) 현재까지 계속 진행됨을 나타내는 현재완료 진행형을 쓴다.
(2) 현재완료 부정문(have(has)+not+p.p.)으로 쓴다.

05 ⓑ 일반동사의 의문문의 시제에 맞춰 과거시제로 쓴다.
ⓔ 시험 시간에 늦은 시점보다 늦잠을 잔 것이 더 이전이므로 과거완료로 쓴다.

CHAPTER 02
조동사

UNIT 01 조동사 (1)

개념 QUICK CHECK p.20

POINT 01 1 b 2 d 3 a 4 c
POINT 02 1 추측 2 허락 3 추측

실전 연습 p.21

1 was able to get 2 can't, be 3 ②
4 ④ 5 ③

1 능력을 나타내는 can은 be able to로 바꿔 쓸 수 있으며, 시제가 과거이고 주어가 I이므로 be동사는 was로 쓴다.

2 '~일 리가 없다'는 강한 부정적 추측의 의미를 나타낼 때에는 can의 부정형인 can't로 쓴다.

3 ②의 may는 허락의 의미로 쓰였고, 나머지는 모두 추측의 의미로 쓰였다.

4 첫 번째 빈칸은 '요청'을 나타내므로 can 또는 정중한 표현인 could를 쓴다. 두 번째 빈칸은 '허락'을 나타내므로 can이나 may를 쓴다. 세 번째 빈칸은 '능력'을 나타내며 다른 조동사 뒤에 나오므로 be able to를 쓴다.

5 ③ 두 개의 조동사를 이어서 쓸 수 없으므로 미래의 능력을 나타낼 때에는 will be able to로 쓴다. (will can't → won't be able to)

개념 완성 Quiz

1 be able to **2** can't **3** 허락, 추측 **4** could
5 might

UNIT 02 조동사 (2) 및 관용 표현

개념 QUICK CHECK p.22

POINT 03 **1** a **2** c **3** b
POINT 04 **1** ○ **2** ○ **3** × **4** ×

실전 연습 p.23

1 ③ 2 must 3 ④
4 I would rather take a taxi than wait for a bus.
5 ④

1 의미상 '~해야 한다'라는 의미로 의무를 나타내는 조동사가 들어가야 한다. used to는 과거의 습관이나 상태를 나타내므로 빈칸에 알맞지 않다.

2 must는 '~해야 한다'라는 의무의 의미와 '~임에 틀림없다'는 강한 추측의 의미를 나타낸다.

3 '~이었다'는 의미로 과거의 상태를 나타낼 때는 「used to+동사원형」을 쓴다.

4 '*B* 하느니 차라리 *A* 하겠다'의 의미를 나타낼 때에는 would rather *A* than *B*로 쓴다.

5 '~할 필요가 없다'의 의미로 불필요를 나타낼 때에는 don't have to를 쓰고, '~하지 않는 게 좋겠다'의 의미로 강한 충고나 경고를 나타낼 때에는 had better not을 쓴다.

개념 완성 Quiz

1 should, ought to **2** must **3** used to
4 would, rather **5** don't have to

UNIT 03 조동사+have p.p.

개념 QUICK CHECK p.24

POINT 05 – (1), (2) **1** 탔음에 틀림없다 **2** 일찍 자지 않았다 **3** 멈췄음에 틀림없다
POINT 05 – (3), (4) **1** might **2** cannot **3** may not

실전 연습 p.25

1 ④ 2 ① 3 should have cried → must have cried 4 ② 5 ③

1 '~했을 리가 없다'는 의미로 과거의 일에 대한 부정적인 추측을 나타낼 때에는 cannot have p.p.로 쓴다.

2 '~했을지도 모른다'라는 의미로 과거의 일에 대한 불확실한 추측을 나타낼 때에는 may(might) have p.p.로 쓴다.

3 '~했음에 틀림없다'의 의미를 나타낼 때는 must have p.p.를 쓴다.

4 첫 번째 빈칸은 과거의 일에 대한 강한 추측을 나타내는 must have p.p.가 알맞고, 두 번째 빈칸은 '~하지 말았어야 했다'는 의미로 과거의 일에 대한 후회나 유감을 나타내는 shouldn't have p.p.가 알맞다.

5 ③은 과거의 일에 대한 강한 부정적 확신을 나타내므로 cannot have p.p.가 되는 것이 알맞고, 나머지는 과거의 일에 대한 후회나 유감을 나타내므로 should have p.p.가 되는 것이 알맞다.

개념 완성 Quiz

1 cannot have p.p. **2** may(might) have p.p.
3 must have p.p. **4** shouldn't have p.p.
5 should have p.p.

서술형 실전 연습 pp.26~27

1 can't come here
2 (1) must be (2) had to get up
3 (1) don't, have, to, bring

(2) cannot, have, cleaned

4 (1) used to wear glasses
(2) would rather play soccer, than watch TV

5 (1) ought(have), to, apologize
(2) may(might), have, left

6 ⓑ → You will be able to speak English well someday.
ⓒ → Lula had better not make the same mistake again.

7 must, have, seen, a, lizard

8 You shouldn't have left the door open.

1 강한 부정적 추측의 의미를 나타낼 때는 can't를 쓴다.

2 (1) '~임에 틀림없다'는 뜻의 강한 추측을 나타내는 must를 쓴다.
(2) 의무를 나타내는 have to를 쓰되, 시제가 과거이므로 had to로 쓴다.

3 (1) 불필요를 나타내므로 have to의 부정형인 don't have to를 쓴다.
(2) 과거의 일에 대한 강한 부정적 확신을 나타내는 cannot have p.p.를 쓴다.

4 (1) 안경을 썼다는 과거의 상태를 나타내는 used to를 쓴다.
(2) 'TV를 보느니 축구를 하는 편이 낫다'는 의미이므로 would rather *A* than *B*로 쓴다.

5 (1) 의무를 나타내는 말 중 ought to나 have to를 사용한다.
(2) 과거의 일에 대한 불확실한 추측을 나타내므로 may(might) have p.p.로 쓴다.

6 ⓑ 두 개의 조동사를 이어서 사용할 수 없으므로 will be able to로 쓴다. ⓒ had better의 부정형은 had better not으로 쓴다.

7 '도마뱀을 보았음이 틀림없다'는 말이 맥락상 적절하므로, 과거의 일에 대한 강한 추측을 나타내는 must have p.p.를 쓴다.

8 '~하지 말았어야 했다'의 의미로 과거의 일에 대한 후회나 유감을 나타낼 때에는 shouldn't have p.p.를 쓴다.

개념 완성 Quiz

1 can't **2** had to **3** don't have to **4** used **5** might **6** better not **7** must **8** should

실전 모의고사

pp.28~31

01 ① 02 ④ 03 ⑤ 04 ② 05 ④ 06 ⑤
07 ⑤ 08 ① 09 ③ 10 ② 11 ④ 12 ②
13 ④ 14 ⑤ 15 ④ 16 ⑤ 17 ② 18 ②

19 (1) had better not hide (2) may be able to solve

20 (1) must not (2) cannot

21 I would rather stay at home than see the movie alone.

22 (1) must have dyed her hair
(2) must have been upset

23 (1) should have kept
(2) shouldn't have hurt

24 ⓒ → will be able to experience

25 (1) can't(cannot) be
(2) may call → may(might) have called

01 '~임에 틀림없다'라는 의미로 강한 추측을 나타내는 must가 알맞다.

02 '*B* 하느니 차라리 *A* 하겠다'의 의미를 나타내는 would rather *A* than *B*가 알맞다.

03 '~할 필요가 없다'라는 의미로 불필요를 나타내는 don't have to는 need not과 바꿔 쓸 수 있다.

04 '~해도 좋다'라는 의미의 허락, '~할 수 있다'라는 의미의 능력, '~해 주겠니?'라는 의미의 요청을 모두 나타내는 조동사는 can이다.

05 빈칸에는 '~해서는 안 된다' 또는 '~하지 않는 게 좋다'는 금지의 뜻을 나타내는 조동사가 들어가야 한다.

06 '~했어야 했다 (그런데 하지 못했다)'라는 의미로 과거의 일에 대한 후회를 나타낼 때 should have p.p.를 쓴다.

07 첫 번째 빈칸은 의무를 나타내는 조동사인 should, 두 번째 빈칸은 '~할 필요가 없다'는 의미의 don't have to가 알맞다.

08 첫 번째 빈칸은 허락을 나타내는 조동사인 can 또는 may가, 두 번째 빈칸은 과거의 일에 대한 강한 추측을 나타내는 must가 알맞다.

09 [보기]와 ③은 허락의 의미를 나타내고, 나머지는 모두 추측의 의미를 나타낸다.

10 ②는 확신을 나타내고, 나머지는 모두 의무를 나타낸다.

11 ④ '~해야 한다'라는 의미로 당연한 의무를 나타내는 ought to의 부정형은 ought not to이다. (→ ought not to play)

12 ② 과거의 습관은 would로 나타낼 수 있지만, 과거의 상태는 used to로 써야 한다.

13 ④ '~하지 않는 게 좋겠다'라는 의미는 had better not으로 나타낸다.

14 ⑤ '~하곤 했다'는 뜻의 과거의 습관은 「used to+동사원형」으로 나타낸다. be used to+-ing는 '~하는 데 익숙하다'는 뜻의 표현이다. (I'm used to going → I used to go)

15 ④ 과거의 일에 대한 강한 부정적 추측을 나타낼 때에는 cannot have p.p.를 쓴다.

16 첫 번째 문장은 과거의 일에 대한 유감을 나타내므로 should have p.p.가, 두 번째 문장은 과거의 상태를 나타내므로 used to가 알맞다.

17 ② might have p.p.는 '~였을지도 모른다'라는 의미로 과거의 일에 대한 불확실한 추측을 나타낸다. 과거의 일에 대한 강한 추측은 must have p.p.로 나타낸다.

18 ⓑ 두 개의 조동사를 이어서 사용할 수 없으므로 must 대신 have to로 쓴다. (will must → will have to) ⓒ would rather *A* than *B*에서 *A*와 *B*는 같은 형태로 쓴다. (to watch → watch)

19 (1) '~하지 않는 게 좋겠다'라는 의미는 had better not으로 나타낸다.
(2) be able to는 능력을 나타내며, 조동사 뒤에 쓰일 수 있다.

20 (1) 수영을 해서는 안 된다는 맥락이 자연스러우므로 금지를 나타내는 must not을 써야 한다.
(2) 아파서 하이킹을 갔을 리가 없다는 맥락이 자연스러우므로 과거의 일에 대한 부정적 추측을 나타내는 cannot have p.p.를 써야 한다.

21 would rather *A* than *B*는 '*B* 하느니 차라리 *A* 하겠다'의 의미를 나타내며 *A*와 *B*는 같은 형태로 쓴다.

22 과거 사실에 대한 강한 추측은 must have p.p.로 나타낸다.

23 과거의 일에 대한 후회나 유감은 should (not) have p.p.로 나타낸다.

24 두 개의 조동사를 이어서 사용할 수 없으므로 미래의 가능을 나타낼 때에는 will be able to로 쓴다.

25 (1) '~일 리가 없다'는 의미의 부정적인 추측은 can't(cannot)로 나타낸다.
(2) '~했을지도 모른다'라는 뜻의 과거의 일에 대한 불확실한 추측은 may(might) have p.p.로 나타낸다.

내신만점 Level Up Test p.32

01 ② **02** ③ **03** ④
04 used to be, would hide
05 (1) should have reminded (2) don't have to call (3) had better come

01 ② 맥락상 '경찰을 불러야 한다'는 뜻이 적절하므로 의무를 나타내는 조동사로 고쳐야 한다. (can't → must, has to 등)

02 ⓐ 조동사는 이어서 쓸 수 없다. (will can → will be able to) ⓓ had better의 부정형은 had better not이다. (had not better → had better not) ⓔ 과거의 습관은 used to로 나타낸다. (was used to → used to)

03 (1)은 과거의 일에 대한 약한 추측을 나타내므로 ⓑ와 같고, (2)는 과거의 일에 대한 강한 부정적 추측을 나타내므로 ⓒ와 같고, (3)은 과거의 일에 대한 강한 추측을 나타내므로 의미상 ⓐ와 같다.

04 used to는 과거의 습관이나 상태를 나타내고, would는 과거의 습관만을 나타낸다.

05 (1) 과거의 일에 대한 후회나 유감을 나타내야 하므로 should have p.p.로 쓴다. (2) '~할 필요가 없다'의 의미를 나타내는 don't have to로 쓴다. (3) 강한 충고의 의미를 나타내는 had better로 쓴다.

CHAPTER 03 to부정사

UNIT 01 명사 · 형용사 역할을 하는 to부정사

개념 QUICK CHECK p.34

POINT 01 1 보어 2 주어 3 목적어 4 목적어
POINT 02 1 × 2 ○ 3 ×

실전 연습 p.35

1 It, to, have **2** (1) a chair to sit on (2) something warm to drink **3** ③
4 ② **5** ⑤

1 주어로 쓰인 to부정사구가 긴 경우에는 가주어 it을 문장 앞에 쓰고 to부정사구는 문장 뒤로 보낸다.

2 (1) to부정사의 수식을 받는 명사가 전치사의 목적어인 경우, to부정사 뒤에 반드시 전치사를 쓴다.

(2) -thing으로 끝나는 대명사를 형용사와 to부정사가 동시에 꾸밀 때는 「대명사+형용사+to부정사」 순서로 쓴다.

3 ③은 to부정사가 형용사처럼 쓰여 뒤에서 명사(a chance)를 꾸며 주고, 나머지는 문장에서 명사처럼 쓰여 ①은 주어, ②와 ⑤는 목적어, ④는 보어 역할을 한다.

4 「be동사+to부정사」가 '~해야 한다'는 의미의 의무를 나타내므로 조동사 must로 바꿔 쓸 수 있다.

5 첫 번째 빈칸은 to부정사의 수식을 받는 a bench가 전치사의 목적어이므로 의미상 자연스러운 to sit on이 알맞고, 두 번째 빈칸은 to부정사의 부정형인 not to be가 알맞다.

개념 완성 Quiz

1 it **2** 형용사, to부정사 **3** 주어, 목적어, 보어
4 be동사 **5** not+to부정사

UNIT 02 부사 역할을 하는 to부정사와 to부정사 구문

개념 QUICK CHECK p.36

POINT 03 **1** b **2** a **3** c **4** d
POINT 04 **1** b **2** c **3** a

실전 연습 p.37

1 (1) visited New York to see (2) grew up to be
2 ⑤ **3** was so sleepy that he couldn't read
4 ③ **5** ④

1 (1) '~하기 위해서'라는 의미로 목적을 나타내는 to부정사를 쓴다.
(2) '~해서 (결국) …하다'라는 의미로 결과를 나타내는 to부정사를 쓴다.

2 부사 역할을 하는 to부정사에서 [보기]와 ⑤는 감정의 원인, ①은 형용사 수식, ②는 목적, ③은 판단의 근거, ④는 결과를 나타낸다.

3 「too+형용사/부사+to부정사」는 「so+형용사/부사+that+주어+can't+동사원형」으로 바꿔 쓸 수 있다.

4 「so+형용사/부사+that+주어+can+동사원형」은 「형용사/부사+enough+to부정사」로 바꿔 쓸 수 있다.

5 첫 번째 빈칸은 감정의 원인을 나타내는 to부정사가 알맞고, 두 번째 빈칸은 「too+형용사/부사+to부정사」 구문을 완성한다.

개념 완성 Quiz

1 부사 **2** 원인 **3** too ~ to ... **4** enough
5 for+목적격

UNIT 03 목적격 보어로 쓰이는 to부정사와 원형부정사

개념 QUICK CHECK p.38

POINT 05 **1** to go **2** to hurry **3** to join
POINT 06 **1** cry **2** to stop **3** throw

실전 연습 p.39

1 ① **2** ①, ③
3 (1) to buy (2) ride(riding) (3) think
4 ⑤ → not to fight **5** ②

1 5형식 문장에서 want, advise, expect, encourage는 모두 목적격 보어로 to부정사를 쓰는데, 사역동사인 let은 목적격 보어로 원형부정사를 쓴다.

2 준사역동사 help는 목적격 보어로 원형부정사와 to부정사를 모두 쓸 수 있다.

3 (1) 동사 allow는 목적격 보어로 to부정사를 쓴다. (2) 지각동사 see는 목적격 보어로 원형부정사나 현재분사를 쓴다. (3) 사역동사 have는 목적격 보어로 원형부정사를 쓴다.

4 사역동사 make는 목적격 보어로 원형부정사를 쓰고, 동사 tell은 목적격 보어로 to부정사를 쓴다. to부정사의 부정형은 「not+to부정사」의 형태로 쓴다.

5 ② get은 사역의 의미를 나타낼 때 목적격 보어로 to부정사를 쓴다. (→ to clean)

개념 완성 Quiz

1 to부정사 **2** 원형부정사, to부정사 **3** 지각동사
4 원형부정사 **5** get

UNIT 04 to부정사의 시제와 수동태, 독립부정사

개념 QUICK CHECK p.40

POINT 07 **1** to have cried **2** to enjoy
3 to be organized **4** to be forgotten
POINT 08 **1** d **2** a **3** b **4** c

실전 연습 p.41

1 ② 2 ⑤ 3 my friends to be blamed
4 to have lost 5 ③

1 「seem to+동사원형」 형태의 단순부정사이므로 「It seems that ~」 구문에서 that절의 동사는 주절의 시제와 동일하게 현재시제로 쓴다.

2 길을 잃고 지갑까지 도둑맞았으므로 '설상가상으로'라는 의미의 독립부정사(To make matters worse)가 들어가는 것이 자연스럽다.

3 to부정사와 의미상 주어의 관계가 수동일 때 「to be+p.p.」 형태로 쓴다.

4 「It seems(seemed) that ~.」 구문에서 that절의 시제가 seem보다 한 시제 앞서므로 「to have+p.p.」 형태의 완료부정사를 쓴다.

5 첫 번째 빈칸은 '솔직히 말하면'을 뜻하는 독립부정사가 들어가야 하고, 두 번째 빈칸은 to부정사와 의미상 주어의 관계가 수동이므로 「to be+p.p.」 형태가 들어가야 한다.

개념 완성 Quiz

1 to+동사원형 **2** to make matters worse
3 to be+p.p. **4** to have+p.p. **5** to be honest

서술형 실전 연습 pp.42~43

1 (1) It is dangerous to swim
(2) to the market to buy flowers
2 (1) in order to get
(2) is, to, leave
3 (1) needed a house to live in
(2) someone to take care of the dog
4 (1) ⓐ → go
(2) ⓑ → to lend
5 (1) eat(eating) an ice cream cone
(2) play(playing) my favorite song
6 to have lost her belongings
7 (1) is too hot to wear this coat
(2) tall enough to get on the ride
8 to solve all the puzzles in five minutes

1 (1) 주어로 쓰인 to부정사가 길면 가주어 it을 쓰고 to부정사구는 문장 뒤로 보낸다.
(2) '~하기 위해'라는 목적을 나타내는 to부정사를 사용해 문장을 완성한다.

2 (1) 목적을 나타내는 to부정사는 in order to나 so as to로 바꿔 쓸 수 있다.
(2) '~할 것이다'라는 의미로 예정을 나타내는 「be동사+to부정사」의 형태로 쓴다.

3 (1) to부정사구인 to live in이 명사인 a house를 뒤에서 수식하는 문장을 완성한다.
(2) to부정사구인 to take care of the dog이 명사인 someone을 뒤에서 수식하는 문장을 완성한다.

4 (1) 사역동사 have는 목적격 보어로 동사원형을 쓴다.
(2) 동사 ask는 목적격 보어로 to부정사를 쓴다.

5 지각동사 see와 hear는 목적격 보어로 동사원형이나 현재분사를 쓰며, 현재분사는 동작이 진행 중임을 강조한다.

6 「It seemed that ~.」 구문에서 주절인 seemed의 시제보다 that절 이하의 시제가 과거완료(had lost)로 한 시제 앞서므로 완료부정사(to+have p.p.)를 쓴다.

7 (1) '너무 더워서 이 코트를 입을 수 없다'는 의미가 되도록 too ~ to ... 구문을 사용한다.
(2) '놀이 기구를 탈 만큼 충분히 키가 크지 않다'는 의미가 되도록 enough to 구문을 사용한다.

8 '~하다니, ~하는 것을 보니'라는 의미로 판단의 근거를 나타내는 부사 역할을 하는 to부정사구를 쓴다.

개념 완성 Quiz

1 It, to부정사 **2** in order to(so as to) **3** 명사
4 동사원형 **5** 동사원형, 현재분사 **6** to+have p.p.
7 too ~ to ... **8** 부사

실전 모의고사 pp.44~47

01 ① 02 ④ 03 ④ 04 ① 05 ④ 06 ⑤
07 ④ 08 ② 09 ② 10 ④ 11 ③ 12 ②
13 ② 14 ⑤ 15 ② 16 ③ 17 ⑤ 18 ④
19 (1) is difficult to remember
(2) It is important to spend time
20 (1) are, not, to, leave (2) brave, enough, to, tell
(3) to, have, fought
21 nothing interesting to see
22 (1) too nervous to say a word

(2) too dangerous for the students to do

23 ⓐ → My parents had the old fence painted.

ⓒ → Last night, I heard the rain fall(falling) on the roof.

24 (1) to move (2) to live in (3) to find

25 (1) I don't have a pen to write with.

(2) apply → to apply

01 사역동사 make 뒤에는 목적격 보어로 원형부정사가 쓰인다.

02 5형식 문장에서 동사 encourage는 목적격 보어로 to부정사를 쓴다.

03 각각 '~와 함께 말하다', '~을 가지고 놀다'의 의미이므로 전치사 with가 들어가야 한다.

04 목적격 보어로 to부정사를 취하지 않는 동사는 사역동사 have이다. have 뒤에는 목적격 보어로 원형부정사가 쓰인다.

05 「It seems(seemed) that ~.」 구문을 「seem+to부정사」 구문으로 바꿀 때, that절의 시제가 주절의 시제보다 한 시제 앞서면 완료부정사(to+have p.p.)를 쓴다.

06 문맥상 '~할 만큼(하기에) 충분히 …하다'는 의미의 「형용사/부사+enough+to부정사」의 형태를 쓴다.

07 to부정사와 의미상 주어의 관계가 수동일 때 「to be+p.p.」 형태로 쓴다.

08 ②는 명사 뒤에서 앞의 명사를 수식하는 형용사 역할을 하고, 나머지는 모두 부사 역할을 하는 to부정사로 쓰였다. (① 형용사 수식 ③ 감정의 원인 ④ 결과 ⑤ 목적)

09 '너무 ~해서 …할 수 없다'는 「too +형용사/부사+to부정사」로 나타낼 수 있으며, 「so+형용사/부사+that+주어+can't+동사원형」으로 바꿔 쓸 수 있다. ②를 제외한 나머지는 '너무 피곤해서 공부를 할 수 없다'는 의미를 나타낸다.

10 [보기]와 ④의 to부정사는 명사를 수식하는 형용사 역할을 한다. ①, ②, ③은 각각 주어, 목적어, 보어로 쓰인 명사 역할을 하며 ⑤는 감정의 원인을 나타내는 부사 역할을 한다.

11 동사 help는 목적격 보어로 원형부정사나 to부정사를 모두 쓸 수 있고, 동사 persuade는 5형식 문장에서 목적격 보어로 to부정사를 취한다.

12 감정의 원인을 나타내는 부사 역할의 to부정사가 알맞다. 지각동사의 목적격 보어로 원형부정사가 쓰이는데 동작이 진행 중임을 강조할 때는 현재분사를 쓸 수 있다.

13 ① to begin with: 우선, 무엇보다도, ③ strange to say: 이상한 말이지만, ④ to tell the truth: 사실을 말하자면, ⑤ to make matters worse: 설상가상으로

14 ⑤ 지각동사의 목적격 보어로는 원형부정사 또는 현재분사가 와야 하므로 to가 들어갈 수 없다. 나머지는 모두 to부정사가 쓰인다. (① 진주어, ② to부정사의 형용사 역할, ③ 목적어로 쓰인 to부정사의 수동태, ④ to부정사의 부사 역할(목적))

15 ② '~하기 위해서'라는 목적을 나타내는 to부정사는 in order to나 so as to로 바꿔 쓸 수 있다. (→ so as to arrive)

16 ③ to부정사의 수식을 받는 명사 music이 전치사 to의 목적어이므로 to부정사 뒤에 전치사 to가 들어가야 한다. (→ to listen to)

17 ⑤ 「so+형용사/부사+that+주어+can't+동사원형」은 「too+형용사/부사+to부정사」로 바꿔 쓰며 부정어 not은 필요하지 않다.

18 ④ 사역의 의미로 쓰인 동사 get은 목적격 보어로 to부정사를 쓴다. (do → to do)

19 (1) 부사 역할을 하는 to부정사로 형용사를 수식한다.

(2) 주어 역할을 하는 to부정사가 쓰인 문장이다. 주어로 쓰인 to부정사가 긴 경우이므로 가주어 it을 쓰고 to부정사는 문장 뒤로 보낸다.

20 (1) to부정사가 be동사 뒤에서 보어처럼 쓰여 의무를 나타낸다.

(2) 「so+형용사/부사+that+주어+can+동사원형」은 「형용사/부사+enough+to부정사」로 바꿔 쓸 수 있다.

(3) 「It seems(seemed) that ~.」 구문을 to부정사 구문으로 바꿀 때, that절의 시제가 seem보다 한 시제 앞서면 완료부정사(to+have p.p.)를 쓴다.

21 「-thing으로 끝나는 대명사+형용사+to부정사」 순으로 쓴다.

22 '너무 ~해서 …할 수 없다'는 의미의 「too+형용사/부사+to부정사」로 문장을 완성한다. 이때 의미상의 주어는 to부정사 앞에 「for+목적격」으로 쓴다.

23 ⓐ 사역동사 have가 쓰인 5형식 문장에서 목적어와 목적격 보어의 관계가 수동이므로 목적격 보어를 과거분사로 쓴다.

ⓒ 지각동사 hear의 목적격 보어로 원형부정사나 현재분사를 쓴다.

24 (1) 문장에서 목적어로 쓰인 명사 역할을 하는 to부정사가 알맞다.

(2) 명사 a big house를 뒤에서 수식하며 형용사 역할을 하는 to부정사가 알맞다.

(3) 「It ~ to부정사」 구문으로 문장 앞에 가주어 It을 쓰고, 진주어인 to부정사구는 뒤에 쓴다.

25 (1) to부정사구의 수식을 받는 a pen이 전치사 with의 목적어이므로 to부정사 뒤에 with를 쓴다.

(2) 동사 allow는 목적격 보어로 to부정사를 쓴다. (apply → to apply)

내신만점 Level Up Test p.48

01 ④ **02** ④ **03** ⑤

04 so difficult that I couldn't answer them

05 (A) helps you (to) become a good writer

(B) advised him to write

01 want, allow, persuade는 목적격 보어로 to부정사를 쓰고, let, have는 원형부정사를 쓴다. help는 목적격 보어로 원형부정사와 to부정사를 모두 쓰는 동사이다.

02 [보기]와 ④는 목적을 나타내는 부사 역할을 한다. ①, ③, ⑤는 문장에서 목적어로 쓰인 명사 역할을 한다. ②는 명사를 수식하는 형용사 역할을 한다.

03 ⑤는 '~하게 되어'라는 의미로 감정의 원인을 나타내는 부사 역할을 한다.

04 「too+형용사+to부정사」는 「so+형용사+that+주어+can't+동사원형」으로 바꿔 쓸 수 있다. 이때 과거시제면 can't 대신 couldn't를 쓰고 타동사 뒤에 목적어를 쓰는 것에 주의한다.

05 (A) 동사 help는 목적격 보어로 원형부정사나 to부정사를 모두 쓸 수 있다.

(B) 동사 advise는 목적격 보어로 to부정사를 쓴다.

CHAPTER 04 동명사

UNIT 01 동명사의 역할과 시제 · 수동태

개념 QUICK CHECK p.50

POINT 01 **1** is **2** inviting **3** entering **4** Not getting

POINT 02 **1** being **2** having wasted **3** being asked

실전 연습 p.51

1 ⑤ **2** sorry for not arriving on time

3 having done **4** ③ **5** ②

1 전치사의 목적어로는 동명사만 가능하고 to부정사는 쓸 수 없다.

2 동명사의 부정은 동명사 앞에 not을 쓴다.

3 that절의 시제(과거)가 주절의 시제(현재)보다 앞서므로 「having+p.p.」 형태의 완료동명사로 쓴다.

4 수동의 의미를 나타내므로 수동형 동명사(being+p.p.)를 주어로 쓴다. 부정이므로 not은 동명사인 being 앞에 쓴다.

5 ② 동명사(구)가 주어로 쓰이면 단수 취급하므로 be동사를 단수형으로 쓴다. (are → is)

개념 완성 Quiz

1 동명사 **2** not+동명사 **3** having+p.p.

4 being+p.p. **5** 단수

UNIT 02 동명사의 의미상 주어와 관용 표현

개념 QUICK CHECK p.52

POINT 03 **1** his **2** her **3** ×

POINT 04 **1** 먹는 데 익숙하다 **2** 두 번 볼 가치가 있다 **3** 울어도 소용없다 **4** 웃지 않을 수 없다

실전 연습 p.53

1 ⑤ 2 are worried about Jake driving their car 3 ③
4 (1) making (2) taking (3) cleaning 5 ④

1 전치사 뒤이므로 동명사가 오고, 동명사의 행위의 주체가 문장의 주어와 다르므로 동명사 앞에 소유격이나 목적격을 써서 의미상 주어를 나타낸다.

2 전치사 about 뒤에 동명사가 들어가야 하는데, 동명사의 행위의 주체가 문장의 주어와 다르므로 동명사 앞에 의미상 주어인 Jake를 쓴다.

3 look forward to에 쓰인 to는 전치사이므로 뒤에 (동)명사가 와야 한다.

4 (1) '~하는 데 어려움을 겪다'라는 의미의 관용 표현은 have trouble -ing이다.
(2) '~하느라 바쁘다'라는 의미의 관용 표현은 be busy -ing이다.
(3) '~하는 데 시간을 쓰다'라는 의미의 관용 표현은 spend+시간+-ing이다.

5 mind는 목적어로 동명사만을 취하며 의미상의 주어가 필요하므로 첫 번째 빈칸에는 「소유격+동명사」의 형태가 알맞다. 두 번째 문장은 '~하는 데 익숙하다'는 의미이므로 빈칸에는 be used to -ing 표현이 알맞다.

개념 완성 Quiz

1 목적격, 소유격 2 앞 3 to+동명사
4 have trouble -ing 5 to+동명사

UNIT 03 목적어로 동명사와 to부정사를 쓰는 동사

개념 QUICK CHECK p.54

POINT 05 1 trying 2 to say 3 going 4 to bring
POINT 06 1 to lock 2 drinking 3 taking

실전 연습 p.55

1 (1) asking (2) to volunteer (3) teaching(to teach)
2 ② 3 ④ 4 ③ 5 ①

1 (1) avoid는 목적어로 동명사만 쓰는 동사이다. (2) decide는 목적어로 to부정사만 쓰는 동사이다. (3) start는 목적어로 동명사와 to부정사를 모두 쓰는 동사이다.

2 choose는 목적어로 to부정사를 쓰고, 나머지는 모두 목적어로 동명사를 쓴다.

3 '(미래에) ~할 것을 기억하다'라는 의미이므로 「remember+to부정사」 형태가 들어가야 한다.

4 첫 번째 문장은 '~한 것을 후회한다'는 의미이므로 목적어를 동명사로 쓴다. 두 번째 문장은 '~하기 위해 멈춰 서다'라는 의미이므로 to부정사를 쓴다.

5 ① give up은 목적어로 동명사만 쓴다. (to study → studying)

개념 완성 Quiz

1 enjoy, keep, avoid 2 plan, hope, choose
3 remember, to부정사 4 동명사 5 동명사

서술형 실전 연습 pp.56~57

1 (1) hates being treated
(2) regrets not taking her parents' advice
2 (1) he → him(his) (2) are → is
3 (1) having been (2) her not coming
4 worried about taking the math test
5 (1) waiting, cleaning (2) singing, to take
6 ④ → forgot to close
7 (1) ⓐ breaking ⓑ his(him) breaking
(2) ⓐ stopped to drink ⓑ stopped drinking
8 hates being told what to do

1 (1) 수동의 의미를 나타내므로 동명사를 수동형(being+p.p.)으로 쓴다.
(2) '~한 것을 후회하다'라는 의미이므로 목적어로 동명사가 쓰이며, 동명사의 부정은 동명사 앞에 not을 쓴다.

2 (1) 동명사의 행위 주체와 문장의 주어가 다를 때 쓰는 의미상의 주어는 소유격이나 목적격으로 쓴다.
(2) 동명사구가 문장의 주어일 때 단수 취급하여 동사는 단수로 쓴다.

3 (1) that절의 시제가 주절의 시제보다 앞서므로 완료동명사(having+p.p.)의 형태로 쓴다.
(2) 동명사의 부정형(not+-ing)을 쓰고, 행위의 주체가 문장의 주어와 다르므로 동명사 앞에 소유격이나 목적격을 써서 의미상 주어를 나타낸다.

4 전치사 about의 목적어가 들어가야 하므로 동명사인 taking으로 쓴다.

5 (1) mind, finish는 동명사만을 목적어로 가지는 동사이다.
(2) keep은 동명사만을 목적어로 가지는 동사이고, need는 to부정사만을 목적어로 가지는 동사이다.

6 '~할 것을 잊다'라는 의미이므로 「forget+to부정사」 형태로 써야 한다.

7 (1) 동명사의 행위 주체와 문장의 주어가 다를 때 소유격이나 목적격으로 의미상의 주어를 쓴다. ⓐ 문장에서 동명사의 주체는 주어인 I이고, ⓑ 문장에서 동명사의 주체는 his(him)이다.
(2) stop은 동명사만을 목적어로 취하는 동사이며 '~하는 것을 그만두다, 멈추다'라는 의미를 나타낸다. ⓐ 문장의 to부정사는 '~하기 위해서'의 목적을 나타내는 부사 역할을 한다.

8 동명사와 행위의 주체인 그(Dave)가 수동의 의미를 나타내므로 동명사를 수동태(being+p.p.)로 쓴다.

개념 완성 Quiz

1 not+동명사 **2** 소유격, 목적격 **3** having+p.p.
4 동명사 **5** keep, quit, consider
6 보어 **7** 동명사 **8** being+p.p.

실전 모의고사 pp. 58~61

01 ②	**02** ③	**03** ④	**04** ④	**05** ③	**06** ④
07 ①	**08** ⑤	**09** ④	**10** ⑤	**11** ③	**12** ④
13 ②	**14** ⑤	**15** ④	**16** ③	**17** ④	**18** ③

19 (1) am sorry for not keeping
(2) admitted having lost
20 (1) not to accept (2) working(to work)
21 (1) used to eating alone
(2) likes being considered
22 (1) his(him), coming, back
(2) watching, thriller, movies
23 (1) using smartphones
(2) Talking(To talk) in a loud voice
24 ⓑ → running, ⓔ → learning
25 (1) taking → to take
(2) Be careful of not being bitten

01 문장에서 보어 역할을 하는 동명사구이므로 writing이 알맞다.

02 동사 promise는 to부정사를 목적어로 취한다.

03 첫 번째 빈칸에는 주어 역할을 하는 동명사나 to부정사가, 두 번째 빈칸에는 동사 enjoy의 목적어인 동명사가 알맞다. 의미상 주어와 관계가 수동이므로 「being+p.p.」 형태가 들어가야 한다.

04 '~하는 것을 멈추다/그만두다'의 의미는 「stop+동명사」로 나타낸다. 의미상 능동이 알맞다.

05 동사 consider는 동명사를 목적어로 취한다. 나머지는 모두 to부정사를 목적어로 취한다.

06 look forward to -ing는 '~을 고대하다'라는 뜻의 관용 표현이고, cannot help -ing는 '~하지 않을 수 없다'라는 뜻의 관용 표현이다.

07 ①은 명사를 수식하는 현재분사, 나머지는 모두 동명사이다. (② 보어 역할, ③ 주어 역할, ④ 목적어 역할, ⑤ 전치사의 목적어 역할)

08 imagine은 목적어로 동명사를 취하는 동사이고, 동명사의 주체가 문장의 주어와 다르므로 she를 소유격 또는 목적격인 her로 써서 의미상 주어를 나타낸다.

09 love, begin, start, continue는 목적어로 동명사와 to부정사를 모두 취하는 동사이므로 빈칸에 알맞다. finish는 목적어로 동명사만 취하는 동사이다.

10 be used to -ing는 '~하는 데 익숙하다'의 의미이다.

11 첫 번째 빈칸에는 '(미래에) ~할 것을 잊다'라는 의미이므로 목적어로 to부정사가 알맞고, 두 번째 빈칸에는 '(과거에) ~했던 것을 후회하다'라는 의미이므로 목적어로 동명사가 알맞다.

12 ④ 주절의 시제보다 앞선 경우이므로 「having+p.p.」 형태의 완료동명사를 쓴다.

13 ② '미루다, 연기하다'는 뜻의 postpone은 동명사를 목적어로 취한다. (→ visiting)

14 '최고의 선수로 선택되는' 것이므로 의미상 수동태를 써야 알맞다. (→ being chosen)

15 이유를 나타내는 전치사 for 뒤에 동명사구를 쓴다. 동명사의 부정형은 동명사 앞에 not을 넣어 나타낸다.

16 ③ '~하느라 바쁘다'라는 뜻의 관용 표현은 be busy -ing이다. (to prepare → preparing)

17 ④ 「try+to부정사」는 '~하려고 노력하다'라는 의미이고, 「try+동명사」는 '시험 삼아 ~해 보다'라는 의미이다.

18 ⓐ spend+시간/돈+-ing: ~하는 데 시간/돈을 쓰다 (to playing → playing) ⓓ 동명사가 나타내는 의미가 수동이므로 「being+p.p.」 형태로 써야 한다. (inviting → being invited)

19 (1) 동명사의 부정형은 「not+동명사」로 쓴다.
(2) 동명사의 시제가 주절의 시제보다 앞서므로 완료동명사(having+p.p.)의 형태로 쓴다.

20 (1) 동사 decide는 to부정사를 목적어로 취하고, 부정의 의미는 to부정사 앞에 not을 넣어 나타낸다.
(2) continue는 동명사와 to부정사를 모두 목적어로 취한다.

21 (1) '~하는 데 익숙하다'라는 표현은 be used to -ing를 사용한다.

(2) 동명사와 주어의 관계가 수동이므로 「being+p.p.」 형태로 쓴다.

22 (1) 전치사 of의 목적어이므로 동명사를 쓰고, 동명사의 행위를 하는 주체와 주어가 다르므로 의미상의 주어를 목적격이나 소유격으로 쓴다.
(2) 동사 enjoy는 동명사만 목적어로 취하는 동사이다.

23 (1) 동사 avoid는 동명사만을 목적어로 취한다.
(2) 문장의 주어로 사용되었으므로 동명사나 to부정사로 쓴다.

24 ⓑ 동사 enjoy는 목적어로 동명사만을 취한다.
ⓔ 전치사 of의 목적어이므로 동명사의 형태로 쓴다.

25 (1) 동사 forget은 '~할 것을 잊다'라는 의미로 쓰일 때 목적어로 to부정사를 취한다.
(2) 전치사의 목적어이고 부정을 나타내며, 의미상 수동이므로 동명사의 수동형(being+p.p.) 앞에 not을 써서 표현한다.

내신만점 Level Up Test p.62

01 ① **02** ④ **03** ①, ③
04 (1) going → to go (2) to see → seeing
05 (1) decided to major in
(2) looking forward to going backpacking

01 동명사를 목적어로 취하는 동사들로 짝지어진 것은 ①이다. like와 love는 동명사와 to부정사를 모두 목적어로 취할 수 있다.

02 동명사의 주체와 문장의 주어가 다르므로 의미상의 주어를 쓰고, 동명사의 시제가 주절보다 한 시제 앞서므로 완료동명사(having+p.p.)의 형태로 쓴다. (I remember her having talked about the strange dream.)

03 ① '~하는 데 익숙하다'라는 뜻의 관용 표현은 be used to -ing이다. (to live → to living) ③ 「try+동명사」는 '시험 삼아 한번 ~해 보다', 「try+to부정사」는 '~하기 위해 노력하다'라는 뜻이다. (tried not making → tried not to make)

04 (1) plan은 to부정사를 목적어로 취하는 동사이다. (2) '~할 가치가 있다'라는 의미를 나타내는 관용 표현은 be worth -ing이다.

05 (1) 동사 decide는 to부정사를 목적어로 취한다.
(2) look forward to에 쓰인 to는 전치사이므로 뒤에 동명사가 와야 한다.

CHAPTER 05 분사

UNIT 01 현재분사와 과거분사

개념 QUICK CHECK p.64

POINT 01 **1** frozen fruit **2** a barking dog
3 a book translated in Korean

POINT 02 **1** a used car **2** cut
3 tired **4** confusing

실전 연습 p.65

1 (1) locked (2) waiting **2** ④
3 ③ **4** ③ **5** ②

1 (1) 분사가 뒤의 명사를 수식하고 있고 의미가 수동이므로 과거분사로 쓴다.
(2) 분사가 앞의 명사를 수식하고 있고 진행의 의미를 나타내므로 현재분사로 쓴다.

2 ④ 문장에서 보어 역할을 하는 동명사이고, 나머지는 '~하고 있는, ~하는'의 뜻으로 진행의 의미를 나타내는 현재분사이다.

3 명사(The science fiction book)를 분사구가 뒤에서 수식하고 있으며, 명사와의 관계가 수동이므로 과거분사를 쓴다.

4 첫 번째 빈칸에는 문장의 주격 보어 역할을 하며 주어와의 관계가 능동이므로 현재분사를, 두 번째 빈칸에는 '~한 감정을 느끼는' 이라는 의미이므로 과거분사를 쓴다.

5 ② '~한 감정을 느끼게 하는'이라는 의미를 나타내므로 현재분사로 쓴다. (→ confusing)

개념 완성 Quiz

1 진행, 능동 **2** 형용사, 명사 **3** 뒤 **4** 과거분사
5 과거분사

UNIT 02 분사구문 만드는 법과 다양한 의미

개념 QUICK CHECK p.66

POINT 03 **1** Turning off the lights
2 Walking along the street
3 Not being hungry

POINT 04 **1** b **2** c 또는 d **3** e **4** c

실전 연습 p.67

1 (1) Hearing the news (2) Listening to the radio
2 ① **3** ②
4 attending, the, same, school **5** ⑤

1 주절과 부사절의 주어가 동일하므로 접속사와 주어를 생략하고, 부사절의 동사를 현재분사 형태로 바꾸어 쓴다.

2 문맥상 조건을 나타내므로, '만약 ~라면'이라는 의미의 접속사 if가 이끄는 부사절이 알맞다.

3 ①은 시간, ②는 양보, ③은 동시동작, ④는 이유, ⑤는 시간을 나타낸다.

4 접속사를 생략하지 않은 분사구문으로, 주절과 부사절의 주어가 같으므로 주어를 생략하고 동사를 현재분사 형태로 쓴다.

5 이유를 나타내는 분사구문이며, 분사구문의 부정은 분사 앞에 not이나 never를 쓴다.

개념 완성 Quiz

1 현재분사 **2** 조건 **3** 동시동작 **4** 주어
5 not+분사구문

UNIT 03 주의해야 할 분사구문 (1)

개념 QUICK CHECK p.68

POINT 05 **1** Having watched the movie
2 Walking down the street

POINT 06 **1** a. Raising **2** b. Seen
3 a. Having spent

실전 연습 p.69

1 (1) Having had a car accident
(2) Having taken the medicine for days
2 Having lived **3** ③
4 ⓐ → (Having been) Offered **5** ③

1 부사절의 시제가 주절의 시제보다 앞선 경우이므로 완료형 분사구문(having+p.p.)을 쓴다.

2 해외에서 산 것이 4개 언어를 구사하는 것보다 먼저 일어난 과거의 일이므로, 완료형 분사구문(having +p.p.)을 쓴다.

3 첫 번째 문장은 주절의 주어와 분사의 관계가 수동이므로 과거분사인 (Being) Left가 알맞고, 두 번째 문장은 능동의 관계이므로 현재분사인 Singing이 알맞다.

4 last year로 보아 분사구문의 시제가 주절의 시제보다 앞서고, 주절의 주어와 분사의 관계가 수동이므로 수동형이면서 완료형인 분사구문으로 써야 한다. 이때 having been은 생략이 가능하다.

5 ③ 주절의 주어와 분사의 관계가 수동이므로 수동형 분사구문을 써야 한다. (→ Seen)

개념 완성 Quiz

1 완료형 **2** having+p.p. **3** being, having been
4 having been+p.p. **5** being+p.p.

UNIT 04 주의해야 할 분사구문 (2)

개념 QUICK CHECK p.70

POINT 07 **1** Mom being sick **2** School being over
3 Dinner being ready

POINT 08 **1** turned **2** coming **3** raised **4** blowing

실전 연습 p.71

1 (1) It raining heavily (2) The room getting dark
2 ③ **3** with his arms crossed
4 ③ **5** ③

1 접속사를 생략하고 부사절의 동사를 현재분사 형태로 바꾼다. 부사절의 주어와 주절의 주어가 같지 않으므로 분사 앞에 부사절의 주어를 쓴다. (2) getting 앞에 being이 생략된 분사구문이다.

2 「with+명사+분사」는 '~한 채로, ~하면서'의 의미로 동시동작을 나타내는데, 명사와 분사의 관계가 능동이므로 현재분사를 쓴다.

3 '~한 채로, ~하면서'의 의미는 「with+명사+분사」의 순서로 나타낸다.

4 부사절의 시제와 주절의 시제가 과거시제로 동일하므로, 분사구문은 being으로 시작하되, 분사구문의 주어와 문장의 주어가 일치하지 않으므로, 주어(The class)가 있는 분사구문으로 표현해야 함에 유의한다.

5 첫 번째 빈칸에는 분사 앞에 요일을 나타내는 비인칭 주어인 It을 써야 한다. 두 번째 빈칸에는 「with+명사+분사」 구문에서 명사와 분사의 관계가 수동이므로 과거분사를 써야 한다.

개념 완성 Quiz

1 앞 **2** 현재분사 **3** with **4** 생략하지 않는다
5 과거분사

서술형 실전 연습 pp. 72~73

1 (1) flying baseball (2) broken window
2 (1) satisfying (2) turned
3 Not wanting to hurt your feelings
4 (1) If you turn left at the corner
(2) Since I had a big lunch
5 (Having been) Bitten by a dog
6 (1) The weather being fine
(2) While walking on the beach
7 (1) Having grown up in Korea, Mike speaks Korean fluently.
(2) (Being) Interested in animals, Sam wants to become a vet.
8 (1) with the front door unlocked
(2) Running fast

1 (1) 공이 날아오는 것이므로 능동을 나타내는 현재분사로 명사(baseball)를 수식한다.
(2) 유리창이 깨진 것이므로 수동을 나타내는 과거분사로 명사(window)를 수식한다.

2 (1) 결말이 만족스럽지 않은 것으로 감정의 이유를 나타내므로 현재분사로 쓴다.
(2) 목적어(your phone)와 목적격 보어와의 관계가 수동이므로 과거분사로 쓴다.

3 분사구문의 부정은 분사 앞에 not이나 never를 쓴다.

4 (1) 맥락상 분사구문이 '~라면'이라는 뜻의 조건을 나타내므로 접속사 if를 쓴다.
(2) 맥락상 분사구문이 '~ 때문에'라는 뜻의 이유를 나타내므로 접속사 since를 쓰고, 완료형 분사구문 형태이므로 부사절의 동사를 주절보다 앞선 시제인 과거로 쓴다.

5 주절의 주어와 분사의 관계가 수동이며 주절보다 분사구문의 시제가 앞서므로 「Having been+p.p.」의 형태로 쓴다. 이때 having been은 생략할 수 있다.

6 (1) 주절의 주어와 분사구문의 주어가 다를 경우 분사 앞에 분사구문의 주어를 쓴다.
(2) 분사구문의 의미를 정확히 전달하기 위해서 접속사를 생략하지 않고 분사 앞에 남겨 두기도 한다.

7 (1) 'Mike는 한국에서 자랐기 때문에 한국어를 유창하게 말한다.'라는 의미가 되도록 완료형 분사구문으로 쓴다.
(2) 'Sam은 동물에 관심이 있어서, 수의사가 되고 싶어 한다.'라는 의미가 되도록 수동형 분사구문으로 쓴다.

8 (1) 「with+명사+분사」는 '~한 채로, ~하면서'의 의미로 동시동작을 나타내는데, 명사와 분사의 관계가 수동이므로 과거분사를 쓴다.
(2) 주절의 주어와 분사구문의 관계가 능동이므로 현재분사를 쓴다.

개념 완성 Quiz

1 능동, 진행, 수동, 완료 **2** 과거분사 **3** not+분사
4 having+p.p. **5** being+p.p.
6 불가능 **7** Being, Having been **8** with, 동시동작

실전 모의고사 pp. 74~77

01 ③	02 ④	03 ②	04 ③	05 ④	06 ①
07 ②	08 ⑤	09 ③	10 ②	11 ③	12 ⑤
13 ④	14 ③	15 ④	16 ⑤	17 ③	18 ③

19 (1) Arriving at the library
(2) Having lost his wallet
20 (1) The children playing in the pool
(2) Not watching TV, I don't know
21 (1) found his buildings interesting
(2) was impressed
22 (1) The weather being fine tomorrow
(2) (Being) Left alone in the darkness
23 ② → Not having eaten
24 ⓑ → Injured in the accident
25 (1) (Being) Born
(2) Having lived in Quebec for a long time

01 '~하는, ~하고 있는'이라는 의미의 능동, 진행을 나타내는 현재분사가 알맞다.

02 주어가 '~한 감정을 느끼는' 의미이므로 과거분사가 알맞다.

03 첫 번째 문장은 목적어와 목적격 보어의 관계가 능동이므로 현재분사가 알맞다. 두 번째 문장은 수식을 받는 명사와 분사와의 관계가 수동이므로 과거분사가 알맞다.

04 ① → Waiting, ② → Leaving, ④ → Getting off, ⑤ → Living 또는 Having lived

05 지각동사(hear)의 목적어(his name)와 목적격 보어의 관계가 수동이므로, 「hear+목적어+과거분사」의 형태로 쓴다.

06 ①은 보어 역할을 하는 동명사이고, 나머지는 모두 현재분사이다. (② 진행형, ③ 명사 수식, ④ 주격 보어, ⑤ 분사구문)

07 주어가 동일하므로 접속사와 부사절의 주어를 생략한 후, 부사절의 동사를 현재분사 형태로 바꾼다. 분사구문에서 being, having been은 주로 생략된다.

08 부사절의 시제가 주절의 시제보다 앞선 경우이므로 「having+p.p.」 형태의 완료형 분사구문을 쓰고, 부사절의 주어와 주절의 주어가 같지 않으므로 분사 앞에 부사절의 주어를 써야 한다.

09 ③ '~을 고려하면'이라는 의미의 관용 표현은 considering이다. (considered → considering)

10 ② 수식을 받는 명사(documentary)가 '지루한 것을 느낀(bored)'것이 아니고, '~한 감정을 불러일으키는'의 의미이므로 현재분사를 써야 한다. (→ boring)

11 시간(~할 때)을 나타내는 접속사를 쓰고, 수동형 분사구문에서 Being이 생략되었으므로 과거시제 수동형으로 쓴다.

12 양보(비록 ~이지만)를 나타내는 접속사를 쓰고, 완료형 분사구문이므로 부사절의 시제를 주절보다 한 시제 앞선 과거완료로 쓴다.

13 첫 번째 빈칸은 접속사와 주어가 생략된 분사구문이므로 현재분사를 쓰고, 두 번째 빈칸은 사역동사(have)의 목적어와 목적격 보어의 관계가 수동이므로 과거분사를 쓴다.

14 ③ 주절의 시제보다 분사구문의 시제가 한 시제 앞서므로 부사절은 과거완료로 써야 한다. (didn't sleep → hadn't slept)

15 「with+명사+분사」 구문에서 명사(her dog)와 분사의 관계가 능동이므로 현재분사를 쓴다.

16 ⑤ 주어(Laura)와 분사와의 관계가 능동이므로 현재분사로 써야 한다. (→ entering)

17 ③ 의미상 주절의 주어와 분사가 수동의 관계이므로 과거분사를 써야 한다. 이때 being은 생략할 수 있다. (Telling → Being told/Told)

18 ⓐ 수식을 받는 명사와 분사와의 관계가 수동이므로 과거분사로 써야 한다. (locating → located) ⓓ 주절의 주어와 같은 분사구문의 주어는 생략한다. (I having → Having)

19 (1) 부사절과 주절의 주어가 동일하므로 접속사와 부사절의 주어를 생략한 후, 부사절의 동사를 현재분사 형태로 바꾼다.
(2) 부사절의 시제(현재완료)가 주절의 시제(현재)보다 앞선 경우이므로 완료형 분사구문(having+p.p.)을 쓴다.

20 (1) 분사가 구를 이루어 명사를 꾸미고 있으므로 분사구가 명사 뒤에 온다.
(2) 이유를 나타내는 분사구문이며, 분사구문의 부정은 분사 앞에 not이나 never를 쓴다.

21 (1) 건물이 흥미로운 감정을 느끼게 하는 것이므로 「find+목적어+목적격 보어(현재분사)」의 형태로 쓴다.
(2) 주어가 '~한 감정을 느끼는' 것이므로 과거분사를 쓴다.

22 (1) 분사구문의 주어와 주절의 주어가 같지 않으므로 분사 앞에 주어를 쓴다.
(2) 주어와 분사와의 관계가 수동이므로 수동형 분사구문(being+p.p.)을 쓰고, 이때 being은 생략할 수 있다.

23 분사구문의 시제가 주절의 시제보다 앞선 완료형 분사구문이고, 부정형이므로 「Not having+p.p.」의 형태로 쓴다.

24 ⓑ 주어와 분사의 관계가 수동이므로 과거분사를 쓴다. (Injuring → Injured)

25 (1) '태어났다'는 수동의 의미를 나타내므로 과거분사를 사용한다.
(2) 부사절의 시제가 주절의 시제보다 앞서므로 완료형 분사구문(having+p.p.)으로 쓴다.

내신만점 Level Up Test p.78

01 ③ **02** ② **03** ②, ④

04 Being shy, I couldn't ask for her autograph.

05 (A) Do you feel depressed
(B) Not getting enough sleep

01 분사구문으로 바꾼 문장은 Not knowing Chinese, she can't understand the lecture.로 2번째로 오는 단어는 knowing이다.

02 ⓒ 사람이 느끼게 되는 감정을 나타내므로 과거분사로 써야 한다. (moving → moved) ⓓ 분사구문의 부정은 분사 앞에 not을 쓴다. (Having not → Not having) ⓔ는 '~한 감정을 느끼게 하는'의 의미가 알맞으므로 disappointing이 알맞다.

03 ⓑ 완료형 분사구문이 쓰였으므로, 부사절의 시제를 주절보다 한 시제 앞선 과거로 써야 한다. (don't sleep → didn't sleep)
ⓓ 주절의 주어와 다르므로 분사 앞에 주어(The weather)를 써야 한다.

04 이유를 나타내는 부사절 As I was shy를 분사구문으로 써서 나타낸다.

05 (A) 주어가 우울한 감정을 느끼는 것이므로 depress를 과거분사로 쓴다.
(B) 능동을 나타내는 분사구문이며 부정형이므로 현재분사 앞에 not을 쓴다.

CHAPTER 06 수동태

UNIT 01 수동태의 의미와 형태

개념 QUICK CHECK p.80

POINT 01 **1** was sent **2** invited
3 is spoken **4** resembles

POINT 02 **1** All life should be respected.
2 The roof is being repaired.
3 His phone has been stolen.

실전 연습 p.81

1 (1) painted (2) is visited **2** The light bulb was invented by Thomas Edison. **3** ④
4 ③ **5** ④

1 (1) 주어가 동작의 주체이므로 능동태이고, 과거 시점의 부사(yesterday)가 있으므로 과거시제로 쓴다.
(2) 주어가 동작의 대상이 되므로 수동태(be동사+p.p.)이고, 일반적인 상황을 나타내므로 현재시제로 쓴다.

2 주어가 동작의 대상이므로 수동태인 「be동사+p.p.+by+행위자」의 어순으로 쓴다.

3 능동태 문장에서 동사가 현재진행형이므로, 수동태로 바꿨을 때 수와 시제를 맞춘 진행형 수동태(be동사의 현재형+being+p.p.)의 형태로 쓴다.

4 첫 번째 빈칸에 들어갈 자동사 happen은 수동태로 쓸 수 없으므로 능동이며 과거시제가 알맞다. 두 번째 문장은 주어가 동작의 대상이 되는 수동태 문장이며 조동사 must가 쓰였으므로 「조동사+be+p.p.」의 형태로 쓴다.

5 ④ 동사 resemble은 수동태로 쓰지 않으므로 The twins resemble their grandfather.로 써야 한다.

개념 완성 Quiz

1 be동사+p.p. **2** by **3** be동사+being+p.p.
4 조동사+be+p.p. **5** 수동태

UNIT 02 4형식과 5형식 문장의 수동태

개념 QUICK CHECK p.82

POINT 03 **1** A parcel was sent to me.
2 Two classes were given to us.
3 Dinner was cooked for us.

POINT 04 **1** is called **2** to study
3 singing

실전 연습 p.83

1 (1) was shown some old pictures
(2) were shown to me
2 ⑤ **3** ④
4 (1) ⓑ → to clean (2) ⓐ → was given **5** ③

1 (1) 간접목적어를 주어로 하여 「주어(간접목적어)+be동사+p.p.+직접목적어+by+행위자」의 형태로 쓴다.
(2) 직접목적어를 주어로 하여 「주어(직접목적어)+be동사+p.p.+전치사+간접목적어+by+행위자」의 형태로 쓰고, 이때 동사가 show이므로 전치사는 to를 쓴다.

2 직접목적어가 주어로 쓰인 수동태 문장이고 동사가 buy이므로 간접목적어 앞에 for를 써야 한다.

3 사역동사의 목적격 보어로 쓰인 동사원형은 수동태 문장에서 to부정사 형태로 바꿔서 「be동사+p.p.」 뒤에 쓴다.

4 (1) 동사 tell의 목적격 보어는 to부정사이므로 수동태로 전환 시 형태 변화 없이 그대로 to부정사로 써야 한다.
(2) 직접목적어가 주어로 쓰인 수동태 문장이므로 동사는 「be동사+p.p.」 형태로 써야 한다.

5 ③ 4형식 문장에서 동사 make는 직접목적어를 주어로 하는 수동태만 쓸 수 있다. (→ A beautiful dress was made for Sally by her mother.)

개념 완성 Quiz

1 간접목적어, 직접목적어 **2** for **3** to부정사
4 to부정사, 분사 **5** buy, make, cook

UNIT 03 주의해야 할 수동태

개념 QUICK CHECK p.84

POINT 05 **1** The game was put off.
2 My proposal was turned down.
3 Don't be looked down on by him.

POINT 06 **1** with **2** of **3** from

실전 연습 p.85

1 (1) was brought up (2) were turned off
2 (1) was turned down by her (2) was put off until tomorrow by the manager **3** ④
4 ③ **5** ②

1 bring up(양육하다), turn off(~을 끄다) 등의 동사구는 한 단어로 취급하여 수동태로 바꾼다.

2 turn down(~을 거절하다), put off(~을 연기하다) 등의 동사구는 한 단어로 취급하므로 동사를 「be동사+p.p.」로 바꾸고 나머지는 그대로 붙여 쓴 후, 뒤에 「by+행위자」를 쓴다.

3 '~으로 유명하다'는 뜻은 be known for, '~로 구성되다'는 뜻은 be composed of, '~로 가득 차 있다'는 뜻은 be filled with로 모두 by 이외의 전치사를 쓴다.

4 '~에 싫증나다'는 be tired of, '~을 돌보다'를 뜻하는 동사구는 take care of이다.

5 ②는 동사구의 수동태 뒤에 행위자를 나타내는 by가 들어가고, 나머지는 전치사 with가 들어간다.

개념 완성 Quiz

1 be동사+p.p. **2** 수동태 **3** for **4** of
5 with

서술형 실전 연습 pp.86~87

1 (1) was being chased (2) will be built
2 (1) was sent to me (2) were laughed at
3 (1) with (2) off (3) at
4 (1) was cooked for us by the Italian chef
(2) were seen to go into the concert hall (by us)
5 (1) The children were forced to learn how to swim.
(2) My sister and I were brought up by our grandparents.
6 (1) is crowded with many people
(2) has been painted red
(3) was made for me by Mom
7 (1) has been taken care of by a kind lady
(2) was sent dog snacks and toys by our volunteers
8 (1) is called (2) has been visited
(3) was designed

1 (1) 수와 시제를 맞추어 과거진행형 수동태인 「was being+p.p.」의 형태로 쓴다.
(2) 미래를 나타내는 조동사가 쓰였으므로 조동사의 수동태인 「will be+p.p.」의 형태로 쓴다.

2 (1) 직접목적어를 주어로 하는 수동태이며 동사가 send이므로, 간접목적어 앞에 to를 쓴다.
(2) laugh at은 동사구이므로 전체를 하나의 단어로 취급하여 수동태로 만든다.

3 (1) be covered with: ~로 덮여 있다 (2) put off: ~를 연기하다 (3) be surprised at: ~에 놀라다

4 (1) 동사 cook은 4형식 문장에서 직접목적어만 주어로 하는 수동태로 바꿀 수 있고, 이때 간접목적어 앞에는 전치사 for를 쓴다.
(2) 지각동사 see의 목적격 보어로 쓰인 동사원형은 수동태에서 to부정사로 바꿔 쓴다.

5 (1) force는 목적격 보어로 to부정사를 취하므로, 수동태로 쓸 때 동사를 「be동사+p.p.」로 바꾼 뒤, 뒤에 to부정사를 그대로 쓴다.
(2) 동사구는 전체를 하나의 동사로 취급하여 수동태로 만든다.

6 (1) be crowded with: ~로 붐비다 (2) 완료형 수동태는 「have/has+been+p.p.」로 나타내며, 5형식 문장의 수동태에서 형용사인 목적격 보어는 「be동사+p.p.」 뒤에 그대로 쓴다. (3) make는 직접목적어만 수동태의 주어로 쓰는 동사이고, 수동태로 바꿀 때

간접목적어 앞에 전치사 for를 쓴다.

7 (1) take care of가 동사구이므로 전체를 하나의 동사로 취급하여 완료형 수동태로 쓴다.
(2) 간접목적어(her)를 주어로 하는 4형식 문장의 수동태로 쓴다.

8 (1) '~로 불린다'라는 의미이므로 수동태를 현재시제로 쓴다.
(2) '최근 수천만 명의 사람들에 의해 방문되고 있다'는 의미이므로 완료형 수동태로 쓴다.
(3) '자유의 여신상이 설계되어졌다'는 의미이므로 과거시제 수동태로 쓴다.

개념 완성 Quiz

1 조동사+be+p.p. **2** to **3** with, at
4 동사원형, to부정사 **5** be동사+p.p.
6 buy, make, write **7** 직접목적어 **8** have been+p.p.

실전 모의고사 pp.88~91

01 ⑤	02 ②	03 ④	04 ③	05 ④	06 ⑤
07 ①	08 ③	09 ④	10 ③	11 ②	12 ②
13 ⑤	14 ②	15 ③	16 ⑤	17 ③	18 ④

19 (1) was called a genius (2) had been stolen
20 (1) My mom was given a flower basket by me.
(2) A flower basket was given to my mom by me.
21 (1) be repaired (2) be taught Chinese
(3) be cooked for the family
22 (1) are being baked for me by Grandma
(2) was asked to go see a musical by Tom
23 (1) must be turned off (2) is allowed to eat
24 ⓑ → Paper should be recycled for the Earth (by us).
ⓒ → A nice pencil case was bought for me by my brother.
25 (1) A box of chocolates was sent to her by Mark.
She was sent a box of chocolates by Mark.
(2) talk → to talk[talking]

01 next Saturday가 쓰였으므로 미래를 나타내는 조동사 will과 수동태 「be+p.p.」가 함께 쓰여야 한다.

02 능동태 문장 The doctor told Mr. Park to stop smoking.에서 목적격 보어가 to부정사구이므로, 「be동사+p.p.」 바로 뒤에 to부정사구가 그대로 온다.

03 능동태의 시제가 과거진행형이므로 시제를 적용하여 진행형 수동태(be동사의 과거형+being+p.p.)로 쓴다.

04 간접목적어가 주어로 쓰인 수동태 문장은 동사 teach를 「be동사+p.p.」로 바꾸고 뒤에 직접목적어를 바로 이어 쓴다.

05 주어가 행위의 대상이므로 cannot 뒤에 「be+p.p.」를 써서 수동태로 만든다.

06 사역동사 make의 수동태는 「be동사+p.p.」 뒤에 목적격 보어인 동사원형(join)을 to부정사로 바꿔 써야 한다.

07 ① 상태를 나타내는 타동사 lack은 수동태로 쓰지 않는다.

08 ③ '~에게 알려지다'는 뜻인 be known to로 써야 한다. be known for는 '~로 유명하다', be known as는 '~으로 알려져 있다'는 뜻이다.

09 첫 번째 문장은 시제가 현재완료이므로 완료형 수동태(has been+p.p.)로 쓴다. 두 번째 문장은 현재 진행 중이므로 진행형 수동태(be동사+being+p.p.)로 쓴다.

10 직접목적어를 수동태의 주어로 쓸 때 동사 send는 간접목적어 앞에 전치사 to를, 동사 make는 전치사 for를, 동사 ask는 전치사 of를 쓴다.

11 상태를 나타내는 타동사 resemble은 수동태로 쓰지 않는다.

12 지각동사 see의 목적격 보어로 쓰인 동사원형은 수동태 문장에서 to부정사 형태로 바뀌어 「be동사+p.p.」 뒤에 쓴다.

13 동사 buy는 직접목적어만을 주어로 쓸 수 있고, 간접목적어 앞에 전치사 for를 쓴다.

14 5형식 문장을 수동태로 만들 때에는 목적어를 주어로 하고, 목적격 보어는 주어로 쓸 수 없다. 주어진 문장은 목적격 보어가 명사이므로 「be동사+p.p.」 뒤에 목적격 보어를 그대로 쓴다.

15 be made of/from: ~으로 만들어지다

16 ⑤ 문맥상 '~라고 여겨진다'라는 뜻이므로 수동태인 is regarded로 쓴다.

17 ③ 4형식 문장에서 동사 make는 직접목적어를 주어로 하는 수동태만 쓸 수 있다. (→ An egg sandwich was made for me by Dad.)

18 ⓑ 동사구를 수동태로 쓸 때는 한 단어처럼 취급하여 같이 붙여 써야 한다. (laughed → laughed at) ⓓ 5형식 문장에서 사역동사 make의 수동태는 목적격 보어를 to부정사로 바꿔 써야 한다. (do → to do)

19 (1) 5형식 문장을 수동태로 쓸 때 명사인 목적격 보어는 「be동사+p.p.」 뒤에 그대로 쓴다.
(2) 과거의 특정 시점보다 이전에 발생했으므로 수동태를 과거완료인 「had been+p.p.」의 형태로 쓴다.

20 (1) 간접목적어를 주어로 하는 수동태이므로, 「be동사+p.p.」 뒤에 직접목적어를 쓴다.
(2) 직접목적어를 주어로 하는 수동태에서는 간접목적어 앞에 전치사를 쓰는데, 동사가 give이므로 to를 쓴다.

21 조동사가 있는 수동태는 「조동사+be+p.p.」로 표현한다. (2) 간접목적어(Suho)를 주어로 한 수동태이므로 be taught 뒤에 직접목적어 Chinese를 쓴다. (3) 직접목적어(Spaghetti)를 주어로 한 수동태이므로 간접목적어(the family) 앞에 전치사 for를 쓴다.

22 (1) 능동태의 시제가 현재진행형이므로, 시제와 수에 맞춰 진행형 수동태(be동사+being+p.p.)로 쓴다.
(2) 5형식 문장의 목적어를 주어로 하여 수동태로 만들고, 목적격 보어인 to부정사는 「be동사+p.p.」 뒤에 그대로 쓴다.

23 (1) 조동사 뒤에 동사구 turn off를 한 단어로 취급해 수동태로 쓴다.
(2) 주어가 no one이므로 not을 사용하지 않고 수동태로 쓰며, allow의 목적격 보어가 to부정사이므로 그대로 to부정사로 쓴다. 이용 규칙이므로 현재시제로 쓴다.

24 ⓐ의 소유를 나타내는 타동사 has, ⓓ의 자동사 appear는 수동태로 쓰지 않는다. ⓒ는 4형식 문장으로, 동사 buy는 직접목적어를 주어로 하는 수동태만 쓸 수 있다.

25 (1) 동사 send는 4형식 문장에서 간접목적어, 직접목적어를 모두 주어로 사용하여 수동태를 만들 수 있다. 직접목적어를 주어로 할 경우 간접목적어 앞에 전치사 to를 쓴다.
(2) 지각동사가 쓰인 5형식 문장을 수동태로 쓸 때 목적격 보어로 쓰인 동사원형 talk는 to부정사나 현재분사로 바꿔 to talk 또는 talking으로 써야 한다.

내신만점 Level Up Test p.92

01 ② **02** ①, ③, ④ **03** ③
04 (1) is filled with a lot of people
(2) is being served by the waiter
05 (A) is looked up to by (B) were pleased with this

01 주어진 5형식 문장을 수동태로 바꾸면 I was made to set the table for dinner by my mother.이다. 사역동사가 쓰인 5형식 문장을 수동태로 쓸 때 목적격 보어는 to부정사로 바꾼다.

02 4형식 문장은 간접목적어와 직접목적어를 각각 주어로 하는 수동태 문장으로 바꿔 쓸 수 있으며, 동사가 give이므로 직접목적어를 주어로 하는 수동태 문장에서 간접목적어 앞에 전치사는 to를 쓴다.

03 ③ 4형식 문장에서 직접목적어를 수동태의 주어로 쓸 때 동사 ask는 간접목적어 앞에 전치사 of를 쓴다. (→ was asked of me)

04 (1) be filled with는 '~로 가득 차 있다'는 뜻이다.
(2) 진행형 수동태인 「be동사+being+p.p.」의 형태로 쓰고 뒤에 「by+행위자」를 쓴다.

05 (A) '~을 존경하다'는 뜻의 동사구 look up to를 한 단어로 취급하여 수동태로 쓴다. 행위자 앞에 쓰는 전치사 by를 빠뜨리지 않도록 주의한다.
(B) '~에 기뻐하다'는 뜻의 표현인 be pleased with를 쓴다.

CHAPTER 07 접속사

UNIT 01 접속사 that, 시간의 접속사

개념 QUICK CHECK p.94

POINT 01	**1** b	**2** c	**3** d	**4** a
POINT 02	**1** until	**2** when	**3** get	

실전 연습 p.95

1 ① **2** ⑤ **3** (1) until
(2) while **4** ⓒ → gets **5** ⑤

1 that절이 문장의 주어인 경우 대개 가주어 it을 주어 자리에 쓰고 that절은 뒤로 보낸다.

2 [보기]와 ⑤의 that은 보어, ①은 주어, ②와 ④는 목적어, ③은 동격의 절을 이끄는 접속사 역할을 한다.

3 (1) '~할 때까지'를 뜻하는 접속사는 until이 알맞다. (2) '~하는 동안'을 뜻하는 접속사는 while이 알맞다.

4 시간의 부사절에서는 현재시제로 미래를 나타낸다.

5 ⑤ 잠자리에 들기 전에 이를 닦으라고 하는 것이 맥락상 자연스러우므로 '~하기 전에'를 뜻하는 접속사가 쓰여야 한다. (after → before)

개념 완성 Quiz

1 it　2 명사절　3 until　4 현재시제　5 as

UNIT 02 이유 · 조건 · 양보의 접속사

개념 QUICK CHECK p.96

POINT 03 ~ 04 A 1 조건　2 이유　3 양보
B 1 because　2 don't　3 Despite
4 Unless

실전 연습 p.97

1 ②　2 As(as)　3 ②
4 ④　5 ③

1 표가 매진되었기 때문에 영화를 볼 수 없었다는 것이 맥락상 자연스러우므로 이유를 나타내는 접속사가 알맞다.

2 첫 번째 빈칸은 '~ 때문에', 두 번째 빈칸은 '~함에 따라', 세 번째 빈칸은 '~일 때'라는 의미의 접속사가 적절하므로 공통으로 들어갈 말은 as이다.

3 if ~ not은 '만약 ~하지 않으면'이라는 뜻을 나타내며 접속사 unless와 바꿔 쓸 수 있다.

4 '비록 ~이지만'이라는 뜻으로 양보의 의미를 나타내는 접속사가 들어가야 한다.

5 ③ 양보를 나타내는 접속사 though 뒤에는 절이 와야 하는데, 절이 아닌 명사구(the cold weather)가 이어지므로 양보의 전치사(구)가 쓰여야 알맞다. (Though → Despite(In spite of))

개념 완성 Quiz

1 since　2 as　3 unless
4 although, though　5 명사(구)

UNIT 03 상관접속사, 간접의문문

개념 QUICK CHECK p.98

POINT 05 1 and　2 nor　3 read　4 have
POINT 06 1 Do you know what he is doing?
2 I wonder if she came back.
3 Why do you believe aliens exist?

실전 연습 p.99

1 ④　2 (1) Not, but　(2) as, well, as
3 (1) what Lisa wants for her birthday
(2) if(whether) he went to the rock concert
4 ②　5 ⑤

1 의미상 '*A*와 *B* 둘 다 아닌'을 뜻하는 neither *A* nor *B*가 적절하다.

2 (1) '*A*가 아니라 *B*'라는 뜻의 상관접속사인 not *A* but *B*를 사용한다.
(2) '*A*뿐만 아니라 *B*도'라는 뜻의 상관접속사인 *B* as well as *A*를 사용한다.

3 (1) 의문사가 있는 간접의문문이므로 「의문사+주어+동사」의 어순으로 쓴다.
(2) 의문사가 없는 간접의문문이므로 「if(whether)+주어+동사」의 어순으로 쓴다.

4 ② 의문사가 있는 간접의문문에서 의문사가 주어인 경우에는 「의문사+동사」의 순서로 쓴다. (→ who won the contest)

5 ⑤ 상관접속사의 *A*와 *B*에 들어가는 두 요소는 문법적으로 같은 형태여야 한다. (meeting → to meet)

개념 완성 Quiz

1 neither *A* nor *B*　2 not *A* but *B*　3 if(whether)
4 의문사+동사　5 think, believe

서술형 실전 연습 pp.100~101

1 (1) It is disappointing that Andrew didn't keep his promise.
(2) The trouble is that my daughter doesn't want to live here.
2 (1) If you leave home now
(2) As soon as she heard the doorbell
3 ⓒ → is over
4 (1) neither, nor　(2) not, only, but, also
5 (1) because of the heavy rain
(2) Although I turned on the air conditioner
6 (1) Unless you go to the party(If you don't go to the party)
(2) after I clean the house

7 (1) will rain → rains
   (2) won't rain → rains
8 (1) why you want to be a school newspaper reporter
   (2) if(whether) you have written any articles before
   (3) if(whether) you are good at talking with people

1 (1) that절을 주어로 써야 하는데, 가주어 It을 주어 자리에 쓰고 that절은 뒤로 보낸다.
   (2) that절을 보어로 써서 문장을 완성한다.

2 (1) '~라면'이라는 뜻의 조건을 나타내는 접속사 if를 사용하여 부사절을 쓴다.
   (2) '~하자마자'라는 뜻의 시간을 나타내는 접속사 as soon as를 사용하여 부사절을 쓴다.

3 시간의 부사절에서는 현재시제로 미래를 나타낸다.

4 (1) '*A*도 *B*도 둘 다 아닌'이라는 의미의 neither *A* nor *B*를 사용하여 문장을 완성한다.
   (2) '*A*뿐만 아니라 *B*도'라는 의미의 not only *A* but also *B*를 사용하여 문장을 완성한다.

5 (1) 문맥상 이유를 나타내는 말이 되어야 하는데 괄호 안의 말이 명사구이므로 because of를 사용하여 문장을 완성한다.
   (2) 주어와 동사가 포함된 절이므로 문맥상 양보의 의미를 나타내는 접속사 although를 사용하여 문장을 완성한다.

6 (1) '만약 ~하지 않는다면'이라는 뜻의 접속사 unless나 if ~ not을 사용한다.
   (2) '~한 후에'라는 뜻의 접속사 after를 사용한다. 시간과 조건의 부사절에서 현재시제가 미래를 대신하므로 현재시제로 쓴다.

7 조건의 부사절에서 현재시제가 미래를 대신한다. unless는 '~하지 않으면'의 의미로 뒤에 not이 쓰이지 않는다.

8 (1) 간접의문문은 「의문사+주어+동사」의 어순으로 쓴다. (2), (3) 의문사가 없는 의문문의 간접의문문은 「if(whether)+주어+동사」의 어순으로 쓴다.

개념 완성 Quiz

1 It **2** as soon as **3** 현재시제 **4** neither *A* nor *B*
5 because, despite **6** after **7** unless **8** whether, if

실전 모의고사 pp. 102~105

01 ④	02 ②	03 ②	04 ④	05 ④	06 ⑤
07 ②	08 ⑤	09 ①	10 ③	11 ②	12 ②
13 ④	14 ②	15 ⑤	16 ④	17 ⑤	18 ③

19 (1) she didn't feel well, she stayed home all day
   (2) he has never been abroad, he speaks English fluently
20 (1) both soccer and baseball
   (2) either soccer or baseball
   (3) neither soccer nor baseball
21 (1) Unless you have the receipt, you can't get a refund.
   (2) It is interesting that some animals can use tools.
22 ⓑ → We will wait until Mr. Davis gives us a call.
   ⓒ → Amy neither speaks nor understands Chinese.
23 (1) Who do you believe donated the valuable painting?
   (2) I'd like to know if(whether) you are going to join us for dinner.
24 (1) While (2) Though (3) As long as
25 (1) ① → where James is
   (2) ⑤ → either

01 서두르지 않으면 늦을 것이라는 의미가 되는 것이 자연스러우므로 '~하지 않는다면'이라는 뜻의 접속사 unless가 알맞다.

02 공부를 열심히 했기 때문에 좋은 성적을 받았다는 의미가 되는 것이 자연스러우므로 '~ 때문에'라는 뜻의 접속사 since가 알맞다.

03 접속사 if는 조건의 부사절에서는 '만약 ~하면', 의문사가 없는 간접의문문에서는 '~인지 아닌지'라는 의미를 나타낸다.

04 주어진 문장과 ④의 as는 '~ 때문에', ①은 '~할 때', ③은 '~인 대로', ②, ⑤는 '~함에 따라'라는 의미로 쓰였다.

05 맥락상 첫 번째 빈칸에는 '~하자마자'라는 뜻의 as soon as, 두 번째 빈칸에는 '~할 때까지'라는 뜻의 until이 알맞다.

06 맥락상 첫 번째 빈칸에는 '비록 ~일지라도'라는 뜻의 although, 두 번째 빈칸에는 '~하는 동안'이라는 뜻의 while이 알맞다.

07 ②는 관계대명사로 쓰여 선행사를 수식하는 that이고 나머지는 모두 접속사 that이다. (① 보어, ③ 동격, ④ 목적어, ⑤ 주어)

08 '*A*뿐만 아니라 *B*도'라는 뜻의 접속사인 not only *A* but (also) *B*를 사용한다. I 뒤에 am이 나오므로 ③ Both — and는 알맞지 않다.

09 의문사가 있는 간접의문문은 「의문사+주어+동사」의 어순으로 쓴다. 질문의 you, your는 대답할 때 I, my로 바뀌는 것에 유의한다.

10 첫 번째 빈칸에는 명사절을 이끌며 문장에서 목적어 역할을 하는 접속사 that이 들어가고, 두 번째 빈칸에는 '~한 후에'를 뜻하는 시간 접속사 after가 알맞다.

11 '*A* 또는 *B* 둘 중 하나'라는 의미를 나타내므로 either *A* or *B*를 써야 한다.

12 의문사가 있는 간접의문문인데 주절의 동사가 think이므로 간접의문문의 의문사를 문장 맨 앞에 쓴다.

13 주어진 문장과 ④는 양보를 나타내는 접속사(although 등)가 알맞다. ①과 ③은 이유(because 등), ②는 시간(when), ⑤는 조건(if)을 나타내는 접속사가 알맞다.

14 ② 의문사가 없는 간접의문문은 「if(whether)+주어+동사」의 형태로 쓴다. (what → if(whether))

15 ⑤ not only *A* but also *B*가 주어로 쓰이는 경우 동사는 *B*(his parents)에 수를 일치시켜야 한다. (enjoys → enjoy)

16 ④ 조건의 부사절에서는 현재시제로 미래를 나타낸다. (will be → is)

17 ⑤ '*A*와 *B* 둘 다 아닌'의 의미를 나타내야 하므로 neither *A* nor *B*를 써야 한다. (→ The movie was neither interesting nor touching.)

18 ⓒ 상관접속사의 *A*와 *B*에 들어가는 두 요소는 문법적으로 같은 형태여야 한다. (→ skating)

19 각각 이유, 양보의 의미를 나타내는 부사절이 있는 문장을 만든다.

20 (1) 축구와 야구 둘 다 좋아하는 경우이므로 both *A* and *B*로 쓴다.
(2) 축구와 야구 중 하나만 좋아하는 경우이므로 either *A* or *B*로 쓴다.
(3) 축구와 야구 모두 좋아하지 않는 경우이므로 neither *A* nor *B*로 쓴다.

21 (1) '~하지 않는다면'이라는 뜻의 접속사 unless를 사용한다.
(2) 가주어 it을 주어 자리에 쓰고 진주어 that절은 뒤로 보낸다.

22 ⓑ 시간의 부사절에서는 현재시제로 미래를 나타낸다. ⓒ 상관접속사의 *A*와 *B*에 들어가는 두 요소는 문법적으로 같은 형태여야 한다.

23 (1) 주절의 동사가 believe이므로 간접의문문의 의문사를 문장 맨 앞에 쓴다.
(2) 의문사가 없는 의문문의 간접의문문은 if나 whether를 사용한다.

24 맥락상 (1)은 '반면에'라는 뜻의 while이, (2)는 '비록 ~이지만'이라는 뜻의 though가, (3)은 '~하는 한'이라는 뜻의 as long as가 알맞다.

25 (1) 의문사가 있는 간접의문문은 「의문사+주어+동사」의 어순으로 쓴다.
(2) 맥락상 '*A* 또는 *B* 둘 중 하나'라는 뜻이 되어야 하므로 either *A* or *B*로 쓴다.

내신만점 Level Up Test p.106

01 ②, ④ **02** ②

03 (1) Though the river was not safe to swim in, he jumped in to save the girl.
(2) Unless you read the instructions carefully, you won't be able to make the model airplane.

04 (1) You eat neither meat(fish) nor fish(meat).
(2) what the ingredients are

01 ② neither *A* nor *B*는 '*A*와 *B* 둘 다 아닌'이라는 뜻이다.
④ while은 이 문장에서 '반면에'라는 뜻으로 대조를 나타낸다.

02 ⓐ는 의문사가 없는 간접의문문이므로 if 또는 whether, ⓑ는 '만약 ~하지 않으면'이라는 뜻의 unless, ⓒ는 '비록 ~일지라도'라는 뜻의 although, ⓓ는 '~ 때문에'라는 뜻의 because/since/as, ⓔ는 목적어절을 이끄는 that이 알맞다.

03 (1) '비록 ~이지만'이라는 뜻의 양보의 접속사 though를 사용한다.
(2) '만약 ~하지 않으면'이라는 뜻의 조건의 접속사 unless를 사용한다.

04 (1) neither *A* nor *B*를 사용하여 문장을 완성한다.
(2) 의문사가 있는 간접의문문은 「의문사+주어+동사」의 어순으로 쓴다.

CHAPTER 08
관계사

UNIT 01 관계대명사의 종류와 역할, 관계대명사 what

개념 QUICK CHECK p.108

POINT 01 **1** friends whom I can trust
2 the table that stands in the kitchen
3 the boy whose mother is an actress
4 the most interesting movie that I've seen

POINT 02 **1** What **2** which **3** what

실전 연습 p.109

1 (1) which (2) whom (3) that **2** (1) who(that) is singing on the street (2) whose(of which) lives are in danger **3** ①
4 what, I, experienced **5** ④

1 (1) 선행사가 동물이므로 주격 관계대명사로 which를 쓴다. (2) 선행사가 사람이므로 목적격 관계대명사로 whom을 쓴다. (3) 선행사가 -thing으로 끝나는 명사이므로 주격 관계대명사로 that을 쓴다.

2 (1) 선행사가 사람이므로 주격 관계대명사로 who나 that을 쓴다.
(2) 관계대명사와 뒤의 명사가 소유의 관계이므로 소유격 관계대명사인 whose나 of which를 쓴다.

3 ②, ③, ④는 목적격 관계대명사, ⑤는 뒤에 분사가 이어지는 「주격 관계대명사+be동사」로 생략할 수 있다. ①은 주격 관계대명사로 생략할 수 없다.

4 선행사를 포함하는 관계대명사 what이 들어가 문장의 목적어 역할을 하는 명사절을 완성한다.

5 첫 번째 빈칸에는 소유격 관계대명사 whose, 두 번째 빈칸에는 선행사를 포함하는 관계대명사 what, 세 번째 빈칸에는 관계대명사 that이 들어가야 한다.

개념 완성 Quiz

1 whom **2** whose **3** 목적격 관계대명사
4 what **5** that

UNIT 02 주의해야 할 관계대명사의 쓰임

개념 QUICK CHECK p.110

POINT 03 **1** the writer for whom I'm waiting
2 the report he is referring to
3 the theater to which we went

POINT 04 **1** who **2** which **3** which

실전 연습 p.111

1 ③ **2** ② **3** ④
4 (1) The boy Ms. Evans is talking to
(2) a writer, which made me surprised **5** ⑤

1 관계대명사가 전치사의 목적어인 문장이며 관계대명사절 끝에 전치사가 없으므로 「전치사+관계대명사」 형태로 쓴다.

2 첫 번째 빈칸은 전치사가 관계대명사절 끝에 있으므로 목적격 관계대명사로 whom이나 that을 쓸 수 있다. 두 번째 빈칸은 전치사가 앞에 있으므로 which만 쓸 수 있다.

3 계속적 용법의 관계대명사가 필요한데 선행사가 앞의 절 전체이거나 사물이므로 which가 적절하다. 관계대명사 that은 계속적 용법으로 쓸 수 없다.

4 (1) 관계대명사 whom이 생략된 관계대명사절을 완성해야 하므로 관계대명사절 끝에 전치사 to를 쓴다.
(2) 앞 문장 전체를 선행사로 하는 계속적 용법의 관계대명사절을 완성한다.

5 ① 「전치사+관계대명사」로 쓰일 때 관계대명사는 생략할 수 없다. (→ a waiting list on which) ② that은 「전치사+관계대명사」로 쓸 수 없다. (→ with which) ③ 관계대명사 that은 계속적 용법으로 쓸 수 없다. (→ which) ④ 선행사가 사람이므로 who(m)으로 쓴다. (→ with whom)

개념 완성 Quiz

1 목적어 **2** who, that **3** which, who
4 선행사+콤마+관계대명사절 **5** 전치사, 관계대명사

UNIT 03 관계부사

개념 QUICK CHECK p.112

POINT 05 **1** the hotel where we're going to stay
2 the year when we met
3 the reason why I'm angry
4 the way I solved the problem

POINT 06 **1** when **2** which **3** where

실전 연습 p.113

1 ② **2** (1) the, reason, why (2) the, month, when **3** ⓑ → the way(how) **4** ③
5 ④

1 관계사 뒤에 완전한 문장이 이어지며 선행사가 시간을 나타내므로, 관계부사 when으로 바꿔 쓸 수 있다.

2 (1) 선행사가 이유를 나타내는 the reason이므로 관계부사 why를 사용하여 문장을 완성한다.
(2) 선행사가 시간을 나타내는 the month이므로 관계부사 when을 사용하여 문장을 완성한다.

3 관계부사 how는 선행사 the way와 함께 쓸 수 없고 둘 중 하나만 쓴다.

4 ③ 빈칸 뒤에 주어가 없는 불완전한 문장이 오므로, 주격 관계대명사인 which나 that을 써야 한다. 나머지는 모두 관계부사 where를 쓴다.

5 ④ 관계사절에 목적어가 없는 불완전한 문장이 나오므로 관계부사 대신 관계대명사를 써야 한다. (when → which)

개념 완성 Quiz

1 전치사 **2** why **3** how, the way **4** 완전한
5 있다

UNIT 04 복합관계사

개념 QUICK CHECK p.114

POINT 07 **1** 오는 누구든지 **2** 네가 무엇을 하더라도
3 네가 좋아하는 디저트는 어느 것이든

POINT 08 **1** whenever **2** wherever
3 However hungry you may be

실전 연습 p.115

1 ② **2** ⑤ **3** ③
4 ① **5** ④

1 '~하는 사람은 누구든지'의 뜻으로 명사절을 이끄는 복합관계대명사 whoever가 알맞다.

2 맥락상 '무엇이 ~할지라도'라는 의미의 복합관계대명사이므로 no matter what으로 바꿔 쓸 수 있다.

3 '언제 ~하든지'의 뜻으로 양보의 부사절을 이끌고, '~할 때는 언제나'의 뜻으로 시간의 부사절을 이끄는 복합관계부사 whenever가 적절하다.

4 첫 번째 빈칸에는 '~하는 곳은 어디든지'를 뜻하는 복합관계부사 wherever가 알맞고, 두 번째 빈칸에는 '어느 것을 ~할지라도'를 뜻하는 복합관계대명사 whichever가 알맞다.

5 ④ 복합관계부사 however는 「however+형용사(부사)+주어+동사」의 어순으로 써야 한다. (However the house is expensive → However expensive the house is)

개념 완성 Quiz

1 양보의 부사절 **2** no matter what **3** whenever
4 whichever **5** 형용사(부사)+주어+ 동사

서술형 실전 연습 pp.116~117

1 (1) The boy who sat next to me in the train
(2) The book whose author won the Nobel Prize
2 (1) which → what (2) where → which(that)
3 (1) Do you have a friend who(that) lives in a foreign country? (2) Let me know the day when (on which) the art exhibition will start.
4 (1) Julia went to the city in which her parents were born. (2) Juila went to the city where her parents were born.
5 (1) which made his mother angry
(2) However hard I try to persuade her
6 (1) which(that) can hold a laptop
(2) why the accident happened
7 Whoever, whenever, wherever, whatever
8 (1) who(that) (2) where (3) when
(4) which(that)

1 (1) 선행사(The boy)를 뒤에서 수식하는 주격 관계대명사절을 완성한다.
(2) 선행사(The book)와 관계대명사의 관계가 소유이므로 소유격 관계대명사절을 완성한다.

2 (1) 관계대명사절의 선행사가 없으므로 선행사를 포함하는 what을 써야 한다.
(2) 관계사절에 목적어가 없는 불완전한 문장이 나오므로 관계부사 대신 관계대명사를 써야 한다.

3 (1) 선행사가 사람이므로 주격 관계대명사로 who나 that을 쓴다.
(2) 관계부사 when을 사용하여 관계부사절로 선행사 the day를 수식한다.

4 (1) 관계대명사가 전치사의 목적어일 때 전치사 which와 whom은 「전치사+관계대명사」의 형태로 쓸 수 있다. (2) 선행사가 장소일 때 in which는 관계부사 where로 바꿔 쓸 수 있다.

5 (1) 계속적 용법의 관계대명사 which는 앞에 나온 문장 전체를 선행사로 취할 수 있다.
(2) no matter how는 '아무리 ~할지라도'라는 뜻의 관계부사 however로 바꿔 쓸 수 있다.

6 (1) 선행사가 사물을 가리키는 대명사이므로 주격 관계대명사로 which 또는 that을 쓴다.
(2) 이유를 선행사로 하는 관계부사 why를 쓴다.

7 첫 번째 빈칸에는 '~하는 누구든지'를 뜻하는 whoever, 두 번째 빈칸에는 '~할 때는 언제나'를 뜻하는 whenever, 세 번째 빈칸에는 '~하는 곳은 어디든지'를 뜻하는 wherever, 네 번째 빈칸에는 '~하는 것은 무엇이든지'를 뜻하는 whatever가 각각 알맞다.

8 (1)은 선행사가 사람이므로 주격 관계대명사로 who나 that을, (2)는 장소를 나타내는 관계부사 where를, (3)은 시간을 나타내는 관계부사 when을, (4)는 선행사가 사물이므로 주격 관계대명사로 which나 that을 쓴다.

개념 완성 Quiz

1 whose **2** 불완전한 문장 **3** when **4** who, that
5 who, which **6** why **7** whatever **8** who, that

실전 모의고사

pp. 118~121

01 ③	02 ②	03 ⑤	04 ④	05 ④	06 ⑤
07 ④	08 ⑤	09 ③	10 ⑤	11 ②	12 ④
13 ⑤	14 ②	15 ⑤	16 ⑤	17 ④	18 ④

19 (1) What, happened, to, him
(2) who, is, from, Ireland

20 (1) The girl whom we met in London sent us an email.
(2) They visited the tower which was built by a famous architect.

21 (1) when (2) How (3) where

22 (1) The lake about which I told you is in Canada. / The lake which(that) I told you about is in Canada.
(2) Whichever he chooses, he won't be satisfied with it.

23 (1) whose hair is long and blonde
(2) when(on which) I won first prize

24 (1) ③ → which(that)
(2) ④ → However hungry you may be

25 (A) where(whose) students volunteer at an animal shelter
(B) Whoever is interested in helping abandoned dogs

01 관계대명사절의 선행사가 없으므로 선행사를 포함하는 관계대명사 what이 알맞다.

02 선행사와 관계대명사가 소유의 관계이므로 소유격 관계대명사인 whose가 알맞다.

03 뒤에 완전한 문장이 이어지고, 앞의 선행사가 장소를 나타내므로 관계부사 where가 알맞다.

04 맥락상 whenever가 '언제 ~하든지'라는 의미로 쓰였으므로 no matter when이 알맞다.

05 첫 번째 빈칸에는 선행사가 사물이므로 주격 관계대명사 which나 that이 알맞다. 두 번째 빈칸에는 관계사절 앞에 콤마(,)가 있으므로 계속적 용법으로 앞에 나온 문장 전체를 선행사로 취하는 which가 알맞다.

06 ⑤는 선행사 his things를 수식하는 목적격 관계대명사 which나 that이 알맞고, 나머지는 선행사를 포함하는 관계대명사 what이 알맞다.

07 ④ 전치사 뒤에는 관계대명사 that을 쓸 수 없다.

08 첫 번째 빈칸은 선행사가 사물이므로 주격 관계대명사 which나 that이 알맞고, 두 번째 빈칸은 선행사가 최상급이므로 관계대명사 that이 알맞다.

09 첫 번째 빈칸은 「전치사+관계대명사」 형태이며 선행사가 사물이므로 which가 알맞다. 두 번째 빈칸은 계속적 용법이며 선행사가 사람이므로 who가 알맞다.

10 첫 번째 빈칸은 뒤에 완전한 문장이 나오므로 관계부사 where가 알맞다. 두 번째 빈칸은 선행사가 「사람+동물」이므로 주격 관계대명사 that이 알맞다.

11 ② 목적격 관계대명사로 생략할 수 있다. ①과 ④는 주격 관계대명사, ③은 「전치사+관계대명사」, ⑤는 계속적 용법으로 쓰인 관계대명사로 생략할 수 없다.

12 ④ whenever는 '~할 때는 언제나'라는 뜻으로 쓰였으므로 at any time when으로 바꿔 쓸 수 있다.

13 ⑤ 관계대명사 that은 계속적 용법으로 쓸 수 없다. (→ who)

14 ⓐ는 '~하는 사람은 누구든지'라는 의미의 복합관계대명사 whoever를, ⓑ는 목적격 관계대명사 which나 that을, ⓒ는 선행사를 포함하는 관계대명사 what을 쓴다.

15 ⑤ 방법을 나타내는 the way와 how 중 하나만 써야 한다. (the way how → the way 또는 how)

16 ⑤ 관계사 뒤에 목적어가 없는 불완전한 문장이 이어지므로 관계대명사 that이나 which를 써야 한다. (where → that(which))

17 ④ 맥락상 whatever는 '무엇이 ~할지라도'라는 뜻이므로 no matter what으로 바꿔 써야 한다.

18 ⓐ 「however+형용사(부사)+주어+동사」의 어순으로 써야 한다. (However the watch is old → However old the watch is) ⓒ 선행사가 있으며 「전치사+관계대명사」의 형태이므로 which를 쓴다. (what → which)

19 (1) 선행사를 포함하는 관계대명사 what을 사용하여 문장을 완성한다.
(2) 선행사가 사람이며 계속적 용법으로 쓰였으므로 관계대명사 who를 사용하여 문장을 완성한다.

20 (1) 선행사 the girl과 we 사이에 목적격 관계대명사가 생략된 문장이다.
(2) the tower와 built 사이에 「주격 관계대명사+be동사」가 생략된 문장이다.

21 (1) 시간을 나타내는 관계부사 when, (2) 방법을 나타내는 관계부사 how, (3) 장소를 나타내는 관계부사 where를 사용한다.

22 (1) 선행사가 전치사의 목적어이므로 「전치사+관계대명사」의 형태 혹은 전치사를 관계대명사절 끝에 쓴다.
(2) '어느 것을 ~할지라도(= no matter which)'라는 뜻의 복합관계대명사 whichever를 쓴다.

23 (1) 선행사와 관계대명사의 관계가 소유이므로 소유격 관계대명사 whose를 쓴다.
(2) 시간을 나타내는 관계부사 when을 쓴다.

24 (1) 선행사가 사물이므로 목적격 관계대명사로 which나 that을 써야 한다. (2) '아무리 ~할지라도'라는 뜻을 나타낼 때에는 「However+형용사(부사)+주어+동사」의 어순으로 써야 한다.

25 (A) 뒤에 완전한 문장이 나오므로 장소를 나타내는 관계부사 where를 사용한다. (이 문장은 소유격 관계대명사를 이용하여 whose students volunteer ~.로도 표현할 수 있다.) (B) '~하는 사람은 누구든지'의 뜻의 복합관계대명사 Whoever를 주어로 사용한다.

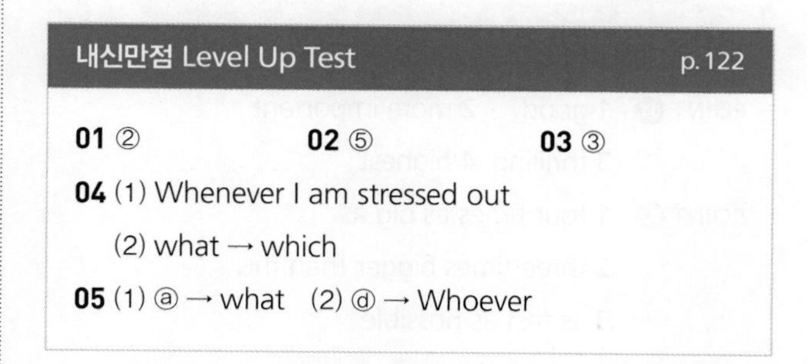

내신만점 Level Up Test p. 122

01 ② **02** ⑤ **03** ③
04 (1) Whenever I am stressed out
(2) what → which
05 (1) ⓐ → what (2) ⓓ → Whoever

01 방법을 나타내는 관계부사를 사용하여 두 문장을 한 문장으로 바꾸면 People want to know how the child could learn three languages.이다. 이때 방법을 나타내는 관계사 how는 the way와 같이 쓰지 않는 것에 주의한다.

02 ⓐ 선행사를 포함하는 관계대명사 what, ⓑ 장소를 나타내는 관계부사 where, ⓒ 「전치사+관계대명사」 형태이므로 목적격 관계대명사 whom, ⓓ 앞 문장을 선행사로 하는 계속적 용법의 관계대명사 which, ⓔ 선행사가 사물이므로 주격 관계대명사 which 또는 that을 쓴다.

03 ⓐ에는 관계부사 where, ⓑ에는 목적격 관계대명사 which (that), ⓒ에는 복합관계부사 whenever가 알맞다.

04 (1) '~할 때는 언제나'라는 뜻의 복합관계부사 whenever를 사용한다.
(2) 계속적 용법으로 앞 문장 전체를 선행사로 하는 관계대명사 which를 쓴다.

05 (1) ⓐ 앞에 선행사가 없으므로 선행사를 포함하는 관계대명사 what으로 고쳐야 한다.
(2) 내용상 '~하는 누구든지'의 의미를 나타내는 whoever가 알맞다.

CHAPTER 09
비교

UNIT 01 원급, 비교급, 최상급

개념 QUICK CHECK p.124

POINT 01 **1** good **2** more important
3 thrilling **4** highest

POINT 02 **1** four times as big as
2 three times bigger than this
3 as fast as possible

실전 연습 p.125

1 (1) yours (2) as (3) lightest **2** older, old
3 four times as tall **4** ④ **5** ④

1 (1) 비교하는 대상을 일치시켜야 하므로 my bag과 your bag 또는 yours로 표현한다.
(2) 「as+원급+as」 구문이다.
(3) 최상급 앞에 쓰이는 the가 있으므로 light의 최상급인 lightest가 알맞다.

2 「비교급+than」과 「배수사+as+원급+as」 형태이다.

3 '~의 –배만큼 …한(하게)'를 뜻하는 「배수사+as+원급+as」로 표현한다. 「배수사+비교급+than」으로 나타낼 수도 있다.

4 ④ 「not as(so)+원급+as」 형태가 되어야 한다. (→ not as scary as)

5 ④ 표에 의하면 휴대전화가 노트북보다 더 비싸므로 The laptop is not as expensive as the cell phone.이나 The cell phone is more expensive than the laptop.이 되어야 한다.

개념 완성 Quiz

1 the+최상급 **2** as ... as **3** 원급
4 가능한 한 빠르게 **5** more 또는 most

UNIT 02 여러 가지 비교 구문

개념 QUICK CHECK p.126

POINT 03 **1** (1) much more expensive
(2) more and more tired
2 (1) cities (2) most interesting

POINT 04 **1** Steve is taller than all the other boys in my class. / No boy is as tall as Steve in my class.

실전 연습 p.127

1 ③ **2** the most moving film that I've ever seen **3** ④ → more and more **4** ④
5 ②

1 very는 원급을 수식하며 비교급을 수식할 수 없다.

2 '지금껏 ~한 것들 중에서 가장 …한(하게)'라는 뜻은 「the+최상급+명사(+that)+주어+have(has)+p.p.」 형태로 표현한다.

3 '점점 더 ~한(하게)'라는 뜻은 「비교급+and+비교급」으로 표현하며, 비교급의 형태가 「more+원급」이면 「more and more+원급」으로 쓴다.

4 최상급의 의미를 나타내는 「부정주어 ~ as(so)+원급+as」는 「비교급+than any other+단수명사」 형태로 바꿔 쓸 수 있다.

5 ① more and more hot → hotter and hotter
③ actress → actresses ④ funniest → funnier
⑤ very → even/much/far/still/a lot

개념 완성 Quiz

1 much **2** the+최상급+명사+(that)+주어+have(has)+p.p. **3** 비교급, 비교급 **4** 최상급
5 최상급

서술형 실전 연습 pp.128~129

1 (1) is, taller, than
(2) as, fast, as
2 three, times, bigger, than
3 one, of, the, most, popular, operas
4 as, big, as / any, other, planet / bigger, than
5 Today is much colder than yesterday. / 오늘은 어제보다 훨씬 더 춥다.

6 (1) 28(twenty-eight) (2) twice, as, many
7 (1) The higher, the colder
(2) lower and lower
8 (1) more exciting than living in the countryside
(2) more dangerous than the countryside
(3) as open and friendly as those in the countryside

1 (1) '~보다 더 …한'의 의미로 써야 하므로 taller than의 비교급 문장으로 쓴다.
(2) '~만큼 …하지 않게'의 의미로 써야 하므로 「not+as+원급+as」의 원급 문장으로 쓴다.

2 '~의 -배만큼 …한(하게)'를 뜻하는 「배수사+as+원급+as」는 「배수사+비교급+than」으로 나타낼 수 있다.

3 '가장 ~한 …(것)들 중 하나'의 뜻은 「one of the+최상급+복수명사」의 형태로 쓴다.

4 「No (other) ~+as+원급+as」, 「No (other) ~+비교급+than」, 「비교급+than any other+단수명사」의 문장 형식을 사용하여 최상급 의미의 문장을 완성한다.

5 비교급을 강조하는 말은 비교급 바로 앞에 위치한다.

6 (1) 4보다 7배 더 많은 수이므로 답은 28이 된다.
(2) 4는 2의 2배인 수이다. 「배수사+as+원급+as」 구문을 활용한다.

7 (1) 위로 올라갈수록 기온이 더 내려가는 것을 표현하므로 「the+비교급, the+비교급」 구문을 사용한다.
(2) 출생률이 점점 내려가는 그래프 추이를 표현하므로 「비교급+and+비교급」 구문을 사용한다.

8 (1) '도시에 사는 것이 시골에서 사는 것보다 더 신난다'는 의미의 비교급 문장이 알맞다.
(2) '도시가 시골보다 더 위험할 수 있다'는 의미의 비교급 문장이 알맞다.
(3) '도시 사람들이 시골에 사는 사람들만큼 개방적이고 친절하지 않다'는 의미의 원급 비교 문장이 알맞다.

개념 완성 Quiz

1 비교급, 원급 **2** as+원급+as, 비교급+than **3** 최상급, 복수명사 **4** 비교급+than, 단수명사 **5** much, a lot **6** twice, times **7** the+비교급, the+비교급 **8** as+원급+as

실전 모의고사

pp. 130~133

01 ③ 02 ⑤ 03 ⑤ 04 ⑤ 05 ② 06 ④
07 ④ 08 ③ 09 ③ 10 ⑤ 11 ③ 12 ②
13 ⑤ 14 ④ 15 ④ 16 ④ 17 ④
18 (1) less (2) most, handsome (3) quick
19 he, can 20 is, the, biggest, island
21 (1) taller, than, any, other (2) as(so), tall, as (3) shorter, than
22 (1) less (2) more (3) least
23 longer than it is from Seoul to Busan
24 (1) The more you exercise, the healthier you will be.
(2) It is one of the most popular TV programs in Korea these days.
25 (1) ran, slower, than (2) ran, twice, as, fast, as

01 ③ '~보다'를 뜻하는 than이 쓰였으므로 비교급이 들어가야 한다. happy의 비교급은 happier이다.

02 ⑤ 동사 work를 수식하기 위해서는 부사가 들어가야 하는데, 비교급을 강조하는 much가 있으므로 efficiently의 비교급이 들어가야 한다.

03 ⑤ strong의 비교급은 stronger이다.

04 ⑤ very는 비교급을 강조할 수 없다.

05 ② 최상급 뒤에는 「of+비교 대상」, 「in+장소나 범위」가 쓰인다.

06 ④ than과 함께 쓸 수 있는 것은 형용사나 부사의 비교급으로 cheap의 비교급은 cheaper, quickly의 비교급은 more quickly이다.

07 세상에서 '가장' 축구를 잘하는 선수이므로 첫 번째 빈칸에는 best가 들어가야 한다. as ~ as에는 원급이 들어가므로 두 번째 빈칸은 good이 알맞다.

08 ③ 아빠는 나보다 나이가 세 배 많으므로 three times as old as me가 되어야 한다.

09 ① → as smart as ② → more expensive than
④ → the more weight you gain ⑤ → one of the best singers

10 ⑤ '다른 어떤 ~보다 더 …한'이라는 뜻은 「비교급+than any other+단수명사」로 표현한다. (→ any other mountain)

11 ③은 남극이 북극보다 더 춥다는 의미이고, ①은 남극과 북극의 추위가 비슷하다는 의미이다. 나머지는 모두 북극이 남극보다 춥다는 의미이다.

12 ②는 러시아가 세계의 다른 나라들만큼 크다는 뜻이고, 나머지는 모두 러시아가 세계에서 가장 큰 나라라는 뜻이다.

13 ⑤ 첫 번째 문장은 Warren Buffett이 세계의 부호들 중 한 명이라는 뜻이고 두 번째 문장은 Warren Buffett이 세계에서 가장 부자라는 뜻이다.

14 ④ '어떤 ~도 –보다 더 …하지 않은'이라는 뜻은 「부정 주어 ~ as(so)+원급+as」로 쓴다. (something → nothing)

15 ⓑ에서 비교급 앞에는 the를 쓰지 않으므로 the를 삭제해야 한다.

16 ⓐ wise → wiser ⓒ longer → long

17 ④ 갈색 가방이 노란 가방보다 더 비싸므로 less가 아니라 more가 되어야 한다.

18 (1) than과 함께 사용할 수 있는 것은 비교급으로 의미상 little의 비교급인 less가 적절하다.
(2) '지금껏 살면서 본 남자 중 가장 잘생긴 남자'이므로 handsome의 최상급이 들어가야 한다.
(3) as ~ as 사이에는 원급이 들어가야 한다. 의미상 quick이 알맞다.

19 '가능한 한 ~하게'라는 의미의 「as+원급+as possible」은 「as+원급+as+주어+can」으로 바꿔 쓸 수 있다.

20 한국에서 '가장 큰' 섬이므로 최상급을 사용해야 한다.

21 (1) 「비교급+than any other+단수명사」로 최상급을 나타낸다.
(2) 「not as(so)+원급+as」는 '~만큼 …하지 않은'이라는 의미로, 「A is not as(so) tall as B」는 'A가 B보다 (높이가) 더 낮다'는 의미이다.
(3) 「비교급+than」 표현을 쓴다.

22 (1) 코끼리가 돌고래보다 '덜' 똑똑하므로 less가 알맞다.
(2) 돌고래가 개보다 '더' 똑똑하므로 more가 알맞다.
(3) 개가 표에서 '가장 덜' 똑똑하므로 최상급인 least를 사용해야 한다.

23 거리는 비인칭 주어 it을 사용하고 비교 표현은 「비교급+than」을 이용한다.

24 (1) healthy의 비교급은 healthier이므로 the healthier가 되어야 한다.
(2) 「one of the+최상급+복수명사」이므로 TV programs가 되어야 한다.

25 (1) Tom의 달리기 기록이 David보다 느린 것으로 나와 있다.
(2) 「배수사+as+원급+as」의 구문을 활용한다.

내신만점 Level Up Test p.134

01 ② **02** ⑤ **03** b, c

04 escaped from the building as soon as they could

05 틀린 부분: ⑤ → good
틀린 이유: 문맥상 '~만큼 …한(하게)'라는 의미가 적절하며, 「as+원급+as」로 표현한다. 비교급 better가 아니라 원급 good이 알맞다.

01 ⓐ very → much/still/even/far/a lot
ⓓ The early → The earlier

02 ⑤ 일개미는 약 반 년을 살고, 여왕개미는 약 3년을 산다고 했으므로 '일개미가 여왕개미의 절반만큼 산다'는 글의 내용과 일치하지 않는다.

03 빈칸에는 비교급을 강조하는 much나 even이 알맞다.

04 「as+원급+as possible」은 「as+원급+as+주어+can」으로 바꾸어 쓸 수 있다. 이때 과거시제이면 can 대신 could를 쓴다.

05 as ~ as 사이에는 원급을 사용해야 하므로 good을 쓴다.

CHAPTER 10 가정법

UNIT 01 가정법 과거와 과거완료

개념 QUICK CHECK p.136

POINT 01
1 아파서 캠핑을 갈 수 없다
2 내가 차가 없어서 너를 데려다 줄 수 없다
3 배가 고프지 않아서 피자를 안 먹는다

POINT 02
1 had been, have made
2 hadn't left, have missed
3 had known, have gone

실전 연습 p.137

1 had	2 ④	3 ④
4 ②	5 ⑤	

1 현재 사실과 반대되는 상황을 가정하여 말할 때 사용하는 가정법 과거는 「if+주어+동사의 과거형, 주어+조동사의 과거형+동사원형」의 형태이다.

2 '만약 ~한다면 …할 텐데'라는 뜻의 가정법 과거가 적절하므로, 동사의 과거형과 의미상 적절한 조동사의 과거형이 순서대로 들어가는 것이 알맞다.

3 과거 사실과 반대되는 상황을 가정하여 말할 때 사용하는 가정법 과거완료는 「주어+조동사의 과거형+have+p.p.+if+주어+had+p.p.」 형태이다.

4 가정법 과거완료는 「if+주어+had+p.p., 주어+조동사의 과거형+have+p.p.」이므로 괄호 안의 말을 배열하여 문장을 만들면 If I had been there, I would have helped you.이다.

5 ⑤ 과거 사실과 반대되는 상황을 가정하여 말할 때 사용하는 가정법 과거완료이므로 if절에 「had+p.p.」 형태가 들어가야 한다. (haven't listened → hadn't listened)

개념 완성 Quiz

1 현재	2 과거형, 과거형	3 과거	4 과거형
5 현재			

UNIT 02 I wish 가정법, as if 가정법

개념 QUICK CHECK p.138

POINT 03 1 저녁에 TV를 보지 못한다 2 그녀는 모델이 아니다 3 나는 키가 크지 않다

POINT 04 1 had arrived 2 had read 3 had seen

실전 연습 p.139

1 had helped	2 ④	3 ⑤
4 ⓐ could speak ⓑ had lived		5 ④

1 '~했더라면 좋았을 텐데'라는 뜻으로 과거 사실에 대한 유감이나 아쉬움을 나타낼 때 사용하는 「I wish+가정법 과거완료(주어+had+p.p.)」 형태가 알맞다.

2 현재 사실에 대한 유감을 나타내는 「I wish+가정법 과거(주어+동사의 과거형)」 형태로 '할머니가 아프지 않으시면 좋을 텐데'라는 의미를 나타낸다.

3 '마치 ~했던 것처럼'의 뜻으로 과거 사실의 반대를 가정할 때 사용하는 「as if+가정법 과거완료(주어+had+p.p.)」 형태를 사용한다.

4 ⓐ '~하면 좋을 텐데'의 뜻으로 현재 사실에 대한 유감이나 이루기 힘든 현재의 소망을 나타내는 「I wish+가정법 과거」 형태가 적절하다. 동사의 과거형이나 「조동사의 과거형+동사원형」으로 쓸 수 있다. ⓑ '마치 ~했던 것처럼'의 뜻으로 과거 사실의 반대를 가정할 때 사용하는 「as if+가정법 과거완료」 형태가 적절하다.

5 첫 번째 빈칸은 과거 사실에 대한 유감이나 아쉬움을 나타내는 「I wish+가정법 과거완료」가 적절하므로 「had+p.p.」 형태가 들어가야 한다. 두 번째 빈칸은 과거 사실의 반대를 가정할 때 사용하는 「as if+가정법 과거완료」가 적절하므로 역시 「had+p.p.」 형태가 들어가야 한다.

개념 완성 Quiz

1 가정법 과거완료	2 동사의 과거형	3 가정법 과거완료
4 가정법 과거	5 had+p.p.	

UNIT 03 혼합가정법, without+명사(구)

개념 QUICK CHECK p.140

POINT 05 1 wouldn't feel 2 would have helped 3 could pass

POINT 06 1 If it were not for 2 If it had not been for

실전 연습 p.141

1 ④	2 ④	3 ②
4 ⑤	5 ③	

1 과거의 일의 결과가 현재까지 영향을 미치는 경우이므로 혼합가정법을 사용한다. 의미상 조건절에는 가정법 과거완료, 주절에는 가정법 과거가 적절하다.

2 뒤에 명사와 가정법 과거가 와서 '(현재) ~이 없다면, …할 텐데'라는 의미를 나타내므로 빈칸에는 but for를 쓸 수 있다.

3 ② 의미상 혼합가정법이 적절하므로 조건절에 가정법 과거완료가 들어가야 한다.

4 주절이 가정법 과거완료이므로 If it had not been for로 바꿔 쓸 수 있다.

5 ③ 의미상 혼합가정법이 적절하므로 조건절에 가정법 과거완료가 들어가야 한다. (→ had worked)

개념 완성 Quiz

1 현재 **2** but for **3** 가정법 과거완료
4 (과거에) ~이 없었다면, …했을 텐데
5 (현재) ~이 없다면, …할 텐데

UNIT 04 주의해야 할 가정법

개념 QUICK CHECK p. 142

POINT 07 **1** get **2** sleep **3** eat **4** pack
POINT 08 **1** Were she our teacher
2 Had I taken your advice
3 Were I tall

실전 연습 p. 143

1 ① **2** ⑤ **3** (1) Were those jeans cheaper (2) Had he known the answer
4 Had, you, been, more, careful **5** ②

1 '–가 ~해야 한다고 요구하다'라는 뜻의 demand 뒤에 이어지는 that절의 동사는 「should+동사원형」으로 쓰며, 이때 should를 생략하고 동사원형만 쓸 수 있다.

2 that절에 3인칭 단수 주어의 동사로 동사원형이 있으므로 앞에 should가 생략되었음을 알 수 있다. 따라서 빈칸에는 이성적 판단, 필요, 당위 등을 나타내는 형용사가 들어가야 한다.

3 if를 생략하면 주어와 동사를 도치시켜야 한다.

4 가정법 과거완료 문장인데 빈칸이 5개이므로 if가 생략된 문장임을 알 수 있다. If가 생략된 「Had+주어+p.p.」 형태를 사용한다.

5 ② If가 생략된 가정법 과거 문장이므로 be동사의 과거형인 were가 들어간다. 나머지는 모두 동사원형 be가 들어간다.

개념 완성 Quiz

1 동사원형 **2** 동사원형 **3** 도치 **4** 과거형
5 동사의 과거형

서술형 실전 연습 pp. 144~145

1 had, not, been, would, have, gone
2 Were I an architect, I would build my own house.
3 (1) 내게 충분한 사과가 있으면 너를 위해 사과파이를 구울 거야. (사과가 있으면 구울 것이라는 사실을 말한 것)
(2) 내게 충분한 사과가 있다면 너를 위해 사과파이를 구울 텐데. (사과가 충분히 없어서 사과파이를 굽지 않겠다는 뜻)
4 (1) had eaten, wouldn't be hungry
(2) hadn't slipped, wouldn't have broken
5 (1) understood (2) had been with me
6 would have visited
7 (1) as if he were (2) as if he hadn't scribbled
8 (1) I had set my alarm clock (2) I had brought

1 가정법 과거완료는 과거의 사실과 반대되는 내용을 포함한다.

2 가정법 과거 문장에서 if를 생략하므로 동사인 were를 주어 I 앞에 쓴다.

3 단순 조건절은 「if+주어+동사의 현재형, 주어+will+동사원형」으로 써서, 특정 조건에 일어날 상황을 설명하는 문장이다. 가정법 과거는 현재 사실의 반대 내용을 표현하며 「If+주어+동사의 과거형, 주어+would/could/might+동사원형」의 어순으로 쓴다.

4 (1) 아침 식사를 안 한 것은 과거이고 배가 고픈 것은 현재 상황이므로 혼합가정법으로 쓴다.
(2) 과거 사실의 반대는 가정법 과거완료로 쓴다.

5 「I am sorry+현재시제」는 현재 이루기 어려운 내용을 소망하는 「I wish+가정법 과거」, 「I am sorry+과거시제」는 과거 사실의 반대를 소망하는 「I wish+가정법 과거완료」로 나타낼 수 있다.

6 Susie가 병원에 있었다는 사실을 몰라서, 방문하지 못했다는 과거 사실에 대한 반대를 가정하는 상황이므로 가정법 과거완료로 쓴다.

7 (1) '개가 사람인 것처럼'의 의미가 되도록 as if 뒤에 가정법 과거를 쓴다.
(2) '낙서를 하지 않았던 것처럼'의 의미가 되도록 as if 뒤에 가정법 과거완료를 쓴다.

8 과거에 일어난 일에 대해 반대 상황을 소망할 때는 「I wish+가정법 과거완료」로 쓴다.

개념 완성 Quiz

1 과거 **2** 도치 **3** 조건절, 가정법 과거 **4** 과거형
5 가정법 과거완료 **6** 가정법 과거완료 **7** 가정법 과거완료
8 가정법 과거완료

실전 모의고사 pp. 146~149

01 ④	02 ⑤	03 ①	04 ⑤	05 ⑤	06 ②
07 ⑤	08 ④	09 ③	10 ⑤	11 ⑤	12 ④
13 ④	14 ⑤	15 ③	16 ④	17 ①	18 ⑤

19 (1) had, taken, would, not, be, ill
(2) hadn't, read, wouldn't, have, been, disappointed

20 (1) could speak foreign languages fluently
(2) she had seen the horror movie

21 (1) as, if, it, were
(2) But, for, living, things, could, exist

22 (1) had studied (2) had he left (if he had left)

23 If I had only one day to live, I would donate all my money. 또는 I would donate all my money if I had only one day to live.

24 (A) (had) advertised (B) had played

25 (1) I were alone (2) I had ordered beef

01 가정법 과거시제로 주절에는 「주어+조동사의 과거형+동사원형」을 사용해야 한다.

02 과거에 일어난 일이 현재까지 영향을 미치므로 혼합가정법을 사용해야 한다. 'Susan이 손을 다치지 않았더라면'이라는 과거의 상황을 가정하고 있으므로 조건절은 가정법 과거완료를 사용해야 한다.

03 이성적 판단, 필요, 당위 등을 나타내는 형용사 뒤에 이어지는 that절의 동사는 should를 생략하고 동사원형을 쓴다.

04 첫 번째 빈칸에는 과거의 일의 결과가 현재까지 영향을 미치는 혼합가정법이므로 조건절에는 가정법 과거완료가 적절하다. 두 번째 빈칸에는 '(현재) ~이 없다면, …할 텐데'라는 의미로 가정법 과거가 적절하며 의미상 부정이 알맞다.

05 ⓔ 가정법 과거 문장이므로 「조동사의 과거형+동사원형」의 형태로 might take가 알맞다.

06 ② 주장, 제안, 요구, 명령, 권고 등을 나타내는 동사 뒤에 이어지는 that절의 동사는 should를 생략하고 동사원형(be)을 쓴다. ① 「as if+가정법 과거」 구문으로, 과거형 were를 써야 한다. ③~⑤ 가정법 과거 구문으로, be동사는 were로 써야 한다.

07 ⑤ 「without+명사, 가정법 과거완료」 구문이다. ① 「I wish+가정법 과거」 구문이다. (→ had) ② 가정법 과거 문장이다. (→ would fly) ③ 「as if+가정법 과거」 구문이다. (→ were) ④ 가정법 과거완료 문장이다. (→ would have bought)

08 ④ 가정법 과거완료로 took는 had taken이 되어야 한다.

09 '(과거에) ~이 없었다면, …했을 텐데'라는 의미를 나타내는 but for나 without, if it had not been for를 쓸 수 있다.

10 '–가 ~할 것을 추천하다'라는 뜻의 recommend 뒤에 이어지는 that절의 동사는 「should+동사원형」으로 쓰며, 이때 should를 생략하고 동사원형(→ watch)만 쓸 수 있다.

11 첫 번째 문장은 가정법 과거의 조건절이므로 were가 알맞고, 두 번째 문장은 가정법 과거의 주절이므로 「조동사의 과거형+동사원형」으로 쓰고, 세 번째 문장은 가정법 과거완료의 조건절이므로 「had+p.p.」로 쓴다.

12 '지갑을 잃어버려 지금 점심을 사 줄 수 없는' 상황이므로 과거의 일의 결과가 현재까지 영향을 미치는 혼합가정법을 사용한다. 조건절에 가정법 과거완료가 들어가야 하므로 hadn't lost가 알맞다.

13 혼합 가정법 문장으로, '(과거에) ~했다면, (현재) …할 텐데'의 의미이다.

14 ⑤ 「without+명사(구), 가정법 과거」 구문으로 will은 would가 되어야 한다.

15 현재 사실의 반대를 가정할 때는 가정법 과거를 써야 한다.

16 ⓓ if절의 동사가 were, had, should인 경우 if를 생략하고 주어와 동사를 도치하여 쓸 수 있으므로 It were는 Were it이 되어야 한다.

17 현재 스마트폰을 가지고 있고, 시간 낭비를 많이 하고 있다는 의미이다. ⑤는 위의 문장만으로는 추측할 수 없다.

18 ⑤ 가정법 과거완료 문장으로, 직설법에서 don't drive는 didn't drive가 되어야 한다.

19 (1) 과거에 의사의 조언을 듣지 않아서 현재 아픈 상태이므로 혼합 가정법 문장으로 쓴다.
(2) 가정법 과거완료는 과거 사실에 반대되는 상황을 가정하여 과거에 대한 유감이나 후회의 뜻을 나타낸다.

20 (1) '~하면 좋을 텐데'라는 뜻으로 현재 사실에 대한 유감이나 이루기 힘든 현재의 소망을 나타낼 때는 「I wish+가정법 과거」로 표현한다.
(2) '마치 ~했던 것처럼'이라는 뜻으로 과거 사실과 반대를 가정할 때는 「as if+가정법 과거완료」로 표현한다.

21 (1) 「as if+주어+were」를 써서 가정법 과거의 문장으로 나타낸다.
(2) '~이 없다면'을 뜻하는 but for와 가정법 과거를 써서 문장을 완성한다.

22 (1) '만약 세 과목을 한 번에 공부했다면 모든 내용이 헷갈렸을 텐데 그러지 않았다'는 내용의 가정법 과거완료이다.

(2) 가정법 과거완료 구문으로, 「주어+조동사의 과거형+have +p.p., if+주어+had+p.p.」 구문에서 if를 생략하고 주어와 동사를 도치시킨 문장이다.

23 가정법 과거 문장이므로, 「If+주어+동사의 과거형 ~, 주어+조동사의 과거형+동사원형 …」의 어순으로 쓴다. 조건을 나타내는 if절은 문두나 주절의 뒤에 쓸 수 있다.

24 (A)는 주절의 동사가 「조동사의 과거형+동사원형」이므로 If 부사절은 가정법 과거인 「If+주어+동사의 과거형」이 오거나, 혼합가정법인 「If+주어+had+p.p.」가 올 수 있다.
(B)는 「I wish+가정법 과거완료」가 알맞다.

25 (1) 현재와 반대되는 소망이므로 「I wish+가정법 과거」를 사용해야 한다.
(2) 과거에 주문하지 않은 것을 후회하고 있으므로 「I wish+가정법 과거완료」를 사용해야 한다.

내신만점 Level Up Test p. 150

01 ② **02** ④ **03** ②
04 ⓓ → wouldn't waste a single minute watching TV
05 had been more careful, wouldn't have broken

01 주절이 가정법 과거완료이므로 조건절도 If it had not been for가 되어야 한다. Without과 But for는 If it had not been for 대신 쓸 수 있다.

02 가정법 과거인 「If+주어+동사의 과거형, 주어+조동사의 과거형+동사원형」으로 말하는 게 알맞다.

03 ⓑ 요구를 나타내는 request 뒤에 이어지는 that절에는 「(should)+동사원형」을 쓴다. locked는 lock으로 써야 한다.
ⓔ 혼합가정법이므로 주절은 「조동사의 과거형+동사원형」이 알맞다. (would have succeeded → would succeed)

04 가정법 과거는 「If+주어+동사의 과거형 ~, 주어+조동사의 과거형(would/could/might)+동사원형 …」의 형태로 쓴다.

05 과거 사실에 대한 후회를 나타내므로 가정법 과거완료(If+주어+had+p.p. ~, 주어+조동사의 과거형+have+p.p. …)로 쓴다.

CHAPTER 11
일치, 화법, 강조, 도치

UNIT 01 일치

개념 QUICK CHECK p. 152

POINT 01 **1** has **2** are **3** are **4** was
POINT 02 **1** studies, studied **2** was
3 rises **4** ended

실전 연습 p. 153

1 ④ **2** ③ **3** (1) will come
(2) would be **4** ③ **5** ⑤

1 「a number of+복수명사」는 복수 취급하고, every가 포함된 주어는 단수 취급한다.

2 each가 포함된 주어와 금액, 거리 단위, 과목명은 단수 취급하므로 단수 동사 is가 들어가고, jeans는 항상 복수로 쓰이는 명사이므로 are가 들어간다.

3 (1) 의미상 미래시제이므로 조동사 will 뒤에 동사원형을 쓴다.
(2) 주절이 과거시제이므로 종속절은 원래 시제에서 한 단계 이전 시제로 바뀌어 의미상 알맞은 조동사 would 뒤에 동사원형을 쓴다.

4 '물이 섭씨 100도에서 끓는 것'은 과학적 사실이므로 주절의 시제와 상관없이 항상 현재시제로 쓴다.

5 ⑤ 「the number of+복수명사」는 단수 취급한다. (are → is)

개념 완성 Quiz

1 복수 동사 **2** 단수 **3** 과거, 과거완료 **4** 현재시제
5 '~한 사람들'

UNIT 02 화법

개념 QUICK CHECK p. 154

POINT 03 **1** there **2** me **3** had cleaned
POINT 04 **1** He asked me where I was going.
2 He ordered me to open the door.
3 She told me not to answer the phone.

실전 연습 p.155

1 (1) she could go (2) you had bought 2 ④
3 ④ 4 ① 5 ③, ⑤

1 인용 부호 안의 1인칭은 주절의 주어에 맞게 바꾸고, 동사의 시제를 시제 일치에 맞게 바꾼다.

2 ④ 직접화법을 간접화법으로 전환할 때 전달 동사가 현재일 때는 시제 변화 없지만 전달 동사가 과거일 경우 시제 일치에 맞게 바꾼다. (am → was)

3 의문사 있는 의문문이므로 빈칸에는 「의문사+주어+동사」의 어순으로 쓴다.

4 부정 명령문을 간접화법으로 바꾸는 경우에는 목적어 뒤에 「not+to부정사」 형태가 들어가야 한다.

5 ① 의미상 의문사 있는 의문문이어야 한다. (→ what) ② 주절의 동사가 과거이므로 시제 일치를 해야 한다. (→ would join) ④ 명령문을 간접화법으로 바꾼 경우에는 목적어 뒤에 to부정사 형태로 써야 한다. (→ to get)

개념 완성 Quiz

1 tell 2 현재 3 의문사+주어+동사 4 to부정사
5 if(whether)

UNIT 03 강조, 도치

개념 QUICK CHECK p.156

POINT 05 1 c 2 a 3 b
POINT 06 1 is the duck 2 she goes
3 does she walk 4 so am I

실전 연습 p.157

1 ④ 2 ③ 3 ⑤
4 have I eaten 5 ②

1 동사를 강조하는 경우에는 「do/does/did+동사원형」을 사용하는데, 시제가 과거이므로 did를 쓴다.

2 It ~ that 강조구문을 사용하여 '…인 것은 바로 ~이다'의 의미를 나타낸다. 강조할 내용인 '티슈 상자 안'을 it was와 that 사이에 넣는다.

3 부정문 뒤에 「neither+동사+주어」를 사용하여 '~도 또한 그렇지 않다'라는 의미를 나타낸다. like를 대신하는 do동사를 써야 한다.

4 부정어를 첫머리에 두어 강조하는 경우, 「부정어+조동사/do동사+주어+동사원형」의 어순이 된다. 현재완료 문장의 경우 have/has와 주어의 위치만 바꾼다.

5 ② It ~ that 강조구문으로 동사는 강조할 수 없다.

개념 완성 Quiz

1 do동사 2 명사 3 Neither 4 도치
5 동사+주어

서술형 실전 연습 pp.158~159

1 (1) has to (2) is
2 (1) Both Tom and I are interested in soccer.
(2) The sick and poor need help.
3 (1) she would exercise regularly
(2) Pluto is not a planet
4 (1) he liked my gift
(2) she was afraid of those bees
5 (1) Chris does like eating chocolate ice cream.
(2) Seldom does he take part in the soccer game.
6 (1) It was my brother who
(2) does he fix things well
7 (1) what I enjoy doing
(2) if(whether) I have been abroad
8 (1) What will I do?
(2) Give me some food.

1 (1) every student가 주어이므로 단수 동사 has to로 써야 한다.
(2) politics는 학문명이므로 단수 동사 is로 써야 한다.

2 (1) both *A* and *B*가 주어로 쓰이는 경우 복수로 취급하므로 am을 are로 고쳐 써야 한다.
(2) 「the+형용사」는 '~한 사람들'의 의미로 주어로 쓰인 경우 복수로 취급하므로 needs를 need로 고쳐 써야 한다.

3 (1) 주절의 시제가 현재에서 과거시제로 바뀌었으므로 종속절의 will을 과거형인 would로 바꿔 써야 한다.
(2) 종속절은 일반적으로 주절의 시제 영향을 받지만 과학적 사실의 경우 주절의 시제의 영향을 받지 않고 항상 현재시제로 쓴다.

4 (1) 직접화법을 간접화법으로 쓸 때 1인칭은 주절의 주어와, 2인칭은 주절의 목적어와 일치시킨다.
(2) 직접화법의 these는 간접화법에서 those로 쓴다.

5 (1) 동사를 강조할 때는 「do동사+동사원형」으로 쓰는데 주어가 3

인칭 단수이면서 현재시제이므로 「does+동사원형」으로 쓴다.

(2) 부정어를 강조하여 문두에 오면 「부정어+조동사(do동사)+주어+동사원형 ~」의 순으로 쓴다.

6 (1) '그것을 고친 사람은 다름 아닌 내 형이었어.'의 의미가 되도록 it ~ that(who) 강조구문으로 쓴다.

(2) 부정어 not only가 문두에 있으므로 주어와 동사를 도치시켜 does he fix things well의 어순으로 쓴다.

7 (1) 의문사가 있는 의문문은 「의문사+주어+동사」의 어순으로 쓴다.

(2) 의문사가 없는 의문문이므로 「if/whether+주어+동사」의 형태로 쓴다.

8 (1)은 의문문의 화법 전환이므로 What will I do?로 바꿔 쓴다. (2)는 명령문의 화법 전환이므로 to부정사 부분을 명령문으로 바꿔 쓴다.

개념 완성 Quiz

1 단수 **2** 복수 **3** 현재시제 **4** 주절의 주어 **5** 도치
6 It **7** 의문사 **8** 명령문

실전 모의고사 pp. 160~163

01 ③ **02** ④, ⑤ **03** ④ **04** ③ **05** ⑤
06 ④ **07** ③ **08** ③ **09** ② **10** ① **11** ③
12 ③ **13** ① **14** ④ **15** ② **16** ② **17** ⑤
18 ③ **19** ③

20 (1) would study hard (2) had broken
(3) discovered

21 (1) where he was from
(2) if(whether) we had seen the movie

22 (1) when he would leave home the following(next) day
(2) he would leave home at 8:00 in the morning

23 ⑤ → to finish

24 (1) It is Yuna that(who) speaks English as well as a native speaker of English.
(2) Yuna does speak English as well as a native speaker of English.

25 (1) Every student who is going to participate is warming up before the event.
(2) to be careful not to get hurt

01 동사를 강조하는 경우와 부정어가 도치되어 문장 앞에 올 때 공통으로 사용할 수 있는 조동사 do가 들어가는데, 주어가 3인칭 단수이므로 does가 알맞다.

02 주절이 과거시제인 경우 종속절은 과거나 과거완료가 알맞다.

03 첫 번째 문장은 주절이 과거시제이므로 종속절은 과거나 과거완료 시제가 가능하다. 두 번째 문장의 「the+형용사」는 '~한 사람들'의 뜻으로 복수 취급하므로 복수 동사가 들어가야 한다.

04 ③은 일반동사로 쓰인 do이고 나머지는 동사를 강조하는 조동사 do이다.

05 sunglasses(선글라스)는 항상 복수 취급하므로 복수 동사 are가 알맞고 나머지는 모두 단수 취급하는 주어(① 하나의 개념, ② the number of ~, ③ 과목명, ④ 병명)이므로 is가 알맞다.

06 주절이 과거시제이므로 시제 일치 원칙에 의해서 lives를 lived로 써야 한다.

07 간접화법을 직접화법으로 바꿀 때 주절과 같은 종속절 주어는 직접화법에서 I로 전환된다.

08 규칙적으로 하는 습관적인 일은 시제 일치에 상관없이 현재시제로 나타낸다.

09 부정명령문을 간접화법으로 바꿀 때 「not to+동사원형」으로 쓴다. bother의 목적어로 Sally를 가리키는 her를 쓰는 점에 유의한다.

10 의문사가 없는 의문문을 간접화법으로 바꿀 때 「if(whether)+주어+동사」의 형태로 쓴다.

11 첫 번째 빈칸에는 '한글이 만들어진 것'은 역사적 사실이므로 과거시제를 사용하며 의미상 수동 형태가 적절하다. 두 번째 빈칸에는 all 뒤에 복수명사가 있으므로 복수 동사가 알맞다.

12 ③ It ~ that 강조구문에서 be동사는 문장 전체의 시제에 맞게 써야 한다. (is → was)

13 ① 「all of+명사」는 명사의 수에 동사를 일치시키는데 furniture는 셀 수 없는 명사이므로 단수 동사인 was가 알맞다.

14 부정어가 문장 앞에 올 때는 「부정어+조동사/do동사+주어+동사원형」의 어순이 된다.

15 ⓐ 현재의 습관은 현재시제로 쓴다. ⓑ 속담은 항상 현재시제로 쓴다. (caught → catches) ⓒ 역사적 사실은 항상 과거시제로 쓴다. (had broken → broke) ⓓ 과학적 사실은 현재시제로 쓴다.

16 '어디에서' 반지를 찾았는지 물어보는 내용이므로 장소(in the drawer)를 강조하는 문장이 가장 적절한 대답이다.

17 ⑤는 '하다'라는 뜻을 가진 일반동사 do의 과거형이고, 나머지는 모두 동사를 강조하는 조동사로 쓰였다.

18 ③ 「so+동사+주어」의 어순이 되어야 하므로 so did she로 써야 한다.

19 ③ 의문사가 없는 의문문의 간접화법으로 Oliver asked me if (whether) I had been to New Zealand.가 되어야 한다.

20 (1), (2) 주절이 현재시제에서 과거시제로 바뀌면 종속절은 원래 시제에서 한 단계 이전 시제로 바뀐다. (3) 주절의 시제가 바뀌어도 종속절이 역사적인 사실을 나타내면 항상 과거시제로 쓴다.

21 (1) 의문사 있는 의문문이므로 「ask(+목적어)+의문사+주어+동사」의 어순으로 쓴다. 시제 일치에 맞춰 are를 was로 쓴다.
(2) 의문사 없는 의문문이므로 「ask(+목적어)+if(whether)+주어+동사」의 어순으로 쓴다. have seen을 한 시제 앞선 had seen으로 쓴다.

22 주절이 과거이면 종속절의 시제는 과거나 과거완료가 되고, 조동사가 있을 때는 조동사를 과거형으로 쓴다.

23 명령문을 간접화법으로 바꾼 경우에는 목적어 뒤에 to부정사 형태가 들어가야 한다.

24 (1) 주어는 It ~ that 강조구문을 사용하여 강조할 수 있으며 that 대신 who를 쓸 수 있다.
(2) 동사는 조동사 do를 사용하여 강조한다. 주어가 3인칭 단수이고 현재시제이므로 does speak가 되어야 한다.

25 (1) every 뒤에 단수 명사와 단수 동사가 온다.
(2) 명령문을 간접화법으로 바꾼 경우에는 목적어 뒤에 to부정사 형태가 들어가야 한다.

내신만점 Level Up Test p.164

01 ② **02** ④ **03** ②
04 (1) so do I (2) neither does Emily
05 (1) Never I dreamed → Never did I dream
(2) will → would

01 It is/was ~ that 강조구문으로 동사는 강조할 수 없다. 동사는 do동사를 사용해서 강조하므로 ② Daisy did drink green tea at the café last Sunday.가 되어야 한다.

02 ⓒ 과목명은 단수 취급하므로 are가 아니라 is, ⓓ The young은 '젊은 사람들'이라는 뜻의 복수명사이므로 likes가 아니라 like가 알맞다.

03 ② who washed → who had washed
의문사가 주어이므로 「의문사+동사」의 어순으로 쓰고, 전달 동사가 과거이므로 시제 일치에 맞게 과거완료 시제를 써야 한다.

04 (1) '~도 또한 그렇다'는 「so+동사+주어」이다.
(2) '~도 또한 그렇지 않다'는 「neither+동사+주어」이다.

05 (1) 부정어 Never가 문장의 맨 앞에 오면 「부정어+조동사/do동사+주어+동사원형」이 되어야 하므로 Never did I dream이 되어야 한다.
(2) 주절의 시제가 과거이면 종속절의 시제도 과거가 되어야 하므로 will이 아니라 would가 되어야 한다.

Final Test

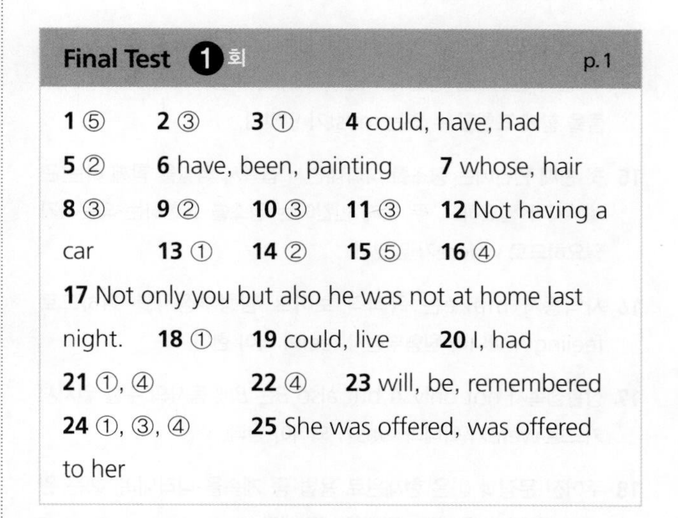

Final Test 1회 p.1

1 ⑤ **2** ③ **3** ① **4** could, have, had
5 ② **6** have, been, painting **7** whose, hair
8 ③ **9** ② **10** ③ **11** ③ **12** Not having a car **13** ① **14** ② **15** ⑤ **16** ④
17 Not only you but also he was not at home last night. **18** ① **19** could, live **20** I, had
21 ①, ④ **22** ④ **23** will, be, remembered
24 ①, ③, ④ **25** She was offered, was offered to her

1 과거보다 먼저 일어난 일이므로 과거완료시제(had+p.p.)가 알맞다.

2 have trouble -ing는 동명사가 관용적으로 쓰이는 표현으로 '~하는 데 어려움을 겪다'라는 뜻이다.

3 조건(~하면)의 부사절을 이끄는 접속사 if가 알맞다.

4 과거 사실과 반대되는 상황을 가정하여 말하는 가정법 과거완료 문장이므로 빈칸에는 「조동사의 과거형+have+p.p.」의 형태가 와야 한다.

5 주어진 문장의 can은 허락의 의미로 쓰였다. ①은 가능성, ③은 요청, ④, ⑤는 능력의 의미이다.

6 과거에 시작된 일이 현재까지 진행되고 있으므로 현재완료 진행형(have been -ing)으로 써야 한다.

7 빈칸에는 접속사와 소유격을 함께 표현할 수 있는 소유격 관계대명사와 이에 이어지는 명사가 함께 와야 한다.

8 첫 번째 빈칸에는 능동을 나타내는 현재분사가 알맞고, 두 번째 빈칸에는 수동을 나타내는 과거분사가 알맞다.

9 ②는 '가능한 ~하게'라는 의미로 「as+원급+as+주어+can」의 형식으로 쓰여야 한다. 비교급 higher가 아니라 원급 high가 알맞다.

10 ③ want는 to부정사를 목적어로 취하는 동사이므로 playing이 아니라 to play가 되어야 한다.

11 명령문을 간접화법으로 전환할 때는 동사 앞에 to를 써서 to부정사로 만든다. 직접화법에서의 부사(구)는 전달자의 입장에 맞게 바꿔야 하는데, now는 then으로 바꿔 써야 한다.

12 주절과 주어가 같은 부사절을 분사구문으로 만들 때는 접속사와 주어를 생략하고 동사를 현재분사 형태로 바꾸는데, 이때 동사가 부정형일 때는 분사 앞에 not을 쓴다.

13 ①은 '무엇'이라는 의미의 의문사로 쓰였고, 나머지는 모두 선행사를 포함하는 관계대명사로 쓰였다.

14 첫 번째 빈칸에는 강한 긍정적 확신을 나타내는 조동사가 알맞고, 두 번째 빈칸에는 강한 금지를 나타내는 조동사가 알맞으므로 이 둘을 함께 표현할 수 있는 must가 알맞다.

15 첫 번째 빈칸에는 장소를 나타내면서 접속사 역할을 함께 하는 관계부사가 필요하고, 두 번째 빈칸에는 장소를 표현하는 의문사가 필요하므로 where가 알맞다.

16 사역동사 make는 목적격 보어로 원형부정사를 취하므로 feeling이 아니라 원형부정사 feel이 와야 한다.

17 상관접속사 not only *A* but also *B*는 *B*에 동사의 수를 일치시키므로 were가 아니라 was가 되어야 한다.

18 주어진 문장과 ①은 현재완료 용법 중 계속을 나타내며, ②는 완료, ③은 결과, ④, ⑤는 경험을 나타낸다.

19 과거의 일의 결과가 현재에 영향을 미칠 때 쓰는 혼합가정문으로 조건절에는 가정법 과거완료가 쓰였지만, 주절에는 현재의 사실과 반대되는 상황을 표현해야 하기 때문에 가정법 과거(조동사의 과거형+동사원형)를 쓴다.

20 현재의 이루기 힘든 소망을 표현하므로 「I wish+가정법 과거(동사의 과거형)」의 형태가 알맞다.

21 ① be satisfied with: ~에 만족하다 ② 간접의문문은 「의문사+주어+동사」의 어순이 되어야 한다. (where was the bus stop → where the bus stop was) ③ mind는 동명사를 목적어로 취한다. (to excuse → excusing) ④ be surprised at: ~에 놀라다 ⑤ expect는 to부정사를 목적어로 취한다. (passing → to pass)

22 As가 이유를 나타내는 접속사로 쓰였으므로 ④ Since와 바꿔 쓸 수 있다.

23 조동사가 있는 문장을 수동태로 바꿀 때는 「조동사+be+p.p.」의 형태가 알맞다.

24 원급과 비교급으로 최상급의 의미를 표현할 때는, 「No (other) ~+as+원급+as」, 「No (other) ~+비교급+than」, 「비교급+than+any other+단수명사」의 형태로 나타낼 수 있다.

25 4형식 문장은 간접목적어와 직접목적어를 각각 주어로 하는 두 가지 형태의 수동태로 바꿔 쓸 수 있다. 간접목적어를 주어로 할 때는 「be동사+p.p.」 뒤에 직접목적어를 이어서 쓰고, 직접목적어를 주어로 할 때는 「be동사+p.p.」 다음에 「전치사(to/for/of)+간접목적어」를 쓴다.

Final Test ❷회 p.3

1 ④ **2** ⑤ **3** ④ **4** ④ **5** would, rather
6 ④ **7** ① **8** ④ **9** something hot to drink
10 ⑤ **11** whenever, I, sing, songs
12 one, of, the, most, famous, places **13** ①
14 ③ **15** ④ **16** Being in trouble
17 틀린 부분: that → which
틀린 이유: 전치사 in이 that 앞에 있고 that은 in과 함께 나란히 쓸 수 없으므로 전치사와 같이 쓸 수 있는 관계대명사인 which로 바꿔 쓴다.
18 ④ **19** had, been **20** ③ **21** ② **22** ④
23 ⑤ **24** she would be home late that day
25 "What are you doing now?"

1 현재완료 시제의 계속을 나타내는 문장으로 문맥상 '내가 8살 이후로'의 의미가 자연스러우므로 ④ since가 알맞다.

2 계속적 용법의 관계사절이 쓰인 문장으로, 선행사가 May로 시간을 나타내며 빈칸 뒤로 완전한 문장이 이어지므로 시간을 나타내는 관계부사 when이 알맞다.

3 '*A*와 *B* 둘 다 아닌'의 의미를 표현하는 상관접속사 neither *A* nor *B*가 알맞다.

4 부사구를 강조할 때는 It ~ that 강조구문을 이용하여 표현한다. '우리 집 앞'을 강조하는 문장이므로 It과 that 사이에 in front of my house를 써야 한다.

5 문맥상 '*B*하느니 차라리 *A*하겠다'라는 의미를 표현하는 would rather *A* than *B*의 표현이 알맞다.

6 비교급 앞에서 비교급을 강조하는 표현으로, even, still, far, a lot 등과 바꿔 쓸 수 있다.

7 ① be afraid of -ing: ~하는 것을 두려워하다 / be left alone: 혼자 남겨지다 ② 과거의 시점을 표현하는 last year가 있으므로 과거형을 써야 한다. (→ visited) ③ 선행사가 「사람+동물」이므로 관계대명사 that을 써야 한다. (→ that are running) ④ 이유를 나타내는 분사구문이 알맞다. (→ Not knowing) ⑤ 수동태가 알맞다. (→ used)

8 주어진 문장의 that은 목적어 역할을 하는 절을 이끄는 접속사이다. ①은 주어 역할, ②는 보어 역할, ③은 동격절, ⑤는 목적어 역할을 하는 절을 이끄는 접속사로 쓰였고 ④는 목적격 관계대명사이다.

9 -thing으로 끝나는 대명사를 형용사와 to부정사가 함께 꾸밀 때는 「대명사+형용사+to부정사」의 순서로 쓴다.

10 ⑤ don't have to는 '~할 필요가 없다'라는 의미이며, 나머지는 모두 금지를 표현한다.

11 '~할 때마다'를 표현하는 복합관계부사는 whenever이다.

12 '가장 ~한 것들 중 하나'를 나타낼 때 「one of the+최상급+복수명사」의 표현을 쓴다.

13 주어진 문장과 ①은 주어로 쓰인 명사 역할을 한다. ②는 감정의 원인, ④는 목적, ⑤는 형용사를 수식하는 부사 역할을 한다. ③은 명사를 꾸며 주는 형용사 역할을 한다.

14 주어진 문장과 ③은 현재완료 경험을 나타내고, ①은 결과, ②, ⑤는 계속, ④는 완료를 나타낸다.

15 반지를 찾지 못한 일(과거)보다 반지를 잃어버린 일이 먼저 일어났으므로 과거완료 시제가 되어야 한다.

16 주절과 주어가 같은 부사절을 분사구문으로 만들 때는 접속사와 주어를 생략하고 동사를 현재분사 형태로 바꿔서 쓴다. be in trouble: 곤란에 처해 있는, 문제가 있는

17 관계대명사가 전치사의 목적어로 쓰일 때 전치사는 관계대명사의 앞이나 관계대명사절의 끝에 올 수 있다. 그러나 who나 that은 「전치사+관계대명사」의 형태로 쓸 수 없다. 따라서 that을 which로 바꿔 쓴다.

18 ④ cannot은 불가능을 표현하고 있으므로 강한 금지를 나타내는 must not과 바꿔 쓸 수 없다.

19 문맥상 주절의 과거시제(was) 보다 이전에 파리에 여러 번 갔었던 것을 표현해야 하므로 과거완료 중 경험을 표현하는 had been이 알맞다.

20 현재의 사실과 반대되는 상황을 가정하고 있으므로 가정법 과거(if+주어+동사의 과거형, 주어+조동사의 과거형+동사원형)의 형태가 되어야 한다.

21 ② 분사구문의 주어와 주절의 주어가 다르므로 분사구문의 주어를 분사 앞에 써야 한다. (→ It being sunny) ③ you 앞에 접속사 that이 생략된 문장이다. 주장을 나타내는 동사 suggest가 쓰여 that절의 should가 생략된 문장이므로 알맞게 쓰였다.

22 ④에는 '만일 ~하지 않다면'이라는 의미의 unless가 알맞으며, 나머지는 모두 if가 알맞다.

23 be satisfied with: ~에 만족하다, be known as: ~로 알려져 있다, be covered with: ~로 뒤덮여 있다

24 간접화법으로 바꿀 때는 콤마와 인용부호를 없애고, 주절의 동사가 과거일 경우 전달문의 동사도 그에 맞게 바꾸고, 인칭대명사와 부사(구)를 전달자 입장에 맞도록 바꿔야 한다.

25 직접화법으로 바꿀 때, 전달문이 의문사 있는 의문문이면 「의문사+동사+주어 ~?」의 어순이 되도록 바꿔야 한다.

Final Test ❸회 p.5

1 ④ 2 ② 3 ③ 4 ④
5 (1) used to (2) had better (3) have to 6 ⑤
7 Having bought a new computer 8 ① 9 ④
10 Sylvia was too strong for me to win the match.
11 It is so amazing that she can speak Chinese like a native. 12 ④ 13 ③ 14 As, soon, as, I, know
15 ③ 16 ⑤ 17 anything, that 18 ①
19 ④, ⑤ 20 to eat → eating 21 ③
22 could not live 23 ④
24 What do you guess she bought?
25 The more you practice, the better you will do.

1 첫 번째 문장은 상대방에게 정중하게 요청하는 문장이고, 두 번째 문장은 과거 사실과 반대되는 상황을 가정하는 가정법 과거의 문장이다. 이 두 가지를 충족시킬 수 있는 것은 ④ Could[could]이다.

2 첫 번째 빈칸에는 동격절을 이끄는 접속사 that이 와야 하고, 두 번째 빈칸에는 her neighbor를 선행사로 하는 주격 관계대명사가 와야 한다. 이 두 가지를 충족시킬 수 있는 것은 ② that이다.

3 주어진 문장은 가주어 It이 쓰인 문장으로 진주어인 to부정사를 뒤로 보낸 형태이다. 따라서 주어 역할을 하고 있는 ③과 쓰임이 같다. ①은 주격 보어 역할, ②는 목적격 보어 역할, ④, ⑤는 목적어 역할을 한다.

4 빈칸 다음에 동명사가 이어지고 있으므로 to부정사를 목적어로 취하는 ④ needed는 알맞지 않다.

5 (1) 이어지는 표현으로 보아 과거의 습관을 표현하는 used to가 알맞다. (2) '~하지 않는 게 좋겠다'라는 의미가 될 수 있는 had

better가 알맞다. (3) '~해야만 한다'라는 의미의 have to가 알맞다.

6 늦었음에도 불구하고 샌드위치를 사러 갔으므로 양보를 나타내는 접속사 Although가 알맞다.

7 그녀가 새 컴퓨터를 산 일이 내게 오래된 것을 준 일보다 먼저 일어난 일이므로 완료형 분사구문 (having+p.p.)의 형태로 써야 한다.

8 ① 현재완료 시제가 알맞게 쓰였다. ② 부정 주어가 쓰였으므로 not이 없어야 한다.(→ so powerful as) ③ as if+가정법 과거나 가정법 과거완료로 쓴다.(→ didn't know 또는 hadn't known) ④ the way와 how는 둘 중 하나만 쓴다.(→ The way 또는 How) ⑤ 조동사가 있는 문장의 수동태는 「조동사+be+p.p.」 형태로 쓴다.(→ must be completed)

9 주절의 시제가 과거일 경우 전달문의 시제도 과거로 바꿔야 하며, 인칭대명사와 부사(구)를 전달자의 입장으로 바꿔야 한다.

10 「so+형용사+that+주어+can't+동사원형」은 '너무 ~해서 …할 수 없다'의 의미로 「too+형용사(+for+의미상 주어)+to부정사」의 형태로 바꿔 쓸 수 있다.

11 That으로 시작하는 명사절이 주어 역할을 하는 문장으로 가주어 It을 사용하여 that절을 뒤에 위치하도록 바꿔 쓸 수 있다.

12 과거 사실과 반대되는 상황을 가정하여 말하고 있으므로 가정법 과거완료의 형식이 되어야 한다. 즉, if절에는 「had+p.p.」, 주절에는 「조동사의 과거형+have+p.p.」가 되어야 한다.

13 to부정사의 주체가 주어와 다를 경우 to부정사 앞에 「for(of)+목적격」의 형태로 의미상의 주어를 나타내는데 성품을 나타낼 때만 of를 쓰고 나머지는 for를 쓴다. ③ rude는 성품을 나타내므로 of가 알맞다.

14 '~하자마자'를 표현하는 접속사는 as soon as이다. 시간의 부사절에서는 미래를 현재시제로 나타내므로 will know가 아니라 know가 되어야 한다.

15 ③ 개가 스스로 훈련을 하는 것이 아니라 훈련을 받는 것이므로 수동태 will be trained가 되어야 한다.

16 ② 현재의 사실은 주절의 시제와 상관없이 항상 현재로 쓰이므로 맞게 쓰였다. ⑤ 역사적인 사실은 주절의 시제와 상관없이 항상 과거로 쓰이므로 had been이 아니라 was가 되어야 한다.

17 '네가 원하는 것은 무엇이든지'라는 뜻이므로 복합관계대명사 whatever 대신 anything that을 쓸 수 있다.

18 ① '중고책'이라는 의미로 과거분사가 맞게 쓰였다. 능동 · 진행의 의미는 현재분사로 쓰고, 수동 · 완료의 의미는 과거분사로 쓰므로 ② → written, ③ → dancing, ④ → playing, ⑤ → given으로 각각 고쳐 써야 한다.

19 ④ 목적격 관계대명사는 생략할 수 있다. ⑤ 뒤에 분사가 이어지는 「주격 관계대명사+be동사」는 생략할 수 있다.

20 stop 뒤에 동명사가 이어지면 '~하는 것을 멈추다'의 뜻이 되고, to부정사가 이어지면 '~하기 위해 멈추다'의 뜻이 된다. 이 문장에서는 '먹는 것을 멈추다'라는 의미가 적절하므로 to eat이 아니라 eating이 되어야 한다.

21 그녀가 시애틀에 도착한 부사절은 과거시제로, 주절은 그녀가 도착하기 전부터 일주일째 비가 내리고 있었으므로 과거완료 진행형 (had been -ing)이 알맞다.

22 If it were not for는 가정법 과거의 표현으로 '~이 없다면'의 의미이다. 따라서 주절에는 「조동사의 과거형+(not+)동사원형」의 형태가 알맞다.

23 ④는 '~할 때까지'라는 의미의 접속사 until이 알맞고 나머지는 다양한 의미를 표현하는 접속사 as가 알맞다. (①, ② ~인 대로 ③ ~ 때문에 ⑤ ~함에 따라)

24 What did she buy?의 의문문이 Do you guess?라는 문장의 일부분이 되는 간접의문문이다. 주절의 동사가 think, believe, guess인 경우에는 간접의문문의 의문사를 문장 맨 앞에 쓰므로 What do you guess she bought?가 된다.

25 '~할수록 더 …하게'는 「the 비교급+주어+동사, the 비교급+주어+동사」의 형태로 쓴다.

빠르게 통하는 영문법 핵심 1200제

LEVEL 3

Answers